The Communist Experience in America

A Political and Social History

HARVEY KLEHR

Transaction Publishers
New Brunswick (U.S.A.) and London (U.K.)

Library of Congress Catalog Number: 2009044442
ISBN: 978-1-4128-1056-2
Printed in the United States of America

Library of Congress Cataloging-in-Publication Data

Klehr, Harvey.
 The communist experience in America : a political and social history / Harvey Klehr.
    p. cm.
 Includes bibliographical references and index.
 ISBN 978-1-4128-1056-2 (alk. paper)
   1. Communism--United States--History--20th century. 2. Communist Party of the United States of America--History--20th century. 3. United States--Politics and government--1919-1933. 4. United States--Politics and government--1933-1945. 5. United States--Economic conditions--1918-1945. I. Title.

HX83.K5495 2010
320.53'22097--dc22

2009044442

For Layla—l'dor v'dor

Contents

Preface

For nearly four decades, my scholarly career has been focused on American radicalism. From one perspective, it appears like an odd choice to be so obsessed with groups and ideas that have failed so consistently and spectacularly. The United States is the only major industrial nation where no socialist or communist movement or party has either come to power or seriously contested for power. Despite the alarums offered by some conservative pundits, the Democratic Party has never embraced even the moderate forms of democratic socialism so common in Europe. The Socialist Party's high point came in 1912 when Eugene Debs, its perennial presidential candidate, received 6 percent of the national vote. The Communist Party achieved some cultural and intellectual panache in the 1930s, but even at the height of its influence, it remained a marginal political movement and was unable to capture the American labor movement.

Why devote one's intellectual life to studying failures? The easy answer—which contains some measure of truth—is that an academic career requires a niche, and I was able to carve out my own among the debris of American radicalism. But that would not account for why so much of what I have written has either appeared in mainstream intellectual publications or engendered debate and controversy that has spread far beyond narrow and obscure academic journals. The fate of the American left touches on much wider themes that go to the heart of still-heated debates about the nature of American society.

Arguments about whether distinctive features of American society, culture, political structure, economic system, or population account for the relative weakness of American radicalism have engaged historians, sociologists, and political scientists for many decades. Such influential concepts as Frederick Jackson Turner's "frontier theory" were linked with the absence of class conflict in America. German sociologist Werner Sombart famously explained that American radicalism foundered "on the shoals of roast beef and apple pie." More critical analysts attributed the failure of the American left to fierce repression, with various red scares and the McCarthy era as prime exhibits. Other commentators have examined American immigration, winner-take-all plurality elections and such cultural values as Lockean individualism or the Protestant ethic as contributors to the failures of the American left.

Although my research began with an effort to contribute to the debate about American exceptionalism, it quickly moved to the study of radical groups, reflecting my evolving interests, but also the realization that radical organizations often created their own opportunities and dilemmas through their own choices. While the environment for radical success has never been especially favorable in the United States, neither has it been hopeless. And the failures of one of the largest and longest-lasting radical groups, the Communist Party, offers many lessons about how political groups can take advantage of or squander these chances.

The opportunity to collect a number of the essays and articles I have written over the years provides a glimpse of how an academic career can be shaped both by an overarching research question and the serendipity of new archival resources. When I began my research in the late 1960s, I could not have dreamed of the material that would become available to scholars by the turn of the century. Nor could I have anticipated that even though my graduate training was in political theory, I would have to learn research techniques more common to sociology or history. And, I would have been astounded to be told of the monetary resources that would be required to answer the research questions that would interest me. Selecting these twenty-seven essays and articles from the nearly sixty I have written is a reminder that much of what I have been able to accomplish is due to the generosity and vision of private foundations committed to excavating inconvenient material from America's past.

These essays also illustrate how fortunate I have been to find scholarly collaborators with similar interests. Ron Radosh and I teamed up to write several articles and one book. For nearly twenty years, John Haynes, twentieth-century manuscript historian at the Library of Congress, has been a friend and co-author. We have been able to research and write far more together than either one of us could have done individually and saved each other from numerous mistakes and misinterpretations.

Revisiting these essays also brings reminders that long familiarity with a topic does not insulate one from being wrong. In the euphoria induced by the collapse of communism in the late 1980s and early 1990s, it was too easy to predict "the end" of the Communist Party of the United States after a seemingly fatal internal split. And John Haynes and I were far too sanguine when we blithely assumed that evidence from Russian archives would convince some of our scholarly opponents that they had been wrong about the relationship between the CPUSA and the USSR or the involvement of certain individuals in espionage. Nostalgia and investments in fixed positions are powerful factors that can trump evidence and we ignore that at our peril.

My interest in the American radical left began in graduate school in the late 1960s. A doctoral student in the Political Science Department at the University of North Carolina, Chapel Hill, I originally intended to study traditional American politics, but became distracted by the upheavals of the era. I considered myself on the political left, but hardly a revolutionary. Some of my friends and classmates, however, were associated with the Southern Students Organizing Committee (SSOC), a spin-off of Students for a Democratic Society. And the political atmosphere on American campuses was charged with anger and rage and much talk of revolutionary upheaval.

Two political events from those tumultuous years gave me my lifetime research agenda. During the 1968 presidential election, a number of radicals, including some I knew, supported George Wallace for president. They certainly had no sympathy for the Alabama governor, but argued that his election would precipitate an American revolution. Their rationale was that a dose of fascism would prepare the way for American radicalism. Although I didn't know it at the time, their strategy of "the worse, the better," had earlier been the policy of the German communists in the late 1920s and early 1930s, who had welcomed Adolf Hitler's accession as German chancellor, on the grounds that they would inherit the government after he failed. Even without the historical knowledge of that catastrophic miscalculation, I sensed that such a course for the American left doomed it to defeat.

After the American incursion into Cambodia in 1970, student protestors held a mass meeting on the Chapel Hill campus. A number of speakers called for a student strike to shut down the university. My advisor, Dr. Lewis Lipsitz, had been one of the most prominent leftists on campus for many years, a target of such conservatives as Jesse Helms, the future senator, then a Raleigh TV commentator, because of his outspoken support for integration and opposition to the war in Vietnam. When Lew urged the crowd not to strike since a university should not be closed down, he was booed.

Convinced that the student left was losing its grip on reality and was likely to fail, I became increasingly intrigued by the question of why the American left always seemed to fail. What was it about America or the left that accounted for "American exceptionalism," the inability of socialists or communists to make inroads comparable to those it enjoyed elsewhere? Such questions were not entirely compatible with the interests of those academics intent on making political science more scientific and behavioral and less historical. Taking a course in American political parties, I wrote a seminar paper on the travails of the Socialist Party and was told by the bemused professor that for an imaginary history course, it would have received an "A," but for a political *science* paper, I had done B-work.

Warned that my interests in American politics were unlikely to meet approval, I decided to major in political theory, attracted by the opportunity to confront Marxism, then all the rage in the academy. And a dissertation topic was directly at hand. Since Marx had insisted that his model predicted the inevitable behavior of every advanced capitalist society, the issue of American exceptionalism was a crucial issue in Marxist thought. I discovered a rich legacy of debate about the nature of American society among Marxist writers.

If the theme of American exceptionalism and the problems that America's capitalistic society raised for Marxism and its variants was one strand of my initial academic interests, the activities of radical groups quickly eclipsed it as a topic for research. A substantial portion of my dissertation dealt with a dissident communist sect, named after its leader, Jay Lovestone, which had been expelled from the CPUSA in 1929 for the alleged sin of American exceptionalism. The Lovestoneites included a number of very talented men, including Bertram Wolfe, the future historian, Will Herberg, later a prominent sociologist of religion, and Lovestone himself, who went on to a career as the American Federation of Labor's fiercely anti-communist advisor on international affairs. Another prominent intellectual figure close to them was Lewis Fraina (Corey), an autodidact who wrote some fascinating essays on American exceptionalism in the 1930s.

I was fortunate to be hired to teach political theory at Emory University. The Political Science Department was both young—there were only three tenured faculty members in 1971—and committed to methodological pluralism. Even though my research interests moved in odd directions, my colleagues tolerated and even rewarded them so long as I published in peer-reviewed journals. While several articles from my dissertation were published, I had to develop a second research project. I became fascinated by the people who had served in leadership positions in the Communist Party of the United States of America. Fraina had been one of the Party's founders, only to be ousted in the early 1920s and assigned to international duties by the Comintern before breaking with communism. Lovestone, Wolfe, and other prominent Communist leaders of the 1920s had likewise been expelled. No one had done any systematic work on the leadership of the CPUSA. What were the social backgrounds of party leaders? Did patterns of recruitment and leadership help to explain the difficulties the Party faced? What kinds of changes occurred among Party leaders over the decades? Was party leadership stable or volatile?

To answer these questions, I used research techniques more commonly associated with sociology than political theory or history, collecting information on members of the Party's Central Committees from 1921 to 1961. Primitive as my database was, it still required several years of patient digging in archives and interviews of dozens of surviving communists and ex-communists to obtain background information on them and their one-time colleagues. Another source of information also became available in the mid-1970s under the federal Freedom of Information law, originally passed in 1966. Slowly and with many redactions justified on grounds of national security, privacy, and other exemptions, it became possible to obtain from the FBI files on individual communists and communist organizations. Several articles and a later book dealt with the social background of members of the American Communist Party leadership, part of my effort to understand whether the internal dynamics of radical groups had contributed to their lack of success.

While awaiting publication of my first book, *Communist Cadre: The Social Background of the American Communist Party Elite*, I received a letter from Theodore Draper, the doyen of historians of American communism. Hoover Institution Press, the publisher, had sent the manuscript to him for an external review and Draper, after writing a blurb, invited me to Princeton, New Jersey to meet with him. It had been more than fifteen years since the second volume of his history of American communism had appeared and he had concluded that he would never be able to finish the final volume on the CPUSA during the 1930s. He asked me if I would be interested in writing it. Thanks to generous support from Emory University, which purchased the voluminous primary source materials Draper had accumulated, and several foundations that enabled me to devote several semesters and summers to full-time research and writing, I was able to complete *The Heyday of American Communism: The Depression Decade*. That experience inaugurated a continuing fascination with the short-lived success and long-term failure of the organization, reflected in a series of articles in both academic journals and such journals of opinion as the *New Republic*.

For a number of years, I wrote an annual summary of the activities of American communist groups for *The Yearbook on International Communist Affairs*. Reading the newspapers and journals of many of the obscure sects that populated the American left was frequently tedious but occasionally produced fascinating tidbits of radical history. They not only included the self-immolation of the CPUSA itself, following Mikhail Gorbachev's failed efforts to reform Soviet communism, but the bizarre spectacle of a group of Maoists turned capitalist entrepreneurs– little did I realize that they presaged the Chinese Communist regime itself – and the eerie example of a Trostskyist party reprising the persecution of a severely wounded World War II veteran who had previously been persecuted by the United States government as a Trotskyist.

Being immersed in the history of the CPUSA involved me in several academic controversies that had a long afterlife. By 1984, when *The Heyday of American Communism* appeared, scholarly interest in the CPUSA had perked up. The implosion of the New Left in the early and mid-1970s had sent many of its activists back to graduate school, where a few began to reflect on the collapse of their hopes for an American revolution. Looking for role models, some of them began to study the Old Left, to which many of their parents had once belonged. Contributing to the burgeoning literature on the CPUSA were the new documentary evidence emerging from FBI files, the greater willingness of old leftists to talk to scholars and allow access to their papers as memories of the McCarthy era faded, and growing skepticism about the American government fueled by Watergate and revelations of FBI misconduct.

The CPUSA, savagely denounced and politically isolated in the wake of Nikita Khruschev's denunciation of Joseph Stalin in 1956, and reduced to a political shell by government prosecution and internal defections, had become an object of nostalgia by the early 1980s. Alger Hiss and the Rosenbergs were widely regarded as victims of a government frame-up. Documentaries appeared in which old communists were hailed as pioneers of civil rights and labor struggles and the battle against fascism. In this atmosphere, my book, critical of the CPUSA's frequent switches in line and supportive of Draper, Irving Howe, and other liberal and socialist historians who saw the party as a pliant tool of Soviet interests, ignited a fierce debate.

Although widely praised in general-interest journals and newspapers, *The Heyday of American Communism* came under attack from academic leftists critical of its "Draperian" anti-communism and concerned that it offered too hostile a view of the CPUSA. That, in turn, prompted Draper, a forceful and talented veteran of many polemical battles, to denounce my and his critics in the pages of the *New York Review of Books*. The ensuing battle between "traditionalist" and "revisionist" historians of American communism has continued for more than twenty years.

The disagreements between the two camps were only partly generational, because some traditionalists, like myself and my long-time co-author John Haynes, were roughly the same age as our revisionist counterparts. To some degree, the combatants were divided by current political loyalties, with most revisionists locating themselves at least on the left wing of the Democratic Party, if not as members of various socialist groupings. But traditionalists themselves ranged from such self-identified socialists as Irving Howe to conservative Republicans. A far more reliable marker was attitudes towards communism. Most of the older traditionalists, even those on the political left, had either been communists or battled them within political, labor, or intellectual organizations and harbored a deep distrust and skepticism about their commitment to democratic values.

Apart from articles defining, defending and analyzing the traditionalist approach to the history of American communism, Haynes and I also found ourselves dealing with blatant distortions of the past. Glorifying the CPUSA, hiding its warts, and apologizing for its crimes became more common as the memories of events faded. In articles detailing how documentaries, reference books and supposedly scholarly works distorted the past, we fought what sometimes seemed to be a losing battle against historical amnesia and the politicized hijacking of history. Even without a present or future in American life, the communist past remained a hot-button topic.

That became even more obvious when my interests turned to the issue of espionage. My entry into the world of espionage came via an introduction to Isaac Don Levine, a long-time stalwart of anti-communist journalism. I had gone to Carlsbad, California in the 1970s to interview Oliver Carlson, an early leader of the Young Communist League, who had known a number of obscure party leaders on whom I was trying to gather biographical information. During the visit, the Carlsons took me to meet Levine and his wife, who had a home nearby. A few years later, while working on *The Heyday of American Com-*

munism, I came across Draper's interview with Josephine Truslow Adams, a mysterious woman who claimed to have served as an intermediary between Franklin Roosevelt and Earl Browder, leader of the CPUSA, during World War II. Learning that Adams, who had testified before a credulous congressional committee about her claims, had later signed a contract to have Levine ghost-write her memoirs, I visited his Maryland house and made use of his marvelous archives. Levine's papers were a treasure trove of information about his long career dealing with communist defectors, informants, and former spies. After his death, his widow donated his extensive archive to Emory.

Another collection of papers that came to Emory precipitated my next major project, a study of the Amerasia spy case. During my research for *The Heyday of American Communism*, I had been allowed to use the private archive of Philip Jaffe, a wealthy businessman who had been a close friend of Earl Browder and received a number of documents from him. Jaffe was an inveterate collector and Emory obtained his large archive, much of which dealt with China. In 1945, he had been the central figure in a prominent spy episode, dubbed the Amerasia case and been indicted by the government. With Jaffe's own papers already at Emory, I made an FOIA request for the FBI file on the Amerasia case and it arrived after several years. Together with Ronald Radosh, who had recently published his groundbreaking study of the Rosenberg case, I began to dig into this murky tale of espionage, government leaks, and McCarthyism. After many delays, our book was finally published in 1996.

By that time, a new resource for scholars had miraculously become available. By 1990, my interest in American communism was waning. The increasingly bitter debates between traditionalists and revisionists seemed to have reached a state of exhaustion, with little new evidence emerging. Communist Party history, which required reading turgid documents and prose, was less and less attractive as a research area. Deciding to try a new genre by writing a biography of an odd young communist who became a prominent newspaperman and later a wealthy businessman associated with Armand Hammer, I began to gather information about David Karr. His glamorous life had taken Karr around the globe and I made plans to visit an archive in Russia, which I had learned contained material dealing with his business activities in the USSR. I arrived in Moscow in the late spring of 1991, just a few months after the failed coup against Gorbachev. Although I was able to interview some of Karr's Russian associates, the promised material on him never materialized. (That biography remains on my research agenda.) But my trip nevertheless turned into a research bonanza.

Spending more than two weeks at the Russian Center for the Preservation and Study of Documents of Recent History, formerly the archives of the Communist Party of the Soviet Union, I had access to the files of the Communist International. As the first American, and one of the first Westerners to examine this material, I felt some trepidation that these documents might force me to retract or repudiate much of what I had written over the past two decades.

Instead, I found general confirmation of most of the themes about which I had been arguing, on the basis of limited sources.

More importantly, I came across scores of top-secret documents that provided evidence of American Communist Party involvement with Soviet espionage. These documents, later collected in two Yale University Press books, opened up a new window on American communism, exposing the Party's deep and intricate ties with Soviet intelligence agencies, confirming the often-derided stories of defectors from Soviet intelligence, and suggesting that Party leaders were complicit in such activities. These books, written in collaboration with John Haynes, an historian working at the Library of Congress with whom I had previously written a one-volume history of American communism, helped move the debate between traditionalists and revisionists from the rarified world of academic journals to the broader pubic stage.

That transition was aided by the decision of the National Security Agency, the CIA, and FBI to release the Venona decryptions in 1995. Having collected cables sent between Moscow and its embassies and consulates in the United States during World War II, American counter-intelligence had spent years decrypting the messages and eventually broken some 2,900 intelligence cables. Although the NSA had been moving towards releasing the Venona material, pressure from Senator Daniel Patrick Moynihan, before whose special committee on reducing government secrecy Haynes and I had testified, accelerated the process. The Venona documents confirmed the guilt of such controversial Soviet spies as Alger Hiss, the Rosenbergs, and Harry Dexter White. Haynes and I wrote about them in another Yale University Press book, *Venona: Decoding Soviet Espionage in America* (2000). When a number of revisionist scholars refused to face reality, we wrote several polemics taking them to task.

I am grateful to all the journals and editors in whose pages these essays first appeared for permission to reprint them here. (Some minor stylistic, spelling and grammatical changes have been made.) Irving Louis Horowitz, whose own career as a scholar, critic, and publisher is a model of an engaged intellectual who has battled all forms of totalitarianism, first suggested collecting some of my essays into a book. Two students at Emory University were of enormous help. Rachel Zelkowitz, then a talented undergraduate, did much of the intitial organization and work getting permissions. Andrew Kirkpatrick, a graduate student, oversaw the scanning and technical work. During my career, I have been fortunate to work with a number of very capable co-authors. William Tompson, an Emory undergraduate, went on to earn a Ph.D. For many years, Ron Radosh has been a valuable collaborator and good friend. John Haynes has been both an intellectual companion and a friend. It is a mark of our collaboration that neither one of us can remember any longer who wrote the first draft of what. My family has been remarkably tolerant of my obsession with communism. I thank my wife, Marcy Steinberg and my sons Ben (and my daughter-in-law Annsley), Gabe, Josh, and Aaron.

Introduction

The essays in this book are organized in four sections, corresponding to four different themes that have concerned me over the years—the issue of American exceptionalism, the history of the Communist Party of the United States and some of the splinter groups that have looked for inspiration to Marxism-Leninism, the debates among historians and other academics about the nature of American communism, and the question of Soviet espionage in America.

The theme of American exceptionalism has a rich history and has attracted interest and insights from numerous academic fields. From Frederick Jackson Turner's frontier theory to Louis Hartz's claim that America's Lockean tradition resulted in a liberal consensus, economists, sociologists, political theorists, and historians have argued for decades about the characteristics of American society that account for its unique socio-political structure. Still others have discounted its uniqueness. American exceptionalism has also resonated in political life, from the Founding Fathers' conviction that they were embarking on a new venture in freedom, through Abraham Lincoln's declaration that America represented the "last, best hope of mankind," to Ronald Reagan's image of America as "a city on a hill." Claims that America had a special mission or message for the world have been part of our nation's self-image.

The belief that America was somehow fundamentally different than Europe posed a serious challenge to Marxism, which insisted that capitalism, wherever it was found, would inevitably be superseded by socialism. American exceptionalism, then, was an issue Marxists had to confront. The first two chapters in this book examine how the founding fathers of the communist movement, Karl Marx ("Marxist Theory in Search of America") and Vladimir Lenin ("Leninist Theory in Search of America"), understood the United States and how they accounted for its seeming differences from Europe and the slow development of socialist movements within its borders. Despite the confidant assertions of both men that it was only a matter of time before American capitalism conformed to the laws of economic development they believed inevitable, America was a disconcerting anomaly for both.

The United States would continue to bedevil American communists anxious to see the growth of a mass radical movement. In 1929, one faction of the Communist Party of the United States (CPUSA) was expelled from the movement

1

and excoriated for the sin of "American exceptionalism," allegedly for having suggested that the United States was immune to the failings of the capitalist system. "Leninsm and Lovestoneism" examines whether such a charge was justifiable. Even in the mist of the Depression, some radicals pondered the anemic growth of left-wing parties and concluded that American society had to be understood on its own terms, not through the straightjacket of Marxist theory. In "Leninism, Lewis Corey and the Failure of American Socialism," I examined one such figure.

Although it never enlisted as many members, elected as many candidates to political office, or published as many newspapers and magazines with as many readers as did the Socialist Party in the first decade of the twentieth century, the CPUSA had, by the 1930s supplanted the SP as the most significant radical movement in the United States. In that decade, it played a significant role in American political and intellectual life, gaining respectability and influence among key segments of the society. Communists either dominated or heavily influenced organizations active among students, immigrants, African-Americans, Jews, farmers, writers, and others. By the end of the decade, communists held key roles within the American labor movement and in some portions of the Democratic Party.

The chapters in the second section of the book examine a number of these issues. "Immigrant Leadership in the Communist Party of the United States of America" traces the pattern of acculturation within the Party's Central Committee. "American Communism and the United Auto Workers Union" looks at the tensions and conflicts that erupted within one of the largest and most powerful CIO unions when communist and union priorities collided. Similarly, "Self-Determination in the Black Belt: Origins of a Communist Policy" is a case study of one of the most controversial CPUSA positions, its support for the right of blacks in the old South to secede from the United States. Tracing the policy back to its Soviet origins was part of my argument that CPUSA policies were overwhelmingly responses, not to American interests and concerns, but to Soviet pressure and doctrine.

Once Russian archives began to be opened to scholars in the early 1990s, the Soviet hidden hand became more exposed. For years, defenders of the CPUSA had dismissed stories of Soviet financial backing for the Party as sensationalistic fantasies purveyed by fanatical anti-communists. The newly available archives, however, quickly provided abundant evidence that the extent of Soviet financing of the CPUSA had, if anything, been vastly underestimated. "Moscow Gold—Confirmed at Last?" was one of the first scholarly examinations of the phenomenon; in the years since, even more detailed information has documented just how pervasive was Soviet financial support for the CPUSA and many of its activities. In the same vein, "Communists and the CIO—From the Soviet Archives" demonstrated that a number of trade union leaders, often accused of being secret communists, had, in fact, been precisely that. The most prominent was Harry Bridges, long-time head of the International Longshoremen's and Warehousemen's Union. Bridges had always denied Party membership, committed perjury numerous times during government attempts to deport him, and won a Supreme Court case by lying.

The opening of Russian archives coincided with the collapse of the Soviet Union. And that, in turn, precipitated the collapse of the CPUSA. For decades, it had limped along, sustained by Soviet subsidies that paid for its publications and its cadre of full-time employees. As Mikhail Gorbachev sought to reform the communist system in the last half of the 1980s, the hardline leadership of the CPUSA bristled, accusing the Soviet leader of ideological deviance. He responded by cutting off the money spigot. When Soviet hardliners staged a coup in 1991, the CPUSA at first applauded. Once the coup failed, it tried to backtrack. Rank and file Party members in the United States reacted with confusion and dismay and a revolt broke out against the leadership. "The End" told this story, but too confidently predicted the demise of the CPUSA; "The CPUSA and the Committees of Correspondence" examined the relationship between the Party and the organization created by the dissidents. Over the years since, the Committees have withered and a number of their members have quietly returned to the CPUSA.

The CPUSA was not, of course, the only Marxist-Leninist organization in the United States. Although the various splinter groups and sects proliferated at a rapid rate, very few of them had either much staying power or significance. That made it all the more remarkable that so many of their leaders or members were people or real talent and ability. A number of adherents of the Lovestoneite and Trotskyist Party schisms of the 1920s went on to distinguished careers in academia, journalism, the labor movement, and even business, most after shedding all or some of their radical views. During the McCarthy era, these sects, like the CPUSA itself sharply contracted. Buoyed by new recruits from the collapse of the New Left in the late 1960s and early 1970s, they once again sprang to life. "Comrades in the Takeover Wars" dealt with one of the oddest remnants, a tiny Maoist sect that had first burst into public life when several of its members were killed by Neo-Nazis and Klansmen in a shoot-out in Greensboro, North Carolina. Several years later it reinvented itself with an audacious—and lunatic—plan to take over American corporations as part of its strategy to communize America. When last heard from, several members were active in Democratic Party politics in New York. "The Case of the Legless Veteran" was the sad story of a long-time Trotskyist who had lost both legs in World War II. He became a minor cause célèbre in the 1950s when the United States government sought to deny him veterans' benefits because of his radical ties. In the 1980s, in the midst of a factional battle among the Trotskyists, his erstwhile comrades framed him for violating Party discipline and expelled him from the movement to which he had devoted his life.

Academic disputes are famously nasty and the controversies about the study of American communism are no exception. In addition to the normal contentiousness of people whose livelihoods are based on arguing and questioning, many of the combatants in this war had personal stakes in the issues. It was not just that many of those writing about American communism had strong opinions about the nature and role of the CPUSA and its relationship with the Soviet Union, but also that a number either were themselves radicals of some stripe or other or ex-radicals. Some came from radical families so that they were writing about their parents or grandparents and the political and moral choices they had made. The articles included in the section on the Revisionism/Traditionalism Debate give a taste of the issues involved in the study of American communism and the often unfortunate ways it played out.

The section begins with a tribute—"A Vigil Against Totalitarianism"—to one of the most distinguished Marxist academics in America—Sidney Hook. A pioneer in the study of Marx, Hook was also a political activist in the 1920s and 1930s. Although once close to the CPUSA, he soon became a pariah and a fierce defender of Leon Trotsky. By the end of the decade, he was in the forefront of intellectual opponents of communism, earning a reputation in succeeding decades as a hardline anti-Communist. Several articles examine how political partisans have distorted the historical record to whitewash the history of American communism, the choices and behavior of American communists, or the activities of anti-communists. Documentary filmmakers have rewritten the past to glamorize aging communists ("Seeing Red 'Seeing Red'"). Authoritative reference works have commissioned members of the Communist Party to write entries on such controversial issues as the Rosenberg espionage case ("Fellow Travelling Is Alive and Well"). Film critics have totally mischaracterized such classic movies as *On The Waterfront* to vilify its anti-communist director Elia Kazan ("On the Waterfront Without a Clue"). One of those film critics, Paul Buhle, has written extensively on American communism with particularly egregious misstatements and efforts to excuse or minimize such activities as Soviet espionage ("Radical History"). Another article, "The Myth of Premature Anti-Fascism," attempts to track down the evidence that the United States government so labeled American communists who fought in the Spanish Civil War and concludes that the phrase is an urban legend created by communists themselves to gloss over their own flirtation with fascism during the period of the Nazi-Soviet pact.

The final four articles in this section deal with the debates between revisionists and traditionalists. Although there is some overlap, the essays were intended for different audiences and have different emphases. "Historiography of American Communism" is a scholarly summary of the controversy. "Professors of Denial" deals with the refusal of partisans of Alger Hiss to accept new evidence of his connections with Soviet intelligence services. "Reflections of a Traditionalist Historian" was originally a paper presented at a panel with Maurice Isserman, a distinguished revisionist historian. "Reflections on Anti-Communism" was a polemic originally given at a meeting of the Pumpkin Papers Irregulars, a group that meets yearly on Halloween to commemorate the Hiss-Chambers case.

Although the revisionist/traditionalist debate preceded the opening of Russian archives and the explosion of new information about espionage, issues of spying quickly became a flashpoint in arguments about American communism. To traditionalists like myself and Haynes, the extensive evidence of assistance by the CPUSA for Soviet spying and the confirmation of the guilt of virtually everyone accused of espionage during the 1940s and 1950s was powerful support for the claim that the CPUSA, whatever its other activities, was in significant measure an adjunct of Soviet policies. Some revisionists hotly disputed the value or reliability of the evidence of espionage or else they minimized its significance. A few went a step further and justified Soviet espionage. In all the discussions, at some point someone raised the specter of McCarthyism.

"The Strange Case of Roosevelt's Secret Agent" represented my first, early venture into the murky world of spying. It cast doubt on the claims that Josephine Adams, an acquaintance of Eleanor Roosevelt, had been authorized by Franklin Roosevelt to serve as a go-between for him with Communist leader Earl Browder during World War II. Adams was a mentally ill fraud who had managed to convince Browder that she was passing along his advice to FDR. I speculated, however, that the Soviet Union might also have been taken in by her delusions, a claim confirmed years later when the Venona material was released. "Spy Stories" was a reaction to an extraordinary event; a lead editorial in the *New York Times* excoriating those of us uncovering stories of espionage from Russian archives for flirting with McCarthyism. Finally, "Reflections on Espionage," written for a conference on Morality and Politics at Bowling Green University, considered the question of espionage in a broader moral context.

After nearly forty years of research on the topic of American communism, I find myself amazed by the variety and richness of the new source material that has emerged from once-secret American and Russian archives, fascinated by the incredible stories and characters whose lives have been uncovered, and depressed by the fierce resistance to new evidence displayed by some scholars. There is no longer any question about the significant role of the Soviet Union in directing the over-all behavior of the CPUSA. Nor does any rational person doubt the key role played by the party and its leadership in aiding and abetting Soviet espionage. Yet, a small but significant cadre of intellectuals remains enthralled by the CPUSA and fiercely resistant to the implications of the new documentary evidence.

Had a far right-wing counterpart of the CPUSA ever attracted comparable support or sympathy from intellectuals and creative artists, academics would be sounding alarums and warnings about the corruptions of our culture. It is easy enough to understand why the left has had an impact among intellectuals far out of its proportion in the general population. Many of the causes championed by the CPUSA over the years, ranging from civil rights to labor organizing to anti-fascism neatly dove-tailed with the enthusiasms, not only of a broader left, but of Afro-Americans, Jews, and others with whom intellectuals have been in sympathy. But one of the enduring fascinations of the CPUSA is how many talented, perceptive people have been willing to overlook or apologize for its alliance with and, indeed, support for one of the two most murderous and barbaric ideologies of human history.

If my original interest in the American radical left was sparked by the question of why America had been spared a successful radical movement, part of what has fueled my continuing obsession with the topic is the same moral outrage that fuels those dedicated to ensuring that the crimes of the Nazis are never forgotten or obfuscated. Communism in practice everywhere in the world came at enormous human cost. Whatever their other virtues or admirable qualities, those who supported or defended it from the safety of the United States need to be called to account. And it has given me a great deal of satisfaction to be able to do so over the course of my scholarly career. The ability to meld my research interests with my moral and ideological ideals has kept me enthusiastic and enthralled by what I have devoted my life to studying and understanding.

Part 1

American Exceptionalism

1

Marxist Theory in Search of America

Marxist theory has, to this day, not been able to inspire a large social movement in America. On the contrary, left-wing groups, during the infrequent occasions when they have thrived, have done so precisely when they were least committed to Marxism. The heyday of socialism came at a time when it most nearly resembled the major American political parties in its hospitality to all shades of left-wing opinion. The Communist Party gained influence in direct proportion as it abandoned Marx for Jefferson and Lincoln and proclaimed Marxism to be twentieth-century Americanism.

A social theory offers a political movement an interpretation of the world. It provides a picture of the past, a map of the present, and a forecast of the future. Marxism, in particular, demands that theory and practice remain intimate. The failure of Marxist practice in America thus casts some doubt on the adequacy of the theory itself. In fact, many people have discovered in the Marxist theoretical armor chinks which supposedly have eliminated it as an adequate guide to American reality. Others have seen America as a deviant example, concluding that Marxism might apply to Europe but not to the United States.

Few people, however, have specifically looked at Marx's analysis of American society to discover where he went wrong. The emphasis tends to be on the differences between the Marxist analysis of capitalism and the actual development of American society. Marx did, however, discuss America and was not as clear as one might expect. In this chapter, I shall examine some of the difficulties that America raised for Marx and Engels and argue that there are actually two Marxist theories of the American past. This suggests that differing Marxist explanations of the American present might exist and might lead to differing projections of the American future although these themes are not pursued here.

The first theory is a product of Marx's writings. The second is largely the product of Engels' pen, although Marx occasionally gave support to it. After

Originally published in *Journal of Politics*, May 1973 and reprinted with permission.

examining these two theories, I shall argue that they do not exhaust the contradictions in the Marxist analysis of America. In particular, the Civil War presented a theoretical problem neither theory could contain. The confusion of Marx and Engels when confronted by American development has been glossed over by their fellows. In the conclusion, I have tentatively suggested some of the reasons for that oversight and a few of the consequences.

In 1860, Karl Marx informed Frederick Engels, his life-long friend and collaborator, that "in my opinion, the biggest things that are happening in the world today are on the one hand the movement of the slaves in America started by the death of John Brown, and on the other the movement of the slaves in Russia."[1] Despite the importance that he attached to events in these two countries, however, Marx never wrote a detailed, major analysis of American or Russian development – or even of a particular phase of their development.[2]

Both Marx and Engels devoted most of their prodigious energy to understanding and influencing events in Europe. In an even more narrow sense, the great bulk of their writing concerns three countries – England, Germany, and France. Neither America nor Russia ever received sustained literary attention. For one thing, they simply were on the periphery of European life, impinging in very important ways on European matters but still distant enough to be ignored on most occasions. A more important, intellectually crucial, reason for this neglect is that the empirical work Marx and Engels did illustrated capitalist development and decay within a limited class of societies.

Marx was convinced that the ultimate fate of capitalist society was socialism. But, how was socialism, this paradise on earth, to descend from the heavens? Marx is not a thinker whose works admit of only one interpretation. At different times he emphasized different themes. And, like most men, in the course of his life he changed his mind about some matters. Nowhere is Marx's ambiguity more apparent than when one asks how he expected capitalism to turn into socialism.

Marx provided at least three models of the transition from the one system to the other.[3] The first was a product of his early writings. Later adopted by Lenin, this model envisioned a revolution made by a small band of conspirators for the benefit of the masses. The second model had two different scenarios. In the *Manifesto*, Marx argued that capitalist economic development would lead to an ever-increasing proletariat facing an ever-decreasing bourgeoisie. Elsewhere, particularly in the *Grundrisse*, Marx abandoned this simplistic, dichotomous vision but retained his belief that socialism would emerge from a revolution made by a majority of the population.

The third model, only occasionally hinted at, postulated a revolution by example. Just as capitalism had bested feudalism by demonstrating its economic superiority, so would socialism slowly eliminate capitalism: "As the co-operative sector continues to grow and the capitalist sector continues to shrink, the socialist era will arrive like a thief in the night."[4] Engels rejected the first model as the product of youthful enthusiasm, and neither he nor Marx emphasized the third model.[5] While socialism was to be a democratic movement, Marx and Engels never specified unambiguously whether the same democratic model would be followed in all countries.

The clearest expression Marx ever made on the question of whether all nations would follow the same path to socialism is contained in a letter written in 1877. Marx attacked those critics who felt they "absolutely must metamorphose my historical sketch of the genesis of capitalism in Western Europe into an historical-philosophic theory of the general path every people is fated to tread, whatever the historical circumstances in which it finds itself."[6] The immediate cause of Marx's letter was the problem of Russian development. A continuing debate was taking place among Russian radicals over whether the Russian village community, a primitive form of collective land ownership, could serve as the nucleus for a socialist society. In short, did Russia have to undergo capitalist development, which would destroy the collective land system, before socialism arrived?

Marx seemed to answer no. He argued that "if Russia continues to move in the path followed up to 1861, it will lose the finest occasion that history has ever offered a people not to undergo all the sudden turns of fortune of the capitalist system."[7] The village community could form the basis for a leap from a primitive to an advanced economic system.

The Russian road to socialism, then, might traverse a different terrain than that of Western Europe. Russian socialism could, depending on events in more developed lands, arise out of the particular institutions of Russian society. When we turn to Marx and Engels' analysis of the United States, however, we find no such clear view of whether this country would undergo, or had already experienced, a course of development comparable in major respects to that of the Old World. While America was frequently used as a convenient illustration of some theoretical point, only once did Marx discuss American development as a theoretical problem.[8] In the last chapter of Volume I of *Capital*, entitled "The Modem Theory of Colonisation," Marx attempted to explain American economic development. Despite their political status, Marx thought that "the United States are, speaking economically, still only a colony of Europe."[9]

In this chapter, Marx points out that there are two kinds of private property. One is founded on the producer's own labor; the other is founded on the employment of the labor of others. The former type is an economic form antagonistic to capitalism; the latter is capitalism's essence. Indeed, capitalism cannot come into existence until private property in land founded on the producer's own labor—the small, independent proprietorship—is abolished or substantially reduced.

> One of the prerequisites of wage labour and one of the historic conditions for capital is free labour and the exchange of free labour against money. . . . Another prerequisite is the separation of free labour from the objective conditions of its realisation-from the

means and material of labour. This means above all that the worker must be separated from the land, which functions as his natural laboratory. This means the dissolution both of free petty landownership and of communal landed property.[10]

In a fully developed capitalist system, private property based on the labor of others is of immeasurably greater significance than the other kind of private property. In colonies, however, independent private property presents a severe problem for aspiring capitalists. The independent laborer "employs that labour to enrich himself, instead of the capitalist."[11]

Capital, Marx points out, is not something tangible but is a relationship between things. Both a capitalist and wage-laborer must establish a productive relationship to each other before capitalism can be said to exist. And, in turn, the productive relationship requires the presence of both capitalists and wage-laborers.

The colonial setting hinders the transformation of the independent producer into a wage-laborer who is devoid of all property but his own labor power. Deprived of all other forms of property, he has been forced to sell his labor power to survive. In order for him to have reached this state, the dissolution of productive forms in which the worker had property in the land, either individually or communally, or in instruments of production, or was himself a "direct part of the objective conditions of production," that is, a slave or serf, must have taken place.[12]

Money available from usury and mercantile wealth provides the starting point of capital, but it cannot begin the productive process alone. Free labor must be available. English capitalism did not begin its life until the landowners dismissed large numbers of retainers and farmers drove out small cottagers. These groups were forced to choose between banditry and selling their labor power. When the first course proved futile, they chose the second.[13] Money formerly used to support these feudal retainers was then made available for exchange.

This primitive accumulation, Marx argues, is the starting point of capitalism. "The expropriation of the agricultural producer, of the peasant, from the soil, is the basis of the whole process" by which capitalism begins its conquest of the world.[14] In a colony such as the United States, money is available from the mother-country to stoke the capitalist fires, but there is a want of the fuel to be burned—wage laborers. The simple reason for this lack is that the agricultural producer cannot be transformed into a wage laborer.

The essence of colonies, or at least of relatively unpopulated colonies such as the United States, is that "the bulk of the soil is still public property and every settler on it therefore can turn part of it into his private property and individual means of production, without hindering the later settlers in the same operation.[15] Since private property based on a man's own labor was widespread, wage laborers were in short supply. And since these independent producers were largely self-sufficient, the internal market for manufactured goods was severely limited:

As in the colonies the separation of the labourer from the conditions of labour and their root, the soil, does not exist, or only sporadically, or on too limited a scale, so neither does the separation of agriculture from industry exist, nor the destruction of the household industry of the peasantry. Whence then is to come the internal market for capital?[16]

A number of other consequences flow from the availability of land at low prices. Capitalism requires a population movement from farm to city as peasants become wage laborers. In the United States, however, the attractions of private ownership made it difficult to retain even wage laborers imported from Europe. The nascent capitalist enterprises in America thus were forced to offer high wages in order to secure a working force:

The wage-worker of today is tomorrow an independent peasant or artisan, working for himself. He vanishes from the labour-market, but not into the workhouse. This constant transformation of the wage-labourers into independent producers, who work for themselves instead of for capital, and enrich themselves instead of the capitalist gentry, reacts in its turn very perversely on the conditions of the labour-market. Not only does the degree of exploitation of the wage-labourer remain indecently low, the wage-labourer loses into the bargain, along with the relation of dependence, also the sentiment of dependence on the abstemious capitalist.[17]

The American working class occupied, therefore, a privileged position in comparison to its European brethren. At least until land was no longer available at moderate prices, American capitalism would be unable to develop unchecked. Marx implies that it is only a matter of time until a colony loses its anticapitalist bias. He argues that

the enormous and ceaseless stream of men, year after year driven upon America, leaves behind a stationary sediment in the east of the United States, the wave of im- migration from Europe throwing men on the labour-market there more rapidly than the wave of emigration westwards can wash them away.[18]

Capital in America was rapidly being centralized, in large part because of the Civil War. As a result, "capitalist production advances there with giant strides, even though the lowering of wages and the dependence of the wage earner are yet far from being brought down to the normal European level."[19]

Would the American wage scale ever be reduced to the European level? Although implying here that eventually it would, elsewhere Marx maintained that needs were culturally determined, so that the wages paid to workers would vary from area to area, depending on historical factors. Unlike the price of other commodities, the price of labor power had a historical component:

The number and extent of his so-called necessary wants, as also the modes of satisfy- ing them, are themselves the product of historical development, and depend therefore to a great extent on the degree of civilisation of a country, more particularly on the conditions under which, and consequently on the habits and degree of comfort in which, the class of free labourers has been formed. In contra-distinction therefore to the case of other commodities, there enters into the determination of the value of labour-power a historical and moral element.[20]

This passage suggests that American wages might always remain higher and satisfy more needs than those paid in Europe.

Marx ended the first volume of *Capital* by remarking that he was not concerned with the condition of the colonies themselves, but with the discovery, by bourgeois economists, that capitalist private property can exist only where individual private property is exterminated. Therefore, he did not consider in any detail whether the peculiar development of capitalism in the colonies would produce social systems different in important respects from those of Europe.

The second theory of American development is hardly a theory. Taken primarily from Engels' work, it does, however, suggest an alternative to the colonial interpretation of American development. Engels, and to some extent Marx, were ambivalent concerning the legacy of feudal society in the American environment.

The discovery of America, Marx announced in *The Communist Manifesto*, was an event of the greatest import for the development of capitalism. It provided "fresh ground for the bourgeoisie" stirring in the interstices of feudal society, was a step towards the establishment of a world market, and a decisive factor in toppling feudal society.[21] American society, according to Engels, "at the very beginning started from a bourgeois basis."[22] While he made no distinction among English, Spanish, and French America, Engels implied that colonization, not independence, inaugurated the reign of the bourgeoisie. For some years later he referred to America as a place "where no medieval ruins bar the way, where history begins with the elements of the modern bourgeois society as evolved in the seventeenth century."[23] America had been settled by the bourgeoisie and peasants, "who ran away from European feudalism in order to establish a purely bourgeois society."[24]

America, according to Marx and Engels, had somehow managed to bypass the feudal stage of development. This event decisively shaped the course of American history and class structure. For one thing, America was spared the cruel transition from feudal to bourgeois society that had convulsed the nations of Europe. Marx had reminded his readers that "capital comes [into the world] dripping from head to foot, from every pore, with blood and dirt."[25] But if America was from its start a bourgeois country, the terrible process of primitive accumulation need not have been so severe.

A consequence of this developmental pattern was that American capitalism lacked the partial and inconsistent nature that characterized the first capitalist economies. Because feudalism had never existed in the United States, a feudal system did not obstruct the full flowering of capitalism: "Capitalist economy and the corresponding enslavement of the working class have developed more rapidly and shamelessly than in any other country."[26] America had been spared such relics as a nobility and a feudal ideology. Even as European thought justified capitalism, surviving bits and pieces of feudal ideology infected the dominant European ideology. In particular, feudal thought had mitigated the harshness of laissez-faire capitalism. Thus, Engels explained the strength of American capitalism partly by "the complete indifference of a society that has grown up on a purely capitalist basis, without any easygoing feudal background, towards the human lives that perish in the competitive struggle."[27] The human costs of capitalism worried Americans even less than Europeans because the latter lived in countries where those obligations assumed within a feudal economy still retained some of their moral force.

Yet, a few years earlier, Engels had thought that America was infected with feudal ideological remnants. Despite its purely capitalistic past, it had "unwittingly taken over from England a whole store of ideology from feudal times."[28] While Americans "did not bring over any medieval institutions from Europe, they did bring over masses of medieval tradition, religion, English common (feudal) law, superstition, spiritualism, in short every kind of imbecility which was not directly harmful to business."[29] If Engels were correct, capitalist development should have been mitigated as it was in Europe, even if not to the same degree.

The bourgeoisie were the historical agents of capitalism. They had revolutionized society, accomplished wonders of production, and had developed the preconditions for the unchaining of the human race from the prison of scarcity. Their economic power had been translated into political power: "the executive of the modern state is but a committee for managing the common affairs of the whole bourgeoisie."[30] Despite their powers, the European bourgeoisie wore their crown uneasily, for among their many splendid creations was a proletariat whose fundamental interests were antagonistic to their own. Even as they reached for political power, after humbling the ancient régime, they recoiled in horror from the spectre of those allies whom they had called into being and without whose assistance they could not win a decisive victory. Caught between the Scylla of the reactionary aristocracy and the Charybdis of the revolutionary proletariat, the European bourgeoisie existed in a politically precarious position.[31]

The singular nature of American economic development—skipping the feudal stage—also had a profound effect on the American class structure. The American bourgeoisie was bolder and more progressive than its European counterparts. Not faced with such obstacles to modernization as a feudal nobility, an established church, and old ideologies, the bourgeoisie was self-confident and untroubled by such doubts as shook their less fortunate brethren across the sea. "A durable reign of the bourgeoisie," Engels remarked, "has been possible only in countries like America, where feudalism was unknown and society at the very beginning started from a bourgeois basis."[32]

Untroubled by enemies to the right, the American bourgeoisie was also fortunate in having little to fear from enemies to the left. The proletariat it faced was not capable of fighting capitalism with all its potential force because "it is quite natural that in a young country, which has never known feudalism and has grown up on a bourgeois basis from the first, bourgeois prejudices should also be strongly rooted in the working classes."[33]

These remarks, put into a logical order, thus leave the impression that America was the bourgeois country par excellence. They do not totally contradict the theory of colonization contained in *Capital*, but they are certainly not congruent with it either. In 1867, Marx was writing of the anticapitalist bias which infected America because of her origin as a country of independent private proprietors. On the other hand, in 1857, prefacing a discussion of the American economist Henry Carey, Marx described America as

> a country in which bourgeois society has not developed from a background of feudalism, but began of its own accord; a country where this society was not the surviving result of centuries of development, but the starting point of a new movement; where the state, unlike all other national structures, was from the start subordinated to bourgeois society and to bourgeois production, and could never pretend to a purpose of its own; where, finally, bourgeois society itself, linking the productive forces of the old world with the gigantic natural terrain of the new, has developed to hitherto unknown dimensions and freedom of movement.[34]

Both the colonization and the pure bourgeois theories were in agreement on the lack of class-consciousness in the American working class. The reasons the theories gave for this peculiar behavior were, however, not at all similar. In the one case opportunities for life as a noncapitalist proprietor were so attractive as to force capitalists to give extraordinary awards to wage laborers, thereby minimizing the extremes of wealth found in Europe; in the other case, workers, like everyone and everything else in America, had been bitten by the capitalist bug and had become infected with bourgeois ideology. In the first case, capitalism was anathema to most Americans, who lived off their own labor and did not exploit another man's; in the other case, capitalism was the beau ideal of the entire country. In the one case, capitalism had been advancing only slowly and with much difficulty; in the other, the American soil had been especially suited for capitalism.

The slow development of the American working class did not appear to worry Marx or Engels unduly, since either one of their theories could account for the delay. The peculiar nature of American society seemed to have been expressly designed for frustrating the growth of a socialist movement. The movement would, Marx and Engels were sure, someday arise. Yet, they were unsure and contradictory as to when this would occur. In 1886, Engels hailed the growing militancy of the working class and ridiculed the earlier hopes of some Americans that class conflict would not appear in the United States, saying that "because there were not, as yet, classes with opposing interests, our-and your-bourgeoisie thought that America stood above class antagonism and struggles."[35]

The earlier opportunities for escape to the land were drying up. Even as late as 1892, however, Engels was advising against the formation of a third party, since

> only when the land—the public lands—is completely in the hands of the speculators, and settlement on the land thus becomes more and more difficult or falls victim to gouging—only then, I think, will the time come, with peaceful development, for a third party.[36]

Even though Marx and Engels confidently expected the eventual emergence of a militant working class, they did not carefully consider what kind of working class could emerge from the particular social structures they had described as existing in America. Nor did they consider whether the privileged position of that class would insure a high standard of living for American workers. Finally, they ignored the implication that the bourgeois attitudes of the working class might permanently dampen class consciousness. Marx and Engels seemed to think that the American working class would, in time, resemble those found on the Continent. Each of the two different pictures they gave of American development, however, suggests that other possibilities existed.[37]

Both the colonization and the pure bourgeois theories account, in one way or another, for the peculiar backwardness of the American working-class. The Civil War, however, and the problem of the South fit into neither theory. The South is an illustration of the gaps in both theories and the difficulties Marx confronted in analyzing America.

Most of the articles Marx wrote on the Civil War deal with the diplomatic intrigue the war engendered in England and with tactical military problems and prospects.[38] The less illuminating of the others treat the Confederacy as a hypocritical state whose ideology could not be taken seriously. Eugene Genovese has pointed out that Marx was unable to confront the Southern ideology as the honest expression of a particular social system.[39] Although studded with sage observations—especially about the decisive influence of the northwestern states—the articles either reveal the shortcomings of Marx's other comments on America or his other work highlights the shallowness of his journalism.[40]

Seeing the Civil War as "a struggle between two social systems, between the system of slavery and the system of free labour," Marx regarded the defeat of the former system as a necessary and inevitable prelude to the full flowering of American capitalism.[41] He felt that certain conditions had to be met before the wage laborer could appear in the marketplace to sell his labor power. The individual could not be an objective part of the conditions of production. The owner of labor power had to offer it for sale, it had to be his to offer, and it had to be sold only for a definite period of time.[42] Slavery certainly failed to meet these specified conditions. It signified an aberration in American development, a detour from America's comfortable, bourgeois course.[43]

While such an analysis of the role of slavery in America may well have been correct, Marx never paused to consider the effects of this aberration, other than that it inevitably would lead to war. If America was from its beginnings bourgeois, as Engels maintained, then the South constituted a glaring exception covering a good portion of the country. If America was a land of anticapitalist private owners, the South still remained an exception.

But if the South was not capitalist, neither was it feudal.[44] Shortly before the war, Marx cryptically remarked that "if we now talk of plantation-owners in America as capitalists, if they are capitalists, this is due to the fact that they exist as anomalies within a world market based upon free labour."[45] Thus, while the planter class "functioned as part of the capitalist world and could not separate itself from the bourgeois economy or ideology," it was part of a social system which was neither capitalist, feudal, or private non-capitalist.[46]

Regardless of its exact classification, the slave system of the South severely modified the nature of American society. Not only did it affect the ideology of both North and South, it also distorted class development, particularly, in the latter. Marx himself was aware of the latent conflict between planters and poor whites, but his reduction of the Southern ideology to simple economic greed led him to anticipate only the possibility of the planters abandoning the poor whites after the war by uniting with the Northern bourgeoisie.[47] He assumed that the Civil War would destroy slavery and pave the way for the complete triumph of capitalism. He did not foresee the strength of the anticapitalist ideology of the South. Combined with the doctrines of white supremacy, the ideology of the postbellum South supported a fierce resistance to the encroachments of capitalism and its corresponding worldview.

When Marx wrote about America he generally ignored the South. He failed to consider its enormous impact on economic, political, and ideological development. When he wrote about the slave South he generally treated it as a temporary phenomenon, whose passing would return America to her preordained course. America was not, however, a country with a single mode of life and a unique set of customs. Neither bourgeois ideology nor capitalist economy dominated all of the American continent. Marx identified at least two precapitalist economic forms—slavery and private property in a farm—but failed to consider their interaction with capitalism.

Despite the shortcomings of Marx and Engels' analyses, they had correctly identified the long availability of free land in an industrializing country, the opportunities for escape from the working class, the absence of most feudal restrictions, a powerful bourgeoisie, a bourgeois-minded working class, and the peculiar mix of nationalities as elements native to America.[48] They did not make clear whether or not these conditions would modify America's path to socialism. Russia, they were willing to concede, might be able to avoid following the footsteps of Western Europe. But America?

As early as 1848, in *The Communist Manifesto*, Marx had contended that the proletarians of every country, "in England as in France, in America as in Germany" had been "stripped of every trace of national character."[49] "As for those wise Americans," Engels sneered in 1886, "who think their country exempt from the consequences of fully expanded capitalist production, they seem to live in blissful ignorance."[50] In 1888, discussing the American labor movement, he opined that "the causes that brought into existence the abyss between the working class and the capitalist class are the same in America as in Europe; the means of filling up that abyss are equally the same everywhere."[51] Again, in 1892, Engels insisted that there was no reason to doubt that America's road to socialism would be any different from that of England or Germany.[52] Such statements have inspired the claim that "while Marx and Engels were clearly aware of the peculiarities of American historical development, they nevertheless pointed out time and time again that America was no exception to the general laws of capitalism."[53]

Unfortunately for the sake of consistency, however, they also pointed out time and again that different nations would tread different paths. Although Engels had hinted that the means as well as the ends would be similar in all countries, neither he nor Marx ever ruled out the possibility of a peaceful transition to socialism in certain countries. Addressing the Hague Congress of the First International in 1872, Marx said that

> we do not assert that the attainment of this end requires identical means. We know that one has to take into consideration the institutions, mores, and traditions of the different countries, and we do not deny that there are countries like England and America and if I am familiar with your institutions, Holland, where labour may attain its goal by peaceful means.[54]

In 1871, commenting on the Paris Commune, Marx implied that different measures might be required in Europe than in America:

> if you look at the last chapter of my Eighteenth Brumaire you will find that I say there that the next attempt of the French revolution will be no longer, as before, to transfer the bureaucratic military machine from one hand to another, but to smash it, and this is essential for every real people's revolution on the Continent.[55]

And, in 1893, Engels speculated that since America had no feudal background and Russia such a pervasive one, "it stands to reason that the change in Russia must be far more violent, far more incisive, and accompanied by immensely greater sufferings than it can be in America."[56]

It is clear from the contradictory assumptions behind their comments, the features of the society left unexplained, and the confusing backtracking that Marx and Engels were never able to fit this country into the great puzzle they claimed to have unraveled. In 1848 and 1886, the class struggle was heating up; in 1852 and 1892, American capitalism was still too immature for such a struggle.[57] The strongest bourgeois ideology in the world bolstered the purest capitalist economy, which was half a slave system while simultaneously sheltering the weakest working class in the industrialized world. A capitalist country from its birth, America was also a colonial, noncapitalist country. Although it had been settled by the bourgeoisie and peasants, as early as 1848 America was absorbing "the surplus proletarian forces of Europe."[58] Bourgeois political institutions were a sham, yet the United States could peacefully introduce socialism.[59]

Inadequate as each may be as a complete explanation of American development, neither the colonization nor the pure bourgeois theories foreclosed the possibility of a theory of American exceptionalism. Either one could be expanded to argue that American history so fundamentally diverged from that of Europe that the American future would also do so. Either one could form the basis for arguing that the American class structure would force alteration of the analytical categories Marx had employed for Western Europe. The development of Marxist thought in America, however, has been dictated in large part by the need of political movements, particularly the Communist Party. Rather than an autonomous theory being used by a political movement, Marxism was transformed into a rationalization for the political program, not even of the American Communist Party, but of the Communist Party of the Soviet Union.

Since its major function became the protection of the supposedly beleaguered socialist homeland, Marxist theory in America did not lead to the development of a theory of American exceptionalism.[60] Since the United States, whatever its past, has become the archetypical capitalist nation in the world for Marxists, they have not, additionally, had much incentive to probe into an explanation which stressed the weaknesses of capitalism. Whatever the problems American capitalism had once encountered, it had seemingly surmounted them in the twentieth century. Consequently, Marx's theory, emphasizing the difficulties faced by capitalists, has been obscured and Engels' theory, emphasizing the difficulties faced by socialists, pushed into the limelight. Political movements are, after all, more likely to attribute their failure to their enemy's strength than to his weakness.

The founding fathers of Marxism anticipated a number of the explanations for the weakness of American socialism later developed by such scholars as Frederick Jackson Turner, Louis Hartz, and Seymour Martin Lipset. Marx and Engels' own work vividly illustrates still another reason for the continual failures of American Marxism—the difficulty of assimilating the American experience to Marxist theory. Marx and Engels were no more successful at this task than their followers. They did, however, haltingly recognize that America diverged in essential respects from Europe. They were unable to consider fully the implications of those differences while their followers have either ignored them or dismissed them as dated. The historical conditions under which American capitalism came into existence, however, have shaped the boundaries within which the socioeconomic system has operated and permanently affected the nature of the class struggle. For that reason alone, the contradictory Marxist theories of American development remain a fruitful theoretical and practical problem.

Notes

1. Marx to Engels, January 11, 1860, in Karl Marx and Frederick Engels, *Selected Correspondence* (Moscow: Foreign Language Publishing House, 1953), 144.
2. Gerald Runkle, "Karl Marx and the American Civil War," *Comparative Studies in Society and History*, 6 (January 1964), 141, alerted me to this interesting lapse.
3. I have relied here on Stanley Moore, *Three Tactics: The Background in Marx* (New York: Monthly Review Press, 1963), and the discussion of the *Grundrisse* by Martin Nicolaus, "The Unknown Marx," in *The New Left Reader*, ed. Carl Oglesby (New York: Grove Press, Inc., 1969), 84-110.
4. Moore, *Three Tactics*, 68.
5. See Engels, "Introduction," to Marx, *Class Struggles in France 1848-1850* (New York: International Publishers, 1964), 15, for the rejection of a minority putsch. See also Martin Buber, *Paths in Utopia* (Boston: Beacon Press, Inc., 1958), for a discussion of the competing systems model in Marx.
6. Marx to the Editors of "Otechestvenniye Zapiski," November, 1877, in *Karl Marx on Colonialism and Modernization*, ed. Shlomo Avineri (Garden City, NY: Doubleday & Company, Inc., 1969), 469. Marx's letter apparently had a wide circulation among Russian radicals. A brief discussion of its history can be found in the editors' comments section of Marx and Engels, *The Russian Menace to Europe: A Collection of Articles, Speeches, Letters and News Dispatches,* ed. Paul Blackstock and Bert Hoselitz (Glencoe, IL, The Free Press, 1952), 274-275. Also see Marx and Engels, "Preface to the Russian Edition of 1882," in *The Communist Manifesto: An Introduction*, ed. Harold Laski (New York: Random House, Vintage Books, 1967), 111-113.
7. Marx to Editors, *On Colonialism*, 468.
8. The bulk of their commentary is found in two sources. Both Marx and Engels corresponded with a number of Americans and, quite naturally, touched on American problems, personalities, and possibilities. Marx also wrote a number of newspaper articles on the Civil War.
9. Marx, *Capital: A Critique of Political Economy*, ed. Frederick Engels, trans. Samuel Moore and Edward Aveling, 3 vols. (New York: International Publishers, 1967), I, 765, fn. 1.
10. Marx, *Pre-Capitalist Economic Formations*, ed. Eric Hobsbawm (New York: International Publishers, 1965), 67.
11. I Marx, Capital, I, 765.
12. Marx, *Pre-Capitalist Economic Formations*, 97-104; *Capital*, I, 714.
13. Marx, *Pre-Capitalist Economic Formations*, 110-111.
14. Marx, *Capital*, I, 716. Marx goes on to point out that "the history of this expropriation, in different countries, assumed different orders of succession."
15. Ibid., 768.
16. Ibid. Marx indicated the effect of capitalism on self-sufficiency. "Capital rapidly creates itself an internal market by destroying all rural subsidiary crafts." *Pre-Capitalist Economic Formations*, 118.
17. Marx, *Capital*, I, 769-770.
18. Ibid., I, 773.
19. Ibid., I, 773.
20. Ibid., I, 171.
21. pp. 132-133. [MISSING MATERIAL?]
22. "On Historical Materialism," in *Marx and Engels: Basic Writings on Politics & Philosophy*, ed. Lewis Feuer (Garden City, N. Y.: Doubleday & Company, Inc., 1959), 63.

23. "The Labour Movement in the United States," in ibid., 491.
24. Engels to F. N. Danielson, October 17, 1893, in *Selected Correspondence*, 545.
25. *Capital*, I, 760.
26. Marx to F. A. Sorge, June 20, 1881, in *Marx and Engels, Letters to Americans: 1848-1895* (New York: International Publishers, 1963), 129.
27. Engels to H. Schlueter, March 30, 1892, in ibid., 242.
28. Engels to Sorge, September 16, 1886, in ibid., 161.
29. Engels to Sorge, November 29, 1886, in ibid., 164. A few months earlier, however, Engels called America a land "with purely bourgeois institutions unleavened by feudal remnants of monarchical traditions." Engels to Mrs. Florence Wischnewetzky, June 3, 1886, in ibid., 157.
30. The praise of the bourgeoisie is in Marx and Engels, *The Communist Manifesto*, 134-138. The quotation about the political power of the class is on 134.
31. Marx, *The Eighteenth Brumaire of Louis Bonaparte* (New York: International Publishers, 1968), 126.
32. Engels, "On Historical Materialism," 63.
33. Engels to Sorge, December 31, 1892, in Herbert Morais, "Marx and Engels on America," *Science and Society*, 12 (Winter 1948), 19.
34. *The Grundrisse*, ed. and trans. David McLellan (New York: Harper & Row, 1971), 48.
35. Engels to Mrs. Wischnewetzky, June 3, 1886, in *Letters to Americans*, 157. This is a curious statement, indeed. Since when had there been an era in America with classes with no opposing interest? Even if it is conceded that the entire society was bourgeois-minded, what about the slaves and the planters, for instance?
36. Engels to Sorge, January 6, 1892, in *Letters to Americans*, 239.
37. At various other times Engels tossed off other obstacles to the development of the American working-class along European lines. He complained in 1892 that the Constitution had the effect of institutionalizing a two-party system. Workers were thus loath to waste their votes on sure losers and a third party was hampered. Similarly, the tariff and a growing domestic market had fostered prosperity which was shared by the working-class. Engels to Sorge, December 2, 1893, in ibid., 258.
38. Engels, who was an avid student of military affairs, wrote many of the latter at Marx's request. They were published under Marx's name, however.
39. "Marxian Interpretations of the Slave South," in *Towards A New Past: Dissenting Essays in American History*, ed. Barton Bernstein (New York: Random House, Pantheon Books, Inc., 1968), 106.
40. See, for example, Marx and Engels, "The American Question in England," in *The Civil War in the United States* (New York: International Publishers, 1969), 7-8.
41. "The Civil War in the United States," in ibid., 81.
42. Marx, *Capital*, I, 169.
43. Marx and Engels, "The American Question," 7.
44. Genovese points out that for Marx the feudal mode of production was characterized by private ownership of property, the retention of the means of production by the laborer, and an economic bounty owed by the laborer to the lord. See "Marxian Interpretations," 112-113.
45. *Pre-Capitalist Economic Formations*, 119.
46. Genovese, "Marxian Interpretations," 112. Engels was confident of "the bourgeois nature of the planters." Engels to Marx, May 23, 1862, in *The Civil War*, 245. On this basis both Marx and Engels expected a postwar alliance between the planters and the northern bourgeoisie.

47. Marx, "The Situation in the American Theater of War," in *The Civil War*, 190.
48. For the last point, see Engels to Schlueter, March 30, 1892, in *Letters to Americans*, 242.
49. Pp. 146-147. In light of what Marx and Engels later had to say about America, the statement is palpably false. In 1886 Engels was claiming that class interests had not existed until just a few years before. In 1857 Marx was admitting that class conflict was far from reaching a virulent form in America.
50. Engels to Wishnewetzky, January 7, 1886, in *Letters to Americans*, 148.
51. "The Labour Movement in the United States," 491.
52. Engels to Sorge, December 31, 1892, in *Letters to Americans*, 244.
53. Morais, "Marx and Engels on America," 6.
54. Hans Gerth, ed., *The First International: Minutes of the Hague Congress of 1872* (Madison: University of Wisconsin Press, 1958), 236.
55. Marx to Dr. Ludwig Kugelmann, April 12, 1871, in *Marx and V. I. Lenin, The Civil War in France: The Paris Commune* (New York: International Publishers, 1968), 86.
56. Engels to F. N. Danielson, October 17, 1893, in *Selected Correspondence*, 545-546.
57. In 1852, Marx had chastised a critic for "taking the 'undeveloped' conditions of the United States for normal conditions." Marx to Joseph Weydemeyer, March 5, 1852, in *Letters to Americans*, 43-46.
58. Marx and Engels, "Preface to the Russian Edition of 1882," 112.
59. Engels put forth the claim that "nowhere do politicians form a more separate, powerful section of the nation than in North America.... It is precisely in America that we see best how there takes place this process of the state power making itself independent in relation to society, whose mere instrument it was originally intended to be." "Introduction" in *Marx and Lenin, Civil War in France*, 20.
60. A theory of American exceptionalism was developed by a faction within the Communist Party in the 1920s. Their exceptionalism was Leninist and not Marxist, however. See Harvey Klehr, "The Theory of American Exceptionalism" (unpublished Ph.D. dissertation, University of North Carolina, 1971). Eric Hobsbawm has pointed out one other instance of Marxist theory being distorted to impede an exceptionalist heresy. He notes that "the fear of encouraging 'Asiatic exceptionalism' and of discouraging a sufficiently firm opposition to (Western) imperialist influence, was a strong, and perhaps decisive, element in the abandonment of Marx's 'Asiatic mode' by the international Communist movement after 1930." "Introduction," in Marx, *Pre- Capitalist Economic Formations*, 60.

2

Leninist Theory in Search of America

Karl Marx once noted that "the country that is more developed industrially only shows, to the less developed, the image of its own future."[1] Surprisingly, prior to World War I, Vladimir Ilich Lenin believed that the developed capitalist nation of America seemed to show Russia a desirable image of her future. While there were enormous differences in social structure, population, and history, Lenin thought America to be a model worth emulating. America was a frequent symbol of Russian backwardness; Lenin compared Marx's comments on nineteenth-century America with twentieth-century Russia. During this era, Lenin's major concern was with the development of a bourgeois revolution in Russia. America stood, therefore, as a positive symbol. Lenin's later writings present a very different image of America. In this chapter I will illustrate these two contrasting images and then offer an explanation for Lenin's shifting perspective of America.[2]

Two Roads of Capitalist Development

Lenin was frequently laudatory about America. He constantly admonished his Russian comrades to remember that their country remained politically, economically, and culturally backward. America illustrated the value of democracy for the class struggle—to make that fight "broad, open, and conscious."[3] The pre-Civil War American economic statistics contrasted favorably with those from early twentieth-century Russia.[4] Even though he was critical of the large gaps existing between blacks and whites in America, Lenin noted that Russian literacy rates were inferior even to those of America's most oppressed group.[5]

Although America presented a model for Russian development, Lenin refused to concede that the American image would inevitably attract Russia. On the contrary, he insisted that without the conscious political effort of the proletariat

---

Originally published in *Polity*, Fall 1976 and reprinted with permission.

Russia would choose another, less desirable, model for development which would condemn Russia to a longer period of inferiority to America.

While convinced that Russia would have to emulate the more developed capitalist nations, Lenin believed that Russia had a choice of models. Russia's feudal elite and nascent bourgeois class had definite interests in steering the nation in one direction; the proletariat had equally compelling interests in another. Having the benefit of historical example both camps could plainly see the advantages and disadvantages of different roads to capitalism. Lacking strong resistance, the nobility and bourgeoisie would choose the road least likely to threaten their own prerogatives.

The very presence of strong feudal elements demonstrated why the American model was not foreordained. America had successfully completed its bourgeois revolution while Russia was still half-immersed in feudal chains. Before all else, this infirmity would have to be removed. Both the working class and the capitalist class had an interest in the capitalist revolution since the former suffered "not so much from capitalism as from the insufficient development of capitalism."[6] The feudal elements also had an interest in guiding capitalism so as to ensure their survival. While the American model offered them little support, the Prussian path to industrialization promised their survival within a capitalist framework. The Prussian model would also prove attractive to the bourgeoisie.

According to Lenin, the bourgeois revolution could be either thorough and wide-ranging or incomplete and limited—either American or Prussian: "The survivals of feudalism may fall away either as a result of the transformation of the landlord economy or as a result of the abolition of the landlord latifundia, i.e., either by reform or by revolution."[7] Reform and revolution referred not only to a difference in the method by which feudalism was abolished, but also to an important variation in the type of bourgeois society that would emerge.

The reform path was the Prussian. It involved a gradual transformation of the feudal landlord system, condemning the peasantry "to decades of most harrowing expropriation and bondage."[8] Even more crucially, the Prussian path meant "the retention of the monarchy and landlordism."[9] Prussia was the symbol for a bourgeois revolution made from the top down, a gradual economic transformation bringing the nation into the modern industrial age but retaining the authority structure of the past. The revolutionary path was the American. It involved the destruction of the landlord economy by means of a policy of nationalization and then division of the feudal estates among the farmers. Most importantly, the American path meant "a bourgeois republic, the absence of landlordism, the creation of a farmer class."[10] The old economic and political elite would be replaced by new groups committed to different values. America was the symbol for a revolution that would alter social and political structures as well as economic ones.

The American path would speed up the development of capitalism in Russia while the Prussian path would slow it down. The former would break feudal ties in the interests of the free peasants; the latter on behalf of the wealthy land-owners. The more thoroughgoing the bourgeois revolution, "the more assured will the proletariat's struggle be against the bourgeoisie and for socialism."[11] The American path would thus insure the earlier arrival and more vigorous prosecution of the struggle between the bourgeoisie and proletariat that would follow. It therefore presented a dilemma to Russia's capitalists. By completely eliminating all feudal vestiges—social, political and economic—the American route ensured a purer form of capitalism but also left the bourgeoisie standing alone to fight the workers. The Prussian path prevented the bourgeoisie from assuming undisputed sway over the country; they were forced to share power and even take a subordinate political role to the aristocracy. While still not completely in control, the bourgeoisie could console themselves with the presence of allies to fight against the working class. The American model left the bourgeoisie helpless to resist proletarian demands in the face of their own ideological pretensions to democracy, universal suffrage, equality, and liberty. The Prussian path permitted the softening of the bourgeois individualistic ethos and a paternalistic regard for the working class likely to dilute the fervor of their hostility to capitalism.

Lenin used both America and Prussia as symbols. The real America had not totally destroyed the relics of slavery, whose survivals Lenin felt were identical with the survivals of feudalism.[12] One of the major themes of *Capitalism and Agriculture in the United States of America,* the longest work Lenin ever wrote on America, was the swifter development of capitalist agriculture in the North and Midwest where slavery had been unknown. In spite of the slight divergence of America from his model, Lenin viewed the United States as the closest embodiment of a purely bourgeois country in the world. There socialism would develop most fully and fruitfully. Consequently, the American path to capitalism promised greater dividends to the working class than the Prussian path. The rapid and thorough democratization of Russian society offered the best hope for a rapid and early victory of socialism. The peasant desire to own land was petty-bourgeois but a necessary step, deserving the support of socialists, as it permitted the flowering of capitalism.[13]

The Failure of American Socialism

Despite his admiration for the American path to capitalism, Lenin did not seek guidance or instruction from the American Socialist Party. Even though he urged Russian radicals down the American road, he turned to the German Socialist Party when seeking strategic models and contrasted the problems of the German and Russian socialists with those of the Americans and the British. Neither Germany nor Russia was a bourgeois democracy. In both countries, socialists existed legally only at the pleasure of the authorities; particularly in Russia, underground work was a necessity. The major reason, however, that Lenin grouped German and Russian socialists together was that there were precious few American, or British, socialists from whom to learn. That country whose example promised the speedy arrival of socialism lagged far behind other, less developed, less bourgeois nations. That country which, according to most Marxist indicators, ought to have been fertile ground for socialists seemed to present especial difficulties.

In Marxist terminology this has been known as the problem of American exceptionalism. Marx and Engels had brooded about the slow development of American socialism and had occasionally suggested that there were special American conditions of one sort or another that had temporarily stalled the march of socialism. Both were confident that the growth of a thriving Socialist party was only a matter of time.[14] Because American socialism was so backward, Marx and Engels had urged its adherents to avoid insisting on theoretical purity. A large, well-established Socialist party in Germany could afford to launch a struggle against opportunism, but the weak sects in America had to concentrate their energies on building a Socialist party of some consequence. They were in no position to drive people out of their party. Lenin followed Marx and Engels in insisting that it would be folly to apply the same tactics in countries facing different problems. Thus, while he admitted that Marx and Engels had urged Americans to avoid sectarianism, such advice, he felt, was inapplicable to the conditions of the Russian socialists.[15]

In countries without an established social-democratic party, Lenin argued, sectarianism was of no value. Like Germany, however, Russia had a long history of proletarian activity in politics. Consequently, opportunism and an undue reverence of parliamentary activity were the major obstacles to the continued growth of both the German and the Russian socialists.[16] In contrast, both in America and Great Britain, "where complete political liberty exists and where the proletariat has no revolutionary and socialist traditions that could be called living traditions," the major task was to develop an independent workers' movement and not engage in sharpening doctrinal differences between socialists of various hues.[17]

As with most of his other comments about America, Lenin was prompted to discuss the country because of a need to solve a Russian problem. Although he thought the American path to capitalism worthy of Russian emulation, he was not prepared to model Russian social-democracy after the American version. If, however, the American path was the quickest route to capitalism and then social-ism, why had not America's revolutionary abandonment of slavery-feudalism hastened the actual development of a Socialist party? Why was Lenin forced to turn to Germany to see a successful socialist movement? Did the German phenomenon mean that the Prussian path would offer socialists greater success? To answer these questions Lenin was forced to explain the failure of American socialism. He did so by formulating his first and least-well-known theory to account for the weakness of socialism in advanced industrial nations.

Lenin's early account of the failure of American socialism contained hints that Marxism itself might be an inadequate guide to the future for socialists.

Socialists in Britain and America could not expect to achieve the successes of their comrades in less developed countries because they were seeking socialist and not purely democratic goals. Because they did not have to struggle for political rights, there was "an absence of any big, nation-wide democratic tasks facing the proletariat." The proletariat was faced with "complete subordination to bourgeois politics." Meanwhile, the socialists faced "the sectarian isolation of groups…from the proletariat; not the slightest success among the working masses at the elections."[18]

In contrast, the relative success of the German socialists, in a less developed country, was an advantageous consequence of their struggling for democracy in an autocratic state. The tensions between the autocratic state, which existed as a result of the failure of the German bourgeoisie to complete fully their revolution, and a capitalist economy fueled the growth of German socialism.[19] Seemingly, then, socialists would thrive where they could plausibly claim to fight for democratic goals. Where political liberty already existed, socialists would find it more difficult to appeal to the population. Political democracy undermined the effectiveness of socialist appeals by permitting the bourgeoisie to depict themselves more favorably.

Lenin had no doubt that the bourgeoisie would not passively await their fate. The English and American capitalists, unable to ally themselves with a feudal nobility, had adopted a liberal ideology, stressing universal values and diluting the notion of class war. This ideology effectively disarmed the working class.[20]

Capitalist ideology, however, was not the only prop of bourgeois rule in America and Britain. The early Lenin explained opportunism among British workers—their alliance with the capitalists—as a consequence of the ability of a small segment to share in the extra-large profits British industry was making in the middle of the nineteenth century. Since the British had enjoyed a near-monopoly in the world market, they had been able to gain excess profits and parcel a small percentage out to a labor aristocracy. But, "these conditions were becoming a thing of the past" as Britain lost her monopoly.[21]

In 1912, Lenin admitted that the American trade union movement also endorsed capitalism. The bourgeois labor movement in America was obviously not a consequence of a world trade monopoly. Instead, it appeared to Lenin that it was due to "the long-standing political liberty" and extensive development of capitalism which had "tended to produce within the working class an aristocracy that has trailed after the bourgeoisie, betraying its own class."[22]

The swift development of capitalism promised by the American path provided, therefore, both the best chance for the triumph of socialism and the development of obstacles to its realization. Lenin was convinced, however, that the impediments to the growth of socialism in America were rapidly being removed. Immediately after noting the conditions which had led to the sorry state of American socialism, Lenin exulted that "in the twentieth century, this peculiar situation in Britain and America is rapidly disappearing."[23] Signs of the turnabout were everywhere: "the American working class is rapidly becoming enlightened, and is organizing in a powerful proletarian party."[24] The circulation of *Appeal to Reason,* a socialist paper, and the large presidential vote for Eugene Debs in 1912 were indications of the march of American socialism.[25] Socialists were beginning to make headway in the AFL.[26] While a Socialist party had been slow to develop in America, once started it would be unstoppable. Before World War I Lenin displayed little sustained interest in America. Aside from *Capitalism and Agriculture in the United States of America,* largely a technical tract written in 1915, Lenin's comments were made in an *ad hoc* fashion. When he did refer to America, his interest was focused less on what he could learn about this country than on what America could tell him about Russia. Even *Capitalism and Agriculture* was written to refute the argument of a Russian social-democrat who had asserted that American agriculture was not becoming more capitalistic.

While critical of the sham of bourgeois democracy, Lenin saw from the United States that it was a valuable weapon in the class struggle. He also noted that socialists involved in the struggle for democracy would find it easier to build mass movements than socialists involved in the struggle for socialism. Democracy, finally, could poison the minds of the working class. Lenin's ambivalence reflected the anomaly of a highly industrialized democracy lacking a strong socialist movement. On the one hand, he might have argued that socialism would never thrive where it could not broaden its appeal beyond economic issues and identify itself with a struggle for political rights. Those nations where the bourgeoisie had successfully completed the fight for democracy might prove perpetually hostile to socialism since large segments of the working class lacked both economic and political reasons to rally behind a Socialist party. On the other hand, Lenin might have discovered a more basic cause for the failure of socialism in those countries where it should have flourished. With the outbreak of World War I, Lenin moved in the latter direction by developing the concept of imperialism.

America and Imperialism

The outbreak of World War I shattered forever the fragile unity of world socialism. When faced with the real problem of supporting their respective bourgeois governments or standing up for the principle of international proletarian solidarity, most socialists opted for national self-defense. The disputes over Bernsteinism, immediate demands, trade unionism, and other issues had divided the world socialist community before, but the reaction of socialists to the war precipitated a new unprecedented crisis. Lenin's response contributed to the split of the socialist community. At the same time, it provided an altered image of the world and of America's role in that world and a coherent rationale for the failure of Marx's predictions about the development of socialism.

While America did not play as prominent a role in *Imperialism* as Britain and Germany, the theme was central to Lenin's evaluation of America from 1917 to his death.

Lenin presented the theory of imperialism as a more logical extension of Marxism. He insisted that Marx and Engels had not been wrong when they predicted socialism would inevitably arrive; they had only underestimated the reserve powers of capitalism. They had not foreseen that capitalism was capable of one additional burst of strength—the era of imperialism. Capitalists discovered a new source of economic vitality abroad. By exporting capital they could revitalize themselves. Instead of steadily falling profits, large-scale unemployment, and an increasingly brutalized proletariat, the bastions of capitalism could enjoy an era of relative prosperity and abundance. The colonial lands offered such rewards since there "profits are unusually high, for capital is scarce, the price of land is relatively low, wages are low, raw materials are cheap."[27]

Imperialism did more than merely solve the economic problem of capitalism. The economic benefits reaped from the possession of colonies enabled capitalists to overcome temporarily a political danger. By permitting workers to enjoy some of the surplus squeezed from the colonial lands, the capitalists reduced their will to struggle for revolution: "Certain sections of the working class, and for a time a fairly considerable minority," were among the beneficiaries.[28] Imperialism was, therefore, a salve for domestic class-conflict.[29]

With the nominal leaders of the working class neutralized, the big capitalists had temporarily avoided that inevitable battle which would sunder their social system. One of the defining characteristics of the age of imperialism, however, was that it was an era of constant capitalist wars for the division of the colonial world. Since the possession of colonies was a matter of economic life and death, capitalist nations would be at each others' throats for the wherewithal to prosper and avoid decay.[30] Since a segment of the working class depended upon imperialism for their own prosperity, some workers were ready allies of the bourgeoisie in such wars.

Before World War I, Lenin had attributed the growth of opportunism among workers in Britain to an earlier form of imperialism which was disappearing as that nation lost her industrial monopoly. In the era of imperialism, however, the pathology of opportunism had now "become common to all the great capitalist countries of Europe, as their colonial possessions expanded, and, in general, as the imperialist period of competition grew and developed."[31] The weakness of socialism in the developed countries was a consequence not of some national peculiarities, but of the structural development of capitalism.

Lenin's view of America accordingly underwent a shift. Indeed, his assessment of the role of all developed capitalist nations changed as backward Russia remained the only country where a socialist government endured. The absence of revolutionary fervor among the workers of the west was attributed to the fact that "class collaboration, repudiation of the dictatorship of the proletariat, repudiation of revolutionary action" were all inevitable consequences of the age of imperialism.[32] Lenin's notion of imperialism attributed the failure of western socialism to a betrayal of the working class by its leadership, encouraging the growth of a conspiracy theory of history. The concept of imperialism obviated the need for Lenin and future Leninists to inquire about the past failure of American socialism. For whatever reasons American socialism had failed in the past, from *Imperialism* onward Leninists had a ready explanation for its more contemporary failures.

Lenin obviously included America among the imperialist nations. He gave the Spanish-American War of 1898 as one of the starting points of the imperialistic age and discussed the American trusts and banks as leading examples of the newly powerful economic institutions.[33] Indeed, he called "the American trusts...the supreme expression of the economics of imperialism or monopoly capitalism."[34] Although America was last among the six great powers both in terms of size and population of colonies in 1914,[35] Lenin still insisted that American imperialism was as bad as that of European monarchies; "has not American 'democracy'...robbed the Philippines, and does it not rob Mexico?"[36] And, certainly, the American intervention in the Russian Civil War seemed to Lenin another imperialistic adventure.[37]

The concept of imperialism promoted a certain vagueness about the timing of the proletarian revolution. On the one hand, imperialism was the final or highest stage of capitalism. At some point during the imperialistic era, the proletarian revolution would occur. On the other hand, imperialism was a temporary salve for capitalism, enabling it to postpone the proletarian revolution. Lenin's comments on America reflected these two possibilities. In 1916, he felt that imperialism in Western Europe and the United States had advanced to the point where "the revolutionary struggle of the proletariat for the overthrow of capitalist governments and the expropriation of the bourgeoisie is on the order of the day."[38] Again, in 1920, Lenin insisted that "in almost all the countries of Europe and America, the class struggle is entering the phase of civil war."[39] Yet, Lenin was also developing the second possibility and in a post-revolutionary "Letter to American Workers" he indicated that he did not expect immediate assistance from the American proletariat.[40]

As the Bolsheviks entrenched themselves in power, Lenin developed the idea that revolutionary assistance from the developed countries was unlikely. In 1920 he argued that "the more complete, lengthy and firmly" the bourgeoisie had ruled a country, the more likely they would have been to install compliant leaders at the head of the labor movement.[41] Russian workers had found it easier to rid themselves of opportunism than European and American workers would because the opportunists in the latter countries were more numerous and better bribed. And "without their leadership of the workers, the bourgeoisie could not remain in power."[42]

While it had therefore been easier to start a socialist revolution in Russia, continuing and bringing it to fruition would be exceedingly difficult. In Russia the human and economic material necessary to create a socialist culture was sadly lacking. Europe, however, and by extension America, had such material, but the proletariat was corrupted by the "higher thinking that comes with culture, and the working class is in a state of cultural slavery."[43] The longer, then, that capitalism had existed in a country and the more complete and thorough its accomplishments, the greater the opposition to socialism would be among the workers. The labor movement would be more thoroughly corrupted and the working class more completely brainwashed. Those conditions Marxists had thought most conducive to socialism were actually, therefore, barriers to its realization. In those places where socialists should have been expected to prosper they would have to struggle against heavy odds.

Imperialism had destroyed much of the distinctiveness of capitalist nations and molded them all in nearly the same image. Marx and Engels had allowed for the possibility that the path to socialism in some countries might not require a violent revolution. The United States, they suggested, was one of those countries that might be able to institute socialism peacefully.[44] Marx had also suggested that in Great Britain socialists might be able to buy up capitalists peacefully, providing compensation for expropriated industries. Lenin refused to concede that either country could peacefully introduce socialism. Marx's comments about Britain had been offered "before Britain had imperialism, when a peaceful transition to socialism was possible."[45] Since that opportunity had been foregone, Britain would be forced to undergo a violent revolution to introduce socialism. When Marx and Engels had spoken of the potential for a peaceful revolution in America, that country too had been different from the capitalist nations on the Continent. The age of imperialism had destroyed that difference:

> Both Britain and America, the greatest and the last representatives of Anglo-Saxon "liberty" in the sense of the absence of militarism and bureaucracy, have today plunged headlong into the all-European dirty, bloody morass of military bureaucratic institutions to which everything is subordinated and which tramples everything under foot. Today, both in England and in America, the precondition of any real people's revolution is the breakup, the shattering of the ready-made state machinery (brought in those countries, between 1914 and 1917, to general "European" imperialist perfection).[46]

Lenin also noted that the absence of militarism and bureaucracy had led Marx and Engels to predict a peaceful transition to socialism but these two factors now existed in both America and Britain.[47]

While the American state machinery had once been relatively weak, this was true only "in its pre-imperialistic days."[48] America was now no different from Germany; in both nations a few major banks enjoyed economic benefits as a result of covert control of the political process.[49] Under the impact of the imperialist war America had been transformed. The "imperialist war is so steeped in blood, so predatory and bestial, that it...has brought the freest democracy of America to the level of semimilitaristic, despotic Germany."[50]

There were certain aspects of American society that Lenin continued to admire. He was convinced that the Russians had much to learn from American technology. His most enthusiastic statement about which capitalist nation could contribute positively to Russia, however, was directed at Germany. In the spring of 1918, Lenin wrote an article justifying state capitalism as a step forward for Russia. He found state capitalism epitomized by Germany; "here we have the last word in modern large-scale capitalist engineering and planned organization, subordinated to Junker-bourgeois imperialism." If that organization were subordinated to a state "of a different type, of a different class content—a Soviet state, you will have the sum total of the conditions necessary for socialism."[51]

Lenin insisted that "in 1918 Germany and Russia have become the most striking embodiment of the material realization of the economic, the productive and socio-economic conditions for socialism, on the one hand, and the political conditions, on the other."[52] They were the two components of socialism—the economic and the political. Lenin eagerly awaited a German revolution which would provide the Russians with the material support they required to build socialism. While they awaited that aid, however, the Russians could "spare no effort in copying it (German state capitalism) and not shrink from adopting dictatorial methods to hasten the copying of it."[53]

The early Lenin had favored the American path to socialism because it had involved the destruction of old political, as well as economic, structures. Writing in the first decade of the twentieth century—after the dawn of the age of imperialism—Lenin had emphasized the difference between the American and Prussian types of capitalism. Writing after he had formulated the theory of imperialism, Lenin opted for the Prussian type and confidently expected that the political aspects of Prussianism could be replaced. Germany's autocratic capitalism had been the product of an incomplete revolution against feudalism. Those democratic structures which had never developed in Germany no longer seemed to Lenin to be crucial aspects of a capitalist system.

American Social Patriots

Why did Lenin alter his view of the United States? Lenin himself would have insisted that he was simply responding to the changing nature of American capitalism. There is evidence to suggest, however, that Lenin was not merely responding to a new form of capitalism but was re-assessing his attitudes towards old concepts. His early positive analysis of America reflected the classic Marxist view of developed capitalist nations as the centers of working-class aspirations. Like other paradigms Marxism included a core set of concepts, an explanation of the world and a set of predictions.[54] The failure of American socialism to develop as quickly as their theory predicted had troubled Marxists.

Lenin himself grappled with the problem and attempted to formulate a solution by focusing on the relationship between democracy and capitalism.

Not every weakness in a theory leads to its abandonment or replacement. For a number of years Lenin had been altering some of Marx's concepts to fit the needs of a Russian revolutionary movement. The outbreak of World War I, however, made it imperative that some comprehensive explanation be made for the seeming collapse of the socialist movements in developed capitalist countries. The failure of American socialism was now ascribed to the impact of imperialism. American socialism, however, had been a failure even before the advent of imperialism; at the most Marxism-Leninism could only explain its failure after America became an imperial power.

More importantly, Lenin's new paradigm distorted the role of various American labor and socialist leaders. Since he felt that imperialism had effaced all significant differences between America and Europe, Lenin was forced to look for European figures and disputes in their American incarnation. He could not, however, decide exactly which American fit which role. One of the keys to the theory of imperialism was the role of the leaders of the labor movement. They were accused of betraying their class interests in return for special advantages from the bourgeoisie. The labor leaders of the Second International had supported their countries' participation in the world war because they personally had a stake in the victory of their respective nations.

The American situation was, however, somewhat different and the early Lenin had realized it. In 1912 Lenin noted that the American Federation of Labor was a relic of the past, a representative of the "liberal-bourgeois traditions that hang full weight over America's working-class aristocracy."[55] Samuel Gompers, the unquestioned leader of the AFL, was "a strong opponent of socialism" who denied the existence of class conflict and pursued "a downright bourgeois policy in the Federation against the socialist one."[56] He and the labor movement he led were prime examples of America's anomalous position within the capitalist world and the source of some concern about the timing and pace of America's transition to socialism. Lenin's first theory accounting for the failure of American socialism had recognized that socialists had not made headway within the labor movement.

As late as 1915, Lenin continued to call Gompers a bourgeois and representative of the working-class aristocracy. In 1918, however, Lenin discovered that Gompers was no longer what he had once seemed to be. Suddenly, the bourgeois labor leader became a fallen socialist. Beginning in 1918, Lenin denounced Gompers as a social traitor for supporting a bourgeois government's war efforts, grouping Gompers with Arthur Henderson, Pierre Renaudel, Philipp Scheidemann, and Karl Renner.[57] Shortly afterwards, he repeated the charge, calling Gompers a social-chauvinist.[58] In early 1919 he accused Gompers, the Mensheviks, Scheidemann, Emil Vandervelde, and Henderson of betraying socialism and linked Gompers with Victor Deiger as a traitor to socialism.[59]

Later that year Lenin accused Gompers of having deserted to the bourgeoisie in return for soft jobs and a niggardly share of their profits.[60] Again, in a 1920 preface to *Imperialism* he included Gompers as a social opportunist along with Eduard Bernstein, Alexandre Millerand, and H. M. Hyndman.[61]

All of the Europeans were prominent and long-time members of socialist parties. Most of them had supported their governments either by entering into wartime unity cabinets or voting for war credits. Gompers had carried on a brief flirtation with socialism in his youth but had been a resolute opponent of any and all ideological intrusions into the labor movement for many years. Within the American Federation of Labor he had been the target for bitter socialist opposition. While such men as Scheidemann, Renaudel, Henderson, et al. had assuredly been key figures in the socialist movements in Germany, France, and Britain, Gompers had nothing to do with the American Socialist party. From Lenin's perspective the Europeans had been traitors to socialism; having once committed themselves to a cause, they had abandoned it. Gompers, however, had never been committed to socialism.[62]

Why did Lenin alter his evaluation of Gompers? Linking Gompers with the European socialists enabled Lenin to imply that what had transpired in Europe had been paralleled in America. If Gompers had betrayed the cause of American socialism, then the inability of socialists to make much headway in the most advanced capitalist nation was not so puzzling. Early in 1918, Lenin noted that in Britain, Switzerland, and the United States, "the workers have a measure of prosperity, which is why it is difficult to shake up the old socialist parties which had been there for decades, had come to power, and had acquired authority in the eyes of the masses."[63] By linking Gompers with the European socialists Lenin was able to avoid re-examining that "peculiar situation" whereby America had never been fertile ground for socialists. The American Socialist party had only come into existence in 1900, had hardly "come to power," and had never become a mass party.[64] The American Labor movement had never been socialist, even in its pre-imperialist days, but had been dominated by bourgeois leaders. The weakness of American socialism could not so easily be laid at the feet of imperialism. While still under the influence of Marxism, Lenin grappled with the weakness of American socialism. Having replaced it with Marxism-Leninism he conveniently excised that difficulty. Although Lenin had eliminated the problem of American exceptionalism in theory, in practice America remained a Marxist wasteland.

Notes

1. Karl Marx, *Capital: A Critique of Political Economy,* ed. Frederick Engels, trans. Samuel Moore and Edward Aveling, 3rd German ed. (New York: International Publishers, 1967), 1: 8-9.
2. For two accounts of Lenin's views on America, see Frederick Barghoorn, *The Soviet Image of the United States* (New York: Harcourt Brace & Company, 1950); and R. Laurence Moore, *European Socialists and the American Promised Land* (New

York: Oxford University Press, 1970). Neither one emphasizes the shift in Lenin's views nor the importance of the concept of imperialism.

3. V. I. Lenin, "The Successes of the American Workers," *Collected Works,* trans. from 4th enl. Russian ed., 45 vols. (Moscow: Foreign Languages Publishing House, 1960), 18:335. All subsequent references to Lenin's works, unless otherwise stated, refer to this edition.

4. "Our Achievements," 18: 596-7.

5. "Russians and Negroes," 18:543-44; and "The Question of Ministry of Education Policy," 19: 137-146.

6. *Two Tactics* of *Social-Democracy in the Democratic Revolution,* 9: 50.

7. "The Agrarian Programme of Social-Democracy in the First Russian Revolution 1905-1907," 13: 239.

8. Ibid.

9. "Some Sources of the Present Ideological Discord," 16: 87.

10. Ibid.

11. *Two Tactics,* 9: 50.

12. *New Data on the Laws Governing the Development of Capitalism in Agriculture: Capitalism and Agriculture in the United States of America,* vol. 22: 24. The second part of this study, never published, was to be on Germany.

13. "Marx on the American 'General Redistribution,' " 8: 323-329.

14. Harvey Klehr, "Marxist Theory in Search of America," *Journal of Politics,* 35 (May 1973), 311-331.

15. Lenin, "Preface to the Russian Translation of *Letters of Johannes Becker, Joseph Dietzgen, Frederick Engels, Karl Marx, and Others to Friedrich Sorge and Others,*" 12: 372-3.

16. Ibid.

17. "Inflammable Material in World Politics," 15: 186. In a more propagandistic mood, Lenin reminded the workers of America that "the American people have a revolutionary tradition." "Letter to American Workers," 28: 69.

18. "Preface to Sorge Correspondence," 12: 364.

19. Ibid., 365-366.

20. "Differences in the European Labour Movement," 16: 347-352.

21. "In Britain," 19:55; and "Harry Quelch," 19: 369-371.

22. "In America," 36: 214-215.

23. Ibid., 215.

24. "Four Thousand Rubles a Year and a Six-Hour Day," 20: 69

25. "The Successes of the American Workers," 18:335-336; and "The Results and Significance of the U.S. Presidential Elections," 18: 402-404.

26. "In America," 36: 214.

27. *Imperialism,* 22: 241.

28. *Imperialism,* 22: 301.

29. "How the Bourgeoisie Utilizes Renegades," 30: 34.

30. *Imperialism,* 22: 293-296

31. "Under A False Flag," 21: 152.

32. "Opportunism and the Collapse of the Second International," 22: 112.

33. *Imperialism,* 22: 195, 287.

34. "A Caricature of Marxism and Imperialist Economism," 23: 44.

35. "Socialism and War," 21: 302.

36. "Disgrace as the Capitalists and the Proletarians Understand It," 24: 221

37. See, for example, "Letter to American Workers," 28: 62.

38. "The Socialist Revolution and the Right of Nations to Self-Determination," 22: 143.

39. "The Terms of Admission into the Communist International," 3 1: 208.
40. "Letter to American Workers," 28:74-75.
41. "Theses on the Fundamental Tasks of the Second Congress of the Communist International," 3 1: 19 1.
42. "The Second Congress of the Communist International," 3 1: 23 1.
43. "Fourth Conference of Trade Unions and Factory Committees of Moscow," 27:4 64
44. See, for example, Hans Gerth, ed., *The First International: Minutes of the Hague Congress of 1872* (Madison: University of Wisconsin Press, 1958), 236.
45. Lenin, "Session of the All-Russia C.E.C., April 29, 1918," 27: 310.
46. *The State and Revolution,* 25: 415416. As with much else, Lenin displayed some inconsistency on this point. Thus, a few years earlier he had insisted that there was a great difference of political forms among the imperialist nations and this "variety will manifest itself also in the path mankind will follow from the imperialism of today to the socialist revolution of tomorrow." "A Caricature of Marxism," 23: 70.
47. *The Proletarian Revolution and the Renegade Kautsky,* 28: 238.
48. *The State and Revolution,* 25: 390.
49. "The Impending Catastrophe and How to Combat It," 25: 334-335.
50. "Extraordinary Sixth All-Russia Congress of Soviets of Workers', Peasants', Cossacks' and Red Army Deputies, November 8, 1918," 28: 156.
51. "Left-Wing Childishness and the Petty-Bourgeois Mentality," 27: 339.
52. Ibid., 340.
53. Ibid.
54. Thomas Kuhn, *The Structure of Scientific Revolutions* (Chicago: University of Chicago Press, 1970) provides a framework for discussing paradigm-change. See also Sheldon Wolin, "Paradigms and Political Theories," in P. King and B. Parekh, eds., *Politics and Experience* (Cambridge: Cambridge University Press, 1968), 125-152.
55. "In America," 36: 214.
56. Ibid.
57. "Letter to American Workers," 28: 75.
58. *The Proletarian Revolution,* 28:286, fn.
59. "Letter to the Workers of Europe and America," 28: 430.
60. "How the Bourgeoisie Utilizes Renegades," 30: 34.
61. "Preface to French and German editions of *Imperialism,*" 22: 192.
62. See Philip Foner, "Samuel Gompers to Frederick Engels: A Letter," *Labor History,* 11 (Spring 1970), 207-211; and John Laslett, "Samuel Gompers to Frederick Engels: An Excerpt From the 1890 S.L.P.-A.F.L. Debate," *Labor History,* 11 (Fall 1970), 531-535. The same point I am making about Gompers is noted by James Weinstein, *The Decline of Socialism in America 1912-1925* (New York: Monthly Review Press, 1967), 187, fn.
63. Lenin, "Extraordinary All-Russia Railwaymen's Congress, January 5-30, 1918," 26: 494.
64. At its peak the party was slightly larger than 100,000 people. It only elected two men to Congress. See Weinstein, *The Decline of Socialism.*

3

Leninism and Lovestoneism

The absence of a thriving socialist movement in the United States has been the subject of much speculation over the past century.[1] America seems to stand alone among industrialized countries in never having developed a socialist party able to command the loyalties of a significant segment of the population.[2] A number of commentators have attributed this lacuna in our political life to some variant of our differences from Europe. The theme of American "exceptionalism" has been a rich source for explanations of the failure of American socialism. American prosperity and class mobility, the absence of classes, the internal frontier, the American Revolution, the egalitarian value structure, the absence of a feudal past—all have been suggested as facets of American exceptionalism.[3] Werner Sombart's classic remark that "on the shores of roast beef and apple pie socialistic Utopias of every sort are sent to their doom"[4] vividly conveys the image of an American fortress remaining staunch against imported doctrines.

Many of the writers who have explained the failure of American socialism by reference to American exceptionalism would doubtless agree with Louis Hartz' assessment of the relative costs to America of the absence of socialism: "European liberalism, because it was cursed with feudalism, was forced to create the mentality of socialism, and thus was twice cursed. American liberalism, freed of the one, was freed of the other, and hence was twice blessed."[5] Socialists, on the other hand, and particularly Marxists, have vehemently disagreed with the idea that the absence of socialism was any kind of blessing other than to the bourgeoisie. Marxists, however, have not been content to deplore the consequences of American exceptionalism; they have denied that America is an exception.

Marxist hostility to the idea that America is so fundamentally different from Europe that American socialism is impossible or unlikely has a long pedigree.

Reprinted from *Studies in Comparative Communism*, v.7, n.4, pp. 3-20, copyright 1974 School of International Relations, University of Southern California, with permission from Elsevier.

Marxism, according to its founder, was both a theory of the inevitable direction of capitalist society and a tool in the hands of those seeking to alter that society. Gabriel Kolko has pointed out that Marxism "accepted a paralyzing and debilitating optimism" which prevented its adherents from considering the possibility of defeat.[6] A commitment to both American exceptionalism and Marxism would seemingly be a contradiction in terms, a recognition that Marxism is not a universally valid scientific theory and that capitalism in at least one country is impervious to disintegration.

Yet during the 1920s the American Communist Party was rent by a dispute over a theory of American exceptionalism. Years after the fracas had been resolved, one of the protagonists, William Z. Foster, recalled that his defeated opponent, Jay Lovestone, had "restated, in Marxist phraseology, the traditional bourgeois theory of American exceptionalism." Foster took that theory to mean "that, in its essence, capitalism in the United States is different from and superior to capitalism in other countries and is, therefore, exempt from that system's laws of growth and decay."[7] One of Foster's opponents, Bertram Wolfe, boasted proudly that "we are more than American exceptionalists. We are exceptionalists for every country in the world."[8]

Historians of the American Communist Party have not agreed on the precise nature of the dispute or its significance. Donald Clark Hodges has accepted Foster's characterization by noting that "we have indirect evidence from the leadership's subsequent abandonment of Marxism-Leninism that the Comintern's charge of right-wing deviations in the late twenties was far from unprincipled name-calling and for the most part was accurate."[9] While not accepting that analysis, Irving Howe and Lewis Coser have argued that the dispute over American exceptionalism generated "one of the very few significant theoretical discussions in the history of the American Communist movement."[10] Theodore Draper has likewise noted that "it precipitated a doctrinal conflict peculiar in its virulence, obstinacy, and significance."[11] Daniel Bell, on the other hand, treated the disagreement between the two groups as a purely factional intrigue devoid of issues.[12] And, in a comprehensive review of literature accounting for the failure of American socialism, D. H. Leon discussed American exceptionalism, but omitted mention of the supposed arch-heretics of exceptionalism, the Lovestoneites.[13]

Several important issues thus exist. What was the Lovestoneite theory of American exceptionalism? In what respects did Foster and Lovestone disagree? Was Lovestone's theory bourgeois or Marxist? If the former, why did so many erstwhile Marxists accept it? If the latter, what was the objection to it? The conclusion I have drawn is that Foster seriously misrepresented Lovestone's position. The theory deviated hardly a whit from orthodox Leninism and was un-Marxist only to the extent that Leninism itself represented a departure from Marxism. Because of its Leninism, Lovestone's theory of American exceptionalism was only a marginally more realistic assessment of America than Foster's theory. Thus, the great debate was little more than shadowboxing. Neither side was swinging at corporeal targets. In large part, this accounts for the failure of American Communism.

The Lovestoneite Theory of American Exceptionalism

The Fifth Plenum of the Communist International, meeting in March 1925, reversed previous Comintern policy by admitting that world capitalism had been partially stabilized. The revolutionary era in world politics had temporarily drawn to a close. For the present, the contradictions inherent in capitalism had been surmounted; the final crisis of capitalism was no longer imminent. On the other hand, the respite was not permanent. The nations of Europe had reached their economic peaks and were inexorably heading toward proletarian revolutions. The period of capitalist stabilization marked a hiatus on this road to ruin. Although spared for the moment, European capitalism would never again be healthy.[14]

This transition from an optimistic to a pessimistic assessment of the opportunities for an immediate world revolution was accompanied by a new view of the relationship between American and European capitalism. In early 1925, the Executive Committee of the Comintern decided that in America alone was capitalism still on the upgrade.[15] By late 1926, Japan and some of the British dominions were added to the list of those capitalist nations still developing economically.[16] If the prospects for an early socialist revolution were dim in Europe, they were even less likely where capitalism was still on the march. In Europe, the stabilization of capitalism had been accompanied by the political defeat of Communist movements. In America, the reverses suffered by the Communist Party were less crucial in decreasing the chances for revolution than the enormous strength and vitality of the capitalist system, enjoying its finest hours in the 1920s.

During 1925 and 1926, American Communists began to seek explanations for the strength of the American economy and the consequent weakness of socialism. The search was led primarily by Jay Lovestone and Bertram Wolfe. Lovestone became the Secretary of the American Communist Party in March 1927 and retained that position until his ouster for the heresy of exceptionalism in May 1929. Wolfe was one of his loyal factional allies and head of the New York Workers School.

The basis of Lovestone's theory of exceptionalism was his assertion that American capitalism was advancing even while European capitalism remained stagnant. By late 1927, Stalin had proclaimed the end of the period of capitalist stabilization in Europe. Lovestone's continued adherence to his theory that American capitalism was advancing thus emphasized America's uniqueness even more sharply. Behind the theory of American exceptionalism, however, stood the theoretical bulwark of orthodox Leninism, the theory of imperialism, the highest stage of capitalism.

The era of imperialism, according to Lenin, was marked by the final effort of capitalism to stave off the inevitable economic collapse. As the opportunities to extract surplus value internally dried up, for the very reasons Marx had cited, capitalists discovered a new source of vitality abroad. By exporting capital they could revitalize themselves. Instead of steadily falling profits, large-scale unemployment, and an increasingly brutalized proletariat, the bastions of capitalism could enjoy an era of relative prosperity and abundance. The colonial lands offered such rewards since "profits were unusually high, for capital is scarce, the price of land is relatively low, wages are low, raw materials are cheap."[17]

The economic benefits reaped from the possession of colonies enabled capitalists to overcome temporarily still another danger that the system itself created. The working class, whose militance was to be the ultimate undoing of capitalism, was neutralized because a small portion of the huge profits being made overseas was doled out to "certain sections of the working class, and for a time a fairly considerable minority."[18] Capitalism's advance was then unhindered by domestic class conflict. The international class solidarity of the workers was replaced by patriotism.

So attractive were the benefits of colonial ownership that a desperate struggle was underway for possession of these backward countries. While the colonies represented a temporary salve for the ills of capitalism, the ensuing wars for these scarce resources propelled capitalism ever more quickly to its doom. The older capitalist nations, having gobbled up the lion's share of the colonies, could no longer survive without these props of their economy. The younger capitalist nations, seeing the enormous benefits conferred by possession of colonies, were eager to receive their fair share. The contradictions "between the development of the productive forces and accumulation of capital on the one side and the division of colonies and 'spheres of influence' on the other side" meant that conflicts between younger and older capitalist countries would be chronic.[19]

The partitioning of the world into the property of various nations was made on the basis of the power of the various participants. As shifts took place in the balance of power and the development of productive forces, wars over colonial possessions formally recorded the relative strengths of the nations. Alliances and periods of peace were, in the age of imperialism, only temporary truces that prepared the ground for the next set of conflicts.[20]

The constant warfare characterizing the age of imperialism also contributed to another ill of capitalism. In the age of imperialism capitalism was unable to develop in an orderly and balanced manner. Instead, "under capitalism the development of different undertakings, branches of industry, or countries cannot be even."[21] The law of the uneven development of capitalism was illustrated most vividly by wars. As colonies, the lifeblood of monopoly capitalism, were won or lost, the rate of economic development in a given country would bounce up or down. Thus, in addition to creating international tensions, imperialism unbalanced capitalist economies.

While Lovestone advanced several reasons for the continuing success of American capitalism, the most important was imperialism. The American empire was "youthful, vigorous, and growing."[22] While the European lands, particularly England, had long since passed their expansionist eras, the United States was still a thriving imperialistic power. One consequence was that "the aggressive role of American imperialism is based on its present strength and precisely on its tremendous, still unexhausted reserve powers."[23] One of Lovestone's allies, John Pepper, drew the proper Leninist conclusion that the major international rivalry would soon be between the United States and Great Britain![24]

The contrast between the vigorous imperialism of America and the older imperialism of Europe meant that economic crises in America were not so immediately debilitating; they were temporary and could be rationalized. Thus, Lovestone felt in 1928 that "we have an economic depression…but American national economy, as such, is not declining fundamentally."[25] Pepper pointed out that the onset of a revolutionary situation in Europe—the end of the era of capitalist stabilization—was not occurring in America because, among other factors, capitalism here was still on the upgrade due to the continued advance of imperialism.[26] In Europe, capitalism had run out of breathing room; in America it still retained options. Room for capitalist expansion still existed both internally and externally. At home, the South remained unindustrialized, providing fresh soil for the growth of capitalism. Abroad, American exploitation of colonial lands was far from reaching its zenith. Latin America, in particular, could be subjected to greater control.[27]

In addition to not having fully developed their imperialistic potential, the Americans had evolved a more efficient capitalist system. Bertram Wolfe pointed out that America had been blessed with an abundance of raw materials and had created an extensive transportation system at an early date in its history.[28] The conjunction of these two factors with the efficiency of the working class[29] enabled the capitalists to gain higher rates of profit on their investments than the Europeans could realize on theirs. The Americans reduced the socially necessary production time by their superior techniques and organization, thus extracting more surplus value from the working class. Additionally, they exploited foreign countries without assuming the cost of administering them. In short, the Americans were simply better capitalists than the Europeans.[30]

The upward course of American capitalism, fueled by the profits from imperialist ventures, required a pessimistic assessment of the short-term prospects for significant gains by the American Communist Party among the working class. Lovestone noted that imperialism had so severely weakened their militancy that domestic conflict was unlikely. Many potential working-class leaders had voluntarily forsworn class warfare owing to the higher wages made possible by imperialism.[31] The weakening of its leadership coincided with the fracturing of the homogeneity of the working class. More foreign-born workers were entering the country illegally. Negroes were migrating North, farmers were abandoning rural life, and the income gap between skilled and unskilled workers was widening.[32] Heavy-industry workers were divided by ethnic and racial hostilities. Consequently, even organizing the unorganized workers within the American Federation of Labor (AFL) was a progressive step.

The development of a labor party, much less a Communist party, was not a viable alternative. The working class was not being radicalized, as in Europe. To pretend that they were could only result in "radical isolation."[33] The petty-bourgeoisie, led by Robert LaFollette, supplied the leadership in the fight against monopoly capitalism.[34] Bertram Wolfe cautioned fellow radicals that American prosperity had minimized the opportunities for independent action.[35]

Neither Lovestone nor any member of his faction claimed that these conditions would be permanent. They did not even expect the hiatus in revolutionary activity to last more than a few years. Every advance of American capitalism brought the day of its destruction nearer. The stronger American capitalism became, the more intense the contradictions of the system. As Max Bedacht, a Lovestoneite, put it, "The very strength of American imperialism becomes the source of its weakness."[36] The export of capital, originally a source of profits, was gradually strengthening America's competitors. Investment in colonial lands produced higher profits but also increased unemployment in the United States.[37]

The Lovestoneites did see some concrete signs that American capitalism had little more room in which to advance. In 1928, John Pepper, after insisting that American problems were different from European problems, listed several indications of an approaching crisis in the United States. Imperialism was beginning to intrude in domestic politics via the tariff, an agricultural crisis was brewing, and a geographical relocation and technological breakthroughs threatened a number of industries. Finally, unemployment was growing.[38]

While the Lovestoneites conceded that the prospects for a labor party had diminished since 1924, they insisted that such prospects were not entirely absent. Lovestone argued that a homogeneous working class was inevitable. The increasing centralization of government would mean that more than ever before the state would reflect and advance the interests of the capitalist class. As a result, the working class would come to recognize, with the help of the Communists, that their interests required them to confront capitalism on the political as well as the economic front. The working class would then be prepared, both physically and psychologically, to seize control of the government.[39]

The Lovestoneite theory of American exceptionalism was firmly bounded by Leninist premises. While the Lovestoneites saw any number of factors to be potential hazards to the health of capitalism, they remained convinced that the final crisis of capitalism in America was not imminent. On the other hand, they were equally adamant in believing that this final crisis was inevitable. The American Revolution was still some time away. John Pepper spoke for his faction in 1928 when he insisted that "there is no revolutionary situation as yet in the United States."[40] American capitalism had not yet reached the apex of its development and thus still retained some powers of expansion. The proper strategy for the Communist Party, in turn, was to tone down its militancy, seek alliances with other radical and liberal groups, and avoid isolating itself from the mass of the working class.

The extent of the Lovestoneites' exceptionalism was their insistence that, at that given moment of history, conditions in America and Europe were fundamentally different. While a socialist revolution might be possible in the one, conditions were not ripe in the other. The Leninist concepts of imperialism and the uneven development of capitalism led logically to such a conclusion. Ironically, Marx had developed a much more daring theory of American exceptionalism, but the Lovestoneites remained entranced with Lenin's version.[41]

Foster's Challenge to Lovestone

While Lovestone saw America on the uphill slope of capitalist development, William Foster and his epigones were convinced that the summit already had been or imminently would be reached. Foster insisted that the Lovestoneite emphasis on the external contradictions of American capitalism—the overriding importance attached to American imperialism—obscured the internal contradictions of the system. Lovestone's habit of looking at America's world role and ignoring the debilitating tensions simmering at home led him to overestimate the staying power of American capitalism. Since Foster was forced to pay obeisance to the Comintern position that American capitalism was on the upgrade, he attacked Lovestone by claiming that while the American economy was still growing, the rate of growth was slowing down as the system neared its peak.[42]

At other times, however, the Fosterites insisted that American capitalism had already reached its apex. It had no more room in which to grow and thus might well begin its downward slide momentarily.[43] While Lovestone and Pepper viewed the 1928 elections as confirmation of the weakness of the American Communists, Foster saw the large vote for Democrat Al Smith as a sign of the impending radicalization of the working class.[44] Foster also criticized Lovestone and his cohorts in control of the Party machinery for neglecting efforts to build new labor unions designed to compete with the AFL for members.[45] If the workers were ready to move to the left, the Communist Party had to be there to greet them.

The debate over American exceptionalism was, then, a debate over timing more than one over fundamental Marxist or Leninist principles. While the Fosterites attacked the Lovestoneites for overestimating the powers of capitalism, the latter kept insisting that the stronger capitalism got, the nearer its ultimate defeat.[46] Strategic differences stemmed from the disparate analyses of the condition of capitalism. The varying estimates of the success of a labor party or dual unions did not reflect differences in principles but differences in tactics.

The only hint of differences in principles came from Foster, who complained about the stress on external contradictions at the expense of internal conflicts. This criticism, however, should more properly have been directed at Leninism than at Lovestoneism, for it was Lenin who had insisted that in the final stage of capitalism imperialistic conflict would play a key role. Foster and most of his co-factionalists had come into the Communist Party from native radical groups, such as the Industrial Workers of the World, or through participation in labor organizing and working-class politics. The Lovestoneites' leadership was college educated and based in New York. Contrary perhaps to expectations, the latter group more accurately assessed the behavior of the working class. The Fosterites were less prepared to accept a pessimistic assessment of the militancy of their fellow workers. The success of Leninism in tsarist Russia seemed to argue that one could never afford to underestimate the militancy of a working class. The lesson that Foster absorbed from Russia was that the strength of American capitalism could be tested only by revolutionary combat.

The debate was more than a sham, but it never seriously involved an attack on Leninist or Marxist theory. For one thing, neither side dealt with Marx's theory of American exceptionalism. For another, Foster was unprepared to extend his critique of Lovestone to an attack on the theory of imperialism. Their mutual commitment to Leninism precluded an original examination of American problems and radical prospects. While both sides argued over whether the peak of American capitalism had been reached, neither could explain satisfactorily how such a peak could be recognized until after a revolution. Since they believed that capitalism was an unstable social system, the only way to distinguish temporary crises from the revolutionary cataclysm was by whether a revolution actually occurred. If there was no successful revolution, the peak had not yet been reached and capitalist society still retained some reserve powers. Unfortunately, a political movement basing its behavior on such predictions would discover too late and at a great cost that its time had not come. Even more tragically, the failure of that movement's revolutionary offensive was likely to have deleterious consequences for a wider circle of people than that group.

Lovestoneites and Leninism

Lovestone's theory was far from incompatible with Leninism. Moreover, additional evidence demonstrates the symbiosis between the two theories and underscores the limited sense in which either was a genuinely fruitful theory of American exceptionalism. First, in a series of articles written in 1926, Bertram Wolfe directly confronted the question of whether Leninism was valid only for Europe or whether it could guide American radicals as well. Having audaciously raised that question, however, Wolfe and his co-author were unable to confront it seriously. They perceived the inevitable death of capitalism and the dawn of an era of proletarian revolution. Just as in Europe or Tsarist Russia, the government was the instrument of a class—a bourgeois dictatorship—and violent revolution was necessary. Wolfe and Jack Stachel attributed the slow development of the working class toward socialism to the opportunities for escape from the proletariat and the impact of a new wave of immigration occurring every generation. As a consequence, the working class lacked a tradition and a culture.[47]

Wolfe set about to give that class a tradition. A 1926 article, "Whose Revolution Is It?," was an effort to demythologize the events of 1776 and place their lessons at the service of the American proletariat. Wolfe readily admitted that the American Revolution had been bourgeois, not proletarian; but he still insisted that it was a precursor of the Leninist type of revolution. The revolutionaries were a minority, used violence, set up dual organs of power, and confiscated land. They had, in short, anticipated the methods of the Russian Revolution. Even though class enemies, they were suitable models for emulation and praise by the working class.[48] Not only was the American proletarian future Leninist, Wolfe seemed to say, but so was the American bourgeois past. And that was why the past offered a lesson to the proletariat.

Six months later, Wolfe chided his comrades for the paucity of their knowledge about American history, politics, political institutions, economic development, and culture. To make an American revolution would require more than nodding familiarity with American society, yet the Communists spent most of their time with their faces resolutely set toward Europe. Citing religion as a major factor in American social development, Wolfe rhetorically asked what the Party knew about Mormonism, fundamentalism, Christian Science, and revivalism. He mourned that "we are without an adequate study of the influence of the frontier on American life."[49]

The effort to discover America never took hold in the 1920s, however, because Leninism had already given the answers to all the important questions that needed to be asked. When the name of the Party's theoretical journal was changed to *Communist,* the editors insisted that "the main purpose and task of the *Communist* will be the 'Americanization' of Marxism-Leninism."[50] What Americanizing the Party would have meant was never faced. Max Bedacht, a Lovestoneite, spoke for his faction when he comfortably assumed that "it is one of the tasks of the Americanization of Marxism-Leninism...to prove that America is no exception to the rule of capitalist development."[51] This attitude relegated Americanism to searching through history textbooks for examples that could justify an American Bolshevik revolution. It involved a search for American experiences that could be conveniently inserted into the revolutionary scenario provided by Lenin. The Lovestoneites had not come near, as Foster had charged, to developing an ideology praising American capitalism or in any way suggesting that the American past made it possible to avoid a revolution. Wolfe's article urging his comrades to discover America had, after all, been entitled "Towards Leninism."

A second indication of the narrowness of the Lovestoneite theory is its use to explain the Great Depression. The Depression formally began just a few months after the Lovestoneites had been expelled from the Communist movement for the ostensible crime of exceptionalism. Throughout the last half of the decade, the Lovestoneites had been skeptical about the proximity of a revolutionary situation in the United States. Downgrading the prospects for crippling domestic class conflicts, they had insisted on the primacy of the external, imperialistic contradictions of American capitalism. The Depression seemed to belie their pessimistic analysis of the opportunities for a radical transformation of American political, economic, and social structures. Had the theory of exceptionalism been what Foster years later took it to be, the Lovestoneites might indeed have had to reexamine their theory.

Lovestone insisted that he and his fellow exceptionalists had not denied that a crisis would strike American capitalism. Since he had always held that an economic crisis was "unavoidable in the near future," the major point of contention between him and his factional opponents had not been whether one would in fact develop.[52] Thus, while the CPUSA viewed the events of 1929 as a phase in the revolutionary epoch, the Lovestoneites were still unwilling to concede that a revolutionary era had yet dawned. The United States was entering a "period of serious depression " which would be characterized by increasing unemployment, wage cuts, and pressure upon the worker but not by a revolutionary upsurge among the populace.[53]

Not every depression or capitalist crisis signaled the onset of a revolutionary period. Marx had sketched a period of constant turmoil as the burden that capitalism bore. By its very nature a capitalist system was unstable. Crisis succeeded crisis, as each new adjustment was upset by the anarchy of capitalist production. The Lovestoneites simply denied that the Great Depression was the final, cataclysmic crisis of capitalism:

> It is absolutely fallacious to conclude that the present economic crisis is already the final, basic crisis of American capitalism ushering in the period of revolution or even marking the beginning of the immediate downward trend of capitalist development in the U.S.[54]

As a consequence of this analysis, the Lovestoneites anticipated a strengthened capitalism emerging from the Depression. The resolution of the temporary strains in the system would allow the forward movement of the capitalist economy to continue. The reserve powers of American capitalism were still available to rationalize the economic system and prevent its breakdown. The Lovestoneites pointed out that "the panic on Wall Street did not come as a result of the decline of American capitalist economy. It came as a result of the very strength of American capitalist economy magnifying and sharpening the contradictions of world capitalism."[55] Far from marking the beginning of a revolutionary situation, the Depression did not even alter the general direction of American capitalism. "The general trend of American capitalism, in its world position, is still upward."[56]

If their reluctance to countenance revolutionary activity strikes one as a decidedly un-Leninist attitude, the Lovestoneites merely insisted that Leninism was a realistic theory which recognized that revolutionary situations were rare moments. An editorial statement in their factional newspaper clearly made the point about the limits of their exceptionalism and their commitment to Leninism. The editorial plainly stated that "American capitalism is not 'excepted' from the general laws of capitalist development as laid down by Marx and Lenin." It was a mark of the Comintern's anti-Leninism that it insisted on applying the same tactics to every country. By doing so, the Comintern was ignoring the implications of the law of uneven development. Lenin never meant to imply by this law that American capitalism could ever be healthy or free of contradictions, but that "at any particular period some national sectors of world capitalism may be on the upgrade while others may be on the decline, while the rate of development of each may be different and continually changing."[57]

Conclusion

The tepid brand of exceptionalism manufactured by the Lovestoneites consisted mainly of an argument over the timing of the inevitable Communist revolutions in Europe and America. Because of specific events or forces, American capitalism was alleged to have greater staying power than European capitalism. This power would avail it little, however, since such past history had no impact on the essential nature of the future. Neither the Lovestoneites nor the Fosterites understood American history, and as erstwhile Marxists they hardly seemed to care.

The Lovestoneites placed great stress on the more deterministic side of Leninism—and Marxism—which emphasized the need for objective conditions to reach a certain point before a country is ripe for revolution. The Fosterites emphasized the voluntaristic element in Leninism, which insisted that the role of a revolutionary is to make a revolution. But both groups ignored the fundamental insight of Marxism that history is destiny—not in the sense that the past foreordains the future, but that the past establishes the boundaries of the possible.

The Lovestoneite commitment to Leninism thus precluded the development of a realistic assessment of America. The intellectual bankruptcy of Leninism is vividly illustrated by an article published in *Communist* shortly after the expulsion of the Lovestoneites for their supposed heresy. The Russian author, V. Mofilev, presented a far more systematic justification of American exceptionalism than Lovestone ever had, yet ran away from his logical conclusions.

Mofilev argued that geographical and physical advantages alone could not account for the extraordinarily high rate of economic development in America. Had it not been for a series of favorable socio-economic conditions, even the vast continent and the unequalled riches of the land would not have sufficed to vault America into world economic superiority so quickly. Mofilev employed an argument that Marx and Engels had relied upon to explain the character of capitalism.[58] Capitalists had taken advantage of favorable social factors to dominate the society. Feudalism never took root in America since "one of the reasons for the revolution of 1775-81" was the destruction of whatever minor feudal vestiges had been transplanted in the New World.[59] Like Marx and Engels, Mofilev considered the absence of a feudal class to be a boon to the bourgeoisie. Additionally, the failure of a parasitic class to emerge in the countryside, outside the South, meant that farm profits remained high even as farm prices stayed low.

While Marx particularly had been concerned about the absence of a sufficiently large pool of workers to stoke the capitalist fires, Mofilev believed that this very weakness had been transformed into a strength by the capitalists. In dire need of labor to conquer the wilderness, the capitalist soon learned that neither servants nor slaves were able to fill the gap between the demand for and the supply of labor. Forced to pay high wages to attract workers, the capitalist saw his workers quickly accumulate enough money to buy the relatively inexpensive farmland.

Since they were thus unable to extract large amounts of surplus value from labor, the capitalists were forced to search for ways to obtain relative surplus value. High wages and a shortage of labor combined to force them to develop technology. "The exceptional rapidity and the extent of this process [mechanization and automatization of production] is the outstanding peculiarity of the economic development of the United States and the most important source of the superiority of its tempo."[60]

The rapid and continuous development of technology in the United States made possible high levels of production. Meanwhile, the consumption market in America kept pace with production. Railroad construction, on a scale dwarfing that of any European country, facilitated exchange and stimulated economic growth. The absence of internal tariffs and the presence of a relatively high external tariff not only aided the growth of industry, but also created a market for its products. The low cost of agricultural products enabled American farmers to compete favorably in foreign markets. These high incomes, together with a light tax burden, meant that farmers enjoyed high purchasing power. Since workers likewise received relatively high wages, the effective demand in America was more than sufficient to absorb production.

To this point Mofilev had developed an ingenious explanation for the rapid development of American capitalism. He claimed that even when the growth rate began to slow down, the reserve powers of capitalism had been sufficient to permit America to avoid many of the difficulties of European capitalism. Despite this evidence, however, he still concluded in Leninist fashion that America's decline would be no different from Europe's. Monopoly capitalism had ended America's charmed life, had transformed it from the promised land of capitalism, and had opened up possibilities for Communism.

Leninism involves an insistence that monopoly capitalism has effaced all differences in the West.[61] History was relevant only as a guide to when a revolution might break out. Such dogmatism was a sure prescription for disaster in a country that had never been fertile ground for socialists. The Lovestoneites were Leninists. Their expulsion from the Comintern signified, not their adherence to a bourgeois theoretical heresy, but their insistence on misinterpreting America for themselves instead of letting the Russians do it for them.

Notes

1. For a good sampling of some of the relevant literature, see D. H. Leon, "Whatever Happened to an American Socialist Party? A Critical Survey of the Spectrum of Interpretation," *American Quarterly,* XXIII (May 1971), pp. 236258. Also see R. Laurence Moore, *European Socialists and the American Promised Land* (New York: Oxford University Press, 1970).

2. The only exception is the brief moment of glory of the Socialist Party early in the century. See James Weinstein, *The Decline of Socialism in America 1912-1925* (New York: Monthly Review Press, 1967). Michael Harrington has recently claimed that the trade-union movement has been America's invisible socialist movement. See his *Socialism* (New York: Saturday Review Press. 1972).

3. See, for example, Louis Hartz, *The Liberal Tradition in America* (New York: Harcourt, Brace & World, 1955); Seymour Martin Lipset and Reinhard Bendix, *Social Mobility in Industrial Society* (Berkeley: University of California Press, 1964); Leon Samson, *Toward a United Front: A Philosophy for American Workers* (New York: Farrar & Rinehart, 1933); Stephan Thernstrom, *Poverty and Progress: Social Mobility in a Nineteenth Century City* (New York: Atheneum, 1969); Frederick Jackson Turner, *The Frontier in American History* (New York: Holt, 1920); Ellen Von Nardoff, " The American Frontier as a Safety-Valve," *Agricultural History,* XXXVI (1962), pp. 123-142.

4. Quoted in Daniel Bell, *Marxian Socialism in the United States* (Princeton: Princeton University Press, 1967), p. 4.

5. Hartz, *Liberal Tradition,* p. 78.

6. Gabriel Kolko, "The Decline of American Radicalism in the Twentieth Century," in James Weinstein and David Eakins (eds.), *For a New America: Essays in History and Politics from Studies on the Left' 1959-1967* (New York: Vintage Books, 1970), p. 198.

7. William Z. Foster, *History of the Communist Party of the United States* (New York: International Publishers, 1952), p. 271.

8. Bertram Wolfe, " Building a Communist Party in the U.S.A." *Workers Age,* 2 (October 15, 1932), p. 7.

9. Donald Clark Hodges, "Introduction," *Revolutionary Age* (New York: Greenwood Reprint Corporation, 1970). Hodges is referring to the political odysseys made by the Lovestoneites. Jay Lovestone served as George Meany's hard-line anti-Communist adviser on international affairs. Bertram Wolfe became a staunch anti-Communist. The careers of some other Lovestoneites are also instructive. Ben Gitlow became a professional informer. Bert Miller (Ben Mandel) was to serve as a research director for congressional committees investigating Communism. John Pepper was recalled to Moscow and disappeared in the purges. Will Herberg wrote several notable works on religion and became an editor of *National Review*.

10 Irving Howe and Lewis Coser, *The American Communist Party: A Critical History* (New York: Praeger, 1962), p. 163.

11. Theodore Draper, *American Communism and Soviet Russia* (New York: Viking Press, 1963), p. 268.
12. Bell, *Marxian Socialism,* p. 133.
13. Leon, "Whatever Happened.".
14. Draper, *American Communist Party.,* pp. 133-140.
15. Charles Ruthenberg, "The Session of Enlarged Executive Committee of the Communist International," *Workers Monthly, 5* (June 1926), pp. 339-342.
16. Draper, *American Communist Party.,* pp. 133-140.
17. V. I. Lenin, *Imperialism: The Highest Stage of Capitalism* (New York: International Publishers, 1939), p. 63.
18. Ibid., p. 126.
19. Ibid., pp. 103-104.
20. Ibid., p. 119.
21. Ibid.
22. Jay Lovestone, " The New America: The American Empire," *Workers Monthly, 4* (July 1925), p. 394.
23. Jay Lovestone, "Some Issues in the Party Discussion," *Communist, 8* (January-February 1929), p. 64.
24. John Pepper, " Speech to Seventh Session of Sixth World Congress of the Communist International," *International Press Correspondence, 8* (August 3, 1928), pp. 785-788.
25. Jay Lovestone, "Some Immediate Party Problems," *Communist, 7* (July 1928), p. 423.
26. John Pepper, "America and the Tactics of the Communist International," *Communist, 7* (April 1928), pp. 219-227.
27. Lovestone, "Some Issues," p. 72.
28. *Bertram Wolfe, "Economics* of Class Collaboration," *Workers Monthly, 5* (January 1926), pp. 117-120.
29. Lovestone "The New America," p. 392.
30. Wolfe, "Economics," pp. 118-119.
31. Jay Lovestone, "Imperialism and the American Working Class," *Workers Monthly, 5* (March 1926), pp. 203-205.
32. Jay Lovestone, "The Present Situation in the Labor Movement," *Communist, 7* (May 1928), pp. 265-278.
33. Lovestone, "Some Immediate Party Problems," p. 425.
34. Jay Lovestone, "Forces and Currents in the Present Political Situation," *Workers Monthly, 5* (April 1926), pp. 249-255.
35. Bertram Wolfe, "A Program for the Period of Prosperity," *Communist, 6* (July-August 1927), pp. 275-286.
36. Max Bedacht, "The Sixth Convention of Our Party," *Communist, 8* (March 1929), p. 102.
37. Jay Lovestone, "Report on the War Question," *International Press Correspondence, 8* (September 1, 1928), pp. 1021-1025.
38. Pepper, " America and the Tactics of the C.I.," pp. 219-227.
39. Lovestone, "Forces and Currents," pp. 249-255.
40. John Pepper, "Locating the Position of CP," *Daily Worker* (May 1, 1928), p. 1.
41. Harvey Klehr, "Marxist Theory in Search of America," *Journal of Politics, 35* (May 1973), pp. 311-331. Marx had enunciated two theories of American development, both of which recognized American differences from Europe. The first theory emphasized that the difficulties faced by capitalism in a colonial state such as America would lead to a privileged working class. The second theory emphasized

that, lacking a feudal structure to destroy, American capitalism had achieved a supremacy unequalled on the continent. Although Marx himself shied away from the implications of his theories, both could lead to a more venturesome concept of American exceptionalism than Lenin's notion of uneven development.

42. William Foster, " Speech to Thirteenth Session of Sixth World Congress of the Communist International," *International Press Correspondence,* 8 (August 18, 1928), pp. 920-922.

43. Draper, *American Communist Party.,* p. 307.

44. William Foster and Alexander Bittleman, "Theses of the Foster-Bittleman Minority," *Daily Worker* (December 25, 1928).

45. William Foster, "The Decline of the A.F. of L." *Communist,* 8 (January—February 1929), pp. 43-58.

46. Jay Lovestone, "Some Issues," pp. 59-80.

47. Bertram Wolfe and Jack Stachel, " Lenin, the American Working Class and Its Party," *Workers Monthly,* 5 (February 1926), pp. 154-160.

48. Bertram Wolfe, "Whose Revolution Is It?," *Workers Monthly,* 5 (July 1926), pp. 287-392. Soon after the Lovestoneites had been expelled, one J. Mo wrote an article attacking the notion that Bolsheviks could learn anything from 1776. To suggest that even tactical lessons could be gleaned was to commit "the error of infantile sickness." Anyone who looked to bourgeois revolutions for lessons for proletarian revolutions "plunges himself into the whirlpool of mechanical and superficial historical parallelism." "Some Clarifications on the Lessons of the American Revolution," *Communist,* 9 (November—December 1930), pp. 1046, 1048.

49. Bertram Wolfe, "Towards Leninism," *Workers Monthly,* 6 (January 1927), p. 679.

50. Editorial statement, *Communist,* 6 (February 1927), p. 763.

51. Max Bedacht, "American Labor at Cross Roads," *Workers Monthly,* 5 (February 1927), p. 726.

52. Jay Lovestone, "Did We 'Hide' the Crisis?," *Revolutionary Age,* 1 (September 1, 1929), p. 5.

53. "Fight Against Unemployment," *Revolutionary Age,* 1 (December 1, 1929), pp. 1-2.

54. "The Economic Situation in the U.S.," *Revolutionary Age,* 1 (March 15, 1930), p. 7.

55. "Order in Wall Street," *Revolutionary Age,* 1 (November 15, 1929), p. 1.

56. "The Economic Situation," p. 9.

57. "Exceptionalism and Leninist Strategy," *Revolutionary Age,* 1 (December 15, 1929), p. 6.

58. Klehr, "Marxist Theory."

59. V. Motilev, " Origin of the Economic Supremacy of the United States," *Communist,* 9 (July 1930), p. 597.

60. Ibid., p. 608.

61. See, for example, Lenin's justification for why a violent revolution was required in the United States and Great Britain, in *The Proletarian Revolution and the Renegade Kautsky* (New York: International Publishers, 1934), p. 21.

4

Leninism, Lewis Corey, and the Failure of American Socialism

For a movement which had so little practical success, American socialism has spawned an enormous literature. Michael Harrington has recently proclaimed that reports of its demise were premature, and that the corpse is alive, well, and living at the headquarters of the AFL-CIO.[1] Harrington's is but the latest in a long line of books and articles searching for the American socialist movement. Most of the searchers are motivated not by necrophilia but by a desire to understand American politics. For many, the key to twentieth-century America is the failure of a socialist party, the broader failure of the left, and the consequent long resistance to the arrival of the welfare state.

Interest in the failure of the socialist movement is also related to current political concerns. Did the American left fail because of its organizational difficulties, its doctrines, its language, its allies, or because it represented an idea whose time had not yet come in America? What can those interested today in social change learn from those who yesterday failed at it? To gain even tentative answers to these questions radicals of various stripes have argued and reargued their pasts. D. H. Leon has recently offered an academic survey of interpretations of the failure of American radicalism.[2] Leon has noted many of the arguments and pointed out a number of the lacunae in our understanding of the radical past. He has not, however, discussed one very cogent explanation of that failure. I wish to exhume this missing explanation, consider its implications, and discuss its importance.

The weakness of American socialism has long bedeviled Marxists. Marx and Engels never provided a clear, unambiguous explanation for the sorry state of socialism in one of the world's most powerful capitalist nations. Their writings actually yield at least two different theories about America.[3] The first,

Originally pubished in *Labor History*, Spring 1977 (http://www.informaworld.com) and reprinted with permission.

contained primarily in the last chapter of the first volume of *Capital*, argued that America's colonial past, particularly the availability of free land and the acute labor shortage, had forced capitalists to reduce drastically their exploitation of workers. Capitalism had been slow to develop in America due to widespread independent proprietorship.[4] The second theory, pieced together from scattered comments of Marx and, especially, Engels, was that America from its birth had been a bourgeois nation. Never having known feudalism, America had developed the purest bourgeois ideology and institutions in the world. Consequently the working class had been imbued with bourgeois prejudices and the bourgeois class itself was much stronger and more confident than its counterpart in Europe.[5]

Lenin was not any clearer about the failure of American socialism than Marx and Engels. He too provided two different explanations for the failure of American socialism. In 1907, in a preface to a collection of letters written by Marx and Engels to a number of friends, including Americans, Lenin first articulated some of the obstacles confronted in America. He argued that the United States and Britain were on a different plane of development than other capitalist countries. As a result, the normal relationships a Marxist would expect between capitalists and proletarians were altered. In these two countries, the "absence of any big, nation-wide, democratic tasks facing the proletariat" meant that the socialists endured "complete subordination to bourgeois politics; the sectarian isolation of groups...from the proletariat; not the slightest socialist success among the working masses at the elections, etc."[6]

In contrast, the relative success of the German socialists, in a less economically developed country was an advantageous consequence of struggling for democracy in an autocratic state. The tensions between the autocratic state, which resulted from the failure of the German bourgeoisie to complete their revolution, and the capitalist economy fueled the growth of German socialism.[7]

A few years later, in 1912, Lenin admitted that the trade union movement in America endorsed capitalism. The presence of a bourgeois labor movement was a consequence of the long-lived alliance between capitalism and democracy. Lenin remained optimistic, however, that the American working class would soon emulate its European brethren:

> The long-standing political liberty and the exceptionally favorable conditions, in comparison with other countries, for the deep-going and widespread development of capitalism...have tended to produce within the working class an aristocracy that has trailed after the bourgeoisie, betraying its own class.... In the twentieth century in Britain and America, this peculiar situation is rapidly disappearing.[8]

Curiously, during the years he compared American socialism favorably to Germany's, Lenin was urging Russian radicals to help direct Russia down the American rather than the Prussian path of development. Feudalism, he felt, could disappear "either as a result of the transformation of the landlord economy or as a result of the abolition of the landlord latifundias, i.e., either by reform or by revolution."[9] The Prussian, or reform path, meant a gradual economic transformation to capitalism without the displacement of the old, politically dominant classes. The American, or revolutionary path, meant a social and political, as well as economic transformation. The latter path would speed up the development of capitalism and hence the arrival of socialism; the former would slow both down.

The contradictions in Lenin's attitude towards America were symptomatic of the difficulties of a Marxist analysis of America. In Marxist terms, America was an anomaly. On the one hand Lenin urged Russia to travel the American path to socialism and on the other he saw the success of the German socialists linked with their differences from America. The American socialists were weak because the fight in America was over socialist demands; the German socialists were strong because the fight in Germany was over democratic demands.[10]

After 1916, Lenin was no longer confused about America. And unfortunately, ever since he provided his answer, few radicals have been confused. The theory of imperialism provided a coherent rationale for the weakness of American socialism. The enormous profits being squeezed out of the colonial lands enabled capitalists to raise slightly the wages of the working class and deflect them from developing revolutionary consciousness. The bourgeoisie was able to bribe the leadership of the working class and thus create a group of "labour lieutenants of capitalism."[11] The theory of imperialism obviated the need for Lenin to inquire why "this peculiar situation" of working-class passivity did not rapidly disappear. It also eliminated the chance of Lenin or any of his followers pursuing the idea that socialism thrive only where it could plausibly claim to fight for democratic as well as socialist goals.

Lenin's earlier explanation was unknowingly resurrected in 1940 by a remarkable and undeservedly obscure figure in the radical movement—Lewis Corey.[12] Corey was an appropriate figure to re-evaluate the American radical tradition: he was involved with all facets of the American radical tradition during his life. He was born in Italy in 1892, and brought to America as a child. Under his given name of Louis Fraina he moved from the Socialist Party to the Socialist Labor Party to the IWW, and back to the Socialist Party once again before playing an influential role in the founding of the Communist Party of 1919.[13] After working in Moscow and Mexico for the Comintern, Fraina abandoned political activities in 1922 and the next year returned to America. In 1926, he began to write under the name of Corey and by the mid-thirties had won a reputation as a Marxist economist. In 1940, he was a leading figure in the founding of the Union for Democratic Action which later became the Americans for Democratic Action. Corey later taught at Antioch College – even though he had never graduated from high school – and served as the educational director of the Amalgamated Butchers Union. At the time of his death in 1953, Corey was fighting a deportation order from the Justice Department. By now a fervent anti-communist, he was charged with being a communist. Even his death was symbolic of the traumas suffered by the American left. As Theodore Draper has noted, "the man who began as Louis C. Fraina and ended as Lewis Corey, provided the complete symbol of the American radical in the first half of the 20th century."[14]

In 1940, Corey published three articles in the *Nation* entitled "Marxism Reconsidered." This reconsideration was continued in two other articles of Corey's appearing in *Workers Age,* a radical sect's paper, under the title "Recreating Socialism." Corey's articles explored the same theme Lenin had first broached, but did not stop at a partial explanation of the weakness of American radicalism. The relationship between democracy and capitalism suggested to Corey that the failure of Marxism in America said more about Marxism than America.

In the light of Russian and American developments since 1917 Corey re-examined Marxism. He argued that Marx had misinterpreted socialism, and that the failure of American radicalism was a result of attempts to graft European theories onto American conditions, and that neither European nor Russian events could fruitfully be transported to America.

It was essential for Corey that socialism in America "must be based upon American traditions, upon American experience, upon American problems."[15] Both American communism and American socialism, however, were impor-tations. Marxism had been a response to peculiar developmental patterns in Europe.

For Corey, searching for an explanation of the weakness of American social-ism obscured the more local question: why had European socialism done so much better? His answer was that Marxism had taken root in Europe because of the backwardness of the continent. While Marx thought that the proletariat would usher in socialism, the strength of European socialism had resulted from the assistance it rendered the bourgeoisie in completing the bourgeois-demo-cratic revolution. In the United States that revolution required no assistance from a socialist movement:

> We must recognize the fact, and build upon the fact that the American working class rejected the older types of European reformist socialism not because it was more backward but because it was ahead of the working classes of Europe. Organized so-cialism was essentially an expression of the democratic backwardness of Europe.[16]

Corey considered the argument that it was Leninism, not Marxism, that was to blame for the failure of American socialism but rejected it. The Russian model of revolution championed by Lenin was applicable to underdeveloped countries, and hence, just as inappropriate an example for America as European socialism. The transformation of socialism into totalitarianism in Russia was not, however, due only to Russian backwardness or Leninism. Corey discerned "elements in a socialist economy that unless conscious measures are taken…may lead towards totalitarianism and not towards socialist democracy."[17] More specifically, the concentration of political and economic power in the same hands would be as inimical to workers under socialism as under capitalism.

American radicals, Corey felt, had failed to appreciate the virtues of democratic institutions because of the European theories through which they viewed these institutions. American socialists would have to promise to insure democracy "with socialist checks and balances." In place of Marx's unity of governmental functions, they would have to argue in favor of a separation of the executive, legislative, and judicial branches. Similarly, economic decisionmaking would have to be decentralized. Trade unions had to remain independent of the state. Different kinds of property would have to be permitted; in addition to nationalized industry, independent small property-owners and cooperatives were needed. In contemporary terms, Corey was calling for a pluralist socialist democracy, with a number of competing power centers.

Corey also argued that socialists would have to reassess their attitude towards democracy if they insisted on remaining Marxists. Marx had, apart from some of his early writings, considered socialism a movement of the majority of the population.[18] In America, however, socialism could not come to power under democratic conditions, since the proletariat was unlikely ever to compose a majority of the population. Holding on to Marxism, then, forced American socialists to abandon democracy and further isolate themselves from the American people.

A proletarian revolution in America would either be crushed by the middle class and the farmers or would be forced to abandon democracy to sustain itself in power. As for the first course, "violence in an advanced country like the United States would be fatal, because the new middle class is large and can dispose of more of today's specialized violence than the proletariat."[19] And the second course would lead in the same direction as Russia.

Reliance on the proletariat as the carrier of socialism was justified only as long as the major struggle in capitalist states was for democratic rights. For this reason Marxian socialism and proletarian parties created in the image of Marxian principles had enjoyed a certain degree of success in continental Europe. Once democratic rights largely prevailed, however, and domestic politics became a struggle for the achievement of socialist goals, the single-minded emphasis on the interests of the working class prevented socialists from making successful appeals to other groups whose support was necessary for obtaining a majority.[20]

Corey attributed the early successes of European socialists to their participation in the struggle for democracy and their more recent failure to their inability to broaden their appeal beyond the trade union movement. The social-democrats were unable to come to power while the Bolsheviks were forced to hold dictatorial power since both remained wedded to Marxist categories. These lessons prompted Corey to insist that "socialists must express and realize the interests of all useful functional groups within society."[21] The failure of American socialists was a failure which European socialists would repeat as they emerged from backwardness—unless, that is, they abandoned Marxism.

While Lenin's theory of imperialism has often been credited—or blamed— for making Marxism a doctrine particularly attractive to undeveloped countries, Corey was insisting that Marxism itself had been attractive to backward capitalist countries-those which had undergone an economic, but not a political revolution. In America, there was little, if any, time-lag between the two revolutions. The working class did not require a separate political movement to batter down the doors to the political arena.

Corey's discussion ignored the distinctive difficulties America presented to radicals. His was not a theory of American exceptionalism. While America's past had differed from Europe's, the future of socialism in both would be similar. From Corey's own observations, however, a more plausible argument could be made that American socialism faced additional obstacles. America's democratic institutions were the creations of elites, not the results of mass political movements. They were designed to insulate elites from mass passion even as they were to provide some measure of popular control. American socialism has faced institutional barriers that the European variant has not. The presidential system encourages two-partyism. The single-member district with plurality election for the House of Representatives likewise limits the ability of third parties to play an independent political role. The timing of America's capitalist and democratic revolutions, in other words, may have created institutions which permanently discouraged hopes of building even a European-style socialist movement.

American socialism has had an embarrassing history of seizing upon doctrines produced in backward lands and dismally failing to adapt them to America. The cults of admiration for Mao Tse Tung and Che Guevara led some radicals to theorize seriously about guerilla warfare in the United States as a step towards socialism. Leninism was the product of a revolution whose first goal was to begin the primitive accumulation necessary to achieve capitalism and yet it became a beacon for a generation of radicals. Marxism, also, Corey suggested, pointed out a path America had already traversed.

Notes

1. Michael Harrington, *Socialism* (New York, 1972).
2. D. H. Leon, "Whatever Happened to an American Socialist Party? A Critical Survey of the Spectrum of Interpretations," *American Quarterly*, 23 (1971), 236-258.
3. This argument is developed at greater length in Harvey Klehr's "Marxist Theory in Search of America," *Journal of Politics*, 35 (1973), 31 1-331.
4. See Karl Marx, *Capital: A Critique of Political Economy*, ed. Frederick Engels, trans. Samuel Moore and Edward Aveling (3 volumes; New York 1967). I, 765-774.
5. See Karl Marx and Frederick Engels, *Letters to Americans: 1848-1895* (New York, 1963).

6. V. I. Lenin, "Preface to the Russian Translation of Letters by Johannes Becker, Joseph Dietzgen, Frederick Engels, Karl Marx and Others to Frederick Sorge and Others," in *Collected Works* (45 vols.; Moscow, 1960-70), vol. 12, 364. For an elaboration of these two Leninist theories, see Harvey Klehr, "Leninist Theory in Search of America," *Polity,* 9 (1976). 81-96.
7. Lenin, "Preface," 365-366.
8. Lenin, "In America," in *Collected Works,* vol 36, 215.
9. Lenin, "The Agrarian Programme of Social-Democracy in the Fit Russian Revolution 1905-1907," in *Collected Works,* vol. 13, 239.
10. On Lenin's contention that socialism was on the American agenda, see "Democracy and Narodism in China," *Collected Works,* vol. 18, 166.
11. See Lenin, *Imperialism, The Highest Stage of Capitalism* in *Collected Works,* vol. 22, 301.
12. In a 227-page interview with the FBI in 1947, whose transcript I obtained under the Freedom of Information Act, Corey discusses his abandonment of communism but does not indicate any discovery of this early Leninist writing. The transcript is a revealing document, particularly insofar as it indicates the FBI's interest in the foreign connections of the early communist movement.
13. The biographical material on Corey is drawn from Esther Corey, "Lewis Corey (Louis C. Fraina), 1892- 1953: A bibliography with Auto-biographical Notes," *Labor History,* 4(1963), 103-131.
14. Theodore Draper, *The Roots of American Communism* (New York, 1963). 302.
15. Lewis Corey, "Recreating Socialism" *Workers Age,* 9 (March 23, 1940), 4. The second part of Corey's article appeared on March 30, 1940.
16. Ibid. Years earlier, Louis Fraina had quite a different perspective on American socialism. In 1919 he charged that the Socialist Party had been compromised from its birth because of Morris Hillquit's opposition to the Socialist Labor Party and its efforts to revolutionize the trade union movement. Fraina accused the SP of supporting Samuel Gompers, criticized it for expelling Bill Haywood, and derided it for running "a petty bourgeois liberal campaign" in 1912. Louis Fraina, International Secretary of the CP of America, "Report to the Executive Committee of the Communist International" in *Manifesto and Program, Communist Parry of America* (Chicago, 1919).
17. Lewis Corey, "Recreating Socialism."
18. See Stanley Moore, *Three Tactics: The Background in Marx* (New York: Monthly Review Press, 1963) and Shlomo Avineri, *The Social and Political Thought of Karl Marx* (Cambridge: Cambridge University Press, 1970).
19. Lewis Corey, "Marxism Reconsidered," *Nation,* 143 (1940), 274. Other parts of the article appeared on February 17 and March 2,1940. Part of Corey's thesis was included in his book, *The Unfinished Task: Economic Reconstruction for Democracy* (New York: Viking, 1942).
20. Carey, "Maoism Reconsidered," 273.
21. Ibid., 274.

Part 2

American Communism and Its Splinters

5

Immigrant Leadership in the Communist Party of the United States of America

American communism has long been popularly associated with foreigners. Radicalism has been seen as an importation or, more accurately, a foreign contagion brought to and spread on pristine American shores by aliens. This perception is not limited to popular superstition. An influential school of historiography has insisted that the theoretical doctrines of communism—and conservatism—are particularly European arriving from a class-conscious, hierarchical society and bearing little relevance to American life (Hartz, 1955).

A substantial number of Americans have, more practically, been convinced that the communists hiding under American beds were mostly foreigners. Congressional committees have expressed their conviction that "the Communist movement in the United States is an alien movement, sustained, augmented, and controlled by European Communists and the Soviet Union" (Divine, 1957: p. 162). A disillusioned former Communist has charged that aliens dominated and directed the CPUSA in the interests of the Soviet Union (Budenz, 1950). Popular stereotypes of the American communist focused on his foreignness. Perhaps one of the reasons so many people found it hard to believe that Alger Hiss could be a communist was that Hiss was so untypical to be cast as one: he was from an impeccably upper-class native American background.

The equation of foreigners with communism has, logically, led to periodic efforts to destroy the latter by ridding the country of the former. Anticommunism has neatly meshed with an older strain of American nativism which has always been hostile to Europe. Nativist efforts to limit immigration, increasingly active as Eastern and Southern Europe replaced Northern Europe as sources of most

---

Reprinted from the *Communist Cadre: The Social Background of the American Communist Elite,* by Harvey E. Klehr, with the permission of the publisher, Hoover Institution Press. Copyright 1978 by the Board of Trustees of the Leland Stanford Junior University

new arrivals, gained even more success when linked to the alleged radicalism of the immigrants. In 1919 the Palmer Raids led to the arrest and deportation of several hundred aliens for links to the newly formed communist parties. Thereafter, deportation of communists was a steady feature of American life. Minimal in the 1920s and 1930s, the deportations picked up considerably after World War II (Clark, 1968; Williamson, 1969).

The Communist Party of the United States of America (CPUSA) has been carefully studied by a host of academics and journalists. Several have provided detailed and fascinating, but incomplete, accounts of the role of the foreign-born in the CPUSA. Nathan Glazer's (1961) exemplary report on the party's social composition, for example, carefully delineates the proportion of party members born in Europe at different times in party history. To understand any organization, however, it is crucial to understand its leadership. Within any communist party there is a sharp distinction between the rank-and-file membership—many only temporary party members—and the leadership or cadres—most of whom were full-time revolutionaries. Of this latter group we know very little.

Historical studies of the CPUSA have made it clear that many of the key figures in the party were born abroad. They have not, however, been able to provide evidence from a reliable sample of the party leadership to suggest precisely what the social composition of that leadership was like.

To what extent were native-born Americans among the party elite? Was the leadership an ethnic mirror of the membership? How rapidly did the CPUSA Americanize its leadership? What consequences did this process have on other leadership characteristics about which the party was concerned—class background, for example. And, most generally, is there any relation between the supposed domination of the CPUSA by the foreign-born and its inability to make much headway in American life?

The Data

To examine these questions we collected data on all individuals who were members of the party's Central Committee between 1921 and 1961. There were several reasons for this choice. First, the committee is the core of the party's leadership. Elected by the national convention, it is the highest constitutional body of the party and has traditionally reflected the territorial and factional balance within the organization. Second, elections to this body occurred at given intervals although this has varied from every year to a seven-year hiatus between conventions. The relative regularity of such elections allows us to examine changes within the leadership and to analyze them within the context of other developments occurring in the party. Third, although the size has varied considerably from election to election, the committee is sufficiently large and visible to be analyzed systematically.

There were some problems in identifying all members of each committee, since some had secret members—usually labor leaders whose public identification as party leaders would have been damaging. Yet, we have been able to identify 212 different Central Committee (CC) members during this period which we believe is a virtually complete list of all those who served on the CC during this period. Finally, by choosing a group of party leaders such as this one we avoided the sample bias which arises from relying on self-selected groups of communists and ex-communists who have provided much of the information upon which several of the studies of the party have been based. Almond's (1954) study is based on a sample of ex-communists. Draper's (1957: p. 200) is limited to one point in time and is based on a nonrandom sample of party leadership.

We gathered information on birthplace and birth date, ethnic and religious background, education, occupation, and certain party career data. Obtaining such information proved extraordinarily difficult. The CPUSA has published little about its leadership other than occasional memoirs and obituaries. Where possible such sources were employed. In addition, we interviewed many communists and ex-communists—some of whom were on the committee. Finally, we made use of information available from the public record concerning the prosecution of the party leadership under the Smith Act and the Subversive Activities Control Act and data obtained from the FBI through utilization of the Freedom of Information Act.

In the next section of this paper we will evaluate the size of the foreign-born component of the CPUSA—both among the membership and leadership. Next we will look at the ethnic divisions within both groups. The following section compares native and foreign-born party leaders in regard to selected socioeconomic characteristics and party career data.

Foreign-Born

There is widespread agreement among historians that, at least in its early years, the overwhelming majority of the CPUSA was "composed of relatively recent immigrants" (Glazer, 1961). The foreign domination of American radicalism had developed after American entry into World War I. Prior to that time, the Socialist Party (SP) of America had been largely a native-born organization (Weinstein, 1967). The development of a left wing in the SP coincided with a sharp increase in the membership of its foreign-language affiliates. These foreign-language federations were designed to provide a congenial home for newly arrived immigrants through which they could remain in touch with events in the old country and participate at least marginally in radical American politics. The federations enjoyed a great deal of autonomy within the Socialist Party and their members, limited by their unfamiliarity with English, had little contact with the American party.

Between December 1918 and April 1919 the Russian, Ukrainian, South Slovak, Lithuanian, and Lettish federations jumped in membership from 12,086 to 22,430 (O'Neal and Weiner, 1947: p. 53). By the latter date, 53 percent of the

108,000 Socialist Party dues payers were in language federations. The impact of the Russian Revolution upon East European immigrants 1 transformed the SP into a largely foreign-born group.

These same federations formed the core of the new communist parties formed in 1919. The language federations also contained the bulk of the party membership in the 1920s. The Palmer Raids, aimed at alien radicals, did not significantly lessen their relative influence within the communist movement. Nathan Glazer (1961, p. 40) has shown that in 1922 only 10 percent of the Workers Party — as the CPUSA was then known — was in the English section: the same percentage as in 1919. While the overwhelming majority of those in the language federations were foreign-born, it is misleading to assume that all members of English-speaking branches were native-born. Many were immigrants who were able to speak English. Whittaker Chambers (1952, pp. 203. 204) noted of his first party meeting at an English branch in 1925: "they were of several nationalities, but broken English, Greek, and Yiddish seemed to be the prevailing languages…. It was called English-speaking…to indicate that the business of the meeting would be conducted in English, however broken." Jack Stachel, organizational secretary of the CPUSA, later admitted that the "so-called English branches included many elements that could hardly speak English" (Draper, 1960, p. 476).

The English-speaking membership was not only small, it was also unstable. While the English-language section "was the heaviest recruiter, it also lost the largest proportion of its recruits" (Glazer. 1961, p. 55; Draper, 1960, p. 188). This condition persisted at least until 1925 when a bare 14 percent of the party was in English branches (Glazer, 1961, p. 40). Such a situation was intolerable for any group wanting to expand its influence in American life and among American workers.

In succeeding years the CPUSA made numerous efforts to transform itself into a more "American" organization. A Bolshevization campaign was begun in 1925 under instructions from the Comintern. Designed to transform the party from a federated to an industrial-based organization, Bolshevization was also aimed at destroying the language federations' role as intermediary between their members and the party and the locus of loyalty of the immigrants. The demise of the federations severely reduced party membership—from 14,037 in September 1925 to only 7,215 in October (Glazer, 1961, p 52), the largest losses occurring in the Finnish Federation. Many of the federation members were more interested in the social and fraternal functions the federations provided than their political activities. When the party was reorganized and the "benevolent society" features downgraded, they left in large numbers (Glazer. 1961).

So few were native-born Americans within the CPUSA during the 1920s, however, that the loss of large numbers of foreign-born members did not significantly increase the former's influence. As late as 1929, the CPUSA was bemoaning its inability to attract more native-born Americans. In a report to that year's party convention Jack Stachel—himself an alien—noted that two-thirds of the membership was still "registered in the various languages" and that only 5,000 were English speaking. In five representative party districts, however, about 88 percent of party members were foreign-born, suggesting that few of the English-speaking members were native-born (Glazer. 1961. P. 59, 60). The same year the Comintern addressed an open letter to the American party, noting that it "has for many years been an organization of foreign workers not much connected with the political life of the country" (Glazer, 1961, p. 59).

During the 1930s the party did make a strong effort to Americanize itself. Its membership also began a steady rise, going from 7,500 in 1930 to 55,000 in 1938 (Glazer, 1961, pp. 92-93). Many of these new recruits were native-born, brought to communism as a result of the Depression or the great labor struggles of the decade. The advent of the Popular Front in 1935 enabled the CPUSA to identify itself with American values and appeal to the native-born. Finally, restrictive immigration legislation enacted in the early 1920s had ensured that fewer Americans would be foreign-born. As the party grew in the 1930s, therefore, its percentage of foreign-born declined, going from 70 percent in 1933 to 61 percent in 1935 to 52.2 percent in early 1936 to an unspecified minority later that year (Glazer. 1961, p. 100; Alperin, 1959).

While there are no reliable statistics available after this period, it is clear that the native-born percentage increased through the 1940s and early 1950s. First, the CPUSA itself made membership more difficult for the foreign-born. The 1929 constitution had opened membership to all persons over eighteen who accepted the program of the CPUSA and the Comintern. In 1938 a new constitution made membership open to citizens and those who declared their "intention of becoming a citizen of the United States" (House Committee on Un-American Activities. 1953, pp. 90, 99). A special 1940 convention called to revise the constitution in response to Congressional passage of the Voorhis Act required members to be citizens and dropped aliens from the party rolls.

Second, those foreign refugees who arrived in the United States during and after World War II were not fertile ground for party recruiting. While some of the refugees from Hitler who managed to enter this country were Communists, they returned home after the war. Many of the postwar refugees were fleeing not only the devastation of Europe but also the Communist takeovers of their homelands and were militantly anti-communist.

As the CPUSA came under attack in the 1950s, however, the greatest defections came from the native-born. The very factors which had contributed to the party's success at Americanizing itself during the 1930s were now reversed. The CPUSA was stigmatized as disloyal and un-American. Instead of an alliance with important sectors of the population, it stood in isolation. Glazer (1961, p. 164) has argued that while the party lost foreign-born members, "since they were somewhat isolated, socially and linguistically and by age from the main stream of American public opinion, the rate of their defection was low." Although there does not seem to be any data available, it is plausible that the older party members, more likely to be foreign-born, were less likely to be discouraged, disheartened, or disgusted with the CPUSA. Many of the old timers clung to the party as a comfortable old age home (Charney 1968). Thus, as the CPUSA shrank in the 1950s—from 20,000 in 1956 to just under 3,000 in early 1958, it is likely that the percentage of foreign-born once again rose (Shannon, 1959, p. 360).

The party leadership was never quite as heavily foreign-born as the membership. For one thing, the language federations which contained the bulk of the party membership in the early years needed some visible native-born leaders for the fledgling organization. Thus, Ben Gitlow (1940, p. 49) recalls that "for all their disdain for the Americans, they realized that without an English-speaking wing they could not organize a Communist Party in the United States." At the very least, leaders of an American Communist Party would have to speak English. Second, a number of the leaders of the language federations returned to Russia; some like Rozins of the Lettish group to positions of responsibility in the new Soviet regime and others like Hourwich of the Russian organization to remove them from meddling in the American party. Finally, the CPUSA desired a more American image and could manipulate its leadership to provide that image far more easily than its membership. Try as it might, the party was for many years unable to attract and retain large numbers of native-born recruits. Within the leadership native-born Americans could be given greater prominence.

Somewhat more than one-third of the 212 central committee members in our sample were foreign-born—almost 40 percent of the 200 for whom we have data on birthplace. More relevant, however, are the figures for each committee since there were huge variations. Figure 1 reveals that while there has been a trend toward a more American-born leadership, it has been neither steady nor uniform. Several specific points bear mention. First, in the party's early years, the leadership was far more native-born than the membership. Second, the same year, 1936, that a majority of the members were, for the first time, native-born was also the year in which the party's leadership finally ceased to have a majority of foreign-born. Symbolically, it was a year after the inauguration of the popular front. Third, it is at least possible that the party leadership was considerably more native-born than the membership in the late 1950s. Two specific periods require some discussion. The 1922-1925 period saw an unusual jump in the percentage of native-born on the CC. During this period the Workers' Party (WP) was establishing itself as a legal arm of American communism. As late as 1922, the CPUSA retained an underground organization which exerted considerable control over the legal organization. Although generalizations are dangerous, the American-born party members were more likely to favor full legality and abandonment of the underground, recognizing that in a public, open movement their own opportunities for leadership would be enhanced (Draper, 1957).

Figure 1
Percentage of American Born on Central Committee

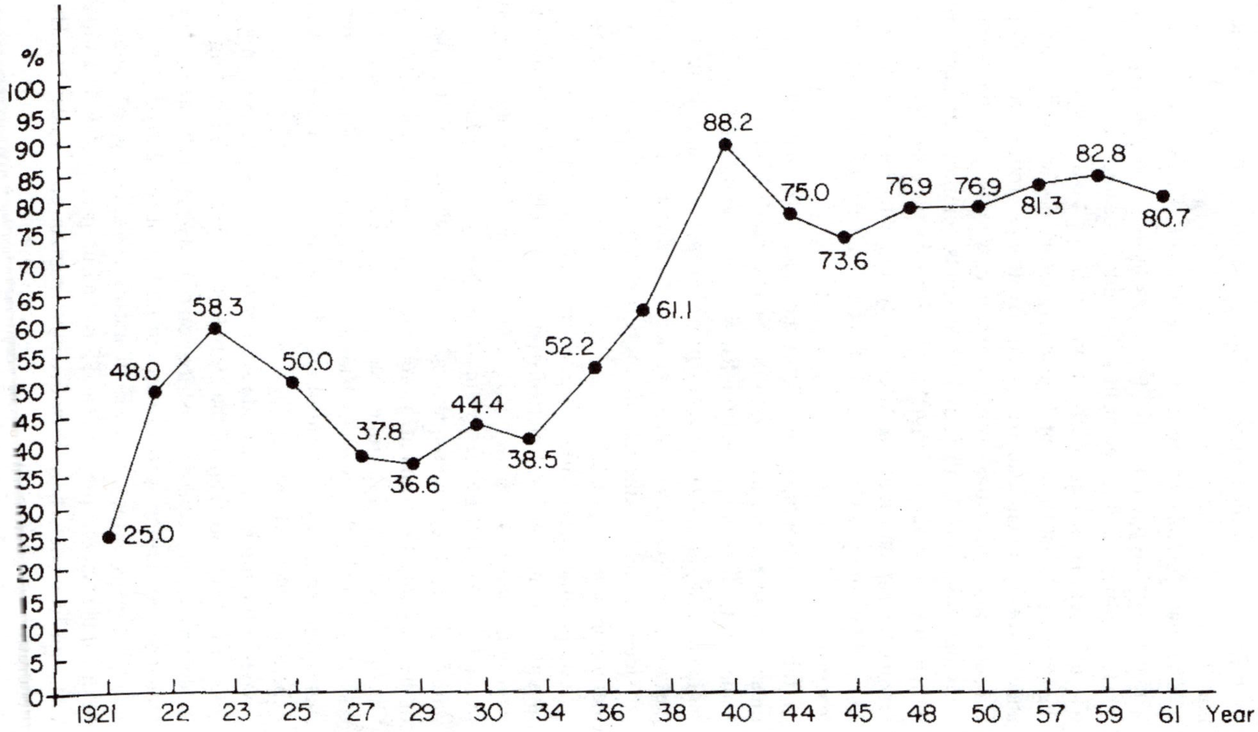

During this same period the remarkable John Pepper arrived in America and immediately leapt into prominence in the party. The indefatigable Pepper zealously preached the necessity of Americanizing the CPUSA and the sudden spurt in the role of the American-born may well be one of his legacies (Cannon, 1962).

The 1940 Central Committee was quite small. It also excluded noncitizens, who had been dropped from the party by a new constitution. As a result, only two foreign-born men served on this committee—neither of whom, incidentally, was a citizen. Both John Williamson and Irving Potash were later deported, the former to Great Britain and the latter to Poland. The words "foreign-born" and "native-born" unite an extraordinarily diverse group of people. A substantial segment of the native-born, for example, were Negroes while others were Jews and still others Anglo- Saxon Protestants. Similarly, the foreign-born are united only by not having originated in America: they came from nineteen different countries and cultures. After briefly summarizing these data, we present some fragmentary comparisons of the comparative origins of membership and leadership.

Table 1 makes graphic the dominant role within the party leadership of those born in the old tsarist empire. Nearly one-half of all the foreign-born leaders of the CPUSA came from Russia or neighboring provinces, excluding Finland. East European countries provided the next largest contingent. The party's foreign-born leadership was heavily drawn from those countries which provided the bulk of American immigration after 1880 and the bulk of the early membership of the CPUSA.

The popular perception of American communism has been that it was imported to this country. Relatively few of the foreign-born leaders, however, were communists when they arrived and it is doubtful many were politically inspired at all. Half of the seventy-nine foreign-born leaders had arrived in America by 1910 and three-quarters by 1915—four years prior to the formation of the communist movement. Moreover, a great many immigrated as children. One-quarter were in the United States by the age of ten while the mean age was 16.4 years. Three-quarters had arrived by the age of twenty-two. While many, or even most, were raised in a foreign culture their formative political experiences were American.

While the foreign-born leadership of the CPUSA reflected in general the foreign-born membership of the party there were some interesting anomalies. Table 2 provides the general distribution of party membership over the various language federations at two times during the party's early years. Bearing in mind that many of those in the English and Jewish language federation should be distributed among the tsarist and Eastern European groups, it is still apparent that some federations never provided much national party leadership. The Lettish Federation which was quite large never contributed many party leaders while the small Polish Federation did. The Finns were seriously underrepresented in

Table 1
Birthplace of Foreign-Born CC Members

Tsarist Empire	(38)	Scandinavia	(8)
Russia	24	Sweden	1
Poland	8	Norway	1
Lithuania	5	Denmark	2
Latvia	1	Finland	4
Eastern Europe	(12)	British Empire	(10)
Yugoslavia	6	Great Britain and Ireland	6
Czechoslovakia	2	Canada	1
Hungary	3	Indies	3
Rumania	1		
Central Europe	(7)	Miscellaneous	(4)
Germany	6	Italy	3
Austria	1	Puerto Rico	1

the leadership, particularly since by 1925 the Finnish Federation enrolled half the party's members. The Germans were overrepresented.

The Letts had been among the earliest and strongest advocates of American Bolshevism. Their guiding spirit, however, returned to Russia where he played a key role in the new Soviet government. All but one of the Polish-born party leaders were Jewish, so many of them may have been of the Jewish Federation or even the Russian. The Finns, for all their numbers and wealthy cooperative institutions, were never very influential within the party hierarchy. Concentrated largely in the upper Midwest, they sought to maintain their own institutions and property and were scorned by many other communists as petty-bourgeois farmers. One second-generation Finnish former communist has suggested that a certain insularity, nourished by a series of labor defeats in the early 1900s and a nationalist-chauvinist exclusiveness, contributed to this lack of Finnish leadership in the top echelons of the CPUSA (Draper, 1960; C. Ross, personal communication, June 29, 1976). Finally, while the German Federation was relatively small, a core of German Marxists had been quite influential in the American radical movement ever since 1848 and a German-language paper had been an early and influential endorser of the communist movement (Draper, 1957).

These figures on birthplace conceal one of the most interesting aspects of the American communist movement: the role played by Jews. Among our sample, 71, or 33.5 percent, of the CC members were of Jewish origin. Moreover, the overwhelming majority of the foreign-born from the area of the tsarist empire was Jewish. As Table 3 makes evident, virtually all of the immigrants from Russia, Poland, Lithuania, and Latvia were Jewish. Two factors in particular may account for this phenomenon. First, the deplorable conditions of Jews in the tsarist empire and the impact of the breakdown in religious and cultural values which took place in the late 1800s led many to transfer their messianic zeal into radical political movements (Howe, 1976). Second, the impact of the Bolshevik Revolution, with its initial promise—and practice—of Jewish liberation from pogroms and discrimination made a great impression. The impact of that cataclysmic event was felt at a time when most Jewish immigrants suffered from crushing poverty and were building a strong labor movement in the garment industry. This combination of events led to a substantial Jewish presence in the Communist Party leadership.

The native-born party leaders were not themselves a homogeneous group. In fact, there was just as much, if not more variation among them than the foreign-born. Virtually all of the twenty-eight native-born Jews were the children

Table 2
Percentage of CPUSA Membership in Language Federations

	October through December 1921	April through June 1922
Tsarist Empire	(54)	(36)
Russian	17	11
Ukrainian	6	4
Polish	3	1
Lithuanian	18	11
Lettish	10	9
Eastern Europe	(11)	(16)
Hungarian	1	2
South Slavic	10	14
Scandinavia	(9)	(14)
Finnish	9	14
Central Europe	(4)	(4)
German	4	4
Others		
English	13	17
Jewish	6	7
Others	3	6
	100 percent	100 percent

Source: Bridgman Convention Documents

of immigrants and were raised in immigrant neighborhoods. Thirty-one of the non-Jewish native-born party leaders were blacks. There were nine German-Americans and nine more of Scandinavian descent and a scattering of people from Eastern and Southern European families. Just more than one-third of the American-born gentiles were of Irish, British, or Canadian descent.

Three-fifths of all the Jews in our sample were born abroad compared to only a little more than one-quarter of the non-Jews. While foreign-born Jews were able to rise to positions of leadership within the CPUSA, foreign-born non-Jews were far less likely to do so. With the exception of the Russian and Hungarian federations, few Jews were in leadership positions of the European language groups. Yet, relatively few of the Scandinavians, Poles, Letts, etc. ever rose to the top ranks of the CPUSA. To answer why, we must turn to the differences between native-born and foreign-born committee members.

Immigrants and Natives

One of the clearest differences between native and foreign-born committee members is when they served on the Central Committee. The CPUSA in the 1920s was largely an organization of immigrants and its leadership reflected that fact. As the years went by, larger and larger proportions of the leadership were American-born. Nearly two-thirds of all CC members in the 1920s were born abroad, compared to only one-fifth in the 1950-1961 period. By 1929, in fact, almost one-half of the seventy-nine foreign-born in our sample had already served on and were off the CC for good.

As these figures suggest, the two groups also joined the CPUSA at different times and probably for different reasons. Table 4 indicates the percentage of native and foreign-born CC members joining at different times. More than half the immigrants were charter party members, joining in that heady period when the lure of the Russian Revolution was strongest. Altogether, more than 90 percent of the foreign-born were already communists by the onset of the great

Table 3
Birthplace of Jewish and Non-Jewish Immigrants

	Jews	Non-Jews
Tsarist Empire	34	4
Eastern Europe	5	7
Central Europe	1	6
Scandinavia	0	8
British Empire	2	8
Miscellaneous	0	4
Total	**42**	**37**

depression. Long before the CPUSA was anything more than a small struggling sect, these people were members. So, for that matter, were more than half the native-born CC members. Table 4 reinforces the key role played in the CPUSA throughout its history by the earliest converts to communism. But, significantly, more than a third of the native-born CC members joined the CPUSA during the depression and another tenth after 1940 —most during World War II and the American-Soviet Alliance. The Depression and the seeming collapse of capitalism was clearly not a motive for the vast number of the foreign-born.

There were some differences between the two groups in the speed with which they advanced in their party careers. Table 5 illustrates the mean number of years between when an individual joined the CPUSA and reached the Central Committee. The scores indicate that when a person joined the Communist Party was crucial in determining how long it would take to reach the CC. Charter party members advanced most quickly: Depression-era party converts had the longest wait. For individuals joining the party through the 1920s, the foreign-born rose to the CC more quickly. For those joining in the 1930s, this relationship was reversed. In a largely foreign-born party foreign-born leaders had some potent advantages. By the 1930s, however, foreign-born potential leaders had a long wait to reach the CC. Even the native-born who joined the CPUSA in this decade had a long wait for party leadership, however.

Table 4
Year Joined CPUSA by Birthplace

	Native born (%)	Foreign born (%)
1919	21.8	54.1
1920-1929	32.7	36.5
1930-1939	36.4	9.4
1940-	9.1	–
Total	**100 (N=110)**	**100 (N=74)**

Table 5
Years to Reach the CC

	Year joined CPUSA			
	1919	1920 to 1929	1930 to 1939	1940 -
Native born	8.9 (N=24)	13.8 (N=36)	16.9 (N=40)	10.9 (N=10)
Foreign born	7.4 (N=40)	11.9 (N=27)	18.6 (N=7)	–

One reported consequence of the CPUSA's heavy concentration of foreign-born membership during its first decade was its working-class character. Glazer notes that two-thirds to three-fourths of the party was proletarian in 1923, in large part because of the foreign-born component. As the party became more Americanized in the 1930s, and particularly in the 1940s, it also became more middle-class (Glazer, 1961). The CPUSA was thus seemingly faced with a paradox: the more it achieved one desirable goal—Americanizing—the more unsatisfactory its "social composition" as a working-class party.

While the party leadership was not as likely as the membership to be employed in traditional blue-collar occupations, a majority of the CPUSA Central Committee members had been working-class prior to their involvement in party work. Most CC members became full-time party functionaries after having some other occupation, but a significant minority moved directly from school into full-time party work and are classified as functionaries in Table 6. There are no major differences between the native-born and the foreign-born in regard to their occupational structure. In both groups a small majority had held such traditional blue-collar jobs as craftsmen, miners, or heavy-industry workers while a sizeable minority were clerks, teachers, journalists, etc.

Significant differences do appear, however, when the native and foreign-born are further subdivided into Jews and non-Jews. Table 6 illustrates that Jews were far more likely to be found in white-collar occupations, whatever their birthplace but the foreign-born were somewhat more likely than the native-born to be in blue-collar jobs. The same was true of non-Jews – although they were less likely than the Jewish CC members to be white-collar workers, the native-born were more likely than the foreign-born. Moreover, those Jews engaged in blue-collar work were usually employed in light industry, such as the needle trades, rather than in heavy industry.

The same pattern is evident when educational differences between native and foreign-born Jews and non-Jews are examined, even though data are not available for one-third of the sample. Considering only those for whom information was obtained, almost 70 percent of the native-born Jews attended college as did a slight majority of foreign-born Jews. On the other hand, less than 45 percent of the native-born non-Jews and only one-quarter of the foreign-born went to college.

These figures provide some clues to the puzzle of why foreign-born Jews rose to positions of leadership in the CPUSA while their non-Jewish counterparts from the language federations did not. Basically, they suggest that foreign-born Jews were more Americanized and assimilated than the non-Jews. A majority of even the foreign-born Jews attended college. Large numbers held white-collar jobs. Many spoke and wrote English well and were, therefore, available for leadership positions in an organization sorely lacking people with such talents.

Still, many foreign-born Jewish CC members were workers with little education. Why did so few of their gentile counterparts rise to leadership when

Table 6
Occupation of CC Members Birthplace and Ethnic Origin

	Jews (%)	Non-Jews (%)	Total (%)
Native born			
White collar	50.0	26.4	31.6
Blue collar	38.5	56.0	52.1
Functionaries	11.5	17.6	16.3
Total	100 (N=26)	100 (N=91)	100 (N=117)
Foreign born			
White collar	41.0	17.2	29.7
Blue collar	43.6	71.4	56.8
Functionaries	15.4	11.4	13.5
Total	100 (N=39)	100 (n=35)	100 (N=74)

Table 7
Party Status of Central Committee Members by Birthplace and Ethnic Origin

	Jews (%)	Non-Jews (%)	Total (%)
Native born			
Stayed	56	63.5	61.8
Left	44	36.5	38.2
Total	100 (N=25)	100 (N=85)	100 (N=110)
Foreign born			
Stayed	61.9	68.6	64.9
Left	38.1	31.4	35.1
Total	100 (N=42)	100 (N=35)	100 (N=77)

the party membership, at least in the 1920s, was largely non- Jewish? The foreign-born Jewish workers emerged from an active and reasonably success-ful labor movement in the garment industry. With scattered exceptions such as the United Mine Workers, heavy industry was not successfully unionized until the 1930s. Most of the non-Jewish immigrants were employed in heavy industry and hence were not unionized until the CPUSA had already removed most foreign-born from the CC.

While many Jewish immigrants were involved in labor organizations as of-ficials or rank-and-file leaders, many of the gentile immigrants were prominent only in their own language federations. In the very early years of American com-munism, federation leaders were prominent but the cost imposed on American communism was almost total isolation from American life and politics. The federations were, by their very nature, inward looking and resistant to involvement in a wider arena (Karni, 1975). Jewish immigrants, paradoxically, were more Americanized or more willing to enter the mainstream of American labor and life. Hence, while the large Finnish Federation produced a few leaders, the Lettish, Lithuanian, Polish federations hardly any, Jewish immigrants moved into positions of leadership.

As the CPUSA collapsed in the 1950s, the foreign-born membership was less affected. Just as their insulation from American society limited their contribution to the party leadership, it also reduced their exposure to the nationwide hostility to communism. Those who had become party leaders, however, were less insular. On the other hand, as party cadres presumably their long training and dedication to communism should have stiffened them to doubts and defection. Were there, in fact, any differences between native-born and foreign-born in regard to leaving the CPUSA?

The foreign-born were, as Table 7 indicates, more likely to remain members of the CPUSA than the native-born but the differences were not large. But, Jews were more likely to leave the party or be expelled than non-Jews. Among Jews, the foreign-born were less likely to leave. Foreign-born Jews, more Americanized than their gentile counterparts, were more likely to abandon the CPUSA.

A special hazard facing the foreign-born CC members was deportation. In addition to the seventy-one committee members who became ex-communists, four were deported and another eight emigrated, most of them not entirely voluntarily. Altogether, just more than 40 percent of the foreign-born CC members left the CPUSA in one way or another.

Conclusion

The leadership of the CPUSA over the forty-year period covered by this was largely native-born. After the mid-1930s the foreign-born no longer dominated the party's leadership. And yet, the CPUSA never was quite able to shake off its image as an organization dominated by aliens and immigrants. In part this image was tattooed to the party during the 1920s when its membership was overwhelmingly and its leadership was largely composed of immigrants.

As a party of immigrants, the CPUSA was not necessarily unrepresentative of the American working class. The immigrants who flocked into the party and dominated its leadership, however, were not entirely representative of the American working class. They tended to have originated in Russia or on her borders and to have joined the CPUSA under the impact of the Russian Revolution. Moreover, the leadership, in particular, was far more Jewish than the membership. Many of those who attacked the CPUSA for being "foreign" undoubtedly had in mind the role played by Jews. Oddly, however, within the party during its early years foreign-born Jews were an Americanizing force.

The large number of foreign-born Jews in the leadership also had an impact on internal party politics. Some foreign-born non-Jews were resentful of the large Jewish role in American communism (C. Ross, personal communication, June 29, 1976; Goldsmith, 1971). The CPUSA also made efforts to reduce the visibility of Jews in the leadership. The impact of these efforts fell largely on native-born Jews, delaying their rise to the CC, although it also may have permanently relegated some foreign-born Jews to the secondary ranks of leadership.

Where the party failed badly was in recruiting native-born Americans. Many of these who did become party leaders were children of immigrants. Few leaders of old American stock ever emerged. Also, very few members or leaders were recruited from southern Europe. To a very large degree American communism was a product of people from one geographical area. Surprisingly, the immigrant party leaders were a fairly well-educated group. A large proportion attended college for at least a brief period in an era when very few Americans did so. The foreign-born party leaders were a capable, upwardly mobile group, either well-educated or active trade unionists.

The immigrant character of the CPUSA did cause the party some difficulties. Many members were isolated by their language and customs. A number of CC members were in constant jeopardy from the government either because they were aliens or because the Justice Department sought to take away their citizenship. In addition to those deported or encouraged to leave voluntarily, many other party leaders were forced to spend time and effort defending themselves in court. William Schneiderman fought a landmark battle to keep his citizenship. Such other party leaders as Martin Young, Henry Puro, and Norman Tallentire successfully staved off expulsion from the U.S. These efforts, however, deflected party attention from its main tasks and may also have prevented the CPUSA from promoting otherwise qualified people for fear of exposing them to government prosecution. Finally, the party's domination by immigrant leaders until 1936 certainly contributed to the party's foreign image and may well have contributed to the series of dismal failures which marked the party's early history.

References

Almond, Gabriel (1954). *The Appeals of Communism* (Princeton, NJ: Princeton University Press).

Alperin. Robert (1959). *Organization of the Communist Party USA, 1931-1938,* Doctoral Dissertation. Northwestern University.

Budenz, Louis (1950). *Men Without Faces: The Communist Conspiracy in the USA* (New York, Harper & Bros).

Cannon, James (1962). *The First Ten Years of American Communism* (New York: Lyle Stuart).

Chambers, Whittaker (1952). *Witness* (Chicago: Henry Regnery).

Charney, George (1968). *A Long Journey.* Chicago, Quadrangle Books.

Clark. Jane Perry (1968). *Deportation of Aliens From the United States to Europe* (New York, Ams Press).

Divine, Robert (1957). *American Immigration Policy, 1924-1952* (New Haven, CT: Yale University Press).

Draper, Theodore (1957). *The Roots of American Communism* (New York: Viking Press).

Draper, Theodore (1960). *American Communism and Soviet Russia* (New York: Viking Press).

Gitlow, Ben (1940). *I Confess: The Truth About American Communism* (New York: E. P. Dutton).

Glazer, Nathan (1961). *The Social Basis of American Communism* (New York: Harcourt, Brace and World).

Goldsmith, William (1971). *The Theory and Practice of a Communist Front.* Doctoral Dissertation. Columbia University.

Hartz, Louis (1955). *The Liberal Tradition in America* (New York: Harcourt, Brace and World).

House Committee on Un-American Activities (1953). *Organized Communism in the United States,* 83rd Congress, 2nd Session.

Howe, Irving (1976). *World of Our Fathers* (New York: Harcourt, Brace and Jovanovich).

Karni, Michael (1975). *Yhteishyva-Or, For the Common Good: Finnish Radicalism in the Western Great Lakes Region 1900-1940,* Doctoral Dissertation. University of Minnesota.

O'Neal, James, and Weiner, G. (1947). *American Communism: A Critical Analysis of Its Origins, Development and Programs* (New York: E. P. Dutton).

Shannon, David (1959). *The Decline of American Communism* (New York: Harcourt, Brace and Company).

Weinstein, James (1967). *The Decline of Socialism in America 1912-1925* (New York: Monthly Review Press).

Williamson, John (1969). *Dangerous Scot: The Life and Work of an American Undesirable* (New York: International Publishers).

6

American Communism and the UAW: New Evidence on an Old Controversy

The issue of Communism has generated more discussion in relation to the United Auto Workers than almost any other union. The UAW was a battleground from its beginnings between contending factions. So long as its Communists remained an integral part of the union leadership, Communists remained a tolerated bloc in the national CIO. Once Walter Reuther routed the Party and its allies, their days in the CIO were numbered.

Never before or since the early days of the CIO has American Communism been so influential in the labor movement. A substantial number of unions, ranging from the National Maritime Union and the International Longshoremen's and Warehousemen's Union to the State, County and Municipal Workers of America and the United Office and Professional Workers were led or controlled by Communists and their close allies. Aside from the United Electrical Workers, however, Party influence was concentrated among the smaller or less successful unions. Neither the United Mine Workers, Amalgamated Clothing Workers, the Steelworkers Organizing Committee or the Textile Workers Organizing Committee had a significant Party presence among its leadership. Had the Party been able to capitalize on its foothold in the UAW, the future history of the entire labor movement might have been quite different.

The Communists' troubles in the UAW began in 1937 when their presence and activities became a major issue in the union's factional war. During that period the Communist Party was assiduously wooing John L. Lewis and doing all it could to cooperate with non-Communist CIO leaders. How, then, had the Party allowed events in the UAW to get so out of control as to lead to a factional war?

Originally published in *Labor History*, Summer 1983 (http://www.informaworld.com) and reprinted with permission

For years the dominant interpretation stressed Communist responsibility for the dispute. Ben Stolberg's early account of the CIO, one of the first attacks on its "infiltration" by the Party, charged that William Weinstone, the Communist district organizer in Michigan, had ordered a continuation of the Chrysler sit-down strike after a settlement had been reached in early April 1937. He further taxed the Party with precipitating the majority of the unauthorized sit-down strikes that bedeviled both the union and General Motors and Chrysler in 1937. According to this version, the union's president, Homer Martin, then launched an anti-Communist drive in self-defense. Both Herbert Harris and Max Kampleman accepted Stolberg's version but none of them offered any proof of the Party's "sabotage."[1]

As scholars began to examine the issue, they focused on the eccentric personality of Homer Martin to account for the conflict. A former college hop, skip, and jump champion and onetime minister, dubbed "the leaping parson," he was a disastrous administrator, an incompetent negotiator, and an insecure leader. Jealous of his position and determined to ward off challengers, he had removed Communist Wyndham Mortimer from control of the union's organizing in Flint in 1936. Early in 1937 he struck up an alliance with Jay Lovestone, a one-time Communist leader but by then a bitter Party enemy. After the Chrysler sit-down strike in early 1937 Martin became convinced that the Communists had fomented rank-and-file resistance to the settlement as part of a campaign to discredit him. He responded by firing, demoting, or transferring most of his enemies, among whom were the Communists, and using the Communist issue to justify his actions.

One of the most careful and thorough accounts of these events, by Bert Cochran, notes that it is very difficult to determine who began the war, Martin or the Communists. Nonetheless, Cochran concludes that while some Party members were active in the unauthorized sit-downs, they acted "in their individual capacities" and were reprimanded by Party leaders. This conclusion puts primary responsibility for the factional war on Homer Martin.[2]

A more recent favorable account of the Party's activities in the UAW by Roger Keeran goes even further, portraying the Communists as the self-effacing and innocent victims of redbaiting: "Some of the issues Martin raised, such as Communist responsibility for wild-cat strikes and general disruption contained no substance and served merely as pretexts for his maneuvers."[3]

Just how innocent were the Communists? Previous studies have relied largely on circumstantial evidence to buttress their claims. Keeran relied in part on an extensive interview with William Weinstone, who directed Party activity in Michigan in 1937 and was still, in 1982, active on its Historical Commission. New evidence is now available, however, to settle part of this old argument. Minutes of several meetings of the Party's Politburo, given to Theodore Draper and now accessible to scholars in the Emory University Library, demonstrate conclusively that the Communist Party itself agreed with the charges made by such anti-Communists as Stolberg. They also illustrate just how hazardous it can be to trust Communists to remember their history honestly because the major culprit singled out by the Party minutes as responsible for the wildcat strikes is none other than William Weinstone.

The Communist Party leadership was as anxious to preserve peace in the UAW as in other CIO unions. The Popular Front required alliances and cooperation with non-Communists, particularly in the labor movement. Moreover, John L. Lewis had personally participated in the Chrysler negotiations; to attack that settlement was to attack him. At the same time, the Party's traditional support for any kind of rank-and-file militancy directed against compromises negotiated by union leaders mitigated against an enthusiastic acceptance of the agreement. For a few hours after announcement of the agreement, some Chrysler workers refused to leave the factories. William Weinstone did not explicitly condemn the Chrysler sit-downers' rebellion at first; he noted that "it was natural" for workers to resent the evacuation and pointed out that their "militancy is one of the strong points of the union." Only after the *New York Times* published reports that the Party was behind the rank and file revolts did Weinstone issue a firm denial: "The charge attributed to Homer Martin that Communists obstructed the recent evacuation of Chrysler plants is absolutely untrue and unfounded."[4]

Weinstone's comments were no mere verbal slip. Just two months later, at a Communist Party Plenum, in remarks published in the Party press, it became apparent that not all Communists agreed about the precise tactics of the Popular Front. Party leader Earl Browder attacked unnamed comrades in Detroit who had made errors in the Chrysler strike. Browder indicated his displeasure with Party figures who "rush into snap judgments on big questions of trade union policy, consider that the trade union leaders have been mistaken or have unnecessarily compromised the workers' demands and from this conclusion pass immediately into a head-on collision with those leaders and the workers who follow them." The Party's line was to remain united behind the strategy laid down by the CIO leadership and John L. Lewis: "Some comrades were entirely in error in thinking they saw intolerable compromises and wrong methods in the settlement of the Chrysler strike."[5]

William Z. Foster, Party chairman and Browder's major rival for leadership, also first admitted that in the Motor City "Communists have too sharply and also incorrectly criticized the progressive elements and thereby needlessly alienated great masses of workers." He then attacked: the greater error, "in the main," was "making too little criticism of progressively-led movements. This Right tendency is manifested, among other examples, by inadequate criticism of Roosevelt and Lewis, and by a failure to put forward our own program (including our revolutionary slogans) in the mass movements led by these men." The Party had to reassert itself, re-establish its separate, revolutionary identity and strike out more on its own, not fearing to denounce even John L. Lewis.[6]

The Party's activities in the next few months suggested that Browder's more cautious policy had been adopted. Bill Gebert, an experienced functionary dispatched to Detroit, tried flattery to assuage Martin: "no small credit for the ten-fold growth of the UAW," he wrote in July, "goes to the international officers of this union, headed by Homer Martin." He soon followed with an article indicating that the Communists wanted the dissolution of all factions within the union and would support Martin for reelection at the 1937 convention.[7] Martin later testified before the Dies Committee that Gebert offered him complete backing if only he would cooperate with the Party: "I was taken up on the mountain, and I was shown the promised land," he related.[8] Even after Martin continued his vendetta against the Communists, Browder wrote him a conciliatory letter, suggesting he had been "misinformed" by Jay Lovestone.[9]

The Party's peace offerings proved futile. Martin, by now dependent on the Lovestoneites, was determined to destroy the Communists and his other enemies. Moreover, the Party's reaction to another wildcat strike brought back a sense of déjà vu. In mid-November a wildcat strike broke out at the GM plant in Pontiac, Michigan. Despite opposition from the UAW Executive Board, the first reports in the *Daily Worker* enthusiastically backed the strikers. The Party Politburo reacted with outrage. Lawrence Emery, the Daily *Worker* correspondent on the scene, reversed field on November 23 and favorably reported that Martin and the Executive Board had successfully ordered the strike to end.[10]

More importantly, Jack Stachel, one of the Party's "labor experts," was given an assignment which suggested the Politburo knew who had encouraged wildcat strikes. He was sent to Michigan to discuss "a number of mistakes and weaknesses that have arisen in Detroit, reflecting a weakness in the application of our People's Front policy." Improvements were promised but Stachel ominously reported back to his colleagues, "As to whether some individuals will be able to make the turn, to continue to remain an obstacle only time will tell." Meeting late in December, the Party's governing body harshly condemned the Michigan Communists, denouncing unauthorized strikes as "against the interests of the workers."[11]

The Communists recognized by now that their relationship with Martin was hopeless and they took steps to insure their future in the UAW. Until the fall of 1937 Walter Reuther, a leftwing Socialist, had been a close Party ally. Reuther, however, gave covert support to the Pontiac strike. In addition, in January 1938 the UAW Executive Board unanimously approved a peace resolution that called for the removal of all U.S. forces from China and passage of the Ludlow Amendment which would have required a national referendum before war could be declared. The Socialist Party, opposed to collective security, had strongly endorsed the steps the UAW now approved. So had the Lovestoneites. Since the Party supported collective security it was horrified that its forces on the board had acquiesced with Martin and the Socialists on this issue: it was a "symbol of the complete confusion and capitulation of all our forces in that Board."[12]

The Party did find a more pliant friend. In late December, the Politburo was informed that "our relationship is established now with F" (Richard Frankensteen, once Martin's ally). After meeting with Foster, Weinstone, and Wyndham Mortimer in April 1938, Frankensteen publicly repudiated Martin, swinging the balance of power in the union to the anti-Martin Unity Caucus. The leaping parson responded by attempting to expel all of his opponents from the UAW. That, in turn, prompted CIO intervention and the eventual ouster of Martin from office.[13]

Their alliance with Frankensteen also emboldened the Communists to open an attack on Reuther. In April 1938, Weinstone and Gebert orchestrated a switch of Communist support from Victor Reuther to Richard Leonard for the secretary-treasurer post of the Michigan CIO Council at a Lansing meeting. They sadly reported to *Daily Worker* readers that die-hard Martin backers had been joined in factional maneuvers by Socialists in the Unity Caucus.[14]

Browder and Foster had visited Moscow in late December 1937 to thrash out their disagreements about a number of Party policies. The results of the meeting were not announced publicly but Browder received Comintern backing for his tactics. Shortly after the Lansing meeting William Weinstone lost his position as Michigan district organizer. Ever since the Party's founding he had held important positions, ranging from district organizer in New York to delegate to the Comintern. After 1938, he was relegated to Party education and second-rank status.[15]

Weinstone's demotion suggests that the Party leaders held him partly responsible for the breakup of UAW unity. There is even clearer evidence to support the charge, however. In March 1939, the Politburo put aside its normal business for an extraordinary, acrimonious debate between Browder and Foster. All of the latter's frustrations and bitterness poured out. He accused Browder of ignoring his talents and ideas and relegating him to trivial tasks. Foster stood alone. Speaker after speaker sniped at him.

Among the major counts in the indictment against Foster were his sins in l'affaire Weinstone. Jack Stachel explained that "nobody can dispute that WWW [William Wolf Weinstone] did not carry out the line of the Party and did serious damage to the Party." Gil Green added, "the errors made by WWW, for example, in Detroit, if continued, if developed elsewhere, if not checked, were errors that could have destroyed the entire position of our Party in the eyes of the wide masses." Bill Gebert confessed that Weinstone's "record in the application of the P.C. [Political Committee] line in a district was more than unsatisfactory...the mistakes in Detroit and there were numerous mistakes committed by WWW primarily, could not be excused." For good measure, he denounced Weinstone's maneuvers at the Lansing meeting. Even Foster admitted that he "agreed without one word of dissent to his being demoted" because Weinstone supported "outlaw strikes."[16]

The Weinstone affair was not regarded as an individual aberration. Foster was reminded that he had "been very sorry for WWW," that "he had a warm feeling for WWW" and had not wanted at first to remove him for threatening the alliance with the CIO and within the UAW. Browder reiterated that the Party's position in the CIO was quite delicate. "Our greatest problem today," he explained, "is breaking down all suspicions in the minds of people who have no other obstacles to collaboration with us except their suspicions. People suspect us of merely biding our time until we can make a coup and stab them in the back." Weinstone's tactics and Foster's criticisms exacerbated those fears. Gene Dennis added that the previous year in Moscow Foster spoke in opposition to Browder and the rest of the Politburo: "allegations were made that the Party is following a line of tailism...following at the tail of Roosevelt and Lewis." The Comintern nevertheless had approved Browder's report. Dmitri Manuilsky himself had praised the Party for breaking with sectarianism and making great strides in its mass work. Foster was barking up the wrong tree if he expected the American Communist Party to alter policies that had achieved such spectacular results and so gratified the Comintern.[17]

The Party was sufficiently worried by this affair and a wave of anti-communism symbolized by the Dies Committee investigations that it did not protest several steps which reduced its influence in 1939. John L. Lewis restricted Harry Bridges' writ as CIO West Coast director to California. Allen Haywood replaced John Brophy as national director. Sidney Hillman and Phillip Murray, the CIO's representatives to the troubled UAW's 1939 convention, served the Party its hardest pill to swallow. With Martin out of the union, his former opponents, now allied against Walter Reuther, had the strength to win the presidency with either George Addes or Wyndham Mortimer. Hillman and Murray wanted a less divisive figure. A Party delegation led by Earl Browder and including Louis Budenz, Bill Gebert, and Roy Hudson ordered the Party fraction at the convention to support the CIO's choice, R. J. Thomas, an old Martin ally.[18]

This episode vividly illustrates that, in spite of its professed desire to get along with non-Communist union leaders, the Party was sometimes unable to avoid trouble. It bore much more responsibility than it cared to admit publicly for the factionalism within the UAW. The anti-communist campaigns of Martin and Reuther were not built on air but had a basis in fact. The former did have reason to suspect that the Party was behind the wildcat strikes. The latter had clear evidence that the local Communist unionists were not free agents.

Homer Martin might well have launched his anti-Communist campaign even if the Communists had not been behind the wildcat strikes. He was a weak and ineffective leader; the Communist issue would likely have been an irresistible weapon to use against his opponents. As it was, the Party's tactics fed his paranoia. Had the Party been able to avoid becoming a major issue in union politics for a while longer, its influence in the UAW might have grown and its future role been different.

This episode demonstrates just how delicate the Party's balancing act had to be during the Popular Front period. John L. Lewis had welcomed Communists into the CIO. One of the unspoken conditions was that they followed his lead. To undermine Martin in early 1937 was to undermine Lewis. The national Party leadership feared antagonizing the CIO leader or leaving him with the impression that Communists were a disloyal opposition prepared to undercut union officers.

The Detroit Communists endangered this understanding by their activities. Local Party activists could not be permitted to jeopardize a policy made in New York and ratified in Moscow, particularly one so important to the whole notion of a Popular Front. There was no tradition in the Communist Party of allowing such local initiative. In addition, there was some suspicion that the Detroit "revolt" was part of an opposition to the American version of the Popular Front. Foster resented Browder's acceptance of a junior and largely silent role for the Party in the CIO and the Popular Front. Whether Foster encouraged Weinstone or the latter had his own objections to the policy is impossible to say. Both the Politburo and the Comintern repudiated the policy. The Popular Front tactics were refurbished and the Party did its best to repair the damage by finding new, dependable senior partners in the UAW.

It is not surprising that neither William Foster, William Weinstone, or the Communist Party have chosen to dwell on this episode. Foster never mentions it in his skewed history of the CPUSA. Weinstone never bothered to inform Keeran. In the recently issued *Highlights of a Fighting History: 60 Years of the Communist Party USA* (one of whose editors was William Weinstone), the single article by Browder, leader of the CPUSA from 1930 to 1945, is prefaced by a denunciation of his "capitulation to the top labor bureaucracy." That the Comintern endorsed Browder's policy is conveniently ignored as is the consequence of Weinstone's and Foster's effort to subvert it.[19] Oral histories are adding significantly to our store of information about American Communism. Historians, however, must be cautious about accepting on faith the stories of men and women who have political scores to settle.

Notes

1. Benjamin Stolberg, *The Story of the CIO* (New York, 1938), 174; Herbert Harris, *Labor's Civil War* (New York, 1940), 136-137; Max Kampelanan, *The Communist Party vs. the C.I.O.* (New York, 1957), 74. I have discussed these issues at greater length in *The Heyday of American Communism: The Depression Decade* (Basic Books, 1984).
2. Bert Cochran, *Labor and Communism: The Conflict that Shaped American Unions* Princeton, NJ 1977), 138. Still another interpretation attributed the wildcats to the workers' pent-up frustrations and management's inability to deal with the new unions. See Irving Howe and B. I. Widick, *The UAW and Walter Reuther* (New York, 1949), *passim*.
3. Roger Keeran, *The Communists and the Auto Workers Unions* (Bloomington, IN, 1980), 194.
4. *Daily Worker,* Mar. 27, 1937, 1, 4; April 6, 1937, 5.

5. Earl Browder, "The Communists in the People's Front," *Communist,* July 1937, 609-610. Keeran mistakenly interprets Browder's remark merely as a slap at rank-and-file Communists employed at Chrysler.

6. William Z. Foster, "Political Leadership and *Party* Building," *Communist,* July 1937, 644.

7. *Daily Worker,* July 9, 1937, 4 July 22, *5*

8. U.S. Congress, House of Representatives, Committee on Un-American Activities. *Investigation of Un-American Propaganda Activities,* vol. 4, 2692. Gebert denied making any such offer. *Daily Worker,* Jan. 10, 1939, 6.

9. *Daily Worker,* Sept. 16, 1937, 1.

10. Ibid.,*Nov.* 17, 1937, 1, Nov. 20, 1, Nov. 23, 1

11. "Politburo Minutes," 12/13/37; "Politburo Minutes," 1/23/37, in Theodore Draper Papers, Emory Univ. Box 1, Folder 47.

12. Cochran, 138; "Politburo Minutes," 1/28/38 in Box 1. Folder 51.

13. "Politburo Minutes," 12/23/37, Box 1, Folder 47, Cochran, 140-143.

14. Clayton Fountain, *Union Guy* (New York, 1949), 84-85; *Daily Worker,* May 10, 1938, 5-6.

15. Browder Interview with Draper, June 23, 1955 in Draper Papers. Browder put the confrontation in Moscow somewhat vaguely in 1937. It appears to have taken place in Jan. 1938.

16. "Politburo Minutes," 3/23/39, in Box 1, Folder 60.

17. Ibid.

18. Wyndham Mortimer, *Organize: My Life as a Union Man* (Boston, MA1971), 162-165.

19. *Highlights of A Fighting History: 60 Years of the Communist Party USA* (New York, 1979), 174.

7

Self-Determination in the Black Belt:
Origins of a Communist Policy

with William Tompson

One of the most curious and fascinating of the many interventions by the Communist International into the affairs of the Communist Party of the United States of America (CPUSA) was its directive that blacks in the southern United States had a right to self-determination. First promulgated in Moscow in 1928 with virtually no discussion in the U.S., self-determination was the subject of another Comintern resolution in 1930. Not until the 1950s did the American Communists formally remove the call for self-determination in the Black Belt from their program, although it had long been all but ignored.

How much did the original 1928 resolution owe to prior discussions of self-determination within the American Communist movement, particularly by Cyril Briggs and the African Blood Brotherhood? Secondly, why were two resolutions necessary? For many years the exact relationship between the two documents—the 1928 and the 1930 Comintern resolutions—has remained unclear, in large part because a full understanding would require access we do not have to Comintern archives.

Numerous scholars have debated these issues over the past thirty years. The extant literature, however, fails to explain adequately the relationship between the two resolutions. Indeed, many of the commentators have misinterpreted or misunderstood what the two resolutions suggest about the relationship between the American Communists and the Communist International.[1] What makes it worthwhile to return to them is the availability of some new primary material. The publication of the first complete run of Briggs' *Crusader* has finally made

Originally published in *Labor History*, Summer 1989 (http://www.informaworld.com) and reprinted with permission.

this crucial publication available.[2] And, in Theodore Draper's papers, located at Emory University, there is a treasure trove of material throwing light on a fascinating dispute within the Comintern about self-determination.

On October 26, 1928 the Executive Committee of the Communist International adopted its resolution on the Negro question in the United States. American Communists did not get around to publishing the resolution until February 12, 1929 when it appeared in the *Daily Worker.* Their hesitation was undoubtedly due to the shock they felt when they read what the Comintern wanted them to do. The CPUSA was ordered to "come out openly and unreservedly for the right of Negroes to national self-determination in the southern states where the Negroes form a majority of the population." The resolution linked the emancipation of American blacks to the struggles of blacks in other areas of the world and optimistically predicted that "A strong Negro revolutionary movement in the USA will be able to influence and direct the revolutionary movement in all those parts of the world where the Negroes are oppressed by imperialism."[3]

The new policy was a typical, if extreme, example of the relative importance of the American Communist Party and the Comintern in deciding upon policy for the U.S. The issue of self-determination had never been discussed in any American Communist meeting, whether of the Politburo or Central Committee. It had never been publicized before its enactment in any organ of the Party press. Virtually all of the Party's black members – there were only about 50—were vocally opposed to the policy.

In later years, American Communists made a frantic search for American roots of self-determination. One of the alleged sources for the idea was Cyril Briggs and the African Blood Brotherhood. In 1917, Briggs had written an article in the *Amsterdam News* entitled "Security of Life for Poles and Serbs—Why Not for Colored Americans?" in which he called for the creation of a forty-ninth state in the Northwest which would provide American blacks with their just portion of the country's land and wealth.[4] Two years later, Briggs, now editor of the *Crusader,* called American blacks "a nation within a nation, a nationality oppressed and jimcrowed, yet worthy as any other people of a square deal or failing that, a separate political existence."[5] By July 1920, however, Briggs had explicitly rejected the idea of a separate state for blacks as "unsatisfactory both to the Negro and the white man." In its place he proposed migration to South America as the solution.[6]

Once Briggs became associated with the Communist Party in 1919 his earlier support for self-determination or a separate political existence for blacks seems to have been toned down. In later years, Briggs claimed that the program of the African Blood Brotherhood, founded in 1919 as the Communist Party's first organization for blacks, included as one of its five demands "self-determination for the Negro in states where he constitutes a majority."[7] A 1922 version of the Brotherhood program, however, the only one available, contains no reference to self-determination.[8] And in 1921 Briggs was calling in the *Crusader* for the "salvation for all Negroes through the establishment of a Universal Socialist Cooperative Commonwealth."[9] This evidence seems to indicate that while the idea of self-determination and a separate black political entity was on Briggs' mind during this period, he was not very consistent in advocating it nor had he formulated the concept in anything like a clear programmatic statement.

Moreover, an examination of Briggs' writings in the aftermath of the Comintern resolution of 1928 does not reveal very much enthusiasm on his part for the new doctrine. In the summer of 1929 Briggs wrote three articles for the *Communist,* the theoretical organ of the CPUSA, on various aspects of the Negro question. Neither "The Negro Question in the Southern Textile Strikes" in June, nor "Our Negro Work" in September made even a passing mention of self-determination, despite the obvious relevance of both topics to the question. "The Negro Press as a Class Weapon," published in August, did mention but only briefly that the matter of self-determination had been raised in the *Amsterdam News* a decade before.

Finally, neither Briggs nor any of his associates played any role in formulating the new line and some attacked it. Otto Hall and Lovett Fort-Whiteman, two prominent figures from the African Blood Brotherhood, did not support the new line in the Comintern debates; after it was issued they denounced self-determination. Briggs' close ally in the Party, Otto Huiswoud, another ABB veteran, openly attacked the policy in the *Communist* in February 1930. Huiswoud declared that it was necessary to take into consideration "the national-colonial character of the Negro question in Africa and the West Indies and the racial character of this question in the United States." He went on to deny that American blacks possessed a language, culture, or economic life distinct from those of white Americans, thus denying them the status of a nation. The only distinguishing characteristic of the Negro, he maintained, was his racial origin. While tactfully avoiding any mention of self-determination, Huiswoud emphasized that the solution to the problems of black Americans was political and social equality.[10] It was probably no accident, as Stalin was wont to say, that Huiswoud was soon withdrawn from American Party work and given new assignments by the Comintern.

Practically the only American black to support the new line forthrightly and vigorously at its inception was the man who had a major role in drafting it, Harry Haywood, brother of Otto Hall and a young student at the Comintern's University of the Toilers of the East. Although Haywood had been a member of the ABB, he admitted in his autobiography that by the time he had joined in 1922, it had already dropped most of its "nationalist revolutionary organization." Nor did Haywood meet Cyril Briggs until he returned from Moscow in the early 1930s. Haywood's account of the development of the self-determination line makes it clear that the influences on him were largely Russian. When he arrived in Moscow to study in 1927, he had no inkling of the concept.[11]

The Comintern, however, had been toying with the idea for some time. In 1922, at its Fourth Congress, the Negro Commission gave American blacks a major role in helping to achieve self-determination for Africa. At the Comintern's Fifth World Congress in 1924, there was considerable discussion of whether the right of self-determination applied to American blacks. The American delegates argued vociferously against the idea and it was rejected. The report of the Congress noted that "it cannot be said that the slogan of the right of self-determination is the solution for all national questions, in which the race question is also involved.... The Program Commission was of the opinion that the slogan of the right of self-determination must be supplemented by another slogan: 'National equality for all national groups and races.'"[12]

Some Comintern leaders were clearly not convinced by this decision. Haywood later noted that one of Zinoviev's aides had instructions to find confirmation for the Comintern leader's belief that self-determination was an appropriate policy. Otto Hall told Theodore Draper of an interview Stalin held with several blacks studying in Moscow in 1925 at which time he criticized the American Communist party for not understanding that blacks were members of an oppressed national minority with some of the characteristics of a nation. Even the vociferous opposition of everyone hearing such suggestions did not deter the Russians from continuing to push their idea.[13]

In Haywood, they found someone willing to be an advocate. At the Lenin School he studied the events of the Irish campaign for independence from Britain and was impressed by the parallels between the position of the Irish and American blacks. Late in 1927 a young Communist International functionary, N. Nasanov, returned to Moscow from the U.S. and began to try to convince Haywood that self-determination was the correct slogan for work among southern blacks. Haywood recounted in his autobiography that Nasanov gradually convinced him of the wisdom of the policy, a process no doubt aided by Haywood's realization that "Stalin was undoubtedly the person pushing the position."[14]

Indeed, Stalin's one theoretical contribution to communism had been on the nationality question. Before the revolution he had authored the Party's position on the treatment of non-Russian nationalities in the tsarist empire and had defined a nation as "a historically evolved, stable community arising on the foundation of a common language, territory, economic life, and psychological makeup, manifested in a community of culture." Considering himself an expert on the national question and regarding his view as the definitive formula, Stalin naturally took a major interest in its application to the United States.[15]

By 1928, no important Comintern decision could be taken to which Stalin objected. Certainly, Nasanov and Haywood, the authors of the resolution on self-determination, were far too junior figures to guide it to enactment. Furthermore, the chairman of the Negro Commission at the Sixth Congress was the Finnish Communist Otto Kuusinen, often used by Stalin as his mouthpiece on important issues. It had been Kuusinen who had written the first articles attacking Trotsky, Zinoviev, and the rest of the left opposition; he later served in much the same capacity when Stalin was crushing Bukharin.[16]

The debate over self-determination at the Sixth World Congress was heated. A number of American Communists, black and white denounced the proposed policy. James Ford, soon to emerge as the CPUSA's leading black figure, argued that "any nationalist movement on the part of the Negroes does nothing but play into the hands of the bourgeoisie by arresting the revolutionary class movement of the Negro masses and further widening the gulf between white and similar oppressed groups." Otto Hall insisted that blacks sought full integration into American society. Sam Darcy, a white delegate, lobbied with Kuusinen, arguing that America was a country of assimilation.[17]

The self-determination issue was complicated by a fierce factional struggle underway in the American Communist Party. Several of the American support-ers of self-determination at the Congress may have hoped to use the issue as a way to attack the dominant group in the CPUSA, led by Jay Lovestone and John Pepper. Harry Haywood was associated with the rival Foster- Bittelman faction; in a discussion article in the *Communist International* printed in Sep-tember 1928, he attacked Lovestone for believing that the northern migration of Negroes or the industrialization of the South would weaken black national consciousness.[18]

Anticipating the need to approve of whatever the Comintern was about to do, Pepper launched a preemptive strike once he learned that the Executive Committee of the Comintern intended to adopt the policy. At the Comintern's Fifth Congress Pepper had denounced self-determination, contending that the only proper policy was "full equality in every respect." In May 1928, he had written the CPUSA's statement on Negro work which had vigorously affirmed the same principle. Sensing that the tide was turning, Pepper now wrote an article calling not merely for self-determination, but for a "Negro Soviet Re-public," an excess that was to cost him dearly and to confuse the reception of the Comintern resolution in the United States.[19]

Because of the delay in publishing the Comintern resolution in the U.S., Pepper's discussion article, written in September and republished in the Party's theoretical organ, was widely viewed as the only authoritative statement of the new line. The Lovestone faction had no interest in publicizing Haywood's article, which came much closer to articulating the new policy than Pepper's. Still in Moscow, Haywood was unable to argue his own viewpoint in the American party. American Communists, in any case, were consumed by their inner-party struggle throughout 1929, a struggle that culminated in May with the ouster of Lovestone from the Party after an extraordinary set of hearings and confronta-tions in Moscow. For months afterwards, the leadership struggle preoccupied high-ranking American Communists.

Thus, despite having the authority of the Comintern behind it, self-determi-nation met with considerable resistance in the United States. It came as a bolt out of the blue, its primary advocates had no standing, its linkage to Pepper's wild call for a Negro Soviet Republic was worrisome, and it got lost in the shuffle of a leadership struggle. An International Labor Defense directive of January 1930 to its district organizers discussed Negro work for five pages without mentioning self-determination once.[20] Huiswoud attacked the policy in the *Communist*.

Nor was the foot-dragging unique to the American Communist. The first International Conference of Negro Workers, meeting in Hamburg, Germany in 1930, included a perfunctory reference to self-determination in its demands, but at no time during the gathering was the matter discussed. The official report indicated that the discussion on the U.S. had focused on racial oppression in general and, specifically, on anti-lynching legislation. Even in Moscow the debate continued. Endre Sik, a Hungarian teaching at the Lenin School, came under attack from Nasanov and Haywood for continuing to espouse the view that American blacks were an oppressed racial minority and that the slogan of self-determination was inappropriate.[21]

Something was dearly needed to remove the questions, doubts, and vacillations. Was the 1928 resolution a call for the creation of a separate Negro republic? What was the relationship between the struggle for Negro liberation and self-determination and the class struggle? Should the Party support Negro separatist movements? Was self-determination only a propaganda slogan?

The Comintern was not oblivious to the confusion and the clear lack of enthusiasm for the new policy. In February 1930, its Anglo-American Secretariat advised the CPUSA of the importance of "clarifying the minds of the party membership on the importance of mobilizing the Negro masses" and of "overcoming the present casual nature of the work among the Negroes." The Party was advised to put the slogan of self-determination at the center of its program.[22] The following month the issue came up for discussion before the Comintern's Political Secretariat, which had before it a draft letter to the American party prepared by Nasanov and Haywood.

We owe our knowledge of this letter to the presence in Moscow of two American Communist leaders, Max Bedacht and Will Weinstone. In the aftermath of Lovestone's expulsion, the CPUSA, unsure of what the Comintern wanted it to do, had dispatched the two to Moscow with a draft Party thesis. Their task was to make sure that nothing in it was objectionable to their Russian overlords. Bedacht and Weinstone sent back frequent cables to their New York colleagues, reporting the advice they were receiving from the Comintern. The Negro question was one of the major items of concern.

Haywood and Nasanov's letter demanded "that self-determination must be turned from propaganda slogan into political action aim," they cabled. It had provoked a sharp exchange; the discussion was "long and hot." On one side were Haywood, Nasanov, and Safarov, the chairman of the Eastern or Colonial Secretariat of the Comintern. Opposing them were the three most prominent

Comintern leaders, Piatnitsky, Manuilsky, and Kuusinen. The latter group opposed any alteration of the formulations of the Sixth Congress. Safarov, the most outspoken advocate of putting more teeth in the resolution, was charged by Kuusinen with trying to repeat "the mistakes of a few years ago." Kuusinen argued that it was "a flight from realities to abstractions" to put the slogan of self-determination ahead of the concrete struggle for Negro rights and against discrimination. Arguing against too extreme a formulation, Kuusinen reminded Safarov that the words "to the point of full separation" had been removed at the Sixth Congress by "a very authoritative Leninist." Haywood confirmed in an interview several years ago that this authoritative Leninist was Stalin; he had prevented the 1928 resolution from calling for the right of self-determination to the point of separation of Negroes from the U.S.[23]

Having invoked the authority of Stalin, Kuusinen carried the day; the Political Secretariat concluded, according to Bedacht and Weinstone, that "self-determination is agitation slogan while aim of immediate action is the concrete fight against Jim Crowism and other discrimination actions of the bourgeois state."[24] Bedacht and Weinstone noted to their fellow Communists that the Political Secretariat had not made any other decisions on other disputed questions—even the separation issue. For now, they warned their American colleagues, they should follow the guidelines of the 1928 resolution:

POLITSECRETARIAT CONSIDERS THAT AT PRESENT TIME THERE IS NO REASON TO THINK STATE SEPARATION OF NEGROES HAS BECOME IMMEDIATE QUESTION IN USA AND THEREFORE AT PRESENT NOT EXPEDIENT FROM VIEWPOINT OF MOBILIZING NEGRO MASSES IN STRUGGLE AGAINST IMPERIALISM TO EMPHASIZE THIS POINT TOO MUCH (STATE SEPARATION). SUCH PLACING OF QUESTION OF COURSE DOES NOT CONFLICT AT ALL WITH CONCEPTION OF COMMUNIST PARTY ON FULL RIGHT OF POPULATION TO SELF-DETERMINATION.[25]

This cable from Moscow, with its warning to "tactically" strike from Negro section "to point of separation," arrived too late, however. The Americans had printed a revised draft thesis that "fully recognizes the right of the Negro masses to self-determination to the point of separation." Luckily for the American Communists, however, the revised draft program still had one more revision to go; this last time they got it right. Communists would "openly and unreservedly fight for the right of Negroes for national self-determination in the South." Earl Browder admitted in the pages of the *Daily Worker* that the elimination of the phrase "to the point of separation" had been prompted by the Comintern.[26]

The relieved Americans felt that they were off the hook. While the CPUSA would call for the right of self-determination, it was not necessary to transform it from a propaganda tool. At the CPUSA's 7th Convention in April 1930 Earl Browder denounced the leftist error that it should be a slogan of action. He confidently noted that the goal of self-determination was "far removed from the realities of development in America and would be wrong."[27]

If the American Communists thought that self-determination had been rendered toothless with the advice and consent of the Comintern, however, they were in for a rude shock. In late August 1930, the Comintern's Negro Commission, chaired by Kuusinen, met once again. Among its members were Browder, William Dunne, Weinstone, James Ford, Nasanov, Haywood, and several others. In his autobiography Haywood reported that with little debate the group approved a Kuusinen-sponsored resolution. This new Comintern statement, however, released in October, totally reversed the private instructions given to Bedacht and Weinstone five months earlier.[28]

The resolution opened by accusing the American Communists of "underestimation of the struggle for the slogan of the right of self-determination." It then proceeded to lay down a new and more radical interpretation of the meaning of the slogan:

> The struggle of the Communists for the equality of the Negroes applies to all Negroes, in the North as well as in the South. The struggle for this slogan embraces all or almost all of the important special interests of the Negroes in the North, but in the South, where the main slogan must be: THE RIGHT OF SELF-DETERMINATION OF THE NEGROES IN THE BLACK BELT... only the fulfillment of their main slogan, self-determination in the Black Belt, can assure them of true equality.

Self-determination included the right of Negroes "to exercise governmental authority in the entire territory of the Black Belt, as well as to decide upon the relations between their territory and other nations." The Resolution also added two other "basic demands" to the right of self-determination, designed to separate the "national-revolutionary" Communist position from the "reactionary Negro separatism" of Marcus Garvey. These two were the "confiscation of the landed property of the white landowners and capitalists for the benefit of Negro farmers" and the merging of all the separate states of the Black Belt into one governmental unit.

Nor was the Comintern finished. It repudiated its previous assurance that self-determination was only an agitation slogan:

> [I]t is also incorrect to say that the Communists are only to carry on propaganda or agitation for the right of self-determination, but not to develop any activity to bring this about. Even if the situation does not yet warrant the raising of the question of uprising, one should not limit oneself at present to propaganda for the demand, 'Right to Self Determination,' but should organize mass actions, such as demonstrations, strikes, tax boycott movements, etc.

In all concrete struggles in the South Communists were instructed "to concentrate the attention of the Negro masses not so much on the general demands of mere equality, but much more on some of the revolutionary basic demands arising from the concrete situation."

Finally, the resolution disavowed Pepper's call for a Negro Soviet Republic. While they supported the right to self-determination, Communists would not necessarily call for separation. "If the proletariat has come into power in the United States," the Comintern fantasized, "the Communist Negroes will not come out for but against separation of the Negro Republic from federation with the United States."[29]

There is no indication whatsoever as to why the Comintern changed its position; the 180 degree reversal performed by Moscow between March and October was never even acknowledged, let alone explained. The concessions made in March had been made in private, and thus the Comintern saw no reason to admit that it had reneged on anything at all. Perhaps Haywood and Nasanov had been politicking in Moscow and had succeeded at last in catching someone's ear. Perhaps Kuusinen had deceived Bedacht and Weinstone for some obscure reason. It is even possible that the concessions made in March did not accurately reflect Stalin's wishes, although it seems unlikely that Kuusinen would have gone so far out on a limb without instructions.

Whatever the reasons, the shift further confirms the made-in-Moscow nature of the self-determination policy. Like the 1928 resolution, this one included instructions that had never been discussed in the U.S. Unlike before, however, this time the Americans dutifully fell into line. There was no factional battle to distract them and little leeway in the words of the new resolution. Self-determination remained a central plank in the Party's program until the inauguration of the Popular Front period in the mid-1930s. By that time it was an obstacle to the CPUSA's efforts to build ties to moderate black groups and it was quietly ignored.

Harry Haywood, the plan's major American supporter, rapidly lost his influence during the Popular Front years. Haywood remained committed to self-determination even after his expulsion from the Party in 1959. When he became a leading figure in the Maoist Communist Party (Marxist-Leninist) in the 1970s, he helped steer that group toward endorsement of the right of blacks to self-determination in the Black Belt.

Most Communists, however, tried to forget the policy. It never produced many results. Party work in the South, never easy, was made even more difficult by the line. Nor did it lead to an influx of black members. As one Party organizer admitted: there was no "revolutionary national movement" of the Negro masses.[30]

However minimal its practical effects, the self-determination line was a potent symbol of the relationship between the Comintern and one of its constituent parties. American Communists allowed foreigners to define and interpret an essential part of their own national history. While they were not totally passive bystanders in the process, their own role was limited to modifying and making marginal alterations in the doctrine. Their private objections and the Comintern's private assurances to meet those objections were not sufficient to enable them to follow the policies they wished to follow.

Notes

1. Among those who have discussed the policy are: Wilson Record, *The Negro and the Communist Party,* (Chapel Hill, 1951), William Nolan, *Communism Versus the Negro,* (Chicago, 1951), Roger Kanet, "The Comintern and the Negro Question: Communist Policy in the US and Africa, 1921-1941," *Survey,* Autumn 1973, Mark Naisson, *Communists in Harlem During the Depression* (Chicago, 1983), Theodore Draper, *American Communism and Soviet Russia* (New York, 1960).
2. *The Crusader,* three vols. (New York, 1987).
3. *Daily Worker,* Feb. 12, 1929.
4. *Amsterdam News,* Sept. 5, 19, 1917.
5. Ibid., Jan. 1918.
6. *Crusader,* July 1920, 5.
7. Notes of Theodore Draper on WPA Writers Project Interview between Carl Offord and Cyril Briggs, Theodore Draper Papers, Emory Univ., Box 21, Folder 3.
8. R. M. Whitney, *Reds In America* (New York, 1924), 190-193.
9. *Crusader,* March 1921, 8.
10. Otto Huiswoud, "World Aspects of the Negro Question," *Communist,* Feb. 1930, 132-147.
11. Harry Haywood, *Black Bolshevik* (Chicago, 1978), 128, 327.
12. Draper, *American Communism and Soviet Russia,* 508.
13. Ibid., 334, Haywood, 134-135.
14. Haywood, 221.
15. Joseph Stalin, *Marxism and the National Question* (New York, 1942), 12.
16. Arvo Tuominen, *The Bells of the Kremlin: An Experience in Communism* (Hanover, 1983), 92, 246-256.
17. *International Press Correspondence,* Oct. 25, 1928, 1346, Oct. 30, 1928, 1393; Draper Interview with Darcy, May 1, 1957, Draper papers, reel 8
18. Haywood's article was never published in English; it is discussed in Draper, *American Communism and Soviet Russia,* 347.
19. Draper, *American Communism and Soviet Russia,* 508, "Policies on Negro Work," *Communist,* July 1928, 418-419; John Pepper, "American Negro Problems," *Communist,* Oct. 1928, 628-638.
20. ILD Memo to all District Organizers, Jan. 23, *1930.*
21. *A Report of Proceedings and Decisions of the First International Conference of Negro Workers,* (Hamburg, 1930); N. Nasanov, "Against Liberalism in the American Negro Question," *Communist,* April 1930, 296-308.
22. Letter of the Anglo-American Secretariat of the Communist International to the American Party, Feb. 15, 1930, Draper Papers, Box 6, Folder 20.
23. Harry Haywood Interview with Harvey Klehr, Oct. 25, 1979.
24. Max and Will Cables, Mar. 30, 1930, Draper Papers, Box 6, Folder 24.
25. Ibid., Mar. 23, 1930.
26. *Theses and resolutions for the Seventh National Convention,* 61: *Daily Worker,* April 21, 1930
27. Earl Browder, "The Bolshevization of the Communist Party," *Communist,* Aug. 1930, 689; *Daily Worker,* April 21, 1930, 6.
28. Haywood, 331-333.
29. "Resolution of Communist International," Oct. 1930, in *The Communist Position of the Negro Question,* 41-56.
30. *Daily Worker,* May 29, 1930.

8

Moscow Gold: Confirmed at Last?

with John Earl Haynes

"Moscow gold" has fascinated students of American communism almost from the very moment there was an American Communist movement. Exposés about its reliance on Soviet financing have periodically embarrassed the Communist Party of the United States of America (CPUSA) but have not deterred party leaders from continuing to rely on Soviet money. A combination of scarce domestic financial resources and ambitious goals persuaded American Communists to accept large donations from abroad in spite of the political and legal risks.

In 1918, Michael Borodin, one of the Communist International's legendary operatives, set out to smuggle Soviet propaganda and money into the United States. One of his couriers was poet Carl Sandburg, who accepted Borodin's request to carry Lenin's *A Letter to American Workingmen* and a $10,000 check to subsidize the fledgling American Communist movement. U.S. Customs officials, informed of the transaction by Sandburg himself, seized the check. Undaunted, Borodin turned to a plan to smuggle some of the tsar's jewels into the United States. Estimated to have a value of $250,000, the diamonds were shuffled from courier to courier. The plan went awry, however, and the jewels' precise fate has never been fully explained. One story has it that after reaching New York, they were used as security for a loan from the Irish Republican movement and deposited in a bank. Later transferred to Ireland, they were returned to the USSR in 1948 after the loan was repaid by the Soviet government. Another account has Borodin called onto a Moscow carpet and forced to account for the disappearance of many of the jewels.[1]

Less dramatic methods of financing the fledgling American Communist party were also common. Louis Fraina was only one of the Comintern's representatives

Originally published in *Labor History*, Spring 1992 (http://www.informaworld.com) and reprinted with permission.

to be given money to use in his mission. Fraina brought $50,000 from Moscow back to North America in 1920 when he became Comintern representative in Mexico. Fraina broke from communism in 1922 and vanished with some of the money. When he resurfaced in New York as a Marxist economist named Lewis Corey in the 1930s, the question of the Comintern's money was a stumbling block to reconciliation with the CPUSA.[2]

Benjamin Gitlow, a party leader in the 1920s, became a vehement anti-Communist after his expulsion from the CPUSA in 1929. In books and congressional testimony, Gitlow charged that the Comintern and the Profintern regularly provided subsidies to American Communists for presidential campaigns, union activities, and the start-up of the *Daily Worker.* Gitlow gave widely varying figures, but suggested that during the 1920s the Soviet provided $250,000 a year. Jay Lovestone, the party's general secretary during the last half of that decade, disputed Gitlow's figures, testifying that the Soviet provided only $25,000 a year.[3]

Other ex-Communists confirmed that Soviet subsidies were commonplace into the mid-1930s. Earl Browder, who led the party in the 1930s, admitted that during the first half of the 1930s, the Comintern provided about 10 percent of the party's funds. A one-time functionary of the Trade Union Unity League testified that his organization was heavily subsidized by Moscow. By the end of the decade, however, the CPUSA had nearly 100,000 members and had developed substantial financial resources of its own. By many accounts, the subsidies were ended during the decade. Browder claimed that he was able to eliminate the subsidy by 1935.[4]

In addition to couriers bringing money to America, the Soviets used a variety of business fronts to transfer funds. Dr. D. H. Dubrowsky, an American Communist who represented various Soviet government agencies in the United States, broke with communism in the late 1930s and testified before the Dies Committee. Dubrowsky claimed that the USSR raised millions of dollars a year in the U.S. through film concessions, insurance claims, estates, and advertising fees for companies doing business with Amtorg (the Soviet foreign trade agency). Some of the money, he charged, was funneled back into the CPUSA.[5]

By the end of the 1940s, American communism was once again on the defensive in the U.S., and Moscow was once again financing a significant percentage of the CPUSA budget. One of the murkier but most spectacular operations involved Morris and Jack Childs, two high-ranking members of the CPUSA. Morris Childs, a one-time member of the Central Committee and editor of the *Daily Worker,* and Jack, a more shadowy figure involved in the party's financial dealings, were recruited by the FBI in the early 1950s. For the next few decades they were the crucial link whereby Soviet money totaling some one million dollars a year was transferred to the CPUSA.

Morris made at least one trip a year to Moscow to pick up funds; Jack received cash from Soviet couriers in New York. Among those involved in their activities to launder these Soviet funds in the 1950s was New York attorney Stanley Levinson, who later became a close adviser to Dr. Martin Luther King, Jr. It was Levinson's connection to Soviet funding of the CPUSA that first led the FBI to wiretap King.[6]

Other reports and hints of Soviet subsidies have surfaced in recent years. Historian Ronald Radosh has written that former California Communist leader Dorothy Healey told him privately that she had brought thousands of dollars for the CPUSA back to the U.S. from the USSR. Healey denied the assertion and demanded a retraction—which was not offered.[7] In 1989 the FBI arrested Alan Thomson, the executive director of the National Council of American-Soviet Friendship, for violations of currency laws. Thomson had received $17,000 from his organization's Soviet counterpart and brought it into the U.S. without declaring it to Customs.[8]

After the failed August 1991 coup against the Soviet government of Mikhail Gorbachev, the Russian government of Boris Yeltsin dissolved the Communist Party of the Soviet Union (CPSU) and seized the archives of its Central Committee. The Russian government renamed the Central Committee's archives the "Center for Storage of Contemporary Documentation," opened some records for examination by researchers early in 1992, and announced plans to make most records available in the future.

Research use of the archives is at present hindered by the Russian government's distraction with more pressing problems and the size, an estimated six billion pages, and largely unorganized state of the records. The Library of Congress, the Woodrow Wilson International Center, and the Hoover Institution are assisting the Committee on Archival Affairs of Russia in organizing this vast collection. Its potential as a source of new historical documentation is illustrated by Librarian of Congress James Billington's announcement that the material includes 4,000 unpublished Lenin letters and extensive Comintern records. In time these documents will allow a more accurate recounting of the history of communism.[9]

The documents reprinted here, however, are byproducts of a Russian criminal investigation rather than historical inquiry. The Russian prosecutor-general is bringing criminal charges against leaders of the August coup and certain leading officials of the CPSU. These documents came to light as part of an investigation into whether the subsidy of foreign Communist parties by the CPSU constituted theft of Soviet government funds.

In October 1991 *Rossiya,* a Russian journal, reported that investigators had discovered that the USSR had given many million of dollars to the CPUSA. On February 10, 1992 Deputy Prosecutor-General Yevgeny Lisov confirmed the story to a Russian parliamentary commission and in a report printed in the Russian journal *Ogonyok.* Lisov presented a seized December 3, 1989, "Top Secret" budget document signed by V. Falin, International Bureau Chief of the CPSU Central Committee. Falin's memo stated,

> The International Fund for Assistance to Leftist Workers' Organizations has for many years been formed from the generous dues of CPSU and a number of other socialist countries' Communist parties. However, since the end of the 1970s, the Polish and Rumanian parties, and since 1987 the Hungarian comrades, have stopped contributing to the fund, owing to difficulties with hard currency reserves. In 1988 and 1989, the Unified Socialist party of Germany, and the Communist parties of Czechoslovak and Bulgaria, without explanation, withheld their portion of dues to the fund. At this point the fund subsisted solely on the contributions of the CPSU. Funds withheld from these three parties amounted to 2.3 million dollars in 1987, or 13 percent of the fund's total.

> The CPSU dues allocated to the International Fund for Leftist Worker's Activities in 1989 amounted to (reference number P144/129 dated 29 December 1989) 13.5 million "hard" rubles, or 22,044,673 U.S. dollars.... Seventy-three Communist parties, workers' parties and revolutionary groups received aid from the CPSU fund in 1989.[10]

Lisov explained, "although the fund was said to be 'International,' the distribution of its funds remained the prerogative of the CPSU Central Committee, more specifically, the Politburo" and that for the 1980s the "amount received by all foreign parties for the ten year period totaled over 200 million dollars."[11] Mikhail Lyubimov, a former agent of the KGB intelligence service, also testified about delivery methods.[12]

Elaborating to the *Washington Post,* Lisov said, "The Politburo would instruct the KGB to arrange the transfers. They were usually delivered in cash through the diplomatic pouch. A KGB agent under diplomatic cover would then hand the money to the local party leader, who would sign a receipt.[13] Lisov asserted that the American Communist party was one of the largest recipients, second only to the French Communist party, and receiving over $20 million in the last decade. Lisov said that the Soviet subsidies of CPUSA continued until 1989 but thereafter were held up in reaction to Gus Hall's criticism of Gorbachev's reforms. (This timing coincides with an obvious financial crisis in CPUSA; the *People's Daily World,* for example, in 1990 dropped from five day-a-week publication to two-a-week and then to one, becoming the *People's Weekly World.*)

As evidence of his assertions, Lisov turned over to the *Washington Post* documents #1, 2, 3, and 4 reproduced here. Michael Dobbs, *Washington Post* Moscow bureau chief, explained "Lisov is currently in possession of the original documents, which he confiscated from the Communist party archives while investigating the coup attempt last August."[14] Lisov reproduced Documents #5 & 6 in *Ogonyok* along with other CPSU and KGB documents listing subsidy amounts for sixteen foreign Communist parties.

Gus Hall and CPUSA refused to affirm or deny to the *Washington Post* the authenticity of the documents or the subsidies. Affirmation would be an embarrassment to CPUSA and, in addition, might raise legal difficulties because of possible violations of federal currency laws or the Foreign Agents Registration Act. Wayne Gilbert, chief of the FBI's intelligence division, said of the Lisov documents, "It's something we're interested in pursuing" and noted that the FBI and Russian officials were discussing the Russian evidence. Gilbert concluded, "You may see some cases down the road that could be indicted and prosecuted."[15]

An anonymous spokesman for the Northern California CP (pro- Hall faction) told a local newspaper, "I think it's part of a general propaganda campaign that's gone on for seventy years. I don't think there's any truth to it. There's a whole series of these things coming out, a whole series of forgeries. The CIA is very good at forging documents."[16] The French CP has also denied the authenticity of the documents. The possibility that the documents are forgeries cannot be dismissed; there have been many forgeries in the tangled history of communism and anticommunism. Our judgment, however, is that these documents are genuine.

Document #1 is an undated letter from Gus Hall to Boris Ponamarev. Ponamarev, a member of the Secretariat of the CPSU Central Committee, was in charge of CPSU relations with nonruling Communist parties. The letter refers to the Reagan administration and speaks of "the 1982 Congressional elections—which start by the New Year." Hall opens the letter with an expression of gratitude for "the very fine vacation and health visit we have had here." These remarks probably place the letter in the late summer or fall of 1981:

Document #1 is a plea for financial aid but does not request a specific amount. Most striking, however, is Hall's understanding of American politics. He speaks of "objective developments, that are reaching qualitative levels, that together are creating the most favorable situation for our party being able to influence the mass upsurge.... Tens of millions have become disillusioned. They are moving towards mass actions, and millions are in an ideological flux." Hall writes this in the first year of the Reagan era, a shift in American politics as conservative as the Eisenhower era of the 1950s and perhaps better compared to the more dramatic shift of the 1920s.

Also striking is Hall's inflated hopes for CPUSA. He suggests that with sufficient money the party could "reach the millions with our message," asserts bright Communist prospects in the labor movement, and claims "our party can be an important and even a decisive factor in influencing and moving these masses" of disillusioned millions. CPUSA did not reach the millions with its message, but, as Document #2 shows, Hall was undaunted:

This letter is also undated but speaks of the "coming August 27, Washington, D.C. mass demonstration," a 1983 event organized by leading unions and civil rights groups to commemorate the 1963 "March on Washington." As did Document #1, this letter asks for money but does not request a specific amount.

Once again, Hall's misunderstanding of American politics and his grandiose conception of CPUSA's capabilities stand out. Hall assured the Soviets, "the main objective and subjective factors are present that can force a change in the political situation in the U.S.... the mass upsurge keeps breaking out into mass actions," and "the potential of the mass upsurge can be turned into a reality if we

Document #1

Comrade Boris Ponamarev,

I want to express our thanks and appreciation to the Central Committee of the Comunist Party of the Soviet Union for the very fine vacation and health visit we have had here. Also our Party places a high value on the ideological vacations the two groups of our comrades who have been in the U.S.S.R. this year.

I greatly appreciated your visit to Barvicka and your very deep and helpful analysis of some of the current world developments and especially your assessment of U.S. Imperialism and the motivating factors behind its present policies of aggression. It will be very helpful in building the mass movement against its criminal policies.

It is in this connection that I want to restate and emphasize what in my opinion is both a responsibility but also an unprecedented opportunity for our party.

There are a number of objective developments, that are reaching qualitative levels, that together are creating the most favorable situation for our party being able to influence the mass upsurge, and political development generally. More than at any moment in recent history. I am convinced that our party can be an important factor in slowing down, stopping and reversing the present reactionary policies of the Reagan Administration.

Tens of millions have become disillusioned. They are moving towards mass actions, and millions are in an ideological flux. Our party can be an important and even a decisive factor in influencing and moving these masses.

Not since the days of the organization of the mass production workers into the C.I.O. unions has our party had such working relation with all levels of the Trade Union movement.

The developments in the peace movement, the womens and youth movements and especially the new potentional are reaching new levels.

And as I indicated in our discussions I believe the 1982 Congressional elections––which start by the New Year, have the possibilities of making a qualitative change in the composition of Congress.

To be able to take full advantage of the new possibilities, especially in the industrial Midwest it is necessary to publish the Daily World both in New York and Chicago––and at a later date also in San Francisco.

And as you Comrade Ponamarev more than anyone else is fully aware that for our party to be able to take full advantage of these new objective developments, depends on our ability to reach the millions with our message, and how big a force we can support.

And this to a large extent depends on our financial resources. Needless to say the continuing escalation of inflation is creating serious problems for us.

In this kind of a situation there is no question a few hundred dollars can make the difference between victory or defeat in a number of Congressional campaigns.

Because of the unprecedented possibility of making a turn in the political developments, and the importance of making a maximum effort I can only urge special consideration for the financial problems that we will face in the coming year,

Comradely,

Document #2

Communist Party U.S.A.

7th Floor • 235 West 23rd Street • New York, N.Y. 10011 • (212)989-4994

Dear Comrades,

Greetings. I know you have endless problems and questions of great significance you have to deal with. But permit me to raise for your thinking an additional question as it is related to the work of our Party in the United States.

How to fully take advantage of and push objective developments to their maximum potential is always a challenge for any Communist Party. Therefore, how to fully utilize the objective developments to turn the present situation in the United States into a more effective struggle against the policies of the Reagan Administration continues to be the central challenge for our Party. The achievement of this goal of course has implications far beyond the borders of the United States. Therefore, I want to briefly give you the assessment of how we see the present situation and the challenge the objective developments present to us.

To begin with, I am convinced that the main objective and subjective factors are present that can force a change in the political situation in the United States. The contradictions and problems that are sharpened by the huge military budgets, the massive government debt, the structural crisis affecting the basic industries, the serious urban crisis, the growing racism, the fear of nuclear war and the general feelings of insecurity and frustration all feed the mass movements and the potential present in the objective situation.

The mass upsurge keeps breaking out into mass actions, while most of its potential is still beneath the surface. There is the great majority sentiment that in one way or another supports every idea that promotes peace. The working class movements are in the process of moving from defensive struggles of retreat to struggles that are offensive in character. We are fully convinced that the victories that resulted from last November's elections against the supporters of the Reagan policies can be turned into meaningful defeats of Reaganites in the coming Presidential elections. The potential of the mass upsurge in the United States is without precedent.

I am convinced that the potential of the mass upsurge can be turned into a reality if we can reach the eyes and ears of the millions with our message. I am personally convinced of this based on my continuing experiences on radio and TV programs that reach millions every week. I am convinced that the millions are receptive to our ideas if we can only reach them.

Our Party has the personnel and cadre to increase our present mass work many times over. As is usually the case, our one single-most serious obstacle to doing this is the lack of financial means.

In a sense we were forced to do it, but we now have the newest printing equipment technology that makes it possible to publish a national daily newspaper in a number of cities simultaneously. This greatly expands our ability to build a mass circulation. But to pay for this equipment we had to launch a campaign to raise a half-million dollars. Even before this innovation, however, the special issues of our paper for special industries and special regional editions have been reaching a circulation of 100,000 copies.

We have writers and technical means now to put out mass pamphlets and leaflets. For relatively reasonable cost, we can purchase time on radio and also TV networks that reach tens of millions.

We have cadre who are willing to work full time for a very minimum wage to organize work in the coming 1984 elections, on organizing the unemployed, in different sections of the peace movement and in the distribution of the press and other literature. But again, we do not have the financial means.

We should assign more cadre to work on the coming August 27, Washington, D.C. mass demonstration for "Peace, equality and jobs," as well as the September Labor Day demonstrations in most of the industrial cities.

Without going into more detail, there are literally hundreds of things we can do that would be effective in building mass movements of struggle and pushing objective developments to their maximum potential.

And, of course it is difficult to think of anything in this world that would have a greater effect on world events than to be able to force changes in the policies of the Reagan Administration. I am convinced that if we were able to fully respond and take advantage of the objective developments we could bring about such changes.

I have never been more convinced of the fact that if we have the means to reach the tens of millions we can very basically influence the direction of political developments in our country. Or, as the old blacksmith saying goes, "one must strike the iron while its hot." I am sure you will give this your consideration.

Comradely,

Gus Hall
General Secretary, CPUSA

Document #3

January 14, 1987

Central Committee, CPSU
Comrade Dobrynin

Dear Comrade,
    I don't like to raise the question of finances, but
when the "wolf" is at the door one is forced to cry out.
    As I indicated before, our special financial crunch
at this moment is the result of a number of special
developments that were forced on us simultaneously.
    First, we are forced to establish a new print shop
outside New York City. This is an expensive operation, but
we had no choice. We know the FBI had a hand in creating
this situation.
    Secondly, the initial cost of starting to publish the
People's Daily World, both in New York and San Francisco
simultaneously, turned out to be a much more expensive
proposition than was originally estimated. Had we known the
initial cost we most likely would not have undertaken the
task. But there is no way we can undo it now without serious
political consequences for our Party.
    And, thirdly, we went all out in the last
Congressional elections, which in my opinion paid off very
well. However, as I am sure you are aware, no matter how
tightly one holds the purse strings election campaigns are a
costly business.
    Of course, what we spend in comparison to bourgeois
candidates is peanuts compared to the average campaign
expense for a U.S. Senator, which is now about $20 million.
    The fact is we were influential and even the deciding
factor in the defeat of some of the extreme Reaganite
candidates.
    And of course, because of inflation, the cost of
everything we do keeps going up.
    The taxes and the upkeep of our headquarters building
goes up every year. Selling the building, which I have often
given thought to, would also be a serious political setback
for the Party.
    And the truth is that in spite of the fact that our
Party raises about twice as much money now than at any time
in our history, we still face a serious crisis.
    We have been forced to cut back in a number of areas.
For example, we have been forced, most reluctantly, to end
the publication of Labor Today, a left trade union
newspaper, because of the increase in the cost of
production. This, in spite of the fact that its circulation
has continued to increase.
    So, in a real sense I cannot overemphasize that the
"wolf is at the door."
    During the past months we have coped with the crisis
largely by borrowing from everyone we could and even
mortgaging homes. And of course going into debt.
    Thus, the cold facts are that we have been able to
function in the past years because of the very generous
contribution of approximately $2 million per year. Once or
twice there have been smaller, special additional
contributions for very specific purposes.
    In order for us to continue functioning effectively
on the present level, the $2 million is needed. But, for us
to get out of the special crisis because of the special
developments, we have to find an additional $2 million.
    I have some idea about the problems, including the
financial requesdts, you comrades must face. And I am sure
everyone believes their problems are most important.
    I can only argue that because our Party works in the
decaying heart of imperialism whatever we do in influencing
events in the United States has an impact on world
developments. And, because of the crisis of the Reagan
presidency, which is deep and chronic now, our Party's work
has had and continues to have a growing impact on the
politics of our country.
    Therefore, in the context of the struggle against
U.S. imperialism and the policies of the Reagan
Administration, our Party must be seen as an important, and
even indispensable, factor.
    I can only hope that in the midst of all the
pressures and activities that you can give this problem your
most serious and urgent consideration.
    With best wishes for the New Year,

        Comradely
        GUS HALL

can reach the eyes and ears of the millions with our message.... [T]he millions are receptive to our ideas if we can only reach them." He goes on to speak of "defeats of Reaganites in the coming Presidential elections. The potential of the mass upsurge in the United States is without precedent." The 1984 election, however, ended with Reagan winning in a landslide.

Document #3, dated January 14, 1987, is a Hall letter to Anatoly Dobrynin. Dobrynin, former Soviet ambassador to the U.S., in 1987 served in the Secretariat of the CPSU Central Committee as its foreign policy adviser and had inherited Ponamarev's duties:

In this letter Hall pleads, "in order for us to continue functioning effectively on the present level, the $2 million is needed. But, for us to get out of the special crisis because of the special developments, we have to find an additional $2 million." This supports Lisov's estimate that the CPUSA received $2 million a year in that Hall writes of that amount as his customary allotment. Hall's receipt of $2 million on March 3, 1987 is confirmed by Document #4:

RECEIVED $2 000 000 (TWO million)

DOLLARS USA

14/3/87

Gus Hall

0929

9.АПР87 00306-он

The Soviet government had a budget cycle, and likely Hall's request for more than $2 million was too late to change CPUSA's 1987 allowance. That Hall's petition may have had some effect may be seen in documents #5 and #6.

Document #5 shows that Hall received $3 million in 1988, up from the prior year's $2 million subsidy. Document #6 accompanied Hall's receipt and is a memo dated April 14, 1988 to Dobrynin from N. S. Lenonov, deputy head of the KGB's First Chief Directorate.[17] It states, "This is to acknowledge the receipt by the U.S. Communist party, the sum of $3,000,000 cash distributed for 1988. The transaction took place in accordance with Decision P-97/48, December 30, 1987. Attached is the receipt on one page, no number dated March 19, 1988. It is top secret and is written in English."[18]

The evidence that has been available hitherto had already persuaded the authors that the CPUSA was regularly subsidized by the USSR. The size of the

RECEIVED $ 3 000 000
(three million US dollars)

19. 03. 88

subsidy as shown in these documents, however, is well in excess of what the authors expected. Two or three million dollars a year is a lot of money for an organization as small as CPUSA. And document #6 indicates that it received 3 million dollars:

In the 1980s, the CPUSA never claimed a membership above 20,000 and its actual membership likely was closer to 10,000 or even less. The size of the subsidies, along with the willingness of Communist cadre to work for low wages, solves the long-standing puzzle of how such a small movement was able to field so many full-time organizers in so many fields and carry on an extensive publications program.

These documents do not answer all of the questions about "Moscow Gold." They do not document Soviet subsidies prior to the 1980s, although in conjunction with the other evidence noted above they support the view that such subsidies were a regular occurrence. Nor do they prove that the American Communist party was nothing but a mercenary hireling of the Kremlin, albeit the financial tie probably bound the CPUSA more tightly to the USSR than it otherwise would have been. It is the authors' view, however, that the vision American Communists had of the Soviet Union was the central source of the loyalty of CPUSA to Soviet interests. A 1934 American Communist poem described the Soviet Union as "a heaven…brought to earth in Russia."[19] The myth that the Soviet Union had built or was building a society of material abundance while eliminating all oppression proved to American Communists that a Marxist utopia was attainable. The description was not hyperbole but the sun around which the world of American Communism turned. To them it followed that the methods used by Soviet Communists would bring a heaven to earth in America as well. Within the limits of their knowledge, American Communists always strove to do what Moscow wanted, no more, no less. American Communists were grateful for Soviet money, but it was not the chief source of their loyalty.

КОМИТЕТ
ГОСУДАРСТВЕННОЙ БЕЗОПАСНОСТИ СССР

Первое главное управление

_14_.04.88   № 157/609

Москва

Совершенно секретно

Лично

ЦК КПСС

Товарищу Добрынину А.Ф.

О направлении расписки

При этом направляем расписку о передаче руководству
Коммунистической партии США 3 000 000 /трех миллионов/
долларов США   в счет ассигнований,
выделенных на 1988 год.

Передача осуществлена в соответствии с решением
П-97/48 от 30.12.87.

Приложение: расписка на 1 листе, без номера, от 19.03.88,
сов.секретно, на английском языке.

Заместитель начальника Первого
главного управления   Н.С.Леонов

20 АПР88 00690-ся

Notes

1. Theodore Draper, *The Roots of American Communism* (New York, 1957), 236-241. In 1918 $10,000 was a lot of money and $250,000 was a fortune. The latter sum may have been intended for Soviet trade representatives as well as for American Communists.
2. Ibid., 294-302.
3. Theodore Draper, *American Communism and Soviet Russia* (New York, 1960), 202-208. A 1921 coded telegram setting out proposed Comintern subsidies for the American Communist press also showed up in evidence at the trial *People vs. Ruthenberg,* see Draper, *The Roots of American Communism,* 339-340.
4. Harvey Klehr, The *Heyday of American Communism: The Depression Decade* (New York, 1984), 376-377.
5. Ibid., 377.
6. David Garrow, The *FBI and Martin Luther King, Jr.: From Solo to Memphis* (New York, 1981), 35-43.
7. Radosh review of *Dorothy Healey Remembers: A Life in the American Communist Party* in *The American Spectator,* January 1991, and Healey's reply, April 1991.
8. Guenter Lewy, *The Cause that Failed* (New York, 1990), 190.
9. Irvin Molotsky, "Russians Get U.S. Help on Baring Soviet Files," *The New York Times,* March 11, 1992
10. Yevgeny Lisov, "Investigation: Greens for Reds," *Ogonyok,* #9 (Feb. 1992) (in Russian).
11. Ibid.
12. Celestine Bohlen, "Gorbachev Enabled Party to Invest, Hearing is Told," *New York Times,* Feb. 11, 1992
13. Michael Dobbs, "U.S. Party said Funded by Kremlin," *Washington Post,* Feb. 8. 1992.
14. Dobbs to Haynes, Mar. 20, 1992, in possession of the authors.
15. Bill Gertz, "Communists in U.S. back on FBI hit list," *Washington Times,* April 6, 1992.
16. Robert Hurwitt, "The Party's Over," *East Bay Express,* Mar. 20, 1992. On February 9, 1992, the Northern California CP voted (152 for, 32 opposed, 8 abstentions) to disaffiliate from the CPUSA. The anonymous spokesman represented the minority that remained loyal to Gus Hall and which claims to be the authentic Communist party of Northern California. See Vivian Raineri, "Vote to disaffiliate from CPUSA," *Corresponder,* 1 (Feb. 1992), journal of the anti-Hall Communist splinter, the Committees of Correspondence.
17. The First Chief Directorate is the KGB's foreign intelligence division.
18. The *Ogonyok* report also quoted the text of a similar KGB memo that accompanied Hall's 1987 receipt (Document #4). It is dated March 31, 1987 from V. A. Kirpichenko of the First Chief Directorate to Dobrynin.
19. Tillie Olsen, "I Want You Women Up North to Know," *Partisan,* March 1934.

9

Letter to the Editor: Follow-Up on "Moscow Gold"

To the editor:

"Moscow Gold: Confirmed at Last?" summarized historical scholarship on the Soviet subsidies of the American Communist movement and reproduced documents confirming Soviet subsidies to the Communist Party of the USA (CPUSA) in the 1980s. Newly discovered Communist International (Comintern) files at the Russian Center for the Storage and Study of Documents of Recent History (RCSS-DRH) are relevant to the issue. Specifically, in the Comintern files is a 1923 financial report from the Communist Party of America (CPA) breaking down Comintern subsidies of $30,950 received in December 1921 and $49,429 received in June and July 1922. The report details amounts spent on the party's English-language press, youth organizing, foreign-language federations and presses, labor organizing, and legal defense costs. The report also notes that $1,000 was transferred to the Canadian Communist Party, $8,330 had been spent extinguishing debts of the United Communist Party that merged with the CPA in 1921, and $239 was spent to extinguish debts of the left opposition that had disbanded in 1922 in response to a Comintern ultimatum. The Comintern files also yielded a Charles Ruthenberg financial statement of subsidies received during June 1 to September 15, 1926 totaling $44,864. Considering the value of a dollar in the 1920s, these sums were substantial. Ruthenberg broke down the uses of the Comintern's funds, with the largest being $13,000 for the *Daily Worker* followed by $5,717 to the Trade Union Educational League.[1] The accounting for 1921 subsidies specified an expenditure of $650 for "propaganda contributions Negro," demonstrating an early Communist interest in this arena. Also located was a 1925 Comintern letter to the American party allocating $2,500 for an upcoming Negro Labor Congress and setting out how the Comintern wanted the money spent.[2]

Originally published in *Labor History*, Fall 1992 (http://www.informaworld.com) and reprinted with permission.

The newly opened Soviet archives show that Soviet subsidies of the American Communist movement began as early as 1919. Recently the RCSSDRH and the Library of Congress exhibited Comintern financial records from 1919 to 1920. The records listed payments for Comintern activity in America to Kotliarov on July 16, 1919 for 209,000 rubles, to Khavkiv on September 30, 1919 for 500,000 rubles, to John Reed on January 22, 1920 for 1,008,000 rubles, and to Anderson on January 31, 1920 for 1,011,000 rubles. Kotliarov, Khavkiv, and Anderson are not known, but John Reed was one of the principal founders of American communism. The date of the payment coincided with Reed's arrival in Soviet Russia as the international delegate of America's newly organized Communist Labor Party. The value of the ruble on foreign exchange markets fluctuated wildly from 1917 to 1922 before the Soviets stabilized the "hard" ruble used for international trade at $1.94. All one can be sure of is that a million rubles was a fortune.[3]

Comintern files also contain numerous letters from American Communist leaders asking for prompter or larger subsidies. "The sum appropriated for us for 1923 is far from enough," American Communist leaders complained. In 1926 the CPUSA cabled "Two thousand dollars necessary for wages to end July.... Send immediately," then said "Failure to send $3860 for conference and organization expenses causing serious demoralization," and later asked for a special subsidy for organizing among miners. A Jay Lovestone cable stated "money unreceived thus paralyzing work...must immediately cable our 17 hundred dollars...Krestintern (Communist farmers' arm) rush 5 thousand for agricultural department war campaign." In 1927 Lovestone bluntly warned Moscow "party penniless." Lovestone could also be demanding; a 1928 cable read, "Bukharin Molotov Insist you execute your promise rendering immediate substantial financial assistance...cable money immediately."[4]

Comintern files also provide some information on how Soviet subsidies reached the American party. A Ruthenberg cable to the Comintern in 1925 complained that "Hammer" had not yet turned over $7,000 that Ruthenberg understood he had received from the Profintern, the Comintern's trade union arm. The Comintern's files also contain a letter from Julius Hammer in New York to his son Armand, then in Berlin, asking Armand to confirm receipt of $6,400 from unnamed friends for transfer to New York. A 1926 Comintern to Ruthenberg message stated that the Comintern was sending $14,777 through Julius Hammer and specifying that $1,500 was to be forwarded to the Canadian Communist Party, $5,777 was to be given to the TUEL, and $2,500 should subsidize publication of various works of Lenin. In addition, Jerrold Schecter, Moscow editor of *We*, an English-language newspaper owned by *Izvestia* and Hearst, and Yuri Buranov, chief of research for Russia's Center for the Storage of Contemporary Documentation (former CPSU Central Committee archive), have quoted an OGPU (Soviet security police) report on Armand Hammer from 1923-1926 Soviet files. The report, comment on granting Hammer certain economic concessions, stated that on a recent trip to the U.S. "Dr. Hammer, at the request of Comintern, carried over and delivered to the Communist Party of America $34,000 in cash."[5]

Finally, the prior essay noted that Alan Thomson, the executive director of the National Council of American-Soviet Friendship, had been indicted in 1989 for evading currency regulations by concealing a $17,000 Soviet cash subsidy that Thomson brought back from the USSR. In June 1992, Thomson pled guilty. His plea agreement included the transcript of the FBI's concealed videotape of Thomson's handover of the $17,000 to an associate who turned out to be an FBI operative. In the transcript Thomson discussed Soviet guidance for his couriering and several Soviet officials involved in the funding "channel," as he termed it.[6]

Although there are details to be filled in, on the main issue the documentation is at this point beyond serious dispute. One can no longer take seriously any scholarship on American communism that does not recognize the role and significance of Soviet funding.

Notes

1. J. Miller to the EC of CI, March 6, 1923, with attached "Disposition of Special Contribution T-1, December 1921, Lewis, Exec. Secy," and "Disposition of Spec. Contributions T-2 and T-3, June-July 1922, LCWheat, Exec. Sec'y," 495:19:608. "Wheat" was a pseudonym for Jay Lovestone; "To the Communist Party of America," February 2, 1923, 495:19:608, "Statement receipts from Comintern Jan 1 to Sept 25th, 1926" signed by Ruthenberg, Oct. 8, 1926, 495:19:613, Russian Center for the Storage and Study of Documents of Recent History, Moscow, Russia. The RCSSDRH is the former CPSU Central Party Archive.
2. Secretariat of the EDDI to the CEC of the Workers' Party of America, Feb. 3, 1925, 495:19:609, RCSSDRH.
3. Comintern accounts, page headed (in Russian) "Corresponding with Krumina's receipts…," document B.3.5a, Library of Congress 1992 exhibit "Revelations from the Russian Archives," Rudolf Pikohya, chairman of the Committee on Archival Affairs of the Russian Federation, estimated the value of the payment to Reed at $1.5 million. Michael Dobbs, "Yeltsin aides seek to link Gorbachev to Terrorism, " *Washington Post* (June 6, 1992).
4. "Dear Mr. Piatnitsky," June 26, 1923, 495:19:608; Henry to Comintern, April 17, 1926, 495:19:613, Cannon to MOPR, Oct. 8, 1926, 495:19:613, "Extracts from Minutes of National Secretariat for America and Canada Meeting of July 7, 1926," 495:19:613, Lovestone to Pepper undated, 495:19:613; From Lovestone, Aug. 12, 1927, 495:19:614; Lovestone to Bukharin and Molotov, Sept. 26, 1928, 495:19:615, RCSSDRH.
5. Ruthenberg to Piatnitsky, June 8, 1925, cable noted as decoded on June 9, 1925, 495:19:612, RCSSDRH; J. Hammer to Armand, Dec. 4, 1925, 495:19:612, RCSSDRH; "To comrade Ruthenberg," April 13, 1926, 495:19:613, RCSSDRH; Jerrold L. Schecter and Yuri A. Baranov, "Documents Tie Hammer to Communists," We 1,7 (June 15-28, 1992).
6. Plea agreement, U.S. v. Alan Thomson, US District Court, Western District of New York, May 21, 1992.

10

Communists and the CIO – From the Soviet Archives

with John Earl Haynes

In the mid-1930s the Communist Party of the USA (CPUSA), in an effort to break out of its isolation, dissolved its explicitly radical Trade Union Unity League and sent its militants into the mainstream unions of the American Federation of Labor and the newly established Congress of Industrial Organizations (CIO). The CIO leadership, needing experienced and dedicated organizers, decided to use the Communists; they played key roles in one large CIO union, the United Electrical Workers, and seventeen smaller CIO affiliates with 1,370,000 unionists, a quarter of the CIO's total membership in 1945. In addition, Communists were partners, although not dominant ones, in the ruling coalition of the million member United Auto Workers (UAW), the CIO's largest and most dynamic affiliate.

Popular hostility to communism was such, however, that most CIO Communists concealed their Communist allegiance. (Ben Gold, head of the small Furriers Union, was one of the few exceptions among high union officials.) The extent, role, and significance of the Communist presence in the CIO have been a perennial source of controversy among historians due to the paucity or ambiguity of historical documentation. The collapse of Soviet communism has opened previously closed Soviet archives to scholars, including the files of the Communist International. The Comintern, as it was known, supervised the activities of foreign Communist parties. The Comintern's records have yielded considerable evidence on who was and was not a Communist.

Originally published in *Labor History*, Summer 1994 (http://www.informaworld.com) and reprinted with permission.

The CPUSA rarely published a list of the members of its ruling Central Committee. Researchers over the years have compiled lists of members but such lists, however, were always incomplete because the party press rarely identified more than a portion of the committee's total membership and because the memories of former Communists were not always reliable. Further, most Central Committees included members whose identities were deliberately kept secret because disclosure would interfere with their activities outside the party. Even in internal CPUSA documents such as transcripts of Central Committee debates or reports these secret members were identified with a pseudonym to protect their identity from informants who had infiltrated the party.

The CPUSA, however, hid little from the Communist International. In the Comintern's files on the American party is a list of the twenty-four full members and fifteen candidate members of its Central Committee, dated January 29, 1938. The Communist Party's Tenth Convention did not take place until the end of May 1938. This list appears to be of those elected at the Ninth Convention, held in 1936. Accompanying the list are nearly thirty pages of biographies prepared by a Comintern official named Belov. He had access to the Comintern's voluminous records on the CPUSA in preparing the biographical sketches, but eleven of the biographies, chiefly of those newly prominent in the CPUSA, include the comment "for the following comrades we have only the reviews given 17 January 1938 by comrades Browder, Foster and Ryan."[1] Earl Browder was general secretary (chief) of the CPUSA, William Foster was the second-ranking figure in the American party's hierarchy, and Ryan (pseudonym for Eugene Dennis) was then the American party's representative to the Comintern. In January 1938, all three men were in Moscow for meetings with Comintern officials.

The list itself uses pseudonyms for secret Central Committee members. Belov's biographies gave the true name along with the pseudonym. The true names show that several of the secret members were trade union leaders. For example, Belov's biography shows that Central Committee member pseudonym "Donaldson" is Donald Henderson, founder and president of the small United Canning, Agricultural, Packing and Allied Workers of America, CIO. On the basis of evidence hitherto available most historians had concluded that Henderson was a Communist, although others disagreed, but no one ever suspected that he was a member of the Central Committee.[2]

Another secret Central Committee member listed is William Mauseth, an International Association of Machinists (IAM) activist at a Minneapolis-Moline plant in Minneapolis, Minnesota. Mauseth later led his union local out of the IAM into the CIO's United Electrical Workers. In 1945, he became the Minnesota director of the CIO's Political Action Committee, but his Communist links led to his removal from that post in 1947. Most historians have regarded Mauseth as a Communist but, as with Henderson, no one knew he was a member of the Central Committee.[3]

A more important secret union Communist is listed under the name "Morgan." Belov identifies Morgan as the pseudonym for Wyndham Mortimer, then first vice president of the United Auto Workers. The biography notes that Mortimer, one of the UAW's influential early leaders, "has been a member of the C.P. USA since 1934, and also a member of the Central Committee since that year." Belov wrote that

> Comrades Browder, Foster and Ryan give Comrade Morgan the following review: 'A sincere and loyal comrade, but too isolated from general party life and from the leadership. This has limited his perspectives. Thanks to his official position [in the UAW] Morgan is not able to actively participate in the work of the Central Committee.'[4]

In 1939 Mortimer was a favorite to become president of the UAW but a factional compromise aborted his candidacy. Although some labor historians have accepted Mortimer's Communist allegiance as established, others have disagreed and no one has suggested that Mortimer served on the CPUSA's Central Committee.

The most controversial secret union Communist listed is "Rossi," who is identified in the accompanying biography as the pseudonym of Harry Bridges. Belov describes Bridges as "President of the Dockers' and Port Warehouse Workers' Union. He is a strong leader of the union movement and a mass worker but up till now has only limited party knowledge and experience."[5] Bridges emerged from the 1934 West Coast maritime strike as the fiery leader of San Francisco dock workers. Under his leadership militant unionism spread to every port on the West Coast, and Bridges' International Longshoremen's and Warehousemen's Union, which he headed until his retirement in 1977, became a powerful force in West Coast labor relations and politics. He appointed Communist militants to dominant positions in his union and used the power and prestige of the union on behalf of Communist causes but always denied membership in the CPUSA.

Harry Bridges was also an Australian. The U.S. government thought he was a Communist and spent nearly twenty years trying to deport him. In 1939, thirty-two government witnesses testified before Harvard Law School Dean James Landis, acting as a special examiner for the Immigration Service. Landis found the evidence insufficient to establish that Bridges was a member of the CPUSA. In 1941 the Immigration Service ordered him deported a second time with a different set of thirty-one witnesses coming forward to give evidence supporting his being a member of the Communist Party. Although this time the examiner supported deportation, a Board of Immigration Appeals reversed the finding, only to have Attorney General Biddle order deportation in 1942. Bridges, protesting that he was not a member of the Communist Party, appealed to the U.S. courts. In June 1945, the Supreme Court in a five to three decision said the evidence was insufficient to establish membership.

Bridges then became a naturalized U.S. citizen. As part of the naturalization process he swore under oath that he was not and never had been a member of the Communist Party. The Justice Deptartment, still convinced of Bridges' party membership, indicted him for perjury in May 1949. In the trial the U.S. prosecutor brought in nearly a dozen ex-Communist Party members who testified to Bridges' membership and the jury found him guilty. However, the Supreme Court in a four to three decision voided the case on a technicality. The government reinstituted denaturalization, but gave up in 1955 after another adverse court ruling.

One of the government's problems in its attacks on Bridges was the quality of its witnesses. At the Landis hearing the clearest evidence of Bridges' membership in the party was given by John Leech, a former official in the California Communist Party. Leech testified that within the party Bridges went under the pseudonym of "Rossi." He stated that the California Party delegation had put forward Rossi for the Central Committee, and the national CPUSA convention had ratified Rossi's election at its 1936 convention. Leech, however, was a strange person; he dressed like a dandy and spoke at interminable length, frequently insisting on pursuing side issues of little relevance to the questions he was asked and about which he appeared to know little. Landis, repelled by Leech's effete manner, accused him of "verbal haemophilia" and doubted his honesty. On the other hand, Landis found Bridges' straightforward denials convincing.[6] The Comintern's records, however, demonstrate that Leech, weird though he was, was telling the truth.

At the 1949 trial, two of the ex-Communist witnesses, Paul Crouch and Manning Johnson, testified that they had been at the 1936 CPUSA convention and had witnessed the convention vote to put Bridges on the party's Central Committee. Crouch and Johnson, who appeared at a number of trials as witnesses against Communists, added that they had seen Bridges himself at the convention, held in New York. In response to the latter embellishment, Bridges' lawyers easily established that Bridges was in California and could not have been physically present. Other witnesses told conflicting stories or had personal or legal problems of their own which damaged their credibility.

Historians have been sharply divided about Bridges' veracity and his closeness to the CPUSA. Some have judged Bridges to have been a party member or so close an ally as to make little difference.[7] Others, however, have vehemently depicted Bridges as an honest man unfairly persecuted by a vindictive government.[8] Whatever the morality or wisdom of the government effort, the Comintern documents would indicate that Bridges was, not only a member of the Communist Party, but a member of its ruling Central Committee. The Comintern documents would indicate he deceived James Landis in 1938, perjured himself before an immigration examiner in 1941, deceived a majority of the Supreme Court in 1945, committed perjury at his naturalization hearing in 1945, and lied once again at his 1949 trial for perjury, as well as deceiving quite a few historians.

This Central Committee membership list changes the context of the debate over the role of Communists in the CIO. Interpretations of that role are of one sort if Bridges, Mortimer, Mauseth, and Henderson were only friendly with the Communist Party or even just casual members. They are of another sort if one accepts the Comintern documents which indicate their commitment to the CPUSA was such that they sat on its ruling Central Committee.

Notes

1. Communist Party of the U.S.A. Central Committee list, with attached biographies signed by Belov, Jan. 31, 1938, 495;74;467, [in Russian] the Russian Center for the Storage and Study of Documents of Recent History (RCSSDRH), Moscow, Russia. The RCSSDRH was formerly known as the Central Party Archives of the Communist Party of the Soviet Union.
2. Henderson's activities in the 1930s are discussed in Lowell K. Dyson's *Red Harvest: The Communist Party and American Farmers* (Lincoln, 1982).
3. On Mauseth's role in Minnesota labor and politics, see John Earl Haynes, *Dubious Alliance: The Making of Minnesota's DFL Party* (Minneapolis, 1984).
4. Communist Party of the U.S.A. Central Committee list, RCSSDRH.
5. Ibid.
6. For a description of Leech and Landis' reaction, see Charles Larrowe, *Harry Bridges: The Rise and Fall of Radical Labor in the United States* (Eastport, 1972), 154.
7. See Max M. Kampelman, *The Communist Party vs. the C.I.O.: A Study in Power Politics* (New York, 1957); Jane Cassels Record, "Ideologies and Trade Union Leadership: The Case of Harry Bridges and Harry Lundeberg," (unpublished Ph.D. diss., University of California, Berkeley, 1954); Irving Howe and Lewis Coser, *The American Communist Party: A Critical History* (New York, 1957); David Saposs, *Communism in American Unions* (New York, 1959); Bernard Karsh and Phillips L. Garman, "The Impact of the Political Left," in Milton Derber and Edwin Young, eds., *Labor and the New Deal* (Madison, 1957); Walter Galenson, *The CIO Challenge to the AFL: A History of the American Labor Movement, 1935-1941* (Cambridge, MA, 1960); Joseph Goldberg, *Maritime Story: A Study in Labor-Management Relations* (Cambridge, MA, 1958); Stephen Schwartz, *Brotherhood of the Sea: A History of the Sailors" Union of the Pacific, 1885-1985* (New Brunswick, N J, 1986); Harvey Klehr and John Haynes, *The American Communist Movement: Storming Heaven Itself* (New York, 1992); Philip Taft, *Organized Labor in American History* (New York, 1964).
8. See Harvey A. Levenstein, *Communism, Anticommunism, and the CIO* (Westport, CT, 1981); David Cante, *The Great Fear: The Anti-Communist Purge Under Truman and Eisenhower* (NY, 1978); Stanley Kutler, *The American Inquisition: Justice and Injustice in the Cold War* (NY, 1982); Bruce Nelson, *Workers on the Waterfront: Seamen, Longshoremen, and Unionism in the 1930s* (Urbana, 1988); Larrowe; Harvey Schwartz, "Harry Bridges and the Scholars: Looking at History's Verdict," *California History* 59 (1980), 84-115.

11

The End

with John Earl Haynes

In December 1991 some 500 people met in Cleveland for the twenty-fifth convention of the American Communist Party. The Cleveland City Council welcomed them with a resolution praising the Party's "proud history in the defense of democracy, civil rights, and peace." The convention was closed, however, not only to the press and public; officials and hired guards kept out even members who lacked leadership-approved passes. Party leaders refused to seat delegates from Communist clubs in New York, Northern California, Massachusetts, the District of Columbia, Alabama, Minnesota, and Wisconsin. These disqualified delegates were among the 900 out of a total membership of 3,000 who had signed an "Initiative to Unite and Renew the Party," which questioned the policies of Party leader Gus Hall.

Delegates inside the convention were treated in similar fashion. When one Hall critic, James Jackson, got up to speak, his microphone was cut off. Herbert Aptheker, a leading Party intellectual, was allowed to address the crowd. A shaken man, he linked the crisis of communism to the fact that it had been "authoritarian, domineering, brutal, and guilty of colossal crimes—not only suppression but also massive human extermination." Aptheker, the former hardliner who had supported the Soviet invasion of Hungary and once called critics of the Communist Party "racist, war-inciting, enemies of humanity, rotten to the core," now found himself on the receiving end of similar invective. Hall's supporters denounced the dissidents, including Aptheker, as "enemies within," "traitors," and "viruses."

When it was over, the convention ratified Hall's continued leadership by a 2-to-1 margin. The Party's new National Committee contained no one from the New York or Northern California districts, the two largest, and excluded every initiative signer including Angela Davis and Aptheker. The Party's newspaper,

Originally published in *New Republic*, March 23, 1992 and reprinted with permission.

the *People's Weekly World*, has yet to say what happened. At the last minute Party officials removed an article by Carl Bloice, an editor and initiative supporter, that included an account of the convention. Hall's lieutenants also accused the editor, Barry Cohen, of tampering with the paper's computer files. They changed the locks on the newspaper's offices and replaced its staff with loyalists. Cohen and the dissidents absconded with the mailing list; they sent subscribers an indignant letter and Bloice's article.

These semicomic death throes were almost entirely a consequence of the Party's ideological and emotional ties to the Soviet Union. The decline of other radical groups and the Party's determination to step up its recruiting had led to a modest but steady growth in membership in the 1980s. By the mid-1980s Communists were edging back into mainstream politics, supporting efforts by Jesse Jackson and the Rainbow Coalition to transform the Democratic Party. A few prominent labor leaders, some city officials, and even a few members of Congress began to associate themselves with Communist-aligned organizations such as the United States Peace Council and the Labor Research Association. At LRA's 1990 awards dinner, for example, both Jackson and New York Mayor David Dinkins spoke.

Then came the sting from the East. Three long-time Party leaders published an article in the *People's Weekly World* revealing that at a CPUSA meeting the day after the attempted coup in the Soviet Union last August, Party officials offered justifications for the coup and Gorbachev's removal, "some not even suggested by the plotters themselves." On an audio tape sent to fellow leaders on August 20, Hall warned that the CPUSA should not join "the bring back Gorbachev bandwagon." The National Board of the CPUSA, the article revealed, then voted to "neither condemn nor condone" the coup. In addition to James Jackson, the authors of the article were Charlene Mitchell, the Party's candidate for president of the United States in 1968, and Danny Rubin, a Party leader since the late 1950s. The three denounced the National Board's action on the coup as "a shamefaced apology for a reactionary, illegal, and indefensible act."

That the Party newspaper would publish so harsh an attack on Hall's leadership was a sign that dissension had reached crisis levels. Because the coup failed quickly and the Party no longer published a daily paper, Hall was spared the embarrassment of a public endorsement of the plotters. By the time the Party's National Committee met on September 8, Hall backtracked, condemning the "illegal, unconstitutional takeover of power," but adding a denunciation of Gorbachev for supporting Yeltsin's "anti-Communist witch hunt." The National Committee rejected the "neither condemn nor condone" formulation by a close vote.

The dissidents then issued their Initiative to Unite and Renew the Party in October. It was no repudiation of the CPUSA's history or even of Soviet communism. It continued to support Marxism-Leninism and expressed no admiration for multiparty democracy or political pluralism. However, it spoke of "a fresh look and making necessary adjustments" in view of events in the Communist world and allowed that "the crisis of the socialist societies in Europe over the last few years makes it evident that there were deep-going flaws in the model of socialism being constructed there."

As mild as this was, the initiative was too much for Hall. After dealing with its signers in Leninist fashion at the Cleveland convention, he assured the faithful: "There is no basic flaw in the theories of Marxism-Leninism or dialectical materialism." He asserted that socialism was in trouble in the Soviet Union due to the "attack by pro-capitalist, right-wing elements" and because under Gorbachev "no one defended socialism, its history and achievements." He charged dissidents in the CPUSA with "right opportunism," and rejected "such concepts as proportional representation and minority/majority positions" that the dissidents wanted as "contrary to the nature of the Party."

What does the future hold for the American Communist Party? The dissidents have formed committees and announced plans for a newsletter, a conference, and participation in the 1992 presidential election. As for the CPUSA, Hall is in firm control, but with the exodus of the dissidents its membership will likely contract sharply. The Party has survived other rifts, but this one is likely to be fatal. Even in 1959 it did not drop below 3,000 members. Moreover, the end of Soviet communism has caused the CPUSA practical as well as ideological problems. Last October Alexander Drosdov, editor of the Russian newspaper *Rossiya*, reported that newly opened Soviet archives indicated that the USSR had provided $21 million in subsidies to the CPUSA over the previous ten years. That's some deficit to make up.

The split leaves the Party at the level of the small Trotskyist sects that do little more than issue turgid newspapers. But for Hall, hope springs eternal. "If you want to take a nice vacation, take it in North Korea," he recently advised. He may soon be in need of one.

12

The Communist Party of the United States and the Committees of Correspondence

with John Earl Haynes

When Soviet communism faced its terminal crisis, the Communist Party of the USA (CPUSA) was only a marginal entity on the edge of mainstream U.S. politics. In the 1930s and 1940s the CPUSA had been the dominant voice of the American left, a force in the labor movement, and a small but significant factor in mainstream politics in New York, California, and a few other states. In the late 1940s, however, anti-communist liberals drove it from labor and liberal institutions, and Washington's Cold War security policies crippled its activities. A near-fatal blow came in 1956, not from American authorities but from Moscow, when Nikita Khrushchev shattered the mental universe of American communism by announcing that Joseph Stalin had committed enormous crimes. The CPUSA lost three-quarters of its members in the two years following Khrushchev's Secret Speech. However, the remnant that survived – about 3,000 – reestablished unqualified confidence in Soviet socialism.

Gus Hall was elected general secretary of the CPUSA in 1959, and under his guidance the party became one of the most loyal pro-Moscow parties in the world. Neither Eurocommunism nor Maoism struck a response in the CPUSA. It played no direct role in the New Left of the 1960s and 1970s, although as the New Left waned, some of its adherents drifted to the CPUSA. The most prominent of these was Angela Davis, whose image as a black feminist revolutionary helped to update the party's image.[1]

The lessening of political strictures against cooperation with communism also allowed American communists to edge back into mainstream politics. In the

Originally published in *Problems of Post-Communism*, vol. 43, no. 4 (July/August 1996).
© 1996 by M.E. Sharpe, Inc. Used by permission.

1980s a few union leaders, city officials, and members of Congress associated themselves with communist-aligned organizations such as the United States Peace Council, the National Alliance Against Racist and Political Repression, and the Labor Research Association. Party activities on college campuses picked up, and a leader of the Young Communist League won the student-body presidency at the University of Massachusetts. Marxist-Leninists reappeared on college faculties, and communist professors sponsored the Marxist Educational Press, which published quasi-academic studies.[2]

Once again, however, events in the USSR determined the direction of American communism. As Mikhail Gorbachev's reforms gathered speed in the late 1980s, Gus Hall became increasingly unhappy. In private conversations and even in several public statements, Hall and his closest associates indicated their skepticism of Gorbachev's reforms and their view that the essential nature of Soviet communism should remain unchanged. In a 1988 CPUSA meeting in Cleveland, Ohio, Hall harshly denounced Gorbachev's decision to allow the Soviet press increased freedom. He centered his attack on *Moscow News*, a weekly paper that enthusiastically backed Gorbachev's reforms. Hall told the CPUSA gathering that he had urged Soviet officials to fire the editor because "he's publishing a lot of nonsense, and I said if you can't do that, burn down the goddamn building. I mean get rid of it. But they laughed, and they haven't done it. *Moscow News* is the worst of their publications."[3] In an even more public example, in a 1989 interview in Newsweek, Hall said, "Under glasnost, the editors have gone wild with untruths, especially about history and capitalism."[4]

Several times in its history Moscow had summarily replaced CPUSA leaders who displeased it. Such direct intervention was not compatible with Gorbachev's reforms, but he saw no reason for subsidizing criticism. So in 1989 Gorbachev cut off the Soviet Union's secret subsidy of the CPUSA. This subsidy had averaged $2 million a year in the 1980s, an enormous sum for a party whose membership was probably less than 5,000.[5] (When in 1992 the Yeltsin government made public the documents about the subsidies, Hall denounced them as forgeries.)

The end of Soviet subsidies produced an immediate financial crisis in the CPUSA. In the late 1980s the party's flagship daily newspaper, *People's Daily World*, was printed on good quality paper with color and photographs and was mailed nationally to subscribers at a price that could not have come close to meeting the actual costs of production and postage. After the cut-off of Soviet funds, the *People's Daily World* shrank in size and quality and had to change its name to *People's Weekly World* because its publication was reduced from five days per week to one. Other party publications suffered similar cutbacks, and the party also reduced its extraordinarily large cadre of paid staff. The tentative signs of acceptance of the CPUSA into mainstream American politics that had appeared earlier in the decade also vanished as Soviet power and prestige crumbled.

With East European communist regimes collapsing and the death knell of the Soviet Union approaching, party morale plummeted even further. Hall reacted by becoming increasingly open in his criticism of any change in the Soviet system. As for Gorbachev's glasnost and perestroika, Hall dismissed them as "basically nothing more than the old social-democratic thinking class collaboration. Internally, it is expressed by those who are for liquidating socialism, one step at a time." Hall insisted that there had been no flaws in the Soviet system and that its growing difficulties simply "stem from human error....While Gorbachev continues to cover it up, I believe the basic cause is in the massive, irresponsible mistakes made three or four years ago, led by Gorbachev." Hall also claimed that he had "on several occasions spoken directly to Gorbachev regarding criticisms of current events in the USSR."[6]

Hall's refusal to reconsider the party's stance produced internal disquiet that boiled over at an August 1990 meeting of the CPUSA's National Committee (formerly the Central Committee). Charlene Mitchell, a member of the National Board (formerly the Political Committee), launched an unprecedented public attack on Hall's leadership, accusing him of stifling debate about the party's problems. Mitchell, one of the most prominent black members of the party's leadership and head of its National Alliance Against Racist and Political Repression, also accused Hall of refusing to deal with the "influence of racism in our party." Mitchell's attack received the support of nine of the twenty-three National Board members, including five of its six blacks.[7]

The failed hard-line communist coup in the Soviet Union in August 1991 set off a factional explosion within the CPUSA. At a CPUSA meeting the day after the coup began, Hall offered justifications for the action and warned that the CPUSA should not support any attempt to bring back Gorbachev. The National Board then voted to "neither condemn nor condone" the insurrection. The coup failed quickly and only the absence of a daily CPUSA newspaper spared Hall the embarrassment of the party press printing his supportive statements about the coup. When the National Committee met on September 8, after Gorbachev had returned to power, Hall backtracked and condemned the "illegal, unconstitutional takeover of power," but added a denunciation of Gorbachev for abandoning Marxism-Leninism and for supporting Yeltsin's "anti-communist witch hunt."[8]

Hall's action infuriated Mitchell and her supporters, who included Barry Cohen, the editor of the *People's Weekly World.* Cohen published an article by Mitchell and two other veteran party leaders, James Jackson and Danny Rubin, denouncing the National Board's first action. "The coup merited a clear-cut condemnation," they stated. That the party newspaper would publish such an attack was a sign that dissension had reached crisis levels. In October 1991, Mitchell's faction released a platform, the "Initiative to Unite and Renew the Party." Eventually, about 900 American communists signed the initiative. As membership then stood below 2,500, this put more than one-third of the party openly in the anti-Hall camp.[9]

The initiative was in no way a repudiation of the CPUSA's history or even of Soviet communism. The document supported Marxism-Leninism, condemned past criticism of communism, vindicated the CPUSA's past defense of the USSR, and, although speaking of internal democracy for the party, expressed no support for multiparty democracy. However, it spoke of "a fresh look and making necessary adjustments" and allowed that "the crisis of the socialist societies in Europe over the last few years makes it evident that there were deep-going flaws in the model of socialism being constructed there."

As mild as this was, the initiative was too much for Hall. He settled accounts with its backers at the American Communist Party's Twenty-fifth Convention, held in December 1991, in Cleveland, Ohio. Hall closed the convention not only to the press and public, but even to party members who lacked leadership-approved passes; party officials and hired Cleveland police kept all others out. Party leaders refused to seat scores of delegates from communist clubs in New York, Northern California, Massachusetts, the District of Columbia, Alabama, Minnesota, and Wisconsin--all areas that supported the initiative. Nor were delegates allowed into the convention given much leeway. James Jackson, a veteran black communist, had first become associated with the party in the 1930s. Imprisoned under the Smith Act in the 1950s, he had served as editor of the party newspaper and international affairs secretary. However, he supported the initiative, and when Jackson got up to speak, his microphone was cut off. When speakers who did get the floor criticized Hall, delegates broke into chants of "Gus, Gus, Gus." When it was over, the convention ratified Hall's continued leadership by a vote of two-to-one. The party's new National Committee excluded every initiative signer, such as Angela Davis, Gilbert Green, James Jackson, Charlene Mitchell, and Herbert Aptheker.[10]

After the convention, Cohen tried to publish an article by Carl Bloice, the *People's Weekly World* Moscow correspondent, describing the convention. Bloice was a prominent black party leader, an initiative supporter, and had written a number of articles supporting Gorbachev's reforms. After the *People's Weekly World* had been sent to the printer, CPUSA officials had the printer remove Bloice's article and inserted an anonymous article praising the convention's rebuff to "factionalism." Hall's lieutenants also changed the locks on the newspaper's offices, named Hall-loyalist Tim Wheeler as its new editor, and brought in other Hall supporters to continue publishing.[11]

"The truth is," the victorious Hall assured his loyalists, "that there are NO systemic flaws in the basic tenets of socialism, no flaws in the basic concept of public ownership of the means of production, no flaws in the concept of a planned economy or production for common good. There is no basic flaw in the theories of Marxism--Leninism or dialectical materialism." Hall asserted that socialism was in trouble in the Soviet Union because under Gorbachev "no one defended socialism, its history and achievements. The slander and vilification of the socialist system went mainly unanswered. This led to mass confusion."

He dismissed dissidents in the CPUSA as guilty of "right opportunism," and rejected proportional representation and recognition of minority/majority positions, reforms that the dissidents had demanded.[12]

Hall also eagerly sought a new revolutionary patron to replace the USSR. For a while the CPUSA hoped that communists would come to power in post-apartheid South Africa and fund a new center for world revolution with South African gold. Hall also visited North Korea, where, he said, "socialism is alive and well and efficient." He told his comrades, "If you want to take a nice vacation, take it in North Korea."[13] In 1991, the communist-aligned Marxist Education Press, having abandoned its program of arranging tours for American faculty to visit East European communist states, sponsored a "Korean—U.S. Scholars Interdisciplinary Colloquium" in Pyongyang.[14] In addition to continued links to foreign communist parties, usually those least changed from pro-1991 days, other foreign movements with which the CPUSA has established friendly relations include Syria's Baath party and the Democratic Popular Front for the Liberation of Palestine. Not surprisingly, the CPUSA makes no secret that it yearns for and expects the reestablishment of communist rule in Russia and the recreation of the Soviet Union.

Hall has stressed his long-favored policy of "industrial concentration," targeting the recruitment of blue-collar workers in heavy industry. Basing his position on a traditional interpretation of Marxism, Hall has said, "Surplus value is generated at the point of production....Workers in basic and mass production industries carry on the class struggle at the point of production."[15] In *Political Affairs*, the party's theoretical journal, a Hall associate stated that the strategy was one of concentrating "our small working-class party's resources on moving the strongest, most advanced, most compact, strategically placed section of our class in order to most effectively move the entire class in an anti-monopoly, revolutionary direction."[16] As one Hall critic noted, the policy has produced virtually no useful results in the last twenty years. In 1991 the party possessed only a single shop club in the entire steel industry; in the Illinois district, the CPUSA's third largest, there were only two industrial workers among the party's 190 members. There are a handful of communists holding local union offices or employed on union staffs, but their numbers are so few and they are so scattered that they do not constitute a force within the American labor movement.[17]

The picture presented in the party's publications and by its leaders, however, is not only optimistic but claims huge successes for the CPUSA since 1991. In December 1994, Hall told the *New York Times*, "There is no question we are now the fastest-growing political organization in America." He declined, however, to give specific figures about membership. Other party leaders spoke of thousands of new recruits and suggested to the *New York Times* that the party's membership was in the 15,000 to 20,000 range. According to CPUSA publications, the party has also raised more than a million dollars from this rapidly growing membership. These claims, however, lack credibility.[18] Indeed, at times

CPUSA leaders appear to be living in a world of fantasy. John Bachtell, head of the party's New York district, announced to its New York state convention that the party was "in the midst of the process of transition to a communist party of millions."[19]

As 1996 began, the CPUSA continued under Hall's leadership with no significant revisions of its ideology or its views that classic Soviet communism is still the model for which socialists should strive. Hall himself is eighty-five years old and has been CPUSA leader since 1959; he is the longest-tenured Communist Party leader in the world today. In addition to Hall, leading CPUSA officials include Political Action Commission chair Jarvis Tyner, Labor Commission chair Sam Webb, New York Party chair John Bachtell, and *People's Weekly World* editor Tim Wheeler. The CPUSA's membership is probably less than 2,000 and may be less than 1,000. The bulk of its membership is over the age of sixty and a majority may be over sixty-five. Although its financial status had been drastically reduced by the end of Soviet subsidies, the party retains substantial capital assets from its more prosperous days, such as its eight-story headquarters building on West Twenty-third Street in New York; those driven out of the Party by Hall claim that he controls party property and assets worth $7 million.[20] The CPUSA, however, is believed to be draining these to maintain its current operations. While the bulk of its elderly membership has only limited income, the CPUSA benefits from a long-established program whereby members bequeath their estates to the CPUSA.

While its ability to draw on capital assets allows it to maintain several publications and a paid staff of a size many times that of larger left-wing organizations, those assets are finite and will be exhausted at some point. Hall adamantly refuses to reconsider the party's traditional ideology or its focus on workers in heavy industry. Unless Hall is replaced by a very different leader, the CPUSA appears likely to remain a living fossil from a bygone era.

The Committees of Correspondence

In ridding the American communist party of dissidents, Hall threw out most of the party's non-elderly leadership. These anti-Hall communists have since formed an organization called the Committees of Correspondence (CoC). On February 9, 1992, a convention of the Northern California District of the CPUSA, one of the party's largest and most active districts, voted to disaffiliate from the party and join the CoC. On March 5, 1992, the party's New York district, its largest, also cut its ties to the CPUSA.[21]

In July 1992 the CoC held a national conference in Berkeley, California, with an attendance of about 1,200.[22] In addition to those who had left the CPUSA, the convention attracted a variety of radicals, leftists, and left-liberals. The conference adopted a statement of principles declaring that the CoC sought "a humane alternative to the anti-human system of capitalism" and that supporters of the CoC "are predominately people with a socialist vision and a Marxist view of history." The CoC statement said the "science" of Marxism was "still evolving" and adherence to Marxism was not a requirement for membership: "We are convinced that we can and must build an organization that is pluralist, embracing members who have theoretical frameworks other than Marxist.... The continuing distinct contributions of liberation theology, environmentalism, feminism, theories of non-violent resistance and multiculturalism, non-Marxist socialism, and others cultivate the common ground for struggle.... People with diverse views are necessary and welcome in this organization on an equal basis: Therefore we are both Marxist and pluralist."[23]

Like the initiative statement, the CoC statement expressed no serious regrets about the past, no view that the Soviet Union or the CPUSA (prior to the 1991 split) had ever been in error. The closest the statement came to recognizing that Soviet communism had flaws was an oblique reference: "We will continue to assess the experience, including both achievements and failures, of the first sustained attempts to build socialist societies in Europe, Asia, Latin America, and Africa."[24]

By August 1992, the CoC claimed a membership of about 1,400, probably exceeding that of the CPUSA. About half of those had been either expelled or resigned from the CPUSA because of their anti-Hall stance. The remainder of the CoC membership was a mix of people who had been close allies of the CPUSA but had found it inexpedient to formally join, as well as a variety of leftists attracted to the idea of a new radical organization with a hard-left but nevertheless broad agenda. California state legislator Barbara Lee (Democrat, Thirteenth Assembly District) became a member of the CoC National Coordinating Committee. Although the bulk of its membership was white, the CoC boasted that its five co-chairs were "people of color" – four African Americans (Charlene Mitchell, Kendra Alexander, Carl Bloice, Manning Marable) and one Puerto Rican (Rafael Pizarro). Mitchell, Alexander, and Bloice had all held high posts in the CPUSA. Marable was a professor of political science and history at the University of Colorado. Pizarro was an organizer for the Local 1199 of the Hospital Workers Union of New York City and a former leader of the Castroist Venceremos Brigade.[25]

Throughout this period CoC members engaged in considerable internal debate over exactly what type of organization it was and what ideology it supported. Without the unity that had once been provided by Moscow, the CoC's membership began to reflect the multitude of agendas of the American left. Many of the CoC's black members had quit the CPUSA and wanted a movement that would insist on the "centrality of the struggle for African American equality." Others wanted to become part of a broad movement of the socialist left; still others looked back to the model of a small disciplined Leninist party. Some spoke of a "green Marxism" focusing on environmental concerns, and a number drifted toward a sort of eclectic leftist activism.[26]

The Minnesota CoC affiliate, led by University of Minnesota physicist Erwin Marquit, called for continued explicit adherence to a Marxist-Leninist theoretical perspective. Marquit commented that many "good" communists still remained in the CPUSA and suggested reconciliation with these communists after Hall left the scene. In June 1993, Marquit and about several dozen of his followers formed the Independent Communists of Minnesota. While not leaving the CoC, they formed the organization to promote a purified Marxism-Leninism, freed of what Marquit regarded as ideological deformations brought on by Stalin and later Soviet rulers.[27]

Hall, meanwhile, has made it clear that, while he is around, there would be no reconciliation with those who split in 1991. Hall denounced the CoC as "a thoroughly petit-bourgeois phenomenon" and accused its members of "ideological collapse, political dishonesty, and simple greed." The *People's Weekly World* has also featured lengthy articles by CPUSA spokesmen repudiating suggestions that the party leave open the possibility of reconciliation with the CoC.[28]

The Committees of Correspondence negotiated with several left-wing organizations about a merger, the most likely partners being the Democratic Socialists of America, the Socialist Party, or Solidarity. A formal merger, however, was not achieved. The CoC's prospects took a blow in 1993 when Kendra Alexander, one of its most dynamic leaders and the mainstay of its California organization, died in an accident. Also, some of the elderly anti-Hall communists who joined the CoC have found it too painful to exist outside the party to which they had devoted their lives: since 1992 a trickle of older CoC members has submitted to Hall and returned to the CPUSA.[29]

On July 22-24, 1994, the CoC held a national convention in Chicago, which it declared to be a formal founding of the Committees of Correspondence as a permanent organization. Angela Davis gave the keynote address. Organizers reported the attendance of 388 delegates (representing 1,500 dues-paying members) and 132 observers. Elected as CoC co-chairs were Charlene Mitchell, Manning Marable, Leslie Cagan, Rafael Pizarro, and Sushawn Robb. Mitchell served as the organization's chief organizer and executive.[30]

The CoC leadership presented to the 1994 convention a statement of principles, later adopted by the body, that endorsed left-wing variants of environmentalism, feminism, multiculturalism, and gay rights along with opposition to colonialism and imperialism. The statement also directly referred to the demise of the Soviet Union, stating that the "collapse makes clear that the socialist ideal cannot be reconciled with authoritarian politics." But again, there were no regrets over past support for Soviet communism. The statement called for the abolition of capitalism and "the construction of strategic democratic alliances between critical sectors of the most exploited and oppressed groups within American society: the working class; people of color, African Americans, Latinos, Caribbean Americans, Asian-Pacific Islanders, Arab and Middle Eastern Americans, Native Americans; women; lesbians, gays, and bisexuals; youth; seniors; the unemployed, the homeless, and people on fixed incomes; all Americans who need social guarantees of health care, quality shelter, and the basic material elements of a decent life."31

The CoC statement endorsed socialism, but gave it no fixed meaning, stating,

> By socialism, we do not mean a social system in which the state dominates everything, or in which authoritarian measures are used to restrict basic human rights for members of society. Socialism without democracy is no socialism at all. Our understanding of socialism is that it is a political, cultural, economic, democratic, and ethical project, a struggle to transform the power relations within a class-divided society, for the benefit of the overwhelming majority of the people. Socialism therefore is not a fixed entity, but the social product of the dynamics of class struggle.[32]

This broad and largely rhetorical definition of socialism reflects the CoC's lack of any unifying vision aside from the goal of complete equality and its hostility toward existing society. The vagueness of its ideological stance also means that while the largest part of its membership is still made up of former CPUSA members, the CoC is losing its ideological distinctiveness as a communist organization. Consequently, the CoC is blending into the far left as just one of the dozens of sometimes competing, sometimes cooperating radical bodies.

Still, because the largest part of its membership and leadership consists of former communists, many of the CoC's organizational ties are to communist and post-communist organizations. For example, the communist parties of El Salvador, Austria, Canada, Great Britain, Spain, the German Party of Democratic Socialism, the Party of Labor of Russia, the South African Communist Party, the Hungarian Socialist Workers Party, and the Refoundation Communist Party of Italy sent either speakers or fraternal greetings to CoC conventions. The latter two parties are hard-line heirs of post-1991 splits in the Hungarian and Italian communist movements. Also, the CoC convention, despite repeated declarations of support for democratic socialism, gave enthusiastic support for Fidel Castro's very undemocratic socialist regime and had kind words as well for Vietnam's undemocratic socialist government. The CoC is emphatically not a social-democratic movement, and its contempt for democracy in the traditional Western sense appears to be little different from that held by the CPUSA.

There have been several court fights between the CPUSA and the Committees of Correspondence over some of the movement's capital assets. While most of the CPUSA's assets were held by the Party directly and remained under Hall's control, some were held by independent entities. In California for many years, communists sponsored a West Coast newspaper, the *People's World* published by the Pacific Publishing Foundation. In the 1980s the paper was merged into the CPUSA national newspaper but the property and financial assets of the *People's World* remained with the Pacific Publishing Foundation. When the CoC split from the CPUSA, the governing board of the foundation supported the CoC and backed a new monthly publication *News for a People's World*. The CPUSA sued, arguing that the Pacific Publishing Foundation's independence was a fiction and its property belonged to the CPUSA. CPUSA spokesmen claimed that the assets under dispute were worth about $1 million, but the defendants said the value was much less. The Party won in San Francisco Superior Court, but in June 1995 a unanimous California State Court of Appeals reversed the decision and handed the property back to the foundation. There has also been a New York case, still in litigation, where a deceased communist left several hundred thousand dollars to executors, who were CPUSA leaders, to use on behalf of radical causes. When some of these executors went with the CoC, the CPUSA sued, arguing that all of the money should be under CPUSA control.[33]

Leaders of the Committees of Correspondence are shaping the organization as a coordinator for the American left, seeking to place its activists in a variety of left campaigns and guide the entire left by providing coherence to the multitude of hard-left agendas and by giving the left disciplined practical direction while avoiding divisive theoretical matters. Given the fractious nature of the American far left and the CoC's own lack of unified ideology, its small membership (1,710 as of October 31, 1994), and limited financial resources (its 1994 budget, including expenditure for its convention, barely topped $100,000—only a fraction of CPUSA expenditures), this may be a task beyond its capacity.[34]

For Further Reading

On the history of the CPUSA before the collapse of the Soviet Union, see Harvey Klehr and John Haynes, The American Communist Movement: Storing Heaven Itself(New York: Twayne Publishers, 1992); Irving Howe and Lewis Coser, The American Communist Party, A Critical History, 1919--1957 (Boston; Beacon Press, 1957); Theodore Press, The Roots of American Communism and Soviet Russia, The Formative Period (New York: Viking Press, 1960); Harvey Klehr, The Heyday of American Communism and Soviet Russia, The Formative Period (New York: Viking Press, 1960); Harvey Klehr, The Heyday of American Communism: The Depression Decade (New York: Basic Books, 1984); Maurice Isserman, Which Side Were You On? The American Communist Party During the Second World War (Middletown, CT: Wesleyan University Press, 1982); and Joseph R. Starobin, American Communism in Crisis,

Notes

1. Along with many New Left figures who joined the CPUSA in the late 1970s and 1980s, Davis was raised in a family with strong CPUSA links; so in a sense she and other "red-diaper babies" were returning to the movement from which they had come.
2. Harvey Klehr and John Earl Haynes, "The End: The CPUSA Expires," New Republic (March 23, 1992): 12-13.
3. Quoted in "American Communists Criticizing Moscow," Up Front 1, 1 (March 1989): 2.
4. Bill Turque, "The Party's Shaky Line," Newsweek (November 13, 1989): 48-49.
5. Soviet documents regarding subsidies to the CPUSA in the 1980s, including receipts signed by Gus Hall, are reproduced in John Earl Haynes and Harvey Klehr," 'Moscow Gold,' Confirmed at Last'?" Labor History 33, 2 (Spring 1992): 279-93.

6. Gus Hall's speech to the CPUSA National Conference on the Working Class, June 29-30, 1991, Chicago, reprinted in *People's Weekly World* (August 3, 1991): 4; Denise Winebrenner, "Gus Hall Examines Roots of Crises in U.S., Soviet Union," *People's Weekly World* (August 17, 1991): 4.

7. Erwin Marquit, "Organizational Crisis of Marxism-Leninism in the USA," October 3, 1992 (copy in possession of the authors). Marquit was a CPUSA leader in Minnesota.

8. "Resolutions of the National Committee of the CPUSA," *Political Affairs* (September-October 1991): 30; "CPUSA Statement on Soviet Crisis," *People's Weekly World* (August 31, 1991): 8; Klehr and Haynes, "The End: The CPUSA Expires."

9. Charlene Mitchell, James Jackson, and Danny Rubin, "If You Ask Me," *People's Weekly World* (September 7, 1991); "Initiative to Unite and Renew the Party" with attached cover letter. October 21, 1991: remarks by Herbert Aptheker, at an extraordinary membership meeting of the Communist Party of Northern California, February 9, 1992 (copies in possession of the authors).

10. Accounts of the convention include Max Elbaum, "Upheaval in the CPUSA: Death and Rebirth?" *Crossroads* (January 1992): 2-5: Marquit, "Organizational Crisis of Marxism-Leninism"; Margy Wilkinson (CPUSA delegate from Northern California), "My thoughts on the twenty-fifth convention CPUSA," December 21, 1991 (copy in possession of the authors); Jay Schaffner, "Dear Mom and Dad." December 22, 1991 (circulated as an open letter, copy in possession of the authors): "CPUSA to Dear Comrades," January 28, 1992 (CPUSA reply to Schaffner open letter, copy in possession of the authors); "Proceedings of the Twenty-fifth National Convention, Communist Party, USA" (copy in possession of the authors); remarks by Herbert Aptheker, extraordinary membership meeting; Barry Cohen, "CPUSA Convention—An Exercise in Exclusion," *Corresponder* 1, 1 (February 1992): 14. The *Corresponder* is the house journal of the Committees of Correspondence.

11. "Tim Wheeler Named Acting PWW Editor." *People's Weekly World* (December 21, 1991): 3.

12. Gus Hall's main report to the twenty-fifth CPUSA convention.

13. Laurie Goodstein, "Octogenarian U.S. Chairman Hall Insists the Party's Not Over Yet," *New York Times* (August 31, 1991).

14. "Professional" column, *Newsletter of Historians of American Communism* 9, 1 (March 1990): 1.

15. Gus Hall's speech to the CPUSA National Conference on the Working Class, June 29-30, 1991, Chicago.

16. Bruce Grant, "Industrial Concentration: Key to People's Advance." *Political Affairs* (December 1991): 18.

17. Marquit, "Organizational Crisis of Marxism--Leninism."

18. Jenny Scott, "Comrades Up in Arras," *New York Times* (December 21, 1994).

19. John Bachtell, "Communist Party USA: 'They should see us now!'" *People's Weekly World* (February 3, 1996): 9.

20. Marquit, "Organizational Crisis of Marxism-Leninism."

21. Kendra Alexander, Chair, Communist Party of Northern California, "Communist Party of Northern California Breaks with CPUSA," press release, February 13, 1992; Barry Cohen, "NY Declaration of Independence," press release, March 9, 1992 (copies in possession of the authors).

22. Accounts of the conference include Eleanor Shapiro, "Radicals Gather at Berkeley to Assess Left Wing's Future." *San Francisco Chronicle* (July 20, 1992); Max Elbaum, "A Jump Start and No Turning Back," *Crossroads* (September 1992); David Kidd, "Important Meeting for American Left," *Canadian Tribune* (July 27, 1992); Marcy Rein, "Reborn Socialists Regroup," *Guardian* (August 12-19, 1992).

23. "Where We Stand," *Perspectives for Democracy and Socialism in the 1990s: Proceedings of the Committees of Correspondence Conference* (New York: Committees of Correspondence, September 1992).

24. Ibid.

25. "Profiles of the NCC Members," *Corresponder* 2, 1 (January 1993): 10-13; Steve Willett, "Final Corrections to the Balloting Committee Report," Committees of Correspondence Conference, July 19, 1992 (copy in possession of the authors).

26. Examples of the diversity of views include Mark Solomon's "Looking Back Before Jumping Ahead," John Henry's "For a Freedom and Liberation Communist Tendency," Eric Fried's "The Genesis of 'Greening the Reds,'" and Michael A. Dover's "Organization and Democracy Cannot Be Separated," all in *Dialogue & Initiative* I (April 1992); Michael Eisenscher's "A Marxist-Leninist Party in Our Future?" Danny Rubin's "Is a Marxist-Leninist Party Needed?" Sushawn Robb's "The Importance of Left Coalitions/Networks," all in *Dialogue & Initiative* 2 (June 1992). *Dialogue & Initiative* was a CoC pre-conference internal discussion journal.

27. "Janet Quaife, Chair of Independent Communists of Minnesota to Dear Friends," March 22, 1994 (copy in possession of the authors).

28. Scott, "Comrades Up in Arms"; Mark Almberg, "An 'Alliance' with the CoC?" *People's Weekly World* (October 3, 1992) is just one of a number of dismissals of any CPUSA relationship with the CoC.

29. "Democratic Socialists of America (DSA)." *Corresponder* 1.7 (November 1992): 14; Barry Cohen. "Outreach," *Corresponder* 2, 2 (February-March 1992): 13; Jay Schaffner, "Report of the National Organizing Committee to the National Coordinating Committee," Committees of Correspondence, January 7, 1994 (copy in possession of the authors); Kendra Alexander obituary, *San Francisco Chronicle* (May 25, 1993).

30. Steve Willett, "Final Report Nominations/Balloting Committee," 1994 Committees of Correspondence Founding Convention, August 6, 1994 (copy in possession of the authors); Max Elbaum, "Settling in For a Long Haul," *Crossroads* 44 (September 1994); Barry Sheppard, "CoC Votes for Mass Workers Party," *Green Left Weekly* [Australia], carried on CoC internet site, August 19, 1994.

31. "For a Democratic and Socialist Future," founding convention of the Committees of Correspondence. July 22, 1994, Chicago (copy in possession of the authors). When adopted, the document was titled "Toward a Democratic and Socialist Future."

32. Ibid.

33. George Cothran, "Communists Sue Former Members Over Property," *San Francisco Weekly* (May 19, 1993): Barry Cohen, "The Strange Case of the CPUSA vs. Rubin, Linton and Aptheker," *Corresponder* 2, 2 (February-March 1992): 20-21: Scott, "Comrades Up in Arms"; "News Publisher Wins in Court." press release posted on CoC internet site, July 13, 1995.

34. "1994 Income Statement, January 1, 1994, Through October 31. 1994" and "CoC Memberships at October 31, 1994" (copies in possession of the authors).

13

Comrades in the Takeover Wars

American radical groups often have a short shelf life. They also have frequently acted in extreme and bizarre fashions. Few, however, have made as complete a turnabout as one small, violence-prone party whose activities led to a shocking moment of murder in 1979. Today, they seem determined to become the first Yuppie Communists.

Six years ago, five members of the Communist Workers Party, a Maoist sect, were gunned down by a band of American Nazis and Ku Klux Klansmen as they prepared to begin a "Death to the Klan" rally in Greensboro, NC. For weeks before the rally, the CWP had taunted white racists as cowards and dared them to appear. The CWP's tactics were based on its belief that the route to a Communist revolution was through armed confrontations with the Klan that would build up the CWP's prestige and eventually lead to armed insurrection. Its rhetoric was strident and its threats bloodcurdling. The CWP regularly denounced its critics as misleaders, cowards and "scum."

Such tactics and language did not prove very successful. Catapulted out of obscurity only by the Greensboro tragedy, the CWP briefly basked in the glow of media attention. Members were often in the news, threatening violence prior to marches and then attempting to disrupt the Democratic National Convention in 1980. Neither a state nor a federal prosecution resulted in any convictions for the killings; the Nazis and Klansmen pleaded self-defense and claimed they were provoked by the Communists. Earlier this year a federal jury awarded civil damages to several victims and next of kin, finding some of the racists and two Greensboro policemen liable for damages.

While the various trials were in progress, little was heard from the Communist Workers Party. The party did endorse Jesse Jackson's presidential bid in 1984, deciding that the five murdered party members "were among the forerunners of multinational unity in the South which Jesse Jackson's Rainbow Coalition is now striving to actualize." Since the CWP had scorned electoral politics and "reformers," that was a breathtaking assertion. There were signs, however, that all was not well in the CWP. Its newspaper, *Workers Viewpoint*, ceased publication in the summer of 1984 amid rumors that the party was reassessing its views.

The reassessment is now complete. And somewhat startling. The CWP has renamed itself the New Democratic Movement, recognizing that Americans are likely to respond more favorably to that name than to a group calling itself Communist. It has decided to combine Marxism-Leninism with American know-how to climb to power. The party's new heroes are the Founding Fathers. In place of such outmoded and foreign concepts as "democratic centralism," "working class" and "socialist revolution," it uses such terms as "accountability system."

The CWP has done more than simply change its language, however. Party leader Jerry Tung has developed a new tactic for achieving power. He advocates entering the Democratic Party and the union movement with the goal of capturing several state governments and union treasuries. Their money would then be used to gain control of American Express Co. (Comrade Tung having perceived that corporate takeovers are easily accomplished these days). Once in control of American Express, the radicals are confident they will run it more efficiently, lower interest rates, and thus drive competitors out of business. Mr. Tung has offered reassurance to any worried executives that their perks are in no danger: "We'll still pay the top managers salaries of two or three million dollars…we don't mind paying an American Express president to beat out VISA or MasterCard and take them over for us."

There is no sign that Wall Street has reacted to this new takeover bid. American Express does not appear to be frantically seeking a white knight. The nation's media have not been filled with speculation about the consequences of communism, Yuppie-style. This new tack is just as loony as the CWP's last one, albeit considerably less dangerous to life and limb. The CWP has demonstrated a maxim of one of its heroes, Karl Marx. Its history has been a movement from tragedy to farce.

14

The Case of the Legless Veteran

It is now thirty-seven years ago that the United States government decided James Kutcher was a security risk because of his membership in the Trotskyist Socialist Workers Party, then on the attorney general's list of subversive organizations. He was fired from his job as a clerk in the Vocational and Rehabilitation Division of the Veterans' Administration in Newark, New Jersey in 1948.

Kutcher no doubt would have remained an obscure victim of a security-conscious government except for one fact. He had lost both his legs in September 1943 when hit by a mortar shell in Italy. That the government would attack a legless veteran made Kutcher a minor celebrity and helped to generate support that ordinarily was not accorded radicals under attack. His case was fought in the courts for a decade; among his lawyers was Joseph Rauh. Kutcher got his job back in 1956; two years later he won back pay. The system of "capitalist justice," which Kutcher and his party so despised, had finally protected his rights, albeit after a protracted struggle and such sensitive actions as trying to cut off his disability pension one week before Christmas in 1955.

Prior to his case, Kutcher was an obscure member of the SWP. By his own admission, he had "no special talents" and did little more than "Jimmy Higgins" work for the party. The campaign on his behalf made him one of the most well-known Trotskyists in the country – a minimal distinction, to be sure, but one the SWP appreciated. Kutcher spoke widely around the country, and the party harped on his case; he wrote a book about his ordeal, and there was even a movie produced about it in 1981. Still, Kutcher remained a devoted rank-and-filer. He had joined the SWP in 1938 at the age of twenty-five; it had been the one great commitment of his life.

In 1983, Kutcher was expelled from the SWP, after forty-five years of devoted service. That in itself is unremarkable; radical movements have a savage history

Originally published in *Dissent*, Vol. 33, No. 1, Winter 1986 and reprinted with permission.

of turning on old comrades for various ideological errors, and longevity in the ranks is rarely allowed to override other virtues. Still, the story of Kutcher's expulsion is fascinating, both for what it tells us of the ethics of at least one radical group, and the ironic counterpoint it provides to Kutcher's treatment at the hands of the U.S. government years ago.

The Socialist Workers party has been in turmoil for the past several years. Hundreds of members have either resigned or been expelled, including a large proportion of the party's veterans whose tenure goes back to the 1930s.

The immediate cause of the dispute was the decision of the party leadership, particularly of General Secretary Jack Barnes, to jettison several core Trotskyist ideas, including the concept of permanent revolution. Barnes has condemned most of the world's Trotskyists as hopeless sectarians and indicated that a new international grouping of communists is in the making, to be led by the Cubans and the Sandinistas. Abandoning their traditional critique of Stalinist regimes as betrayers of revolution, the SWP has accepted Cuban leadership of the world revolutionary movement. Since the Cubans are, in turn, devoted clients of the Soviet Union, the SWP has become more pro-Soviet, even going so far as to mute its traditional defense of Soviet dissidents.

Kutcher was one of the many SWPers who were unhappy about the new course. In 1981, he abstained in the voting for the leadership's resolutions at the party convention. Nonetheless, he has resolutely maintained that he was not disruptive and did not violate any organizational rules or resolutions, even those he opposed. This point is important because the SWP, despite its name, is a Bolshevik organization that operates according to the rules of democratic centralism. There is supposed to be complete freedom within the party for discussion of all issues, but once a decision is made members are obligated to obey it.

The SWP has an elaborate and rather restrictive set of organizational norms. Discussion of the party's program is prohibited except for a three-month period prior to the party convention. Factions are prohibited. "Tendencies" are allowed to operate under the supervision of the party leadership, thus giving it the right to oversee the deliberations of any dissenters. Members are prohibited from discussing internal party matters with nonmembers.

Kutcher was not expelled for running afoul of any guidelines. He was framed on a different charge.

On August 14, 1983, the New York-New Jersey district membership met to hear reports on recent developments in the SWP. Four members of the National Committee had just been suspended as a result of inner-party turmoil. The National Convention, required to be held every year, had been postponed for a year, meaning that intraparty discussion of the abandonment of basic tenets of Trotskyism had not been able to take place. Expecting trouble from critical members, the party leadership appointed Dick McBride, a National Committee member, to act as a security guard at the meeting. According to McBride, during the discussion he saw Kutcher, seated in his wheelchair at the back of the hall, punch Berta Langston, another party member, with no provocation. Fearing an escalation of the conflict, McBride did not intervene and Langston moved away. One week later, McBride filed charges against Kutcher for committing violence against a comrade.

Kutcher was devastated. All that had happened, he protested to his branch organizer, was that Langston had stood in front of his wheelchair, blocking his view of the speakers. He had touched her on the back "either with my right index finger or, possibly, with that and the middle finger." When she turned around, he had silently indicated that she should move and she had done so. Kutcher was shocked by this "nightmare." He "turned hot with anger, feeling under intolerable pressure, isolated, helpless, humiliated and in despair." He asked if a friend could come to the trial with him. The answer was no. "I had," he recalled, "the same feeling many years ago when the government was persecuting me, but at least some of the time the government witch-hunters pretended I had some rights."

Three witnesses testified before the investigating committee – McBride, Langston, and George Breitman, a long-time SWP leader and friend of Kutcher's who gave Kutcher's version of the affair. McBride repeated his charges. Langston confirmed Kutcher's story in every detail, asserting that the charges were "completely baseless." Nevertheless, Kutcher's SWP branch concluded that McBride's version was correct, thus taking the word of a bystander over that of the two participants in the event. Because the severity of the violence was in doubt, Kutcher was only censured. Most of the report of the trial, however, charged that Kutcher had used violence and insulted women comrades in the past.

Kutcher, who had not been present, was particularly upset about the new charges, since he had not been informed of them prior to the trial. Despite their promises, SWP leaders refused to send Kutcher the trial transcript or allow him to see the report. Even though the branch members had heard the report the night of the trial – and Kutcher would also have heard it had he been well enough to attend – the party decided that he might circulate it outside the party and hence damage SWP security. In short, thirty-five years after the government labeled him a security risk, his SWP comrades agreed.

Emotionally distraught, Kutcher pleaded that he was unable to meet with an SWP delegation assigned to discuss his errors. On September 20 he was found guilty of violating party discipline for this infraction and instructed that he would be expelled if he did not meet the delegation by October 5. Kutcher wrote the party a plaintive letter, stating that he was not being defiant but had not attended the meeting because "I simply couldn't, physically or emotionally." He begged that his emotional turmoil be regarded as a legitimate excuse. He got no answer. When the deadline passed Kutcher was expelled. In April 1984, the National Convention rejected his appeal.

Despite his shabby treatment by the party to which he had devoted his life, Kutcher remained a true believer. "My loyalty to the party remains unchanged," he wrote in his appeal to the National Convention. He indicated that he did not want to be held responsible for any misuse of his case by enemies of the party. He now gives his allegiance to a Trotskyist splinter group, the Fourth Internationalist Tendency, composed of a few hundred people expelled from the SWP, including Breitman. Kutcher has been very ill, hospitalized for months because of his ailments. He may not live to realize his dream of being readmitted to the SWP.

It should come as no surprise that Marxist-Leninist groups, which demand strict adherence to every detail of every regulation by private organizations or the government, evince no strong attachment to such procedure themselves. Luckily for Kutcher, his former comrades only have the power to expel him from their ranks.

Part 3

Revisionism/Traditionalism Debate

15

A Vigil Against Totalitarianism

Particularly since the Vietnam War, often blamed on America's obsession with communism, anticommunism has rarely been fashionable in American intellectual circles. And few intellectuals were as obsessed with communism as Sidney Hook. It is, therefore, not surprising that he has not fared well in recent historical or autobiographical accounts of American life in the 1900s. In his autobiography, Irving Howe complained that on the communist issue "within that first-rate mind there had formed a deposit of sterility, like rust on a beautiful machine."[1] Alan Wald has charged that Hook was the model for those intellectuals who "became fanatical adherents" of the anticommunist ideology that marked America's transition from isolationism to imperialism.[2] Judy Kutulas chided such "extreme anticommunists" as Sidney Hook, who kept badgering "progressives" like Corliss Lamont about the political positions they had taken in the 1930s.[3]

Unlike many of his academic critics, Sidney Hook's knowledge of and hostility toward communism grew out of his own experience with the Communist Party. His long life intertwined with the issue of communism, from his early infatuation to disillusionment and his final deep hostility. At every stage of his professional life, he confronted communism and communists – as friends and allies, as subjects of study and friendly criticism, as intellectual rivals, and, finally, as relentless enemies. Hook was a passionate and fearsome polemicist who skewered communists and their allies for many years over many issues. While he gave no quarter, he was spared none either. At various times he was called a "Fascist and ally of Fascists," "a dirty, four-letter word," a "baboon of imperialism," an "American National Socialist," a "hook-worm," and a "counterrevolutionary reptile."

The recently published *Letters of Sidney Hook* provides, with two exceptions, a representative sample of Hook's initial flirtations and later confrontations with

Originally published in *Academic Questions* Summer 1996 and reprinted with kind permission of Springer Science and Business Media.

communism. The first letter in the anthology is dated 1929 and was written to his parents from Moscow, where Hook was working at the Marx-Engels Institute on a Guggenheim Fellowship. He praises the Soviet Union for nurturing the "seeds of the future."

By this time, Hook had already accumulated a decade of procommunist activity, not illustrated in this volume. As a student at City College of New York he was a founder of the Social Problems Club, where young communists and socialists adulated the new Soviet state. Although he never joined the Communist Party of the United States of America (CPUSA), Hook collaborated with it during the 1920s. Not only was his first wife a Party member, but Hook himself translated Lenin's *Materialism and Empiric Criticism* for International Publishers, the CPUSA's publishing arm, when he was still a graduate student. (The first edition, released in 1927, acknowledged Hook's contribution. Later editions, prepared when he had become persona non grata in the communist world, deleted his name, although sloppy editing left it in the book's index.)

In his autobiography, *Out of Step: An Unquiet Life in the 20th Century*, Hook admitted that in 1929 he was blind to the repression already a part of Soviet life. His faith in socialism and the USSR and his support for Soviet policies and educational theories persuaded him that whatever problems existed were the result of a society in transition, one that was overcoming the legacies of the past. When he returned to America, he continued to collaborate with the Communist Party, without sharing its ultrarevolutionary views.

Beginning in 1929, communist parties around the world, under orders from Moscow, had inaugurated the so-called "Third Period," during which they expected revolutionary upheavals in the capitalist countries. In addition to setting up separate, dual unions to compete with the AF of L, the CPUSA denounced socialists as social fascists and insisted that they were far more dangerous than were fascists themselves.

In spite of his scorn for these fatuous ideas, Hook joined with fifty-three other distinguished American intellectuals in 1932 to endorse the communist presidential ticket of William Z. Foster and James Ford. In his autobiography, Hook notes that, when he got around to reading Foster's campaign statement, *Toward Soviet America*, he was appalled at its antidemocratic tone. If so, he must have been curiously and uncharacteristically inattentive to communist rhetoric in the preceding three years. Unfortunately, the *Letters* are silent about this episode and Hook's close collaboration with the CPUSA.

The League of Professional Groups for Foster and Ford produced a widely read manifesto, *Culture and the Crisis*, but began to splinter apart soon after the election. The CPUSA tried, after a fashion, to entice Hook, whose writings on the Hegelian foundations of Marxism and efforts to reconcile Marxism with pragmatism had already established him as a talented Marxist thinker. He discussed his critique of orthodox Marxism with Earl Browder and other communist leaders and tells in his autobiography of a remarkable meeting in which Browder urged him to go to work for the CPUSA setting up an espionage network of scientists. In January 1933, the CPUSA's intellectual commissar, J. Jerome, launched an attack on Hook titled "Unmasking an American Revisionist of Marxism." But in March, Browder, while continuing to attack Hook, also printed his rejoinder to Jerome, the only time the Party dignified the views of an "enemy" in its theoretical journal.

Party orthodoxy could not, however, abide Hook or such other League heretics as Lewis Corey and James Rorty for long. And Hook finally concluded that the doctrine of social fascism was both stupid and dangerous, its having already contributed significantly to the triumph of Nazism in Germany. He joined with A. J. Muste in 1933 to form the American Workers Party (AWP), a Marxist revolutionary group whose unstated goal was to take communism away from the communists. For the next several years, Hook actively tried to build an alternative to the CPUSA, an effort doomed to failure. His unhappy experience in helping to broker the merger of the AWP with the Trotskyists (the Workers Party, created in late 1935) convinced him that revolutionary politics was a dead end. Hook also briefly became a public figure in this period; an article he wrote in 1934, originally titled "Communism Without Dogmas," was changed by the editor to "Why I Am a Communist." Eschewing subtle distinctions, the Hearst press in New York led a campaign to oust Hook from his teaching post at New York University. The dean at NYU defended his controversial philosopher on the grounds that Hook was only a "half-baked Communist."

Despite all the criticisms he had made of both communism and the CPUSA, Hook did not focus his attention or his critique on the Soviet Union until the Moscow purge trials led to his involvement, along with John Dewey, in attempting, first, to secure asylum for Leon Trotsky and then to investigate the charges made by the Soviet regime that Trotsky was a spy and traitor who had plotted to kill Stalin. To defend Trotsky's right to a hearing was to declare oneself an enemy of the Soviet Union and, in the view of many American intellectuals, most of whom were not communists, to ally oneself with fascism. Hook's old friend Corliss Lamont fervently defended the trials and all other manifestations of Soviet power. He signed manifestos denouncing Hook and John Dewey as fascists and became a cheerleader for the GPU, the Soviet secret police, praising the quality of Soviet justice. Hook's "extremism" in reminding Lamont and other fellow travelers of their enthusiasms earned lifelong enmity.

From the mid-1930s through the end of the 1940s Hook was prominently identified with a string of organizations dedicated to combating Stalinism in American intellectual life. The League of Professional Groups had been only one of the first communist efforts, and by no means the most successful, to attract intellectuals, writers, and artists to its orbit. When the Communist International finally abandoned the Third Period in 1935 and inaugurated a Popular Front, a number of new and seemingly more moderate organizations sprang up. The League of American Writers, the American Artists Congress, the American Committee for Intellectual Freedom and Democracy, and the Hollywood Anti-Nazi League, among others, enlisted hundreds of prominent figures who supported worthy causes, relentlessly and unconditionally defended the Soviet Union as a bulwark of democracy, and slandered its critics.

Sidney Hook took the lead in response. He devoted himself to exposing the lies and evasions of these groups and their supporters. He wrote to prominent people on their letterheads and asked if they really agreed with the statements being issued in their names. He badgered the "innocents" who lent their good names to questionable causes. He organized like-minded intellectuals to combat communist propaganda about the United States or the Soviet Union.

Tangling with Sidney Hook in argument was a sobering experience. In one series of letters to Jerome Davis, a Yale academic whose firing because of his political views had led to protest by the American Association of University Professors, Hook noted that he himself had worked to overturn Yale's decision. When Davis not only refused to help the Trotsky Defense Committee but also signed a letter prepared by the Communist Party denouncing it, Hook refused to accept his rationalizations, which included Davis's denial that the statement said what it said and went on to doubt that the Soviet Union persecuted anyone who was innocent. With impeccable logic and barely concealed scorn, Hook noted that his "first guess that either your name had been forged or that you had signed in carelessness" must have been in error and concluded that Davis had repudiated the very ideals he had once defended. When the Trotsky Defense Committee was attacked on the grounds that it constituted interference in the internal affairs of the Soviet Union, Hook responded that American liberals did not hesitate to interfere similarly in the internal affairs of Nazi Germany or other rightwing violators of democracy.

The Committee for Cultural Freedom (CCF), founded in 1939, denounced totalitarianism of both the Left and the Right. Such heresy earned it a concerted attack by some 400 communists and fellow travelers, including Corliss Lamont, I.F. Stone, Dashiel Hammett, Harry Ward, and Lillian Hellman, who called the equation of the Soviet Union with Nazi Germany a "fantastic falsehood" and labeled Hook, Dewey, and other members of the CCF "Fascists and allies of Fascists." Published one week before the Nazi-Soviet Pact, the attack contributed to the discrediting of Stalinism in the American intellectual community, exposing its fatuousness and viciousness.

After World War II, Hook revived the American Committee for Cultural Freedom to respond to the communist-orchestrated and inspired Cultural and Scientific Conference for World Peace at New York's Waldorf-Astoria Hotel in 1949. Rebuffed by organizers unwilling to allow him to present a paper defending the autonomy of science and protesting the notion that there existed "party" or "class" truths, Hook determined to expose the communist line dominating the affair. Displaying a talent for publicity, he succeeded in embarrassing astronomer Harlow Shapley of Harvard and a number of other prominent intellectuals who had given the event their support. Shapley retaliated by using his influence to keep Hook out of the American Institute of Arts and Sciences for many years.

Perhaps the most controversial aspect of Hook's relationship with communism was his position on the employment of communists in American universities. His experiences with the CPUSA had convinced Hook that communists were not free agents, or heretics, but conspirators, obliged to carry out the Party line. Accordingly, he insisted that, while they deserved constitutional protections, they had no right to jobs which required an open mind and commitment to the pursuit of the truth. He believed that there was a prima facie case that a member in good standing of the CPUSA was unfit to serve on a university faculty. In contrast to the McCarthyites, Hook insisted that it was the responsibility of college faculties, not congressional committees or public pressure, to judge their colleagues. He also denied that such faculties should actively seek to discover communist affiliations. If a case arose, however, Hook believed that it would be up to the faculty member to demonstrate that he was fit to teach and was not using the classroom as a forum or trimming his teaching and research to fit Party positions.

In an age when using the classroom as a bully pulpit to advance a professor's political opinions is commonplace, when not just courses but entire departments proudly advertise their commitment to one or another oppressed group or ideological perspective, when the idea that academics are engaged in a search for the truth sounds like a quaint pre-postmodernist illusion, Hook's demand that the professoriate take seriously its collective responsibility for the educational enterprise sounds otherworldly and repressive. Hook was right about the nature of the CPUSA. It was a conspiratorial organization. On balance, he was wrong about communist academics. Most were not conspirators, but naive, although a few were dishonest men and women who betrayed their calling. With few exceptions they posed little threat to the academic community, or at least not enough to justify efforts to remove them, although the exposure of their views was entirely appropriate.

Sidney Hook paid a price for his convictions, both when he was a "communist" and when he was an anticommunist. The youthful Hook, a Jew with a reputation as a radical, could never hope to gain an appointment at a prestigious American university. The older Hook, never willing to back down from a fight—indeed, pugnaciously seeking out conflict—sacrificed professional prestige and put off academic work to combat communism. In the academic world, he was, he wrote to a friend, about as popular as a porcupine: "God knows I'd like to keep my mouth shut and pen quiet for a while, but unfortunately when I do nobody else does (with a few exceptions, of course). The result is that even when my colleagues agree with me, they don't like me."

Sidney Hook never stopped arguing. Devoted to discovering the truth and committed to democratic values, he may have done more than any other

American intellectual to combat one of the great evils of the twentieth century. Our country and our culture are the better for his confrontations with communism.

Notes

1. Irving Howe, *A Margin of Hope* (New York: Harcourt, Brace, Jovanovich, 1982), 210.
2. Alan Wald, *The New York Intellectuals* (Chapel Hill: University of North Carolina Press, 1987), 5.
3. Judy Kutulas, *The Long War* (Durham, NC: Duke University Press, 1995), 200.

16

Seeing Red *Seeing Red*

Seeing Red: Stories of American Communists is a very sympathetic portrayal of the political activities of a group of ex-Communists and a few current Party members, all of whom came of age during the 1930s. The film has received generally respectful reviews and was nominated for, but did not receive, an Academy Award for Best Documentary. The filmmakers, James Klein and Julie Reichart, veterans of the New Left, have frankly admitted that they sought political lessons from the collapse of the Old Left and the movie has been used for fundraisers around the country by the Democratic Socialists of America. The Communist Party has complained that *Seeing Red* adopts the political perspective of the John Gates "wing" of the Party, which largely left it in the late 1950s and has criticized the movie for leaving the impression that the present-day CPUSA is irrelevant.

In recent years there has been a spate of documentaries on old radicals and radical movements, ranging from the gentle Jewish anarchists of *Free Voice of Labor* to the tough organizers of *The Wobblies*. Like most of these films, *Seeing Red* is a blend of interviews and documentary footage. Such movies run a great danger of distorting the historical record. It is not only that it can be risky to trust the memories of old people about events of forty or fifty years ago. The faces and voices of these old radicals are often so arresting and striking that the audience wants to believe their accounts. Moreover, the filmmakers naturally pick and choose what interviews to include—Klein and Reichart did 400 and used only fifteen. Because most Americans know very little about American radicalism, they are ill-equipped to judge either how representative the interviewees are, how accurat the filmmakers have been. In the case of *Seeing Red*, the answers are that the Communists are not entirely representative, their recollections are presented in a confusing way and Reichart and Klein have dramatically and seriously distorted the historical record.

Originally published in *Labor History*, Winter 1985 (http://www.informaworld.com) and reprinted with permission.

American Communism was largely an immigrant phenomenon. Not until 1935 was a majority of the Party native-born. A substantial number even of these Communists were the children of immigrants. Approximately 30-40 percent of the Party was Jewish and there were a substantial number of Finns. In a *Cineaste* interview Klein explained that they balanced the interviews to reflect how "broad the Party was." That may make for a more interesting and varied movie, but it also leaves a distorted impression, especially insofar as only three of the fifteen are Jewish and not one of these makes any mention at all of their background. There is not a mention of the immigrant, big-city milieu out of which American communism arose. In fact, there is virtually no discussion of just what led any of the fifteen to join the Party or when they signed up. Were they from radical homes? Did they join the Party under the spur of the Depression? Because of the rise of fascism? We never learn.

Most confusing of all is *Seeing Red*'s treatment of the 1930s. To be a Communist in 1931 was rather different than to be one in 1938. The film never hints that the CPUSA was a revolutionary party for half the decade and a reformist one for the remainder. It glosses over the simple fact that the Party line changed rather dramatically not just in the mid-1930s but in 1939 as well. As a result, the nature of the Communist movement is hopelessly confused. It is hard to know if those interviewed simply ignored this point or whether Reichart and Klein chose to omit it. In either case, it results in "stories" which are ahistorical.

The narrator presents Party members as people who had decided "to challenge the very fabric of their society" by joining the CPUSA. They were, it is suggested, revolutionaries who had constructed a thoroughgoing counter-culture. Dramatic archival footage of Communists battling the police on the streets of New York, militant protesters confronting authority, and hunger marchers demanding relief are used to reinforce the image of an organization not afraid to do battle with the government.

On the other hand, in a rather jarring counterpoint, there are clips of May Day demonstrators waving American flags and Communist organizers building the CIO. The narrator discusses Communist support for Social Security and one ex-Communist, Marge Frantz, explains that she and her comrades considered themselves "small d democrats."

Both of these contradictory images were true but obviously not at the same time. *Seeing Red* does not explain that the CPUSA was revolutionary from 1929 to 1935 because the Communist International ordered such policies. It did confront police and participate in pitched battles on American streets. It did call for the overthrow of capitalism and made no bones about its contempt for "bourgeois democracy." Communist demonstrators did not wave American flags or celebrate American culture. (Questioned by a congressional committee in 1930, Party leader William Foster proudly noted that Communists had only one flag and it was red.) Not so coincidentally, the Party made very little headway in America during this period, even though it was the height of the Depression.

Although *Seeing Red* suggests that it was natural to become a Communist during this era, relatively few people did and even fewer stayed in the Party.

How many of the fifteen interviewees joined the CPUSA during this "Third Period?" Since the Party was not interested in reform, what attracted them? Were they really just another group of democrats? How did they feel about calling Norman Thomas and the Socialist Party social-fascists? We never learn.

From late 1935 to 1939, the Communist Party, in line with Comintern direction, called for a Popular Front against fascism. It no longer challenged the very fabric of American society but attempted to join the political mainstream. By 1937, it had enthusiastically endorsed the New Deal and Franklin Roosevelt, both of which it had harshly denounced earlier in the decade. Earl Browder explained that Communism was twentieth-century Americanism and Thomas Jefferson a precursor of Karl Marx. The Party faithful lustily sang the Star-Spangled Banner at Madison Square Garden rallies. Communists seemed indistinguishable from liberals, particularly since so many now remained silent about their true political allegiance. Under these conditions, the Party prospered, growing to nearly 100,000 members.

How many of the fifteen interviewees joined *this* Communist Party? Since it was the Party's proudest claim to fame that it was prematurely anti-fascist, how did they react to the Nazi-Soviet Pact in 1939? Were they jarred by the return to the hard-line anti-New Deal policies of the early 1930s? The narrator briskly justifies the pact in a sentence or two as an understandable Soviet response to Western intransigence and merely notes that things were confused until Hitler's attack on Russia and America's entry into the war once again allowed American Communists to regain their bearings. How did these "small d democrats" respond when Gil Green, still a Communist today, and a consultant for *Seeing Red,* explained in 1940 that France and Nazi Germany were essentially similar regimes and Communists could not choose between them?

The absence of any historical perspective contributes to errors in both fact and interpretation in *Seeing Red.* Some are minor, but cumulatively they leave a distorted picture of American Communism.

Some examples:

1. There is documentary footage of Dorothy Healey organizing agricultural workers during a 1937 strike in California; the narration and context implies that workers were responding to Communist leadership and positions. At the time, however, Healey was working for a CIO union and the strike was hardly revolutionary. A 1934 strike, led by a Communist union in which she took part, was crushed.
2. The camera pans over a photograph of a smiling, enthusiastic group of young radicals. They are not, however, Communists, since several are brandishing the *Workers Age*, a publication of the radical splinter group led by Jay Lovestone. The CPUSA regarded the Lovestoneites as renegades and akin to fascists.

3. The narrator explains that the Party-dominated Unemployed Councils "effectively pushed for social security and unemployment insurance." In fact, the Party sent a representative to testify before Congress against those Roosevelt Administration measures. The Communist proposal for unemployment insurance, made in the Third Period, demanded that it be administered by workers' councils and the Party called for a vote *against* the bill which became law even though the only alternative was no law at all.
4. The narrator explains that the Communist Party "protested lynchings and worked for voting rights" in the South. Totally ignored is the most controversial Party program for Negroes-self-determination in the Black Belt. Designed in Moscow and imposed on the Party in 1930, it remained Communist policy for most of the decade.
5. Documentary footage from the early 1930s is intermixed with footage from the late 1930s. At one point, Oscar Hunter talks about the John Reed Clubs marching on May Day; a film clip of a May Day parade follows but it is apparently from the late 1930s, after the John Reed Clubs had been liquidated on Party orders.
6. Documentary footage and contemporary interviews are used to suggest that Communists who defied the House Un-American Activities Committee and Senator Joseph McCarthy did so because of their belief in civil liberties. Neither the narrator nor any of the interviewees touch on the Party's opposition to civil liberties for "fascists" or its support for the prosecution of Trotskyists under the Smith Act in 1941.
7. A segment on post World War II anti-communism features Texas Congressman Martin Dies in footage from an earlier period.

Seeing Red caricatures anti-Communism. It uses footage from a dreadful anti-communist movie, vignettes of Richard Nixon and J. Edgar Hoover and an incredible scene of Herbert "I Led Three Lives" Philbrick teaching that Communists are "lying, dirty, shrewd, murderous and determined." The movie implies that anticommunism attracted only fools, knaves, or frauds. The CPUSA was hated and despised for good and bad reasons; this film simply pretends the good reasons did not exist. One ex-Communist admits that the Party and its members ignored the relationship between ends and means and thus justified a lot of "crappy little things" but no concrete examples are offered. The Party's zig-zag lines and assaults, both verbal and organizational, on other groups, particularly those of a left-wing or liberal bent, either go unmentioned or are treated as minor blemishes on an otherwise spotless record. But it was the organizational structure and the tactics of the Party and its loyalty to one of the two most murderous regimes in all of human history (the narrator delicately notes that Stalin murdered "thousands") which made anti-communism so powerful a force. And it was the Party's history which had alienated so many of its previous allies, even if it does not excuse the persecution suffered by many Communists during the McCarthy period.

Most of the people Reichart and Klein interviewed left the Communist Party as a result of Khrushchev's revelations of Stalin's crimes. They vividly testify to the shock and outrage they felt. Dorothy Healey admits that she had been "a little Stalin" in her Southern California bailiwick (although the film does not mention that she remained in the CPUSA until the early 1970s). But Healey also adds that she has no regrets—only "enormous pride"—for what she and her generation did, a sentiment seemingly shared by most of the ex-Communists and the filmmakers. What some of them regret is that they were not more willing to question the Soviet Union or their Party's undemocratic structure.

It may well be that these people were drawn to the Communist Party by the noblest of motives and a high degree of idealism. They fought many good fights and exhibited large doses of courage and idealism. Their lives, however, have a tragic dimension which *Seeing Red* largely misses. Joining the Communist Party was a political choice which had political consequences. There were other radical groups one could join in the 1930s. There were earlier revelations of Stalin's crimes than those of 1956. There were frequent changes in Party policy. Reichart and Klein are so intent on showing that Communists can be ordinary people—laughing, singing, dancing—and probing how their subject "felt" (after one Spanish Civil War veteran describes seeing his comrades die at Jarama, Reichart asks him, "how did you feel about that?") that they skip over the far more important issues of what the American Communist Party did to the American left and how it used and misused the idealism of a generation. Both on historical and interpretive grounds *Seeing Red* is a major disappointment.

17

Fellow Traveling is Alive and Well: The Rosenbergs' New Apologist

with John Earl Haynes

Published last year in twenty-four volumes, the *American National Biography* has been justifiably praised by reviewers. It received the American Library Association's Dartmouth Medal as the best reference work of the year. Sponsored by the American Council of Learned Societies, the *ANB* replaces the venerable but out-of-date *Dictionary of American Biography*, first issued in 1928 as a standard biographical resource, and is already on the shelves of thousands of school and academic libraries.

A reference work like the *ANB* is expected to offer reliable information and reflect the consensus of the best scholarly thinking, not to offer one-sided interpretations or disputatious views. Entries are carefully vetted and edited through several iterations. What, then, possessed the editors of the *ANB* to print a bizarre, even absurd, entry on Julius and Ethel Rosenberg, who were convicted for espionage on behalf of the Soviet Union and executed in 1953?

For scholars who know the Rosenberg case, the *ANB* entry is either a source of amusement, embarrassment, or irritation, but no reputable scholar can take it seriously as an accurate summary of what is known about the Rosenbergs or their case. For example, it has been common knowledge for years that both Rosenbergs were Communists and that Julius was an active figure among student Communists at CCNY. The *ANB* entry camouflages this information behind euphemisms (Julius was "active in left-wing student circles") and evasions (he was fired from the Signal Corps for being a Communist but "he denied" it).

Without actually saying so, the entry suggests they were religious Jews, both raised in "orthodox Jewish families" and that "Julius also received religious

Originally published in the *Weekly Standard*, April 10, 2000 and reprinted with permission.

instruction at Downtown Talmud Torah and Hebrew High School." Although the two abandoned their youthful Jewish orthodoxy for communism—a loyalty they retained until their execution—this goes unmentioned in the essay. But the author's conclusion of the case having an "anti-Semitic subtext" remains. A student unfamiliar with the Rosenberg case, exactly the audience that will consult the *ANB,* will come away with no knowledge of their actually being Communists but with the definite impression that they were executed because they were Jews.

The entry offers an equally distorted version of the Rosenbergs' trial, portraying the evidence against them as weak and probably perjured. It devotes several laudatory paragraphs to writers and books that uphold their innocence and, in contrast, dismisses with a single sentence the most detailed and scholarly account of the case, Radosh and Milton's *The Rosenberg File,* which found them guilty. As for new evidence from Soviet archives and interviews with Julius Rosenberg's KGB control officer, the essay cavalierly and incorrectly dismisses such material as "discredited." Even more dishonestly, there is no mention that Walter and Miriam Schneir, longtime defenders of the Rosenbergs, reluctantly admitted several years ago that Julius was indeed a spy.

Those who have concluded that the Rosenbergs committed espionage are denounced as "conservative writers" and "conservatives and Anti-Communist or Cold War liberals" for whom their "unquestioning belief in the Rosenbergs' guilt" was "a kind of loyalty oath." In contrast, upholding the innocence of the Rosenbergs was "the most significant expression of resistance to the spread of the domestic Cold War in the United States" by "radicals and anti-Cold War liberals."

The author of this tendentious essay is Norman Markowitz, a tenured professor at Rutgers University and one of the few academicians who writes for the *People's Weekly World*—the newspaper of the Communist Party of the United States—and its theoretical magazine, *Political Affairs.* He specializes in personally attacking not only those "conservative" scholars who have dared to suggest the right side won the Cold War, but also liberals and former allies who have been persuaded by new evidence of the CPUSA's involvement in Soviet espionage, offering party-line justifications and rationales for his conclusions. Back in the early 1980s, at a meeting of the Historians of American Communism, an academic group in which both of us have been active, Markowitz announced to all that he was most proud of having just joined the CPUSA, surely one of the prime examples of jumping onto a sinking ship.

It is no surprise, of course, that some of the last Marxist-Leninists in the world reside in American universities. But ideological zealots with axes to grind are not usually picked to write entries on controversial political figures for a standard reference work. The Rosenberg entry has some incongruous wording, and this may reflect the *ANB* editors' belated realization that they had made an unfortunate choice in an author. The first sentence of the essay reads

"Rosenberg, Ethel (28 Sept. 1915-19 June 1953), and Julius Rosenberg (12 May 1918-19 June 1953), spies," followed by an essay devoted to the message that they were not spies. (Even more bizarre, the online version of the *ANB* calls them "accused spies," as if they had not even been convicted.) And after many paragraphs devoted to arguing for the Rosenbergs' innocence, the essay ends with a non-sequitur: "The Rosenberg case has remained subject to debate and reinterpretation."

But to scholars of the Rosenberg case the main points are not subject to debate. The evidence available in the 1950s was enough to sustain their conviction. And more recent documents available from Russia and the Venona files make clear that Julius headed an extensive Soviet espionage apparatus, engaged in atomic spying, and his wife Ethel not only knew about his activities but actively assisted her husband. About the only disputed question is whether the death penalty was excessive.

Norman Markowitz may be so ideologically blind as not to see this, but the editors of the *American National Biography* should have been more clear-eyed. Scholars will be unaffected by Markowitz's absurdity, but the ANB's editors have allowed this distortion of historical fact to be palmed off on many thousands of unsuspecting students for decades to come.

18

On the Waterfront without a Clue

with John Earl Haynes

On the Waterfront is one of the most honoured films in Hollywood history. The 1954 release reaped eight Oscars for best film, best actor, best director, best screenplay, best supporting actress, best cinematography, best art director, and best editing. It has also generated frequent controversy because its director, Elia Kazan, had testified before the House Committee on Un-American Activities just two years before the movie was released. Kazan "named names" of associates who had belonged to the Communist Party with him in the 1930s.[1] Denounced as an informant, he went on to make a movie that justified "squealing."

A significant section of the Hollywood community never forgave him. When the Motion Picture Academy gave Kazan a lifetime achievement award in 1999, there were organized protests outside the awards ceremony and a substantial segment of the audience refused to applaud when Martin Scorsese and Robert DeNiro made the presentation to the infirm, eighty-nine-year-old Kazan, who died in 2003.[2]

Kazan's decision to name names, his subsequent defense of his actions and his refusal over the years to apologize have provoked intense controversy. Although *On the Waterfront* was commonly interpreted as Kazan's justification for his decision, some critics have insisted that informing on Communists and informing on mobsters are not comparable, and thus Kazan's rationale for his actions is unpersuasive. Whatever one's opinion of Kazan or his movie, it is an arguable point. A new book, however, goes beyond arguing about the moral validity of Kazan's actions by distorting nearly everything about *On the Waterfront*.

Blacklisted: The Film Lover's Guide to the Hollywood Blacklist is a directory of films "written, directed or produced" by victims of the blacklist or by those

---

Originally published in *Film History*, v. 16, n. 4, 2004, produced by Indiana University Press and reprinted with permission.

who escaped it by offering friendly testimony to HUAC.[3] Its authors, Paul Buhle and Dave Wagner, have written numerous books on Hollywood radicals and, in Buhle's case, on a variety of themes in American radical history filled with factual errors, dubious claims, and incorrect information, much of it serving to present American Communists as innocent victims of a repressive American society. Many of these errors, however, deal with topics so esoteric that most readers cannot judge for themselves just how egregiously he violates basic standards of accuracy.

In their book, Buhle and Wagner demonstrate with stunning clarity in one short entry just how driven they are by ideological blinders. *On the Waterfront* was based on Malcolm Johnson's Pulitzer Prize winning reporting series (twenty-four articles) published in the *New York Sun* in 1949. Later published in book form as *Crime on the Labor Front*, the series described the domination of International Longshoreman's Association locals in New York by organized crime.[4] In 1950, Governor Thomas Dewey ordered the New York State Crime Commission to investigate corruption on the docks, and recommended reforms. The commission immediately ran into an obstacle – only a few longshoremen were willing to testify about conditions on the docks. Enough evidence emerged of mob control of the waterfront, however, to lead to the creation of a permanent Waterfront Commission to oversee labor relations and weed out criminal elements.

The film is set in the context of the New York State Crime Commissions' investigation. It depicts the dilemmas of Terry Malloy, played by Marlon Brando, a washed-up boxer working as a longshoreman who, driven by love for Edie (Eva Marie Saint), and advised by an activist priest (Karl Malden, modeled on Father John Corridan of New York's St. Xavier Labor School), comes to realize that the longshoreman's code of silence, supposedly allowing the dock workers to take care of their own problems without outside interference, actually served to protect gangsters who controlled the local union. Risking both violence from the mob and ostracism by family and friends, Terry testifies against John Friendly (played by Lee J. Cobb), the union's corrupt boss.

Left-wing critics have seen the movie as an apologia for "naming names." Script-writer Budd Schulberg had also been a candid witness before HUAC.[5] Both he and Kazan seemed to be suggesting that, like Malloy, as members of the Communist Party they had been complicit in a criminal conspiracy. Remaining silent only served the interests of the criminals. Telling the truth allowed Terry to break the grip of the mob and serve the interests of the hardworking men they had exploited.

Buhle and Wagner declare that the movie was the "friendly witness" *High Noon*, but they get virtually everything about it wrong. Their first claim is that "it is only after the audience's identification with Terry is complete that it is finally revealed that the 'gangsters' are officers of the dockworker's union." In fact, the identification of the local as gangster-controlled takes place early in the film, long before Terry becomes a sympathetic character. More outrageously, Buhle and Wagner solemnly intone, "the Longshoreman's union, the ILA, was not in the hands of gangsters but of their bitter enemies on the Left, who are the real targets of the film." In reality the national and local leadership of the International Longshoreman's Association (part of the AFL-American Federation of Labor) was overwhelmingly and stridently anti-Communist. Further, a substantial number of ILA locals, particularly in New York, were mob-run as the Crime Commission documented and the film depicted.

Indeed, so entrenched was the mob in the union that the AFL expelled the International Longshoreman's Association and attempted, unsuccessfully, to create a rival gangster-free union. Buhle and Wagner add more historical fiction to their account, writing that when the film was made in late 1953, "the Republican governor of New York and the Eisenhower administration were attempting to assert direct political control over the New York waterfront unions as the first step in acquiring control...of unions nationwide. The target on the docks was the hiring hall, the source of union power, hard-won during the Depression. Dewey and the feds wanted the state to take over the hiring halls, fingerprint and register longshoreman [sic.] and blacklist "undesirable" workers. It hardly seems a matter of chance that this very issue is at the centre of the film." But *the ILA didn't have hiring halls*. An entirely different union, the left-wing International Longshoremen and Warehousemens Union led by Harry Bridges on the West Coast, did, but on the East Coast the ILA used a system called the "shape-up."[6]

Under the "shape-up" system ILA-approved foremen held informal dockside meetings with crowds of longshoremen without a job that day. Job tokens were then passed out by the foremen until all jobs were assigned. As the movie documents, the ILA-sanctioned shape-up was a source of corruption.

The foremen distributing the job tickets sometimes demanded wage kickbacks, others gave preference to family and friends, and corrupt ILA officials denied jobs to union members who challenged their control of the local. One of the most dramatic scenes in *On the Waterfront* depicts the shape-up, with a crowd of desperate longshoremen pleading with a mean-spirited foreman and being forced to abase and humiliate themselves to get a day's work. Nor are Buhle and Wagner right about the "Republican governor" attacking the hiring hall. The New York crime commission, which had been created by Governor Dewey, denounced the shape-up and urged the creation of a joint union-shipper hiring hall as a solution.

The tendentious Buhle-Wagner review concludes with a denunciation of *On the Waterfront* as an "unapologetically anti-union" film. Only critics who cannot differentiate a Communist from a mobster and a mobster from a union leader could be so obtuse. With so careless and inaccurate a description of one of the most famous films ever made by a Communist or ex-Communist, one can only imagine how Buhle and Wagner's *Blacklisted* deals with the other 900 or so entries.

Notes

1.   Kazan discusses and defends his testimony in Elia Kazan, *Elia Kazan: A Life* (New York: Alfred A. Knopf, 1988), and Elia Kazan, *Kazan: The Master Director Discusses his Films: Interviews with Elia Kazan*, with Jeff Young (New York: Newmarket Press, 1999).
2   For contrasting views of the episode, see Richard Cohen, "A Salute to Elia Kazan," *Washington Post*, 26 January 1999, and David Thomson, "What Elia Kazan Won't Hear at the Oscars," *Washington Post*, 21 March 1999.
3.   Paul Buhle and David Wagner, *Blacklisted: The Film- Lover's Guide to the Hollywood Blacklist* (New York: Palgrave Macmillan, 2003).
4.   Malcolm M. Johnson, *Crime on the Labor Front* (New York: McGraw-Hill, 1950).
5.   Budd Schulberg, *On the Waterfront: A Screenplay* (Carbondale: Southern Illinois University Press, 1980) includes an "afterword" by Schulberg discussing the controversy about the movie and his earlier participation in the CPUSA.
6.   The ILWU, created in the 1930s as part of the CIO, had driven the ILA from the West Coast but never managed to displace the AFL's ILA on the East Coast. By 1950, however, the ILWU had left the CIO, one step ahead of being expelled due to its Communist leadership.

19

Radical History

with John Earl Haynes

In Israel's war of independence in 1948, American Communists were deeply involved in the covert shipment of arms to the new state of Israel, and Communists were prominent among those Americans wounded or killed in battles protecting Israel from Arab attack. How do we know this? It says so in a standard reference book found in hundreds of American libraries. The *Encyclopedia of the American Left,* published by Oxford University Press, was selected by *Choice* and *Library Journal* as one of the ten best reference books published in 1990. It sold so well that a second edition appeared in 1998. Reference books are expected to summarize the scholarly consensus and to present reliable information. In fact, these claims about the role of American Communists in Israel's founding, made in the second edition, have no basis whatsoever in any historical literature. Yet this and other distortions in this reference work have gone unchallenged by the historical profession.

This last year has not been good for the reputation of American historians. The first exhibit: Joseph Ellis, a professor at Mount Holyoke College, winner of a National Book Award for his biography of Thomas Jefferson and the Pulitzer Prize for *Founding Brothers.* The *Boston Globe* discovered that, contrary to what he told his classes and claimed in interviews, Ellis had never fought in Vietnam, worked in the civil rights movement in Mississippi, or even been a high school football hero. Embarrassed by revelations that Ellis had lied to his students, Mount Holyoke after some hesitation suspended him for a year without pay and lifted his endowed chair.

Ellis's classroom transgressions were bad enough, but at least no evidence has come forward regarding irregularities in his books and scholarly works.

Originally published in *New Criterion*, June 2002 and reprinted with permission.

But not long after Ellis had been identified as a fantasist, the best-selling author and historian Stephen Ambrose was exposed as a plagiarist. Fred Barnes of the *Weekly Standard* noted the disturbing similarity between passages in *The Wild Blue,* his popular account of B-29 combat missions over Europe, and a previously published book, Thomas Childers's *Wings of Morning.* Sleuths quickly unearthed four additional Ambrose books with substantial borrowing from other writers dating back to 1975. Coming just weeks after the considerable success of the World War II miniseries *Band of Brothers*, based on his book, the charges received considerable attention. Ambrose, a former professor at the University of New Orleans, admitted the unauthorized borrowing, explained that his books are researched and written by a team of employees, expressed mild remorse, and suggested that the plagiarism issue was something that academics took too seriously. His publisher did not seem overly concerned that its best-selling author repeatedly used other writers' words.

While journalists were scouring Ambrose's books, another high-profile scholar, Doris Kearns Goodwin, came under fire for the same offense. Formerly a professor of government at Harvard, the best-selling author of *the Fitzgeralds and the Kennedys* and a Pulitzer Prize winner for *No Ordinary Time* about Franklin and Eleanor Roosevelt still serves on the Board of Overseers of Harvard University, an institution that takes student plagiarism very seriously. Goodwin confessed to extensive, unattributed, and improper use of material and to making a private financial settlement to Lynne McTaggart, author of a biography of Kathleen Kennedy. Goodwin's embarrassment was compounded not only because she was forced to admit to additional acts of plagiarism in other books but also because she had previously publicly chastised Joe McGinness for improperly borrowing from *her* own work. She attributed the plagiarism to her sloppy note-taking methods. Goodwin stepped down from service as a commentator on *The NewsHour* with Jim Lehrer, but, despite calls from the *Harvard Crimson* for her removal, she remains on the Harvard Board.

The most serious recent charges of academic fraud, however, were leveled at the Emory University historian Michael Bellesiles. In 2000, reviewers hailed his *Arming America: The Origins of a National Gun Culture* as a major work of scholarship destined to change the terms of the debate on firearms in American life. Bellesiles claimed that he had demonstrated that gun ownership was a far less common phenomenon in early American life than had been widely assumed, and his publisher advertised the book as a direct challenge to the National Rifle Association and its values. In addition to a glowing front-page review in the *New York Times*, *Arming America* was praised by academic historians and pundits and received the prestigious Bancroft Prize, awarded by Columbia University for the best book in American history. Within a year, however, disturbing questions about Bellesiles' use of sources and data began to emerge. Critics were unable to find not merely some of the documents he cited, but some of the document *collections* he had claimed to have examined. Skeptics also discovered he had not quoted accurately from records they did unearth, and they were unable to verify a number of his claims. Quantitative historians demonstrated that figures he had calculated about the percentages of colonists who owned guns were mathematically implausible and based on flawed sampling techniques. By the end of 2001, Emory University had undertaken an investigation to determine if he had committed fraud, and, if so, how he should be penalized.

The charges against Bellesiles are of a different magnitude than the sins of Ellis, Ambrose, and Goodwin. Whatever their culpability, none has been accused of inventing documents or deliberately misquoting or mischaracterizing historical evidence in the service of an ideological cause. But such actions, while certainly not common among historians, are, unfortunately, not once-in-a-blue-moon occurrences.

Paul Buhle is a faculty member in American Civilization at Brown University and one of the luminaries in the study of American radicalism. Like many of his colleagues in this area, he has impeccable radical credentials. He attended the University of Illinois, where he became a socialist and activist in Students for a Democratic Society during the 1960s. At a brief stop-over he started *Radical America*, a journal devoted to American history and popular culture, before arriving at the University of Wisconsin in Madison in 1967 for further graduate training. While his SDS colleagues turned to violence and increasingly apocalyptic rhetoric, Buhle nurtured *Radical America*, which was supported by grants from left-wing foundations and devoted to "throwing monographs at an intellectually keen audience" instead of bombs.

Even before he received his Ph.D. in American history in 1975 for a dissertation entitled *Marxism in the US 1900-1940*, Buhle had made a mark as a prominent figure among New Left historians. Since then he has written, co-authored, or edited at least eighteen books and innumerable articles. He writes for such journals as *Radical History Review*—a publication that plainly states it "rejects conventional notions of scholarly neutrality and 'objectivity,' and approaches history from an engaged, critical, political stance"—and contributes regularly to *Tikkun*. As the history profession has become increasingly politicized in recent decades, Buhle has increasingly written for more mainstream journals, including the prestigious *Journal of American History*, and has contributed to the Organization of American Historians' professional *Newsletter*. He founded and continues to direct the Oral History of the American Left at the Tamiment Library of New York University, an ambitious effort to develop an extensive archive of interviews with hundreds of radical activists. Along with his wife, his fellow Brown historian Mari Jo Buhle, a recipient of a MacArthur Foundation "genius grant," and Dan Georgakas, Buhle co-edited the *Encyclopedia of the American Left*.

There is no reason why radical historians cannot do good history; one can disagree with the conclusions another historian has reached, dispute the significance he places on certain facts, or challenge the interpretive framework he uses, and still recognize that he has illuminated a problem, or uncovered new information, or challenged old preconceptions. Years ago, in *Radical America*, Buhle himself insisted that radical historians had to be scrupulous about their facts. Criticizing the discipline of history, he nonetheless praised many of its practitioners by noting, "The most important positive feature we see is that, through imposition of fairly rigorous standards of evidence, the profession has helped to produce a great mass of historical writings which, although they may often ask trivial questions, nevertheless provide data that is generally reliable."

Where he once gloried in standing on the margins of the historical profession, Buhle now claims to inhabit the middle of a broad stream. In a featured essay in the *Newsletter*, he wrote: "Every scholar has a perfect right to political and personal views: rigidly anticommunist, Communist or (for the great majority of us) 'other.'" Leave aside the less than perfect balance-anti-Communists are rigid while Communists are just, well, Communists. Focus instead on the suggestion that Paul Buhle works in the mainstream of some wide scholarly consensus that lies between the rigidities of anti-Communists and Communists. In fact, the span of acceptable politics in Buhle's worldview is far left of center. He is willing to put Stalin on the left as an extremist, but only if one agrees that Harry Truman is an extremist of the right. Writing in *Radical History Review* in 1994, Buhle judged Truman as "America's Stalin" and went on to declare, "when the judgment of the twentieth century's second half is made, every American president will be seen as a jerk. After Truman, Nixon yields only to Reagan—still another Truman heir—as the jerkiest of all."

Apart from the coarseness of the writing, how accurate is the radical history produced by Paul Buhle? A review of some sections of the *Encyclopedia of the American Left* shows that it is about as accurate as *The Great Soviet Encyclopedia*. Take the issue of the funding of the Communist Party, USA by the Soviet Union, by now about as established and uncontested a "fact" as one could imagine. (Among other evidence are the receipts signed by the party leader Gus Hall for millions of dollars handed over to him by KGB couriers.) The first edition of *The Encyclopedia of the American Left* gave little attention to the issue of Soviet funding of American Communism. When the second edition appeared in 1998, after abundant documentation of Soviet subsidies had been published, Buhle felt compelled to offer a convoluted and deceptive account of the issue.

He first noted that secret ties between immigrant radicals and their homelands were not unusual. In the nineteenth and twentieth centuries, Germans, Irish, and other ethnic Americans were constantly sending money back to comrades in their homelands and "inevitably, legal niceties were avoided." Of course, this was money *from* America to foreign countries, not the other way around. He did allow that the Bolshevik revolution had changed this pattern in some ways. But, while there were Soviet subsidies to American Communists, he insisted that most of the money still flowed the other way from Americans to the USSR; "the overwhelming flow of money went from American shores to the Soviet Union, mainly for specific campaigns, such as food support in the early 1920s and war relief in the 1940s." But this deliberately confuses apples and oranges. The huge amounts of funds, openly raised and openly sent to the USSR for famine relief in the early 1920s and war relief in the 1940s, cannot be compared to Moscow's clandestine subsidies to a revolutionary political movement within the United States. Further, the bulk of the famine and war relief was not even from immigrant radicals as Buhle implies but from a broad spectrum of Americans motivated by humanitarian concerns. For example, Herbert Hoover, no friend of Bolshevism, spearheaded the Russian famine relief campaign in the early 1920s.

As for the specific monies transferred to the CPUSA by the KGB, Buhle is silent. Instead, in another entry written with fellow coeditor Dan Georgakas, he attributes the CPUSA's ability to support a daily newspaper, despite a lack of advertising and a paucity of members, not to Soviet subsidies, but partly to "the strength of library subscriptions in the Soviet Union and its bloc." In contrast to these relatively benign-sounding library subscriptions, Buhle tries to divert attention by pointing to CIA funding of an ex-Communist leader: "Heavily funded by CIA sources,... Jay Lovestone, now fervently anti-Soviet, used his personal network of associates to shape labor's own counterintelligence agency. Millions of dollars were passed to friendly labor officials in Europe, particularly in France and Italy. Later, connections between the CIA and heroin gangsters reputedly began in a complex alliance against French Communists."

East bloc libraries and institutions did purchase thousands of subscriptions to CPUSA publications. But these were a lesser indirect subsidy of American Communist activities and were not in the same league with Soviet delivery to the CPUSA of millions of dollars in cash subsidies, subsidies that go unexamined in *The Encyclopedia of the American Left*. Moreover, whatever the merits or morality of the CIA funding of Jay Lovestone's anti-Communist activities, there is far less documentary evidence to support the charge that the CIA was linked to "heroin gangsters" than to evidence demonstrating Soviet subsidies to the CPUSA to support espionage.

Diverting attention to the CIA is Buhle's favorite tactic when confronted by stories of Soviet money. He is not careful whether the stories are true or not. In one essay published in the *Newsletter*, he linked the CIA-funded American Committee for Cultural Freedom to the "highly prestigious scholarly series 'Communism in American Life.'" According to Buhle, the Communism in American Life series "was secretly planned by the board of the American Committee for Cultural Freedom, with generous funding arranged for a handful of scholars." The Communism in American Life books were critical of the CPUSA, and linking them to the CIA was Buhle's way of discrediting them. Yet Buhle's cited source, Sigmund Diamond's *Compromised Campus*, made no such charge. Diamond, a vociferous critic of the ACCF, discussed the attempt of the ACCF to play a role in the Communism in American Life project and its recommendations for authors. But Diamond also wrote that the Fund for the Republic, creator of the Communism in American Life project, rejected the proposals from the ACCF, and he says nothing about CIA funding of the project. Contrary to Buhle's assertion, there is no evidence that the series was planned by the ACCF or that the CIA arranged the funding.

It is not only on the issue of funding that the *Encyclopedia of the American Left* engages in falsification and obfuscation. The new evidence from Moscow archives has documented not only extensive Soviet financing of the CPUSA but also direct Party participation in espionage against the United States. Those like Buhle who have devoted their lives to trumpeting a distinctly American, independent radicalism have been discomfited by these revelations. Rather than confront the issue, they have dissembled.

The first edition of *The Encyclopedia of the American Left* did not have an entry for "Secret Work." Enthusiasts for American Communism long had ridiculed stories of a party underground and Communist involvement in espionage told by ex-Communists such as Whittaker Chambers, Louis Budenz, and Elizabeth Bentley. By the time the second edition appeared in 1998, the documentary material emerging from Russian archives had established that the CPUSA had an underground secret apparatus that cooperated with Soviet intelligence. The Venona documents, deciphered cables between KGB spies in the United States and Moscow, began to appear in 1995 and further confirmed the widespread participation of American Communists in espionage. The issue had to be confronted, so for the 1998 edition Buhle wrote an entry on "Secret Work."

Buhle admitted that some top-level Communists were aware of Soviet espionage but found a convenient scapegoat: the same Jay Lovestone, party leader in the late 1920s, who had also served as his foil on the issue of funding. Lovestone was a handy villain because he indeed had connections with Soviet intelligence, but chiefly because after the mid-1930s he became a leading anti-Communist and in the 1950s assisted the CIA: "A handful of trade union officials-most prominent among them, Jay Lovestone, former Communist Party leader and future associate of the Central Intelligence Agency (CIA)—and some liberal intellectuals apparently traded secret communications with the Soviet regime in the 1930s, but the substance of them involved personal information without any great importance or high-level security connections." Buhle loathes Lovestone because he became an anti-Communist. By implying that the only Communist leader who spied for the USSR also spied for the United States, he tried to suggest that the whole issue was at least morally equivalent. But, of course, when Lovestone aided the CIA, he was an American citizen helping an American security agency, hardly the same thing as an American citizen assisting a hostile foreign power such as the Soviet Union.

Nor was Lovestone the most significant CPUSA leader to participate in Soviet espionage. Earl Browder and Eugene Dennis, who led the CPUSA from

1930 to 1959, a period during which the party was far more important than it had been during Lovestone's brief reign in the 1920s, were closely connected to Soviet intelligence. Buhle never names the "liberal intellectuals" he says also engaged in Soviet espionage, possibly because there were none. Nor does Buhle explain why they or anyone else would use espionage channels to provide, as he writes, "personal information" to the USSR.

When he turned to the issue of espionage in the 1940s, Buhle's essay in the *Encyclopedia* first justified spying and then trivialized it. Buhle first stated that the Office of Strategic Services, America's chief World War II intelligence agency, gave a new dimension to left-wing secret work by hiring radicals and thus "unleashed an unprecedented flurry of left-wing spy activity, some of which inevitably continued into the Cold War era." But he never explained why it was "unprecedented" or why it "inevitably" continued. Likewise, he noted that the employment of so many left-wingers on the atomic bomb project "virtually ensur[ed] the passage of some highly classified information to a power which at the time was a formal ally." Once again, he eschews any effort to explain who spied, or why any left-winger would inevitably be a source of information for the USSR. One obvious implication is that the American government was responsible for whatever espionage took place because the atomic bomb project and the OSS hired left-wingers. Buhle does not seem to recognize that his assumption that left-wingers would "inevitably" want to assist the USSR by turning over secret information provides a very powerful rationale for the Truman administration's Loyalty-Security Program that Buhle himself despises.

Regardless of the inevitability of Communists spying for the Soviet Union, Buhle dismisses the significance of the espionage issue: "Such intrigues had almost no role in the day-to-day activities of the American Left, save for the need of Communists to deny the existence of spying by or for the Russians and for anti-Communist socialists to insist upon its central importance to American Communists at large." But how can what Buhle calls "an unprecedented flurry of left-wing spy activity, some of which inevitably continued into the Cold War era," be irrelevant to historical debates over whether the CPUSA was a legitimate participant in domestic politics during the Cold War era? Further playing down the importance of espionage, he reduces the "secret apparatus" to "rumors circulated within and without the Left concerning possible Russian agents" and adds speculation that "American Communist leaders may have informally assured members that the Russians could penetrate the renowned American security state.... Garrulous old-timers who had served in the Spanish Civil War and World War II sometimes hinted and even bragged about what they might be able to do in a moment of international crisis."

Immediately after belittling the significance of "such intrigues" involving the Soviet Union, Buhle suggests that there was more significant "secret work" committed on behalf of Israel by American Communists: "Little was said within the Left or outside it concerning the largest incident of illegal activity: the shipment of arms and assorted war materials to the new state of Israel." Apart from its irrelevance to the issue of Soviet espionage, the question of American Communist covert assistance to Israel in 1948 is presented without any supporting evidence. Neither of the two sources Buhle provides at the end of his entry says a word about the issue.

His further claim that "among those Americans wounded or killed in battles protecting Israeli gains from Arabs, Communists played a prominent role" is unsupported by any evidence. Yehuda Bauer, the distinguished Israeli historian, called the claim "sheer nonsense." The former national president of the American Veterans of Israel, Simon Spiegelman, labeled it "absolutely false," noting that most of the forty Americans and Canadians who died in 1948 were actually connected to one of the right-wing Israeli political movements. The most thorough account of the Jewish role on the American left does not mention any such volunteers. American Communists would have trumpeted this sacrifice in the late 1940s, but there is no evidence they ever did. *Jewish Currents*, a magazine founded by ex-Communists whose writers and editors have run innumerable articles about Israel and Communism, has never mentioned "the prominent role" played by American Communists fighting and dying in the Israeli War of Independence.

We contacted *Jewish Currents* regarding Buhle's claim of Communists fighting in the Israeli war of independence. The magazine in turn got in touch with several veteran radicals, including the *Daily Worker's* correspondent in Palestine in 1947-1948, who unanimously dismissed the assertion as laughable or outrageous.

We also contacted Professor Buhle directly and asked for the documentary basis for the claim. Buhle responded that it was based on oral history interviews but he could remember only the name of one of the interviewees and was not sure if that was the correct one. We obtained a copy of the interview from the Tamiment Library at New York University. It contained no support for the *Encyclopedia*'s assertion. Additional inquiries to Professor Buhle requesting the documentary basis for the published claim in the *Encyclopedia* produced no specific sources.

It was Labor Zionists and the Jewish Joint Distribution Committee that coordinated the vast majority of the fundraising and arms shipments that went to Israel in 1947-1948, not, as Buhle implies, American Communists. The Czech Communist government shipped arms to Israel, and there are rumors of IRA contributions. Some stray American Communists might even have been involved. But how could this constitute the "largest incident of illegal activity" on the part of the Left? Even if one or two oral history interviewees claimed to know a stray American Communist who fought and died in Israel, how could a responsible historian accept it as the truth in the absence of any documentary evidence? And even if there were one or two such obscure people, how did they become transmogrified into playing "a prominent role"? A handful of American radicals immigrated to Israel in the 1950s to escape McCarthyism in the United States. But there is no evidence of how many were Communists or how many were killed or wounded in subsequent Israeli wars. By 1950, the CPUSA, which had supported the founding of the state of Israel in large part because the Soviet Union had done so, was actively hostile to Israel and all manifestations of "Jewish nationalism," in parallel with a similar Soviet shift.

Nor, of course, are the two cases—American Communists secretly spying against the United States for Stalin, and American Communists secretly working for Israel—comparable, even if the latter were true. An American Communist who moved to Israel and fought in its armed forces was not violating any American law. An American Communist who secretly turned over classified U.S. government information to representatives of another government was breaking the law and betraying his country. Buhle's unsupported and spurious claim functions in *The Encyclopedia of the American Left* as a distraction from the issue of secret work by the CPUSA on behalf of the USSR.

Buhle concluded his exercise in damage control by speculating that the collapse of both the USSR and "the Cold War leadership of the American labor movement" might turn up new "documentation of secret relationships between Americans and either the K.G.B. or the C.I.A." Only in the mind of a left-wing extremist who equated Harry Truman with Joseph Stalin could American trade unions assisting an American government agency be equated with American Communists assisting Stalin's USSR Buhle added, "as of the late 1990s, documents examined in the Soviet Union or reprinted for scholars offered little that was new in regard to illegal or secret work by Soviet sympathizers." In fact those documents have revealed a great deal that was both new and illuminating to anyone with eyes to see. It was simply that Buhle did not want to see, and so he shut his eyes and pretended nothing was there.

Buhle is not the only contributor to the *Encyclopedia* of *the American Left* whose ideological enthusiasms are far stronger than their analytical abilities or truthfulness. The editors display a penchant for authors whose preferred method of dealing with unpalatable material is to ignore it. One entry on Finnish-American radicalism reports on the thousands of American Finns, mostly Communists, who moved to Soviet Karelia in the early 1930s but conveniently forgets to mention that hundreds of them were murdered by Soviet political police during Stalin's purges. No Holocaust denier could do better. There has been no uproar about the lies and distortions in this mendacious reference work and no one has called Paul Buhle to account for his peculiarly creative facts about American Communists fighting in the Israeli War of Independence. If he truly does inhabit the mainstream of the historical profession, it is in deep trouble.

20

The Myth of Premature Antifascism

with John Earl Haynes

In *1984,* George Orwell gave the Ministry of Truth the task of rewriting history. Under the slogan "who controls the past controls the future," an army of scribes modified documents, changed textbooks, and rewrote old newspapers to ensure that history conformed to every shift of the ruling party's political line. Left-wing American historians have likewise been busily engaged in altering the past to buttress their conviction that Communists are the real heroes of modern history. Of all the historical myths promoted by the American left, few have been more fiercely protected than those about the Spanish Civil War, lionized as "the Good Fight": a heroic struggle between fascism and antifascism, and the Communist-led International Brigades, a band of selfless volunteers whose brave deeds were immortalized in stirring songs (they won the battles, but we had all the good songs, Tom Lehrer noted).

In this narrative, the American volunteers of the Abraham Lincoln Brigade confronted the fascist menace in 1937, years before the outbreak of World War II finally roused the American government and the public from the torpor of isolationism and appeasement. An often-cited part of the story is that the veterans of the Lincoln Brigade, rather than being hailed for the prescience of their antifascism, were given the pejorative label "premature antifascist" and punished by an American government even then blinded by hatred of communism. *The Encyclopedia* of *the American Left,* an Oxford University Press reference book found in many libraries, states that after the United States entered World War II, many of the Lincoln Brigade veterans volunteered for the American armed forces but "in a foreshadowing of the McCarthy period, the armed forces designated the Lincolns 'premature antifascists' and confined them to their bases."

Originally published in the *New Criterion*, September 2002 and reprinted with permission.

This assertion is a ubiquitous refrain in historical literature during the last thirty years. Ellen Schrecker, a historian at Yeshiva University, wrote that in World War II the Lincoln veterans "were, in the [U.S.] Army's bizarre terminology, 'premature antifascists,' subject to harassment by military intelligence officers and, in many cases, sent to special camps where they were treated almost like prisoners of war." Fraser Ottanelli of the University of South Florida insisted that the veterans "in the witch hunts of the 1950s were disparagingly referred to as 'premature antifascists.'" Robin Kelly, a professor at New York University, wrote, "rather than applaud these men and women for risking their lives in a battle America would officially join in 1941, Lincoln Brigade veterans were hounded by the FBI, a variety of 'un-American activities' committees, and labeled 'premature antifascists.'" Robbie Lieberman of Southern Illinois University stated that the Americans who fought in Spain "faced problems later because of what the government labeled their 'premature antifascist' stance." Professor Bernard Knox (Harvard and Yale) confidently stated, "Premature Antifascist was the label affixed to the dossiers of those Americans who had fought in the Brigades when, after Pearl Harbor (and some of them before) they enlisted in the U.S. Army. It was the signal to assign them to noncombat units or inactive fronts and to deny them the promotion they deserved."

Despite all these confident assertions, "premature antifascism" is a myth. Not only is there no evidence that the United States armed forces ever used the phrase "premature antifascists" to describe those Americans who fought in Spain, there are indications that it was Communists and the veterans themselves who first employed the term. Moreover, many of the veterans were also "interim profascists" who in obedience to Soviet instructions dropped their anti-Nazism in September 1939 and opposed resistance to Fascist aggression while Germany conquered most of Western and Central Europe. Only when the Nazis turned against the USSR in June 1941 did the veterans of the Abraham Lincoln Brigade rediscover their antifascism.

No one has to this day located any documentary evidence that any American government agency coined or used the phrase "premature antifascist" to apply to Americans who fought for the International Brigades. Not until the early 1990s when our research took us into FBI, OSS, and U.S. Army records, the "dossiers" about which Knox had spoken, did it occur to us that there was no documentary support for the charge that had been repeated routinely for years. We examined thousands of pages and realized that the term "premature antifascist" did not occur. Government security agents rarely used euphemisms when describing Communists and other radicals and certainly nothing as coy as "premature antifascist."

Struck by the absence of "premature antifascist" from government files, we checked references to the phrase in scholarly literature. We could not find a single citation to a specific government document. Instead, we found claims with no source, claims with citations to secondary works which had no source, and claims citing an oral history interview with a Lincoln veteran, usually made thirty or more years after the alleged event. In most of these cases, the veteran claimed that some government investigator had used the term in his presence or that he had seen the term stamped on his U.S. Army personnel records. But no one ever produced such a stamped personnel record. There was, moreover, no uniformity about what agency used the term and when it originated. Some scholars and veterans claimed the FBI was the instigator; others pointed to the post-World War II House Committee on Un-American Activities, and, most commonly, still others insisted it was U.S. Army counterintelligence in World War II. Nobody, however, produced a specific document.

One book that promoted the term, dramatically entitled *The Premature Antifascists*, was based on 130 interviews with American volunteers done between 1979 and 1985. In these interviews a snide volunteer claimed that "the first time that [he] heard the expression 'premature antifascists'" came when military security officers interviewed him in 1942. Another says, "I realized how much 'the premature antifascists' as we were called, contributed to save the honor of America" but he did not indicate who did the calling.

Peter Carroll, an independent scholar with a loose association with Stanford University, published *The Odyssey of the Abraham Lincoln Brigade* in 1994. One chapter, entitled "Premature Antifascists," appears to have an indirect but at least contemporaneous documentary source for the governmental origins of "premature antifascist." Carroll discussed the experiences of two Lincoln veterans, Milton Wolf and Gerald Cook, in the U.S. Army in World War II. Both were assigned to Fort Dix, New Jersey, but inexplicably received no orders to report for basic training. Carroll writes:

> Inquiries about the unusual delay brought mystified responses, until Wolff mentioned to a clerk that they had been in Spain. "Oh, that's a different story!" exclaimed the friendly sergeant, who finally found their records in a special file. A few nights later, Wolff and Cook sneaked into the office and read their papers. Printed on the corners were the letters "P.A." The next day, a clerk explained the initials: "premature antifascists." Thus they discovered a euphemism that would become part of anti- Communist rhetoric of the next decade. Service in the Spanish war qualified the Lincolns for that honor.

Although he is a professionally trained historian and author of several widely used American history textbooks, Carroll does not use the usual scholarly apparatus for documenting material in his book, and it is difficult to identify clearly the source for this story. It appears to be a letter Milton Wolff wrote on July 29, 1942 that is located in a collection of Spanish Civil War correspondence at the University of Illinois at Urbana-Champaign. While this letter is not a government document, it would, nonetheless, be contemporaneous indirect evidence if Wolff in a private letter in 1942 made a claim of seeing the label "P.A." on his military personnel records. We wrote to the University of Illinois to obtain a copy of that letter, but it could not be found. We then wrote Dr. Carroll. He replied that he had seen the letter in Milton Wolff's possession and had just assumed that Wolff had later sent it to the University of Illinois. He also said "I doubt that these letters include the phrase premature antifascist." He provided, however, no alternative source for the "P.A." story in his book. Later when the issue was raised on an Internet historical discussion list, he provided this explanation:

> I cannot explain the "missing letters," since I read them before they were sent by Milton Wolff to the University of Illinois. However, I am certain that none of the letters referred specifically to the term "premature antifascist." My source for that reference was my interviews with Wolff himself. As he told me the story about ten years ago, he and another Lincoln veteran, Gerry Cook, were detained at Camp Dix (New Jersey) in June 1942, soon after they had enlisted in the U.S. army. To their dismay, other recruits were routinely being shifted to other camps for basic training, but they remained unassigned. Frustrated by this situation, they entered the camp's office at night and found their names on cards with the initials PA. The next day, they confronted a clerk with that information, and he supposedly said something like "oh, that's why you're not being shipped out." Prompted by the recent flurry of interest in this matter, I reinterviewed Wolff yesterday (May 24, 2000) about this issue. He now told the story differently. Only Cook actually broke into the office, so that Wolff could not, in fact, testify to the authenticity of the PA story. But he was sure that something in their records prompted the clerk's response the next day.

Carroll's new explanation effectively discredits the story he presented in his book. The source of the "P.A." story was an interview given forty-eight years after the incident and abandoned eight years later.

We also placed inquiries in the *Newsletter* of the Historians of American Communism in 1998 and on several history internet discussion lists in 2000, asking for a citation to a specific document showing that some government agency had labeled International Brigade veterans as "premature anti fascists." We received many responses, but *none* provided a citation to a specific government document. New York Polytechnic University Professor Marvin Gettleman, then executive director of the Abraham Lincoln Brigade Archives, responded in 1999 with the comment that while no document had been found "that may be because the relevant FBI files have not yet become publicly available.... But be assured that the search you call for is underway." In 2002 he posted a message on an internet discussion list devoted to the Abraham Lincoln Brigade indicating that as yet no such document had been located.

Some respondents cited oral history interviews and personal conversations, all from decades after the events in question and none adequate to document the claim. Others cited secondary sources, all of which we checked and none of which cited a primary source document. A few respondents suggested archival collections that *might* contain such documents. In so far as those could be checked, we did so and found no documents. The burden of proof that the government originated the "premature antifascist" label for Americans who fought for the International Brigades rests with those making the assertion. And the burden has not been met. Documentary evidence ought to be readily located in the many thousands of pages of World War II military personnel records and OSS records dealing with these individuals. FBI records are less open, but the Freedom of Information Act has made much material available. Congressional investigating committee files contain copies and excerpts from executive branch investigative reports. Despite extensive searches in appropriate archival collections by many people, no documentary evidence has surfaced. At a minimum, the claim made by numerous scholars that U.S. security agencies commonly labeled or stamped the records of Americans who served in the International Brigades with the term "premature antifascist" is false.

That does not preclude the possibility that some government agent on some occasion may have used the term or even written it in a document or reported that some third party used the term. Some such document may turn up some day. But until such documentation is located, the handful of oral history claims about this matter, assertions made thirty or more years after the events in question, are not sufficient to override the absence of direct documentary evidence and the near complete absence of indirect contemporaneous corroboration. That so many scholars and a pretended reference work such as *The Encyclopedia of the American Left* have disregarded scholarly standards in regard to "premature antifascism" is a symptom of the myopia that exists in the academic world on issues that touch upon American Communism. When we publicly asked for documentation of the claims advanced about "premature antifascism," Peter Carroll was "amazed that serious scholars are so exercised about the origins of the term. It seems to me that the important point is that the U.S. Army during World War II did discriminate against Communists or suspected Communists, including Lincoln Brigade veterans.... Does it matter what they called 'them'?"

Yes, it does matter. Historians are not free to shade the truth, create dramatic illustrations out of their imaginations, or manipulate the evidence in the service of what they believe is some other truth. "Premature antifascist" appears repeatedly in the 1940s, 1950s, and into the 1960s as a proud *self-reference* by Lincoln veterans, Communists, and others of the Popular Front left with only a single indirect claim during World War II that the government had invented the term. (In 1944, a magazine article claimed that the FBI used this label but provided no specifics and no examples.) As one of the respondents to our Internet queries stated, "You will *never* find the term in official records because it was used by people who opposed Hitler 'too early' as in the Spanish Civil War as a self-deprecating term for their own ability to see ahead and the U.S. Govt's inability to see what Hitler was planning." It was a way of claiming credit for being antifascist in the late 1930s before antifascism became fashionable following America's entry into the war in December 1941.

But it was also in part camouflage to cover the opposition of the veterans and their supporters to assisting the anti-Hitler belligerents during the period of the Nazi-Soviet Pact. Only after 1970 did historians begin to blame the government for originating the term. Just as Peter Carroll contributed to the myth about premature antifascism, he has distorted the refusal of the Communist veterans (and most were Communists) of the Abraham Lincoln Brigade to fight against fascism from 1939 to 1941.

In his book Carroll wrote that sometime in the spring of 1941 and prior to the German invasion of the USSR on June 22, William Donovan, an adviser to President Roosevelt on intelligence, arranged a meeting with Milton Wolff through "Dinah Sheean." At the meeting,

> Donovan told Wolff that British intelligence officers, working in the United States, wanted assistance in establishing contact with resident aliens from southern and eastern Europe—Italians, Greeks, Yugoslavs, Austrians, and Hungarians—who would be willing to help the partisan resistance fighters in German-occupied countries. Donovan asked if the Lincoln veterans, particularly those with language skills, would participate in such an operation. Wolff agreed to find out. He knew that before undertaking such work individual volunteers would want the sanction of the Communist Party. Steve Nelson referred him to Eugene Dennis, an important party official.... Dennis gave his consent and assured Wolff that the party would cooperate, provided the scheme was kept secret. According to Wolff, in other words, the highest level of the American Communist party authorized clandestine operations that violated the avowed noninterventionist line.... The party's acceptance of Donovan's overture to Wolff thus represented an audacious departure from its previous distrust [of the U.S. government].

Carroll went on to relate that with the CPUSA's "permission granted," Donovan introduced Wolff to two British agents named Bryce and Bailey who asked Wolff to recruit "reliable antifascists to place behind enemy lines in Greece, Yugoslavia, and the Balkans." Carroll concluded, "So, at a time when the Communist party officially opposed American involvement in the war, Wolff started a recruitment program on behalf of British intelligence" and was paid a salary plus expenses. After the United States entered the war in December 1941, Donovan asked Wolff to redirect his recruits from British intelligence to the American Office of Strategic Services, headed by Donovan himself. Wolff later entered the OSS and as an OSS officer worked with anti-Nazi partisans in Italy.

Carroll's account dramatically whitewashes the historical image of both the CPUSA and the Veterans of the Abraham Lincoln Brigade (VALB is the veterans organization of the Americans who fought in Spain in the International Brigades). Both groups' acceptance of the Nazi-Soviet Pact had always been a historical embarrassment to their admirers. In the late 1930s Communists had been in the forefront of the fight against fascism. But the Nazi-Soviet Pact changed everything. From September 1939 to June 1941, when Hitler invaded the Soviet Union, the CPUSA dropped its support for an antifascist Popular Front. It denounced President Roosevelt's efforts to aid Britain, France, and other nations at war against Germany and opposed FDR's reelection in 1940. The

Veterans of the Abraham Lincoln Brigade, led by Milton Wolff, tacked in parallel with the CPUSA and opposed all assistance to the anti-Nazi belligerents.

After the Nazi attack on the Soviet Union in June 1941, all this changed. The CPUSA once again donned the cloak of antifascism, and the VALB called for American intervention in the war. Carroll's story of the Communist Party and the VALB covertly continuing to fight fascism makes the case that antifascism remained at the heart of both groups' world view, even when it conflicted with Soviet foreign policy. In this account, Wolff, the last commander of the Lincoln Brigade in Spain and chief of the VALB, secretly realized the error of the Soviet position and began helping the British before the Nazi attack caused Moscow to change its policy. Even more dramatically, Carroll asserts that Eugene Dennis, then the de facto number two figure in the CPUSA hierarchy, sanctioned Wolff's actions with the support of other party leaders. Thus, "the highest level of the American Communist party," as Carroll put it, had also seen the error of the Soviet position and possessed sufficient independence from Soviet control that it gave permission for Wolff to work for British intelligence and recruit Communist veterans of the International Brigades for British covert operations.

If it were true, Carroll's story would require a major revision in thinking about American communism. But is it true? The answer is no. Everything that Carroll related occurred, but it took place *after* June 22, 1941, not before. With CPUSA permission, Wolff agreed to assist British covert operations but only *after* the Nazi invasion of the USSR and only *after* Wolff and the CPUSA concluded that assisting the British was in concert with the post-June 1941 Soviet policy of all-out support for the anti-Nazi war effort.

Carroll based his account on a 1988 interview with Milton Wolff. He claimed it was corroborated by other interviews, but cited only one, an undated interview with Irving Goff, a Lincoln veteran and fellow Communist whom Wolff recruited for this covert work. Carroll failed to cite a single document in support of the story, nor did he attempt to fit his account within the historical context about British covert operations in this period. In fact, there is abundant evidence that Carroll's timetable cannot be accurate.

The Comintern archive in Moscow contains a May 1942 report by Eugene Dennis about Wolff's work for British intelligence and the American OSS. The report confirms that Diana Sheean (Carroll mistakenly spells her name Dinah) set up a meeting between Donovan and Wolff, that Donovan asked Wolff to recruit International Brigade veterans for the British, that Wolff got CPUSA sanction for the project, and that Wolff set up a recruiting operation funded first by the British and then, after December 1941, by the OSS. However, this document placed the Donovan-Wolff meeting in *November* 1941, well *after* the Nazi invasion of the USSR, and not before as Carroll would have it. The change of date robs the story of its ability to revise the history of the CPUSA and the VALB during the Nazi-Soviet Pact period. This document is corroborated by other 1942 documents in the Comintern archive. The NKVD judged that

Wolff's recruiting might allow American intelligence insight into Communist networks in the United States and ordered it stopped. In the Comintern archive one finds a Comintern directive to the CPUSA to end the recruitment operation and a subsequent report from Dennis that Wolff had shut down his activities as directed. So, not only is Carroll's story wrong but the documentary evidence is that Wolff and the CPUSA refused to cooperate with American intelligence to fight fascism at the behest of Soviet intelligence even when the U.S. and the USSR were allies.

In 1982, the historian Maurice Isserman reported that Eugene Dennis's widow, Peggy, and the veteran Communist Gilbert Green told him that Eugene Dennis had met with and furnished Donovan with information on possible recruits for the OSS *after* the Nazi invasion of the Soviet Union. While Carroll reports that Goff corroborated Wolff's pre-invasion dating, this is contradicted by a 1964 Goff interview with the historian Robert Rosenstone where he said that he had been recruited for OSS work shortly before Pearl Harbor and well *after* the Nazi invasion. *All* of these sources support a fall 1941 date for these activities and contradict a pre-Nazi-Soviet pact date.

Wolff's 1988 claim that he worked for the British prior to the Nazi invasion of the Soviet Union is not even supported by his own testimony to the Subversive Activities Control Board in 1954. Wolff appeared as a witness for the VALB which was contesting the SACB proposal to list it as a Communist-front organization. He proudly testified that he had worked for British military intelligence and the OSS in 1941 and 1942 and that his work for the British had been at the initiative of General Donovan, then a leading White House adviser. While his testimony was vague on the precise timing, he clearly placed his work for the British in the latter half of 1941, perhaps starting as early as July but still *after* the Nazi invasion of the USSR.

Even more damning, Eugene Dennis, who played a central role in the Carroll version of the story, was not *in* the United States during most of this period and could not have met with Wolff during the period claimed. The outbreak of war in Europe in September 1939 had disrupted the usual channels of communications between the CPUSA and the Comintern. The frequent visits of high party officials to Moscow became difficult. But in the spring of 1941, the CPUSA dispatched Dennis to Moscow. The reports Dennis prepared and personally delivered before the Comintern leadership in Moscow in April 1941 are in its archives. The earliest is dated April 1, 1941 and the latest June 18, 1941. Given the conditions of wartime travel in 1941, Dennis had to leave the United States no later than mid-March to reach Moscow by the first of April. He did not return to the United States until after the Nazi invasion.

Could Wolff's meeting with Donovan and his consultation with Dennis have occurred prior to Dennis leaving for Moscow in March 1941? No, it could not. Carroll is vague about his dating of the Wolff-Donovan meeting; he says only that it was prior to the invasion of the Soviet Union and likely in the late spring or early summer. It could not have been earlier than May because in Carroll's account Donovan relayed a British request for aid in recruiting "resident aliens from southern and eastern Europe—Italians, Greeks, Yugoslavs, Austrians, and Hungarians—who would be willing to help the partisan resistance fighters in German-occupied countries." Germany did not invade Yugoslavia and Greece until April 1941 and the British expeditionary force sent to Greece was not forced to withdraw until May. It was not until August 1941 that the British learned that significant remnants of the shattered Yugoslav army were regrouping under the command of Colonel Draza Mihailovich and not until September that they received reliable information about Communist partisans organizing under Josip Tito. The British Special Operations Executive (SOE) sent a small team into Yugoslavia in September 1941 to evaluate the possibility of British aid. Encouraged by their report, the British began preparing SOE units for deployment. The availability of recruits with appropriate language and ethnic backgrounds in North America persuaded the SOE to train its Balkan teams in Canada and it opened "Camp X" near Toronto in December 1941. This timing fits a Donovan approach to Wolff in the autumn of 1941, not prior to the German invasion of the USSR.

Carroll also reports that Donovan introduced Wolff to two British intelligence agents, one of whom was named Bailey. During most of 1941, S. W. Bailey worked out of the SOE Istanbul office. After the autumn 1941 decision to send SOE teams to Yugoslavia, he traveled to North America sometime in *late* 1941 to recruit men of Balkan background. Histories of the Canadian role in SOE recount his meetings with Canadian Communist party officials in early *1942* to recruit Canadian Communists who had served in the International Brigades. Bailey was not in North America before the Nazi invasion of the USSR; he could not have met with Wolff until late 1941.

Wolff's own words and actions in 1941 also contradict his later claims. He delivered the keynote address to the Veterans of the Abraham Lincoln Brigade's convention in May 1941 when Nazi Germany had conquered most of Western and Central Europe. Wolff mentioned Hitler only once, in a sentence that denounced as equally evil Roosevelt, Hitler, Churchill and Mussolini. The chief target of his speech was FDR'S policy of providing assistance to Great Britain, then the only major power fighting Hitler. Wolff told the convention,

under the dishonest slogan of anti-fascism, he [President Roosevelt] prepares the red-baiting, union-busting, alien-hunting, anti-Negro, anti-Semitic Jingoistic road to fascism in America: we accuse him. Turning with cynical calculation on his own lies and false promises, he drags the American people, despite their repeated expressed opposition, closer and closer to open participation in the imperialist slaughter in which the youth of our country will, *if* he has his way, join the 1,000 British seamen of the H.M.S. Hood, the 30,000 German bodies floating in the Mediterranean, the bloody and bloated corpses on battle fields the world over, for the greater glory of foreign trade and the brutal oppression of free people at home and abroad: we accuse him. Franklin Demagogue Roosevelt we accuse; tirelessly and until the people hear and understand, we accuse him....We fight against the involvement of our country in an imperialist war from which the great majority of the American people can derive only misery, suffering, and death. We stubbornly oppose every move of Roosevelt and the war-mongers in this direction, and call on the American people to organize and make vocal their deep and sincere opposition.

Nor was this all. Some Americans who had fought in Spain with the International Brigades criticized the Nazi-Soviet Pact. Wolff had them expelled from the VALB and continued to treat them with scorn for the next fifty years. Wolff claimed in 1988 that his public adherence to the Nazi-Soviet Pact was feigned but there is no documentary evidence to support him and a great deal that demonstrates that his assertions are not credible.

Equally false is Carroll's claim that prior to the Nazi invasion of the USSR, Eugene Dennis and "the highest level of the American Communist party" secretly dissented from the Nazi-Soviet Pact and supported aiding the British in opposition to Soviet policy. Not one word of such dissent has ever surfaced, either in the recollections of Communist leaders or the reports they sent to the Comintern. Dennis had a lifetime record as a Moscow loyalist. At the very time Carroll has Dennis undercutting Moscow's policies in the United States, he was actually in Moscow bragging to the Comintern about the enthusiasm of the CPUSA's campaign to defeat Roosevelt's policies of assisting Britain.

Peter Carroll currently serves as chairman of the Abraham Lincoln Brigade Archives (housed at New York University), a project that combines research on the ALB with hagiography and efforts to honor Brigade veterans. His own efforts at whitewashing the veterans' subservience to Stalinism and gilding their efforts to claim victim status do not rest on any evidence or scholarly foundation. It may be appropriate to honor the Spanish Civil War veterans for their bravery but it is simply not true that the vast majority were independent of the Communist Party and its rigid ideological line.

21

Historiography of American Communism: An Unsettled Field

with John Earl Haynes

Although the Communist Party, USA (CPUSA) never became a major player in American political life, it has always been a controversial body whose activities evoked tremendous passions among both supporters and opponents. During the 1930s, the CPUSA played a significant role in a number of organizations, crusades and campaigns which helped to shape American life. These included the creation of industrial unions, the resistance to fascism and the struggle over the proper scope of governmental activism in social and political life which gave rise to the dominant New Deal coalition of President Franklin Roosevelt. Communists led or were part of the leadership of unions which enrolled a quarter to a third of the membership of the Congress of Industrial Organizations (CIO). This was an impressive achievement for a small movement, although sometimes it looms disproportionately large in histories which brush over the fact that at least two-thirds of CIO members were in unions led by non-Communists and that Communists had only a toehold in what remained the largest trade union body, the American Federation of Labor (AFL). In their Popular Front mode, Communists also achieved a significant although limited entry into mainstream politics in some regions, notably the states of New York, California, Washington, Michigan, Minnesota, Wisconsin, Oregon, and Illinois. Again, however, in most areas of the country Communists had no significant role in electoral policies.

In 1948, Communists and their allies mounted a bold bid to seize the leadership of American liberalism by creating the Progressive Party and backing Henry

Originally published in *Labour History Review*, v. 68, n.1, April 2003, copyright Society for the Study of Labour History and reprinted with permission.

Wallace for the American presidency. But the Cold War was already setting in and the effort failed badly, destroying Popular Front liberalism in the process. As American-Soviet conflict intensified, and particularly during the Korean War when American troops were directly engaged with Communist forces, the CPUSA became the pariah of American society. Hostility to Communism increased as evidence accumulated of extensive Russian espionage against the United States. Congressional committees investigated the extent of Communist influence in a number of institutions, and anti-Communism gained a high degree of political saliency among both liberals and conservatives. Communists were ejected from the trade union movement, the Democratic Party and most liberal political institutions. Increasingly isolated and damaged by sustained governmental harassment, the party tore itself apart when Khrushchev's confirmation of Stalin's crimes and the Hungarian revolution shattered the faith of many members. Its peak membership in the late 1930s was about 88,000. By 1958, it was down to 3,000 and as an organization never again played a significant role in American life.

In America's intellectual life, however, Communism and anti-Communism have continued to loom large. Over the past fifty years an enormous number of books and articles have been published dealing with American Communism. Sometimes it seems as if never have so many written so much about so few. The 1987 *Communism and Anti-Communism in the United States. An Annotated Guide to Historical Writings* listed more than two thousand books, articles, and dissertations.[1] If a new edition were prepared today, it would contain twice as many citations.

The first substantial group of scholarly works on the CPUSA, the Communism in American Life series, the product of a grant from the Fund for the Republic, appeared in the late 1950s and early 1960s.[2] One of the most difficult tasks faced by the authors was simply to gather documentary source material. Little was available, apart from newspaper stories and the records of congressional investigations. Theodore Draper, in particular, was indefatigable, interviewing scores of ex-Communists, gathering internal party documents from expelled party leaders like Earl Browder and rummaging in long-forgotten Communist publications.

Not everyone was happy with the results. Some conservatives objected to the liberal and left-wing assumptions of many of the authors and thought some volumes understated the extent to which liberals cooperated with Communists in the Popular Front era of the 1930s. And several volumes suffered from the limited availability of archival documentation and the dearth of supporting monographic studies of particular incidents and controversies. But many of the books uncovered fascinating material and they remain useful as well as pioneering works. In particular, Draper's two volumes, *The Roots of American Communism* and *American Communism and Soviet Russia,* recreated the political and organizational history of the CPUSA to 1929 with a detail and understanding still unsurpassed. Although most of the authors were left-of-center, all shared an anti-Communist perspective. Many were veterans of bruising battles with Communists and their allies in trade unions, intellectual organizations and political groups while some had gone through the CPUSA and learned to distrust it. The only one-volume history of the CPUSA written in this era, Irving Howe and Lewis Coser's *The American Communist Party, A Critical History,* although not part of the same series, shared its anti-Communism, reflecting the authors' prior experience as critical Trotskyists.[3] All of these books argued that the American Communist Party was subordinate to the Soviet Union, possessed a totalitarian ideology, could not by its nature be a "normal" participant in a democratic polity, and had no legitimate place on the democratic left.

Beginning in the early 1970s, the study of American Communism began to attract new attention. After several years of euphoric self-confidence that an American revolution was imminent, New Leftists, many of them the children of Communist parents, confronted the reality of an emphatically non-revolution-ary America governed by Richard Nixon. Returning to graduate school after several years of political organizing and agitation that had left in its wake failed radical splinter groups disconnected from American life, some of them began to try to understand the American radical past. A cadre of more sympathetic researchers found old Communists more willing to talk about their pasts in an America farther away from the fears of McCarthyism. By the mid-1970s, with the Vietnam War over, Richard Nixon disgraced and American internal security agencies reeling from revelations of official misconduct, the anti-Communist consensus that had dominated American life was shattered.

New documentary sources also became available. The Freedom of Infor-mation Act, passed in 1966, partially opened government files to scholars. Privately held collections of CPUSA material also became available. Moreover, new modes in historiography broadened the scope of inquiry. Oral history aficionados located scores of old activists and encouraged them to tell their stories. Memoirs and autobiographies abounded. Biographers found aging veterans, some with source material, others with memories of the wrongs they felt had been done to them, eager to justify their lives and struggles. Emphasis on ethnic history stimulated fresh research on a variety of immigrant groups in which Communists had been active. Social and cultural historians decried the previous emphasis on politics and explored the lives, mores and social milieu of American Communism.

Maurice Isserman, the author of *Which Side Were You On? The American Communist Party During the Second World War,* explained the leitmotif of this new generation of historians who criticized Draper and his generation of historians:

> the new history of Communism has examined particular communities, particular unions, particular working class and ethnic cultures, particular generations, and other

sub-groupings within the party. Though critical of the CP's authoritarian internal structure, and its overall subservience to the Soviet Union, the new historians have been alert to the ways in which the American CP was shaped by the environment in which it operated and by the people who enlisted under its banners.... The new Communist history begins with the assumption that nobody was born a Communist, and that everyone brought to the movement expectations, traditions, patterns of behavior and thought that had little to do with the decisions made in the Kremlin or on the 9th floor of Communist Party headquarters in New York.... [T]he new historians of Communism are willing to see American Communists…as a group of people involved in, shaping, and shaped by an historical process.[4]

The "new historians," more often termed "revisionists,"have poured out hundreds of essays and books on an astounding array of topics: Communist influence on folk music, drama, poetry, Communist activity among ethnic Jews, Finns, Italians, blacks, Mexicans, Slavic immigrants, as well as among Alabama sharecroppers, Midwestern wheat growers, New York dairy farmers, professional social workers and socially conscious lawyers, even on Communist influence in sports, and scores of studies of Communist activities in the labour movement.[5] They emphasized the heroic battles Communists had fought, the severe repression they had endured, and the progressive causes they had enriched.

Some of this new work uncovered previously unknown or unappreciated incidents or offered interesting new perspectives on American Communism. But it also provoked a debate about the nature of the CPUSA and the most appropriate way to study its history. How much significance should be attached to the activities of the CPUSA at the local level? How reliable were oral histories and how much credence should be given to interviews often conducted by politically sympathetic interviewers? How much autonomy did individual Party units have? Given that the CPUSA was a *political* party and, moreover, one so obsessed with ideology that it judged not only public policy issues but literature, art, music and even family relationships with political criteria, how appropriate was the disparagement of political history and the privileging of social history? To what extent was the CPUSA an instrument of the Soviet Union?

On the latter point, some revisionists, like Isserman, conceded the Russian tie, but most minimized its seriousness or brushed it off as largely symbolic, in stark contrast to the "traditionalist" approach of the Communism in American Life historians. In *The Roots of American Communism* (1957) Theodore Draper summarized a central element of the traditionalist view in his description of the CPUSA's shifts in policy in the 1920s:

> The first change of line was every other change of line in embryo. A rhythmic rotation from Communist sectarianism to Americanized opportunism was set in motion at the outset and has been going on ever since. The periodic rediscovery of 'Americanization' by the American Communists has only superficially represented a more independent policy. It has been in reality merely another type of American response to a Russian stimulus. A Russian initiative has always effectively begun and ended it. For this reason, 'Americanized' American Communism has been sporadic, superficial, and

short-lived. It has corresponded to the fluctuation of Russian policy; it has not obeyed a compelling need within the American Communists themselves.

He concluded that within four years from its founding, the American Communist party had been "transformed from a new expression of American radicalism to the American appendage of a Russian revolutionary power."[6] Thirty-five years later we restated this interpretation in *The American Communist Movement. Storming Heaven Itself*:

> Every era in the history of the American Communist movement has been inaugurated by developments in the Communist world abroad. The Russian Revolution led to the formation of the first American Communist party. Soviet pressure led to the abandonment of an underground Communist party. Comintern directives led American Communists to adopt an ultrarevolutionary posture during the late 1920s. Soviet foreign policy needs midwifed the birth of the Popular Front in the mid-1930s. The Nazi-Soviet Pact destroyed the Popular Front in 1939, and the German attack on the Soviet Union reconstituted it in 1941. The onset of the Cold War cast American Communists into political purgatory after World War II, and Krushchev's devastating expose of Stalin's crimes in 1956 tore the American Communists apart.... Within the limits of their knowledge, American Communists always strove to do what Moscow wanted, no more, no less.[7]

In contrast to the international context in which traditionalists put American Communists, many revisionists took a determinedly national approach. Only a few compared or contrasted American Communism with Russian Communism and many treated Russian Communism as an irrelevancy.

Taken as a whole, revisionist literature was strong on the periphery and weak at the core. Individual Communists working in one area were in the forefront while the Communist *Party* remained in the background, often a vague presence. Revisionist literature offered a Communist movement where local autonomy, spontaneity and initiative ruled and orders from the center were ignored. This literature often conveyed the impression that there were two Communist Parties. One consisted of the CPUSA headquarters in New York to which was attributed the regrettable part of Communist history: subordination to Moscow, support for Stalin's purges, cheers for the Nazi-Soviet Pact, contempt for political democracy, and fervent belief in Marxism-Leninism. The other Communist Party consisted of idealistic rank-and-file Communists who rooted themselves in the wants and needs of the workers, were inspired by the populist traditions of the American past, and paid little attention to Earl Browder in New York and even less to Joseph Stalin in Moscow. In most revisionist accounts, rank-and-file Communists were not Marxist-Leninist in any meaningful way. They were just passionate supporters of trade unions, principled opponents of racism, and steadfast enemies of fascism. The only factor that seemed to distinguish them from other socialists and radicals was that they were more passionate, principled, and steadfast than others on the left, inspiring Theodore Draper to comment that revisionists produced a "genre of books about Communists-without-communism."[8]

Revisionists also gave extraordinary attention to Communist influence on the arts, literature, entertainment and cultural matters. The harsh side of Communism virtually disappeared, as illustrated by Michael Denning's *The Cultural Front: The Laboring of American Culture in the Twentieth Century.*[9] In the benign and romantic Popular Frontism of *The Cultural Front,* Stalin, the Gulag, and the Great Terror faded into the background along with most conventional politics and even the CPUSA itself as an institution. What was left was softly politicized art, literature, music, cinema, and theater that is politically sensitive, on the side of the people against the interests of big business, and treated as the authentic heart of the American left. The impact of Communism and Popular Front styles on the cultural arts cannot be gainsaid, and *The Cultural Front* presented an impressive analysis of Popular Front cultural modes. But for those who regard the history of Communism as chiefly about politics and power, *The Cultural Front* was a sideshow.

While praising *The Cultural Front,* even some revisionists were uneasy with Denning's extreme purging of politics from history. Peter Rachleff, a labor historian, remarked that his focus on culture issues was so tight, "Denning averts his gaze from the moment of the mid-1930s, the moment when wholesale social change was most possible in America." Denning replied, "for cultural history that gaze leaves us looking forever at *Waiting for Lefty,* asking why he never turned up. For me, the question is no longer why Lefty didn't come, but why he came in the forms he did.... The issue raised by the cultural front is less its political failure in the mid-1930s than its cultural success, the ways it continued to live after the defeat of the social movement." Denning's call for recognition that in radical terms the Popular Front had failed politically while succeeding culturally, however, discomforted many revisionists who habitually presented the Popular Front era as a heroic model for contemporary left politics.[10]

Despite the tide of revisionist works, traditionalist studies continued to appear in the 1970s and 1980s. Joseph Starobin's *American Communism in Crisis, 1943-1957* presented a political and institutional history of the CPUSA from the high point of Browderism to the party's near extinction in 1957.[11] Starobin had been a senior CPUSA official in the late 1940s and early 1950s who became an academic after he left the movement. His personal knowledge of many of the events and the personalities of the CPUSA significantly augmented the still thin documentary record for the postwar period. Harvey Klehr, following Draper's model, extended the political and institutional history of the CPUSA into the 1930s with *The Heyday of American Communism: The Depression Decade.* But this text also cast a wider net with coverage of Communist activity in the labor movement, among students and blacks, its influence among intellectuals, and its Popular Front relationship with elements in the New Deal coalition.[12]

Klehr's critical study of the party at the height of its influence irritated revisionists, setting off a fierce series of polemics. They condemned its critical view of the CPUSA and its "Draperite" qualities. Draper retaliated, insisting that the revisionists, whom he described as "left-wing intellectual yuppies," had warped their findings to serve their own radical sympathies and had mis-characterized the basic facts of Communist history.[13] In 1993, twelve revisionists published essays in *New Studies in the Politics and Culture of U.S. Communism.* One of the editors, Michael Brown, dismissed the writings of Draper, Starobin, and Klehr as not scholarship at all. Their books revealed "an almost palpable pathos," were "predicated on a profound philosophical malaise," were "outside of social science" and were only "an extraordinary overtly tendentious type of satire." Brown linked the reappearance of "orthodox" historical writings about Communism in the 1980s to "the introduction of a durable fascist element at the centre of the United States polity," presumably meaning that Ronald Reagan's election was somehow equivalent to the rise of Adolf Hitler. In contrast, he praised the work of Maurice Isserman, Roger Keeran, Paul Lyons, Mark Naison, and Ellen Schrecker, commenting that "what appears to be sympathy" for American Communism in their writing "is in fact simply a willingness to accept responsibility for the only perspective from which a critical historiography can proceed."[14]

Most revisionist articles and books dealt with a limited geographic area, a short time span, a single incident, a specific ethnic or racial group, a particular union, or some other partial aspect of Communist history. And the analytic perspective offered is often disconnected from any broader attempt at interpreting Communist history, coming close to the limitations of a railroad excursion ticket, "good for this trip only." Isserman, while defending the revisionist approach as a needed corrective to the traditionalist focus on the CPUSA as a political institution, recognized the misleading impression that could be conveyed collectively by the multitude of specialized studies. He commented, "it would be a mistake to regard the Communist Party at any point in its history as if it had been simply a collection of autonomous, overlapping sub-groupings of Jews. Finns, blacks, women, longshoremen, East Bronx tenants and baseball fans, who were free to set their own political agenda without reference to Soviet priorities."[15]

Indeed, in its heyday the CPUSA was highly centralized and run by a full-time, paid bureaucracy controlled by a hierarchy answerable only to a tiny group of top leaders who were themselves vetted and often picked by Moscow. Isserman's sensible stipulation received only pro forma acknowledgement from most revisionists who continued to produce numerous articles and dissertations in which American Communism resembled a loosely organized American evangelical Christian denomination where each congregation interprets the gospel as it wishes. Only a few revisionist studies centred on the institution of the CPUSA and even fewer dealt with the party over a lengthy period.[16] There is no revisionist equivalent to the traditionalist, one-volume histories that cover the entire history of the party from origins to irrelevance and must, consequently, provide a comprehensive narrative and unified interpretive stance.[17] And, decidedly, it is difficult to imagine a revisionist-style interpretation that could deal coherently with the party from origin to finish.

Even those revisionist accounts that deal with only a segment of party history run into difficulties. Fraser Ottanelli's *The Communist Party of the United States from the Depression to World War II* is a revisionist answer to Klehr's *The Heyday of American Communism.* Ottanelli argued, "the course of the CPUSA was shaped by a homespun search for policies which would make it an integral part of the country's society as well as by directives from the Communist International." The party's process of Americanization during the Popular Front years "was initiated and defined, in its various phases, by United States Communists," while the Communist International's activities merely "provided new opportunities and more room to maneuver."18 In the course of his book, Ottanelli largely presents Communists as independent of their party headquarters and Moscow almost disappears from view.

Ottanelli's treatment of the Nazi-Soviet Pact illustrates just how problematic such a position is. In the late 1930s the Party had centred its successful Popular Front policy around an international alliance against Nazi aggression and support for President Roosevelt. Given its subordination to Moscow, the Nazi-Soviet Pact of 22 August 1939 required a rapid shift. The CPUSA did not hesitate for even one day and immediately endorsed the Pact without reservation. The Communist International (Comintern), however, had not given any forewarning and party leaders had to guess about the full implications of the agreement. Initially the CPUSA presented the Pact as a blow against war. Earl Browder told the *New York Times* that it made "a wonderful contribution to peace" and the *Daily Worker* proclaimed, "German fascism has suffered a serious blow."19 That notion ended with the German attack on Poland on 1 September. Assuming that Moscow still opposed Nazi aggression, however, American Communists cheered Polish resistance and Browder announced on 3 September that the party gave "full moral, diplomatic and economic help for the Polish people and those who help Poland defend its national independence."20 But a few days later the Comintern informed the CPUSA that this was a wrong guess and provided guidance on the proper interpretation of the Pact; one central point was no support for Polish resistance or Polish national independence. Obediently, the Party immediately denounced the Polish government as fascist and lost any interest in Polish independence.

The Comintern's guidance, however, did not deal with domestic policy. Browder sought to salvage what he could of the Popular Front alliance by opposing Roosevelt's policy of supporting Britain and France in the war against Germany but continuing to support FDR's domestic policies. In mid-October, the Comintern informed Browder that this was an incorrect interpretation and ordered a complete break with Roosevelt. Browder and the CPUSA complied at once. American Communists, who had been among the earliest to campaign for a third-term FDR presidential candidacy, turned against him and attempted to sabotage his 1940 election by using their positions in liberal and labor organizations to block assistance to the Roosevelt campaign. The lesson of this episode is the primacy of Moscow's wishes over domestic American considerations. Yet to Ottanelli the episode proved the reverse: "the unwillingness of American Communists to accept the implications of the new course of Soviet policy is in itself an unequivocal refutation of any notion that the United States Communists automatically aligned themselves to the 'twists and turns' of Moscow's policies."[21] Where he sees maverick independence, we see a scant few weeks of wrong guesses about what Moscow wanted, promptly and willingly corrected when instructed.

While it is not difficult to differentiate "traditionalists" from "revisionists," the latter category includes scholars with a variety of views that sometimes clash. Those revisionists who take the view that the CPUSA was almost never wrong have denounced those who, while judging the party's history positively, have been critical of aspects of CPUSA history. For example, Isserman offered a positive portrayal of the attempt by Earl Browder to Americanize the party during the Second World War. Moscow, however, had denounced Browder's reforms, and he was ousted in mid-1945, and "Browderism" became a Communist heresy. His positive views on Browderism earned Isserman a rebuke from Rutgers University historian Norman Markowitz, author of *The Rise and Fall of the People's Century: Henry A. Wallace and American Liberalism, 1941-1948*. Markowitz labeled Isserman as one of a "new group of anti-Communist caretakers" for his favorable views of the Browderist deviation.[22] Although Mark Naison presented a highly positive portrayal of Communist activities in *Communists in Harlem During the Depression,* he also noted the party's subordinate relationship to Moscow.[23] The latter emphasis angered University of North Carolina professor Gerald Horne, author of *Communist Front? The Civil Rights Congress, 1946-1956.* He denounced Naison for writing "rot" and practising "bad scholarship."[24] Markowitz and Horne published these attacks in *Political Affairs,* the theoretical journal of the CPUSA itself. Isserman, for his part, differentiated "new historians" of his sort from revisionists such as Markowitz and Horne who were closest to the CPUSA's self-perception of its history.

Many revisionist historians explicitly stated their radical loyalties, their admiration for Marxism-Leninism and their hatred of capitalism. Paul Lyons, whose 1982 *Philadelphia Communists, 1936-1956* has often been cited as a model "new historian's" grassroots study, stated that he regarded Communists as "people committed to a vision of social justice and a strategy of social change that make them my political forebears. And like my biological parents, they merit a love that includes — in fact, requires — recognition of their faults and errors. Needless to say, such a love also rests on an honoring." He described his book as a "contribution" toward "socialist cultural hegemony."[25] Ellen Schrecker declared, "I do not think that I conceal my sympathy for many of the men and women who suffered during the McCarthy era nor my agreement with much (though not all) of their political agenda."[26] And Norman Markowitz enthusiastically endorsed the Communist "dictatorship of the working class," calling it "a higher form of democracy."[27]

Often, but not always, this benign view of Communism is coupled with hostility to the United States. University of Michigan Professor Alan Wald, a literary scholar and author of *The New York Intellectuals,* wrote,

> United States capitalism and imperialism remain absolute horrors for the poor and people of color of the world, and ultimately hazardous to the health of the rest of us. Therefore, the construction of an effective oppositional movement in the United States remains the most rewarding, and the most stimulating, task for radical cultural workers. That is why I choose to assess the experience of Communist writers during the Cold War era from the perspective of learning lessons, finding ancestors, and resurrecting models of cultural practice that can contribute to the development of a seriously organized, pluralistic, democratic, and culturally rich left-wing movement.[28]

New York University Professor Robin D. G. Kelley, author of *Hammer and Hoe, Alabama Communists during the Great Depression,* has never hidden his radical views.[29] When asked his reaction to the September 11, 2001 terrorist attack on the United States, Kelley, a professor at New York University, thundered a call for war not against the terrorists but against the American state:

> In 1932, a group of French and Caribbean Surrealists got together and wrote a brief called "Murderous Humanitarianism," vowing to change "the imperialist war, in its chronic and colonial form, into a civil war." I say the same thing: We need a civil war, class war, whatever, to put an end to U.S. policies that endanger all of us.[30]

The Archives Open

By the early 1990s, assisted by the consensus in historical circles that the McCarthy era represented the most disgraceful episode in American life and fading memories of a Communist menace, the revisionist interpretation of American Communism was in the ascendant. Most of the graduate students working in the area treated anti-Communism as a vestigial product of a benighted era. They laid the failure of the CPUSA at the feet of a repressive American regime that had spied upon, disrupted, and destroyed a radical movement that embodied the best impulses of American democracy. Then the Soviet Union collapsed, its archives were opened to scholars and the historians of American Communism had to confront mountains of new information. In addition to a treasure trove of reports and minutes from American Communist bodies and similar reports and minutes from Comintern bodies supervising and overseeing American Communism, there was extensive correspondence between the Comintern and American Communists. The archives contained copies of Comintern orders, reports from Comintern representatives in America who supervised the CPUSA, reports from the American party and thousands of pages of transcribed testimony of American Communist officials who journeyed to Moscow each year to appear for days before Comintern commissions that questioned them regarding the movement in America. The numerous files also preserved the actual headquarters records of the CPUSA itself, from its origin to 1944, including protocols of the political bureau meetings, reports from district organizers, records of the labour secretariat, the various ethnic immigrant affiliates and letters to and from the Party's representative to the Comintern. The history of American Communism, heretofore pieced together from snippets of such material and extensive reliance on newspaper accounts, personal interviews and American government files, was once again in play.

That traditionalists would find more to support their arguments in the Moscow archives than revisionists was only to be expected. Revisionists had adopted a largely favorable view of the Communist movement, and veteran Communists over the years had already said everything they could that was positive or ex-onerative about the movement. The CPUSA, like other political bodies, had never been inclined to hide what it saw as its positive accomplishments (or the self-exculpatory justifications for things that went wrong). No one really thought that the CPUSA had hidden away in Moscow a trove of documents about un-known incidents that made it look good. No one expected to find in Comintern files a report that the American party's Political Bureau had secretly sent a stern letter to Comrade Stalin expressing doubts about the Moscow Trials of senior Bolsheviks and demanding that Bukharin and Zinoviev be given an opportunity to defend themselves before an unbiased commission. Nor did anyone expect to find documents showing that the CPUSA's leaders even discussed, much less agonized, over the possibility of breaking with Moscow over the Nazi-Soviet Pact. At best, some might have hoped that CPUSA leaders privately expressed some independent views before acceding to Comintern orders.

The new archival material has bolstered the traditionalist perspective. We have published four books using the newly available material as well as a number of essays. *The Secret World of American Communism* documented the long-dis-puted existence of the CPUSA's covert arm, the complicity of some American Communists in the execution of at least one and perhaps other Americans who served in the International Brigades in Spain, as well as the party's co-opera-tion with Soviet intelligence agencies in the early 1940s. *The Soviet World of American Communism* documented secret Soviet funding of the CPUSA from 1919 to 1988, party compliance with Comintern directives on ideology, on party organization and in support of the Stalinist purges, the long-suspected but unconfirmed Soviet origins of the "Duclos article," Comintern selection of party political bureau membership in the 1930s and supervision of CPUSA policy statements. *Venona: Decoding Soviet Espionage in America* combined Moscow archival material with newly declassified American decryptions of the Second World War Soviet intelligence agency communications to detail the unexpectedly extensive use of the CPUSA as an institutional auxiliary to Soviet espionage. *Red Scare or Red Menace? Communism and Anticommunism in the Cold War Era* surveyed the interaction between the CPUSA and its opponents with particular attention to the key role of liberal and left anti-Communists.[31]

The evidence of extensive CPUSA cooperation with Soviet espionage also united what had been largely separate areas of historical writing. Until the appearance of *The Secret World of American Communism, Venona,* and Allen Weinstein and Alexander Vassiliev's *The Haunted Wood: Soviet Espionage in America — the Stalin Era,* based on KGB archival material, the history of Soviet espionage had been treated apart from the history of American Communism.[32] Most revisionists ignored it entirely and even traditionalists had believed that the CPUSA as an institution had had only a minor role in Soviet spying. Now with espionage clearly part of the Party's own history, it had to be taken into account. Maurice Isserman remarked,

> The "new" history of American Communism and what might be called the new history of Communist espionage need not be mutually exclusive, let alone antagonistic, historical inquiries. If this reviewer were to rewrite *Which Side Were You On?* today, it would certainly be influenced by the revelations contained in books like *Venona* and *The Haunted Wood.* By the same token, some of the concerns and themes raised by the new history of American Communism are not irrelevant to those who seek to decipher the mixture of faith and breach of faith that created a romance of the clandestine among some American Communists during World War II.[33]

The new archival resources prompted several historians to shift perspectives. James Ryan's 1981 dissertation on Earl Browder, the long-time chief of the CPUSA, argued that at his core he was a Kansas Populist-in-a-hurry and thoroughgoing American. In 1993, Ryan, then revising this dissertation for publication, examined the Comintern and American Communist party records and shifted markedly toward a traditionalist stance. His 1997 book, *Earl Browder: The Failure of American Communism,* stated, "it is difficult to overstate the significance of these materials. They offer a perspective on American radicalism available nowhere else."[34] Vernon Pedersen's 1987 master's thesis, a study of the Communist Party of Indiana, had been firmly in the revisionist camp. But after a research stint at the newly open Moscow archives he concluded: "the opening of the Russian archives confirmed the traditionalists' long-held claims."[35] Pedersen's 1993 dissertation on the Maryland Communist Party, published in 2001 as *The Communist Party in Maryland, 1919-57,* combined a focus on the local activities of rank-and-file Communists with a clear-eyed understanding of the CPUSA's centralized nature, anti-democratic ideology, and subordination to Moscow.

Maurice Isserman, one of the most prominent revisionists, dealt with the new evidence seriously from the first. When *The Secret World of American Communism* appeared, he stated, "No one will be able to write about the CPUSA in the future without reference to this volume.... [T]he Comintern documents that Klehr, Haynes and Firsov have uncovered are almost surely the real thing.... Interpretation will vary: the documents will stand." That is not to say Isserman accepted a traditionalist view of the CPUSA. He insisted, "For my own part, what has always interested me in the history of the CPUSA had been the *conflict* between the 'democratic, populist, and revolutionary' beliefs of individual Communists, and its decidedly undemocratic purposes and conduct imposed on the party from abroad."[36] Other revisionists, however, were less impressed with the new documentation and more reluctant to adjust their views. Ellen Schrecker saw no reason "that the past 30 years of scholarship [the revisionist consensus] will need to be rewritten." She went on to criticize the Cold War "triumphalism" of people like Klehr, Haynes, and Radosh, depicting it as part of a "broader campaign to delegitimize professional scholarship" instigated by conservative foundations.[37]

Thus far, only a few revisionists have published studies making use of the new archival resources. Most have been narrowly focused, avoided dealing with the party as a political institution, and conceded considerable ground to the traditionalist perspective, albeit usually without acknowledging any shift. Edward Johanningsmeier's 1994 *Forging American Communism: The Life of William Z. Foster,* a biography of a leading figure in the party from the 1920s to the 1950s, restated the revisionist thesis but with a slight qualification: the CPUSA's "rank-and-file membership did not act completely autonomously, even though it is now clear that the relationships between shop-floor and community-level organizers and the party hierarchy were characterized by a significant degree of independence" and Foster was "in the end, profoundly American."[38] The qualification "did not act *completely* autonomously" (emphasis added) was his ever-so-slight retreat from earlier revisionist insistence on American Communism's autonomy. However, concentrating as it does on Foster's life, the book does not directly address the question of local party or rank-and-file independence. And as to whether Foster was "profoundly American," Johanningsmeier noted that after chastisement by Stalin and the Profitern in 1929, Foster never again deviated from Moscow's leadership and "recomposed his Utopian vision in the 1930s to conform with the totalitarian ethos of Stalinism." He stated that Foster's "radicalism was based on a powerful and genuine alienation from the central assumptions of American politics" and later quoted an evaluation of Gerhard Eisler, onetime Comintern representative to America, that Foster and Eugene Dennis, who jointly led the CPUSA from 1945 to 1959, "interpret American problems as foreigners."[39]

James Barrett made more extensive use of Moscow archives than Johanningsmeier for his 1999 *William Z. Foster and the Tragedy of American Radicalism.* Although taking a revisionist perspective, he gently criticized Johanningsmeier for minimizing the importance of the Comintern in shaping Foster's views: "his own instincts and ideas were constrained and often distorted by the exigencies of international communist politics...[by the late 1930s] he seemed to become more fixed on the Soviet line and more rigid in his understanding and application of Marxism-Leninism." Barrett interprets Foster's life as a lamentable conflict between indigenous radicalism and a foreign import, eventually won by the latter.[40]

In his 1972 dissertation on the CPUSA and black Americans, Mark Solomon minimized the role of the Comintern, arguing, for example, that African-Americans "virtually originated the idea of Black Belt self-determination," referring to the CPUSA's controversial stand in the late 1920s and 1930s that the black population of the American South had the right to national independence.[41] After extensive use of the archives, Solomon remained sympathetic to the CPUSA but more realistic. In his 1998 *The Cry Was Unity: Communists and African Americans, 1917-1936,* he insisted that some Comintern directives and orders "were reminiscent of a parent's tough love for an errant child" and others "provided a needed sense of distance and perspective to straighten out muddles in national parties." Nonetheless, he conceded that American Communists often confused "Soviet state interests with a loftier internationalism," that "more often than not led to willing acquiescence to foreign-made decisions that were often applied reflexively in the United States."[42] He also now acknowledged that the Black Belt thesis originated in Moscow.

The most recent full-scale defence of revisionism is Ellen Schrecker's *Many Are the Crimes: McCarthyism in America* (1998). It is a large book, encompassing both extensive archival research (although none in the Moscow archives) as well as a broad reading of the secondary literature. The book has several themes, but its chief one is to reinforce, as she describes it, the academic world's "near-universal consensus that much of what happened during the late 1940s and 1950s was misguided or worse," referring to American post-Second World War anti-Communism.[43] In several venues she has stated her outrage that the new evidence from Moscow and the renewed vigour in the traditionalist interpretation has "given new life to liberal anticommunism." Speaking to the American Historical Association, Ellen Schrecker warned, "the rehabilitation of Cold War liberalism is a central tenet of the triumphalist discourse about communism and anticommunism." Elsewhere, Schrecker and Isserman assailed the idea that Cold War liberalism was owed any credit for its struggle against Communism; on the contrary, they insisted, "cold war liberalism did not, in fact, 'get it right.'"[44]

Schrecker realized that the American scholarly world's consensus that postwar opposition to Communism was "misguided or worse" assumes the revisionist view that the CPUSA was a normal, albeit radical, political movement, rooted more in American traditions than subordinate to Moscow, and had no serious involvement with Soviet espionage. For example, David Caute's influential 1978 book *The Great Fear: The Anti-Communist Purge Under Truman and Eisenhower,* had placed in emphasized type, "*There is no documentation in the public record of a direct connection between the American Communist Party and espionage during the entire postwar period.*"45 The new evidence contradicted this assertion and undermined the "near-universal consensus" on anti-Communism. Consequently, in bringing the revisionist interpretation up to date, Schrecker offered an account of the CPUSA that took cognizance of the new evidence.

She provided a harsher assessment of the CPUSA than earlier revisionists. She admitted that the CPUSA was not a collection of independent spirits: "discipline was central to the CP's identity" and

> In their political work (and for many activists in their daily lives as well) Communists were expected to comply with party directives. Even during its more reformist phases, where there was little difference between the aims and actions of the 'big C' and 'small c' Communists, the American Communist party never abandoned its demand for conformity. It was — in theory and in ways that shaped the behavior of its members — a tightly organized, highly disciplined, international revolutionary socialist organization.

Schrecker added, "its quasi-military culture precluded real debate. Members of a vanguard party, lower-level cadres actually prided themselves on their discipline. As one labour organizer recalled, 'edicts were handed down and we didn't examine them.'" She also agreed that the CPUSA required its trade union militants to put party policy above union goals despite the high price that required, writing that the CPUSA's "demand that its labor cadres back the Progressive Party destroyed whatever influence the party had within the mainstream of the labor movement." As for the party's relationship with the USSR, Schrecker stated, "it was unthinkable for American Communists to defy what they interpreted as a directive from the Soviet Union." On the matter of spying, she says, "it is clear that some kind of espionage took place during the 1930s and 1940s" and "as the evidence accumulates, it does seem as if many of the alleged spies had, indeed, helped the Russians."[46]

A traditionalist scholar could have written these observations: they abandon much of the revisionist stance on the nature of the CPUSA. But, having said these things, Schrecker then "privileges" Communists. Their shortcomings receive understanding or excuse because their intentions were good. Spying for Stalin, for example, was not so bad and, in any case, preventing Soviet espionage was worse than tolerating it: "were these activities so awful? Was the espionage, which unquestionably occurred, such a serious threat to the nation's security that it required the development of a politically repressive internal security system?" She then praises the motivation of the spies:

> the men and women who gave information to Moscow in the 1930s and 1940s did so for political, not pecuniary reasons. They were already committed to Communism and they viewed what they were doing as their contribution to the cause…[and]…it is important to realize that as Communists these people did not subscribe to tradi-

tional forms of patriotism: they were internationalists whose political allegiances transcended national boundaries. They thought they were "building...a better world tor the masses," not betraying their country.[47]

The main theme of her book, however, was the "crimes" of anti-Communism. While she asked that scholars take "a more nuanced position and go beyond the question of guilt or innocence," on such matters as the CPUSA's participation in Soviet espionage, when it comes to anti-Communism there was no nuance. Schrecker depicted in a negative light all varieties of opposition to Communism. Fervid opposition to Communism, Schrecker explained, "tap[ped] into something dark and nasty in the human soul."[48]

To Schrecker, the "term *McCarthyism* is invariably pejorative," and she applied it to any opposition to Communism. In addition to Joseph McCarthy, his allies and imitators, she insisted there were "many McCarthyisms" including "a liberal version...and there was even a left-wing version composed of anti-Stalinist radicals" since "Socialists and other left-wing anti-Communists functioned as a kind of intelligence service for the rest of the [anti-Communist] network.[49] Consequently, weighed in the balance and found guilty of McCarthyism are Harry Truman, the liberal Americans for Democratic Action, the AFL, the CIO (its non-Communist majority under Philip Murray and Walter Reuther), Trotskyists, Lovestoneists, Socialists, Roman Catholics, *Partisan Review*, and the "New York intellectuals," Sidney Hook, Hubert Humphrey, Morris Ernst, Norman Thomas, and other leading lights of the non-Communist liberal and left community.

Many Are the Crimes held anti-Communism responsible for most of the ills of American society since 1945. Schrecker indicted anti-Communism for destroying the civil rights movement's ties to the "anti-imperialist left," thereby having "deprived the African nationalists of their main American ally, thus indirectly strengthening that continent's colonial regimes." It was responsible for legal restrictions on trade union power and, she added, "debilitating as Taft-Hartley was, it was not solely responsible for labor's disastrous failure to replenish its ranks. Here, again, the anticommunist crusade bears much of the responsibility, for it diverted the mainstream unions from organizing the unorganized." Anti-Communists also get the blame for the failure of national health insurance, government inefficiency, and incompetent American foreign intelligence and diplomacy. Anti-Communism also retarded feminism, held back research in natural science, crippled American higher education, drove talented musicians from major orchestras, and compelled serious painters to abandon realism for modernism by "destroy[ing] the artistic vision of the Popular Front, marginalizing entire schools of representation and severing the connection between art and social responsibility." Opposition to Communism even gets the blame for dull television programming and for having caused Hollywood to promote "the good guy/bad guy polarization of the Westerns, the unthinking patriotism of the war movies, the global triumphalism of the bible epics, and the constricted sexuality of the romantic comedies."[50] Too many are the crimes!

Schrecker's book demonstrated that part of the focus of the historical debate is shifting from Communism to anti-Communism. She recognized that the new evidence destroyed key points of the revisionist interpretation of CPUSA history. What she vehemently rejected, however, was any shift in perspective on anti-Communism. Yet traditionalists are unwilling to divorce anti-Communism from Communism. There was no anti-Communist party around which the movement was built nor a core anti-Communist ideology. Anti-Communists were defined by what they were against rather than what they were for. Instead of a single anti-Communism, there was a multitude, each with different objections to Communism. The various wings of anti-Communism did not follow a common agenda aside from their shared opposition to Communism or even approve of each other. Consequently, any historical treatment of anti-Communism has to be keyed to the historical treatment of Communism. The new evidence about the CPUSA bears directly on the perspicacity, tactics and rationale of their anti-Communist opponents.

Conclusion

The historiography of American Communism is today very unsettled. The revisionist domination, achieved in the 1970s and 1980s, has been shaken, but not shattered. Revisionists easily outnumber traditionalists and dominate the most prominent American historical journals. But the newly available archival evidence has invigorated traditionalists, and revisionists are in retreat. A new academic journal, *American Communist History,* was launched in 2002 with an editorial board balanced between traditionalists and revisionists.[51] The editorial board also includes a sprinkling of foreign scholars as well in an attempt to lessen the isolation of American historians from others working in Communist history. The U.S. Library of Congress's purchase of a microfilm copy of the CPUSA records (fond 515) held by the Russian State Archive of Social and Political History (RGASPI) has made more than 435,000 pages of party headquarters records more easily available to American researchers, particularly graduate students with limited travel budgets. The Library of Congress is also a partner in the International Computerization of the Comintern Archive project (Incomka) that will within a year or two make available as computer images one million pages of the Comintern archive, including files particularly rich in American-related material (the Anglo-American Secretariat and the American Commission).[52] There is every reason to expect that the history of domestic American.

Notes

1. J. E. Haynes, *Communism and Anti-Communism in the United States: An Annotated Guide to Historical Writings* (New York: Garland, 1987).

2. The Fund for the Republic was a private foundation headed by the former president of the University of Chicago, Robert Hutchins. The books in the series are: T. Draper, *The Roots of American Communism* (New York: Viking Press, 1957); R. W. Iversen, *The Communists and the Schools* (New York, Harcourt Brace, 1959); D.A. Shannon, *The Decline of American Communism: A History of the Communist Party of the United States Since 1945* (New York. Harcourt, Brace, 1959); T. Draper, *American Communism and Soviet Russia* (New York, Viking Press, 1960); C. L. Rossiter, *Marxism: The View from America* (New York, Harcourt, Brace, 1960); R. L. Roy, *Communism and the Churches* (New York: Harcourt, Brace, 1960); N. Glazer, *The Social Basis of American Communism* (New York, Harcourt, Brace, 1961); F. S. Meyer, *The Moulding of Communists: The Training of the Communist Cadre* (New York, Harcourt, Brace, 1961); D. Aaron, *Writers on the Left: Episodes in American Literary Communism.* (New York, Harcourt. Brace and World, 1961); E. Latham, *The Communist Controversy in Washington: From the New Deal to McCarthy* (Cambridge, MA: Harvard University Press, 1966).
3. I. Howe and L.A. Coser, *The American Communist Party: A Critical History, 1919-1957* (Boston: Beacon Press, 1957). Also sharing the approach of the Communism in American Life series was M. M. Kampelman, *The Communist Party vs. the CIO: A Study in Power Politics* (New York: F. A. Praeger, 1957).
4. M. Isserman, "Three generations: historians view American communism," *Labor History,* 26, 4, 1985, pp. 539—40; M. Isserman, *Which Side Were You On? The American Communist Party During the Second World War* (Middletown, CT: Wesleyan University Press, 1982).
5. Again, most of the revisionist studies of Communists in the labour movement tend to avoid a broad perspective. One of the exceptions is H. A. Levenstein, *Communism, Anti-Communism, and the CIO* (Westport, CT: Greenwood Press, 1981), the revisionist response to Kampelman, *Communist Party vs. the CIO* and B. Cochran, *Labor and Communism: The Conflict That Shaped American Unions* (Princeton, NJ: Princeton University Press, 1977).
6. Draper, *Roots*, p. 395.
7. H. Klehr and J. E. Haynes, *The American Communist Movement: Storming Heaven Itself* (New York: Twayne, 1992), pp. 4, 179.
8. T. Draper, "Life of the party," *New York Review of Books*, 13 January 1994.
9. M. Denning, *The Cultural Front: The Laboring of American Culture in the Twentieth Century* (London and New York: Verso, 1997).
10. P. Rachleff, "Understanding legacies, understanding possibilities," *Labor History,* 39, 3, 1998, pp. 330-34; M. Denning, "The future of the cultural front'." *Labor History,* 39, 3, 1998, pp. 334-37. *Waiting for Lefty* was a Clifford Odets play of the era where the action takes place while the players and the audience await the return of a strike leader, Lefty.
11. J.R. Starobin, *American Communism in Crisis, 1943-1957* (Cambridge, MA: Harvard University Press, 1972).
12. H. Klehr, *The Heyday of American Communism. The Depression Decade* (New York: Basic Books, 1984). Other traditionalist studies from the 1970s and 1980s include H. Klehr, *Communist Cadre: The Social Background of the American Communist Party Elite* (Stanford, CA: Hoover Institution Press, 1978); L. K. Dyson, *Red Harvest: The Communist Party and American Farmers* (Lincoln: University of Nebraska Press, 1982); A. S. Kraditor, *"Jimmy Higgins":The Mental World of the American Rank-and-File Communist, 1930-1958* (New York: Greenwood Press, 1988); J. E, Haynes, *Dubious Alliance: The Making of Minnesota's DFL Party* (Minneapolis: University of Minnesota Press, 1984).

13. T. Draper, "American communism revisited," *New York Review of Books,* 9 May 1985; T. Draper, "The popular front revisited," *New York Review of Books,* 30 May 1985. For another critique of revisionism from a left-wing, anti-Stalinist viewpoint, see J. Jacobson, "The Soviet Union is dead, the 'Russian question' remains: Part I: The Communist Party — myth and reality," *New Politics.* 5. 2 (n.s,) 1995, http://www.wpunj.edu/newpol/issue18/jacobs18.htm.

14. M. E. Brown, "Introduction: the history of the history of U.S. communism," in M. E. Brown, R. Martin, F. Rosengarten and G. Snedeker (eds), *New Studies in the Politics and Culture of U.S. Communism* (New York: Monthly Review Press, 1993), pp, 21, 28, 31. Other authors in this volume included Rosalyn Baxandall, John Gerassi, Marvin Gettleman, Gerald Horne, Roger Keeran, Mark Naison, Stephen Leberstein, Ellen Schrecker, Annette Rubinstein, Alan Wald and Anders Stephanson. Keeran is best known for a major revisionist work on trade union history. R. Keeran, *The Communist Party and the Auto Workers' Unions* (Bloomington: Indiana University Press, 1980). Wald, who has a Trotskyist orientation, later disassociated himself from what he termed Brown's "oddball opinions" and suggested that few revisionists shared Brown's views. See A. M. Wald, "Search for a method: Recent histories of American communism." *Radical History Review*, 61, 1995, p. 173, n. 10.

15. Isserman, "Three Generations," pp. 544-45.

16. Isserman's own *Which Side Are You On?* is one of the few party-centred studies, and it focuses on the six-year period from late 1939 to 1945 with only brief summaries for the pre- and postwar periods.

17. The two traditionalist, one-volume studies are Howe and Coser, *The American Communist Party* and Klehr and Haynes, *The American Communist Movement.*

18. F. M. Ottanelli, *The Communist Party of the United States: From the Depression to World War II* (New Brunswick, NJ: Rutgers University Press, 1991), pp. 4, 213.

19. *New York Times*, 24 August 1939; *Daily Worker,* 23 August 1939.

20. Browder report to CPUSA national committee, quoted in *Daily Worker*, 5 September 1939.

21. Ottanelli, *The Communist Party of the United States*, p. 194.

22. N. Markowitz, "The new Cold-War 'scholarship.'" *Political Affairs,* 62, 1983. pp, 27-38; N. D. Markowitz, *The Rise and Fall of the People's Century: Henry A. Wallace and American Liberalism, 1941-1948* (New York: Free Press, 1973).

23. M. Naison, *Communists in Harlem During the Depression* (Urbana: University of Illinois Press, 1983).

24. G. Horne, "Communists in Harlem during the Depression," *Political Affairs,* 63, 1984, pp. 36-38. Horne's major works include G. Horne, *Black and Red: W. E. B. Du Bois and the Afro-American Response to the Cold War, 1944-1963* (Albany, NY: State University of New York Press, 1986); G. Horne, *Communist Front? The Civil Rights Congress, 1946-1956* (Rutherford, NJ, and London, Fairleigh Dickinson University Press and Associated University Presses, 1988); and G. Horne, *Black Liberation/Red Scare. Ben Davis and the Communist Party* (Newark: University of Delaware Press, 1993).

25. P. Lyons, *Philadelphia Communists, 1936-1956,* (Philadelphia: Temple University Press, 1982), pp. 18, 238.

26. E. Schrecker, *Many are the Crimes: McCarthyism in America* (Boston: Little, Brown, 1998), p. xviii.

27. N. Markowitz, MARKOWIT@cac-fas1.rutgers.edu, "FDR and socialism," 14 November 2001, in H-1918-45, archived at www2.h-net.msu.edu/lists/.

28. A. Wald, "Communist writers fight back in Cold War America," in P. Goldstein (ed.,). *Styles of Cultural Activism. From Theory and Pedagogy to Women, Indians,*

and Communism (Cranbury, NJ: University of Delaware Press and Associated University Presses, 1994). Wald's works include A. M. Wald, *Writing from the Left. New Essays on Radical Culture and Politics* (London and New York, Verso, 1994); A. M. Wald, *The New York Intellectuals: The Rise and Decline of the Anti-Stalinist Left from the 1930s to the 1980s* (Chapel Hill, University of North Carolina Press. 1987); A. M. Wald, *Exiles from a Future Time: The Forging of the Mid-Twentieth-Century Literary Left* (Chapel Hill, University of North Carolina Press, 2002).

29.   R.D.G. Kelley, *Hammer and Hoe: Alabama Communists During the Great Depression* (Chapel Hill: University of North Carolina Press, 1990); R.D.G. Kelley, *Race Rebels. Culture, Politics, and the Black Working Class* (New York and Toronto: Free Press and Maxwell Macmillan, 1994).

30.   R. Neumann, 'The empire strikes back." *Village Voice,* 3-9 October 2001, http://www.villagevoice.com/issues/0140/neumann.php. While anti-Americanism is predominant among revisionists, we note that not all reacted to the mass murders of 11 September with a call for radicals to launch civil war. Mark Naison responded by stating, "if anyone said anything about America's imperialist activities making it the moral equivalent of the Taliban and Al Qaeda I would beat them up," quoted in R. Perlstein, "Left falls apart as center holds." *New York Observer,* 25 October 2001.

31.   H. Klehr, J. E. Haynes, and F. I. Firsov, *The Secret World of American Communism* (New Haven, CT: Yale University Press, 1995); H. Klehr, J. E. Haynes, and K. M. Anderson, *The Soviet World of American Communism* (New Haven, CT: Yale University Press, 1998); J.E. Haynes and H. Klehr, *Venona: Decoding Soviet Espionage in America* (New Haven, CT: Yale University Press, 1999); J. E. Haynes, *Red Scare or Red Menace? American Communism and Anti-Communism in the Cold War Era* (Chicago: Ivan R. Dee, 1996).

32.   A. Weinstein and A. Vassiliev, *The Haunted Wood: Soviet Esponage in America – The Stalin Era* (New York: Random House, 1999).

33.   M. Isserman, "They led two lives," *New York Times Book Review*, 9 May 1999.

34.   J. Ryan, "Earl Browder and American communism at high time: 1934-1945," Ph.D. thesis. University of Notre Dame, 1981; J. G. Ryan, *Earl Browder: The Failure of American Communism* (Tuscaloosa: University of Alabama Press, 1997), p, xi.

35.   V. Pedersen, "Riding the wave: The Indiana Communist Party, 1929-1934," MA thesis, Indiana State University, 1987; V. L, Pedersen. *The Communist Party in Maryland, 1919-57* (Urbana and Chicago: University of Illinois Press, 2001), p, 3.

36.   M. Isserman, "Notes from underground," *Nation,* 12 June 1993.

37.   E. Schrecker, "Post-Cold War triumphalism and historical revisionism," conference presentation, American Historical Association, Boston, 2001. Radosh, a former young Communist and New Leftist activist, particularly irritates revisionists. His major works include R. Radosh and J. Milton, *The Rosenberg File: A Search for the Truth* (New York: Holt, Rinehart, and Winston, 1983); H. Klehr and R. Radosh, *The Amerasia Spy Case. Prelude to McCarthyism* (Chapel Hill: University of North Carolina Press, 1996); R. Radosh, M.R. Habeck, and G.N. Sevostianov, *Spain Betrayed: The Soviet Union in the Spanish Civil War* (New Haven, CT: Yale University Press, 2001).

38.   E. P. Johanningsmeier, *Forging American Communism: The Life of William Z. Foster* (Princeton, NJ: Princeton University Press, 1994), pp. 6-7.

39.   Johanningsmeier, *Forging American Communism,* pp. 284, 307.

40.   J. R. Barrett, *William Z. Foster and the Tragedy of American Radicalism* (Urbana: University of Illinois Press, 1999), pp. 4-5.

41. M. Solomon. 'Red and black: Negroes and communism, 1929-1932', Ph.D. thesis. Harvard University, 1972. published as M.I. Solomon. *Red and Black. Communism and Afro-Americans, 1929-1935* (New York. Garland, 1985). The quotation is from the latter's preface.
42. M.I. Solomon. *The Cry Was Unity: Communists and African-Americans, 1917-36* (Jackson: University Press of Mississippi. 1998), pp. xxiii-xxiv.
43. Schrecker, *Many Are the Crimes,* p. x. Her other works include: E. Schrecker, *No Ivory Tower: McCarthyism and the Universities* (Oxford: Oxford University Press, 1986), and E. Schrecker, *The Age of McCarthyism. A Brief History with Documents* (Boston: Bedford Books of St. Martin's Press, 1994).
44. Schrecker, "Post-Cold War triumphalism"; E. Schrecker and M. Isserman, "The Right's Cold War revision: current espionage fears have given new life to liberal anticommunism." *Nation.* 24 July 2000.
45. D. Caute, *The Great Fear: The Anti-Communist Party under Truman and Eisenhower* (New York: Simon and Schuster, 1977), p. 54.
46. Schrecker, *Many Are the Crimes,* pp. 5-6, 10, 18, 22, 36, 166.
47. Schrecker, *Many Are the Crimes,* pp. 178-9, 181.
48. Schrecker, *Many Are the Crimes,* pp. xviii, 46, 178-9.
49. Schrecker, *Many Are the Crimes,* pp. x, xii, 75-6.
50. Schrecker, *Many Are the Crimes,* pp. 375-6, 381, 399, 402.
51. See http://www.tandf.co.uk/journals/routledge/14743892.html.
52. The Incomka product will be available at the Library of Congress in the United States and at its partner organizations: RGASPI, the national archives of France, Germany, Italy, Spain (Ministry of Edncation and Culture), Switzerland and Sweden, and the Open Society Archives in Hungary. The Incomka product includes an electronically searchable database to the finding aids (opisi) of the entire Comintern archive at RGASPI.

22

Professors of Denial

with John Earl Haynes

Since the end of the Cold War, documents released from American and Soviet archives have convinced most Americans that long-disputed spy charges against Alger Hiss, the Rosenbergs, Lauchlin Currie, and Harry Dexter White, among others, were accurate, and that hundreds of Americans worked for Soviet intelligence services during the 1930s and 1940s. What has gone largely unnoticed is the frantic rear-guard action by a handful of academics to discredit the new evidence and exonerate these onetime spies. While some who insisted that Hiss and the others were innocent have finally given up the ghost, others concede Hiss and company's guilt but urge us to see their espionage as an expression of true American patriotism. And a few holdouts have refused to admit that the evidence from Russian and American archives is, in fact, overwhelming. Meanwhile, a depressingly large number of high school and college history textbooks still present the Rosenberg and Hiss cases as unresolved or ambiguous and minimize the extent of Soviet spying.

Some of these battles about the extent of Soviet espionage are fought online at H-HOAC, an academic discussion list for those interested in the history of American communism, and H-DIPLO, which is devoted to diplomatic history. There one finds such figures as Grover Furr, professor of English at Montclair State University, ardent defender of Joseph Stalin and the Moscow Purge Trials; Roger Sandilands, an English academic who is the biographer and defender of Lauchlin Currie, a White House aide who assisted Soviet espionage; and David Lowenthal, an American-born, British academic, who has taken up the lost cause of his late brother John, a Rutgers law professor who, until his death last year, stoutly maintained not only that Alger Hiss was innocent of espionage, but that Whittaker Chambers was a fantasist who had invented the tale of his own spying. These holdouts have been joined by a retired KGB general, Julius

Kobyalev, who insists that Hiss was not a spy, while nostalgically applauding the greatness of the KGB and lamenting the fall of the USSR.

One piece of evidence recently cited on H-HOAC emerged during an unusual libel trial in Great Britain. John Lowenthal published an article in a British journal in 2000 attacking the methods used and conclusions reached in *The Haunted Wood*, a book by Allen Weinstein and Alexander Vassiliev. After the fall of the Soviet Union, the SVR, successor to the KGB, signed a lucrative contract with Crown Publishers to bring out a series of books. A retired KGB officer with security clearances would be allowed access to a selected segment of intelligence files and would coauthor a book with an American writer. Vassiliev and Weinstein produced this study of Soviet intelligence operations directed against the United States in the 1930s and 1940s. When the SVR regained much of its clout in 1995, it grew less cooperative, and the project ran into trouble. Vassiliev prudently left Russia before the book was published and settled in Britain. Angered by Lowenthal's charges, he sued for libel and lost the case in 2003.

One document introduced at the trial was a handwritten memo by Vassiliev, summarizing and quoting from a report written in December 1948 by Anatoly Gorsky, chief ("resident" in KGB jargon) of the KGB station in Washington at the time of Elizabeth Bentley's defection in 1945. This memo has been trumpeted by the diehards as proof of Hiss's innocence. In fact, it is another damning link in the long chain of evidence that establishes Hiss's guilt. The memo enriches our knowledge of Soviet espionage and provides further confirmation of stories told by such former spies as Chambers, Bentley, Hedda Massing, and Louis Budenz.

Vassiliev lost his libel suit, but this had less to do with the merits of his work and more to do with his foolish decision to represent himself without professional counsel as well as his poor judgment in treating criticism as libel in the first place. His notes are, of course, not the best evidence; it would be much preferable to have Gorsky's original report, but that is not likely to be soon released by the SVR, which deeply regrets allowing any access to its archives and has been trying to discredit what information is already out.

In a section of the memo titled "Failures in the U.S.A. (1938-1945)," Gorsky noted five groups of agents that had been compromised by defectors from Soviet espionage. The first was "Karl's Group." "Karl" is identified as Whittaker Chambers, and the group includes Alger Hiss (code-named "Leonard"), Donald Hiss (code-named "Junior"), Henry Wadleigh, Frank Reno, William Pigman, Joseph Peters, Harry Dexter White, Felix Inslerman, and a number of others whom Chambers himself identified. Indeed, of the twenty-one names listed in Karl's group, who are all identified by code name and real name, Chambers discussed fifteen in his testimony and his autobiography, *Witness*. And, without providing names, he mentioned three minor participants whose jobs match the positions of three others on Gorsky's list.

Because the code name for Hiss given in the deciphered 1945 KGB cables (the Venona decryptions) was "Ales," and because earlier KGB memos discussed in *The Haunted Wood* referred to Hiss as "Lawyer," several thehards on H-HOAC and H-DIPLO astoundingly found the Gorsky memo exculpatory. But the KGB frequently changed cover names. That Hiss has a new one in this memo does not prove his innocence; his mere inclusion is yet additional proof that Chambers was telling the truth and that Hiss was a Soviet source.

Gorsky's memo also documents a number of agents compromised by the defection of Hedda Massing, who quietly dropped out of KGB service in the late 1930s but did not provide the FBI with an account of her activities until 1947. Among those Gorsky listed as compromised was Laurence Duggan, a senior State Department official who committed suicide when faced with inquiries from the FBI about his work for the Russians. Other Soviet sources Gorsky thought were at risk included those known to senior Communist party officer Louis Budenz, a *Daily Worker* editor whose conversion to Catholicism was dramatically reported in the *New York Times* in 1945. Budenz, whose account of his own connections to Soviet intelligence has been disparaged by many historians, knew a number of Communists selected to infiltrate and disrupt the American Trotskyist movement.

The memo's largest group of names – counting forty-four – come from two large networks of agents supervised by Elizabeth Bentley. Bentley began talking to the FBI in late 1945. In her statement to the FBI and later in congressional testimony, she discussed all but six of the forty-four on Gorsky's list. Several agents she named who were not also identified in the deciphered Venona messages turn up in Gorsky's memo, including Joseph Gregg, Robert Miller, William Remington, and Bernard Redmont (former journalist and professor at Boston University).

Finally, Gorsky listed a group of Soviet sources compromised by Alexander Koral, a New York school district maintenance engineer and KGB courier who broke under FBI interrogation in 1947 and provided a partial account of his group. Among those potentially compromised by Koral, Gorksy noted, was Byron Darling, a physicist who had the KGB code name "Huron." Huron appears in the deciphered Venona cables as a KGB source involved in scientific espionage, including work on the atomic bomb project. The FBI was never able to identify Huron's real name. In 1953, Darling, then teaching physics at Ohio State University and working on a U.S. Air Force research contract, refused to answer questions about secret links to the American Communist party in testimony to the House Committee on Un-American Activities. Ohio State fired him. Darling left the country and taught physics for the rest of his career at Laval University in Canada. He has been lionized by some historians of the McCarthy era as an innocent man hounded by neanderthals for his innocuous political beliefs. In fact, Darling was no martyr, he was a spy.

The Gorsky memo reminds us that historians who underestimate the extent of Soviet espionage in America fail to comprehend just how serious an issue the loyalty of government employees was. That this damning list of spies is cited by a handful of academics to clear the name of anyone on it shows that hope springs eternal among a dwindling band of espionage-deniers. Increasingly, these people resemble the pathetic remnants of the Imperial Japanese Army who refused to believe that the emperor had surrendered and continued to wander the jungles of Southeast Asia for years after 1945. They, at least, had the excuse that they were out of communication with the real world.

Originally published in the *Weekly Standard*, March 21, 2005 and reprinted with permission.

23

Reflections of a Traditionalist Historian

My friend and co-author, John Haynes, recently updated the bibliography he first published in 1987 on American Communism. Then, it included more than 2,000 items. The most recent iteration is up to 9,000 items and every day brings new entries. The last few years have seen a new publication, *American Communist History*, brought into existence through the ministrations of Dan Leab, former editor of *Labor History*. This new journal, Dan informs me, does not lack for high-quality submissions. An H-Net list devoted to the topic began in March 2003, has more than 300 subscribers and generates regular posts and considerable controversy. Only five years ago, the *New York Times* Sunday magazine had a cover story on the raging wars about Senator Joseph McCarthy and the issue of Communist espionage among scholars and a lead editorial in the *New York Times* around the same time inaccurately denounced some unnamed historians who were accused of attempting to rehabilitate the late senator. The *New York Times* does not often deign to notice academic disputes, much less weigh in on their merits, unless they involve plagiarism, fraud, or Alan Sokol fooling the editors of *Social Text*, so the newspaper's intervention was a clear sign that the issue of American Communism continues to strike a nerve even as it recedes further and further into the past.

One of the reasons the issue of American Communism remains so raw is that so many of those who have studied it bring political passions and commitments to their work. Much of the first burst of scholarly attention to the CPUSA came in the late 1940s and 1950s in response to the transformation of the Party from a significant factor in some areas of American life into a pariah and subject of governmental and societal attack. The first generation of scholars of the CPUSA were bitter political opponents of Communism—either one-time Party members like Theodore Draper, former Trotskyists like Irving Howe, or Social Democrats like Daniel Bell. They had lived through many of the events they wrote about,

Originally published in *American Communist History*, December 2005 and reprinted by permission of the pubisher (Taylor & Francis Ltd, http://www.tandf.co.uk/journals)

participated in struggles against Communists and bore the scars earned in those battles. Forced to rely on a limited amount of primary data, they were able to produce often-valuable and still useful scholarship in significant part because of the fund of personal knowledge they brought to the topic.

Although critical of the Party, most of this first generation were men who still considered themselves on the political left. The next generation of scholars to turn its attention to Communism was also largely self-identified as leftist but was harshly critical of people like Bell, Glazer, and, especially, Draper. Like the first group, many of its members had been active in radical causes, in this case, the New Left of the 1960s and early 1970s. In contrast to the first generation, whose connection to universities generally came later in their lives, after long careers on the fringes of political activism such as journalism, this new cadre of scholars came to the study of American Communism at a younger age. While few had any direct experience with the Communist Party, they had generally gone back to graduate school after immersion in one of the myriad of New Left groups and after the collapse of hopes for a new, vibrant American radicalism had ended.

Their study of American Communism was often linked to a search for a model on how to transform American society. The political was personal. A handful, like James Prickett, found a picture of how to build a revolutionary movement in the ultra-revolutionary Third Period; others like Maurice Isserman celebrated the Popular Front. The personal was also political. For some their study of American Communism was, in part, linked to filial piety and family connections; it was their parents, grandparents or other relatives about whom they were writing. Relying on oral histories and old activists more willing to talk now that the dangers of McCarthyism had eased, buttressed by the breakdown of the anti-Communist consensus in the wake of the Vietnam War, and often inspired by the new emphasis on social history, they produced a startling variety of local studies sharing the assumption, as Isserman put it, that "the American CP was shaped by the environment in which it operated and by the people who enlisted under its banner" more profoundly than by "its overall subservience to the Soviet Union."[1]

There were divisions among those who called themselves revisionists or "new historians of American Communism."[2] As already noted, different eras of the Communist past came in for different evaluations. Some revisionists largely abandoned political history, leading to accounts of American Communism without the political impulse that had led the CPUSA to politicize, not only art, literature and music, but even family relations. While Isserman had conceded the Soviet ties, others brushed them off or denied them altogether. In Paul Buhle's eyes, there were really two American Communist parties. One was headquartered in New York where a handful of Stalinist warhorses cheered Stalin's purges and political repression, took orders from Moscow and faithfully promised to carry them out, passionately believed in Marxism–Leninism and practiced a repressive form of democratic centralism. The other party was out in America where idealistic rank-and-filers shrugged off New York headquarters as out of touch, cared little about Earl Browder, less about Joseph Stalin, and fought the good fight for democratic unions and racial integration and opposed fascism. Another small group of revisionists went further, praising Stalin and the Soviet Union. Norman Markowitz, for instance, included Isserman as part of a "new group of anti-Communist caretakers," along with myself, and Gerald Horne castigated Mark Naison for writing "rot" in his revisionist account of the CPUSA in Harlem.[3]

While the great majority of this second generation of scholars of Communism were "revisionists," there were a handful of traditionalists who adopted the perspective first enunciated by Draper—including Lowell Dyson, John Haynes, and myself. We agreed with Draper that the first and most important thing to know about the CPUSA was that it was dependent on the Soviet Union for its vision, its policies and its direction, or, as Haynes and I put it in *The American Communist Movement*, "every era in the history of the American Communist Movement has been inaugurated by developments in the Communist world abroad."[4] The CPUSA was not an independent political organization but an appendage of a foreign body. Like the revisionists, there were differences among the traditionalists. A number, perhaps the majority, were not employed in universities. Most were happy to identify themselves as anti-Communists, although its sources varied. Some traditionalists identified with left-wing critiques of Communism; others retained both a respect and affection for what used to be called "Cold War" liberalism. By the turn of the century, one could even find a handful—a tiny handful—of students of the topic who actually defended Joseph McCarthy, although the number of revisionists who were cheerleaders for Communism dwarfed them. Depending on their perspective, traditionalists blamed American Communism for destroying the prospects for a viable American left, subverting other organizations or advancing foreign interests at the expense of American democracy.

I do not want to rehash the arguments and polemics that characterized this debate during the late 1970s and 1980s. Both sides could find evidence to support their position, although it will surprise nobody if I say that I think the revisionist evidence was weaker and subject to more difficulties. While they could point to isolated cases of independence, moments when the Party seemed to be either a little ahead or a little behind Moscow, the problem was precisely that these were isolated and could easily and plausibly be attributed to communication difficulties or garbled orders or an unusually brazen local Party official soon brought to heel. Some flexibility was sometimes allowed on tactics but creativity was largely limited to those times when Moscow's line emphasized creativity and independence. It was—and is—telling that no revisionist produced a single-volume history of the CPUSA in which he or she would have to maneuver around the periodic revisions of line occasioned by orders from Moscow, but instead focused on one era, one locale or one issue. Still, revisionist monographs illuminated the Party's role in a variety of venues and exposed a great deal of its previously unknown or unappreciated history. Whatever one's disagreement with their conclusions or caveats about some of their judgments, they were based on solid research and respect for the norms of scholarship.

The opening of Russian archives and the availability of a treasure trove of material on the CPUSA from both the Comintern archive and the CPUSA archive itself have given fresh impetus to the study of American Communism. In this regard, everyone who studies this topic owes a major debt of gratitude of John Haynes, who represented the Library of Congress in the negotiations to microfilm the CPUSA collection and place a copy of it in Washington, where it is available to graduate students and faculty under conditions far more expeditious for research than Moscow, and for his role in encouraging the digitalizing of a large portion of the Comintern archive as well. On the one hand, this vast infusion of new material promises to enrich the specific, local studies of the CPUSA and its constituent units by providing the internal documents and memos that help make sense of the public record and scattered internal material previously available. The most valuable portion of the revisionist scholarship, that looking at particular episodes or policies, will certainly be enhanced. On the other hand, I think that the overall result of this new material is to confirm the argument made by traditionalists and even strengthen it. Let me iterate several ways it has done this.

First, there has been the confirmation of the substantial Soviet and Comintern role in financing the CPUSA. Moscow gold was not some myth or invention of right-wing lunatics. Throughout the 1920s the small, struggling CP was kept afloat by money from abroad which financed not only a variety of Party programs, but cadres, enabling the CPUSA to outstrip its rivals on the left. While the financing decreased in the 1930s as the Party grew, it reemerged with a vengeance in the 1960s via the Childs brothers. Although some revisionists tried to downplay the significance of this monetary support or labeled it "old news," it reinforced the argument that the CPUSA had many strands tying it to Moscow.

Secondly, there was confirmation of the Comintern's role in making, unmaking and influencing Party leadership. This had not been as controversial an issue between revisionists and traditionalists, largely because the CI's hand in the manipulations of the 1920s was widely accepted and the Soviet role in the ouster of Earl Browder in 1945 was so blatant. But it has been strengthened and deepened by new information indicating that the CI vetted and interfered with choices for the Politburo and Central Committee, even during the Popular Front. The infamous Duclos article of 1945 was first written by Russians in Russian and appeared in a classified Soviet publication. One prominent revisionist, Jim Barrett, in his excellent biography of William Z. Foster, based in no small part on material from the Russian archives, notes that Foster, originally willing to defy the Soviets, over time became "more fixed on the Soviet line and more rigid in his understanding and application of Marxism-Leninism." He interprets Foster's life as a conflict between an indigenous radicalism and a foreign import, eventually won by the latter.[5]

Thirdly, there has been confirmation of the overall Comintern supervision of the Party's positions and views. Mark Solomon altered his 1972 conclusion that the idea of "Black belt" self-determination was the creation of African-American Communists after examining the archives, concluding that the doctrine originated in Moscow and illustrated how "Soviet state interest" and the CPUSA's lack of independence "more often than not led to willing acquiescence to foreign-made decisions that were often applied reflectively in the United States." In our work Haynes and I showed that even when it came to its vaunted slogan, "Communism is Twentieth Century Americanism," the CPUSA willingly dropped it at the insistence of the Comintern.[6]

Fourthly, there is the issue of espionage. It played a very minor role in the dispute between traditionalists and revisionists. While most traditionalists believed that Hiss and the Rosenbergs were guilty, they also agreed that espionage was, at most, a very minor part of the Communist movement, largely because they thought Party officials were too shrewd or cautious to risk involvement. Most, but not all, revisionists thought that the spy charges of the 1940s and 1950s were part and parcel of a Red Scare that targeted innocent people. Take the autobiographical book that Steve Nelson produced with Jim Barrett and Rob Ruck in 1981. Nelson dismissed the allegations about his role in Soviet espionage as "pretty hokey stuff" and his collaborators obviously did not press him to respond to the documentation available in committee hearings of the House Committee on Un-American Activities, regarded as an obviously unreliable source. The new material now available—much of it obtained by Katie Sibley—makes clear it was not; Nelson was deeply involved in efforts to obtain material from the Radiation Lab in California and was in direct contact with the NKVD.[7]

Some revisionists have honestly and directly acknowledged the importance of the new material that has emerged from both Russian and American archives. Some have acknowledged it but attempted to minimize its significance. While it is certainly true that only a few hundred CPUSA members spied for the Soviets, and the vast majority of people who joined the Party had no connection with espionage, it is also true that the Party leadership was directly involved in these activities; a special Party group, the underground apparatus, coordinated activities with the NKVD and GRU and the relationship was close enough for the former to adopt the code name "Fellowcountrymen" for CPUSA members. Revisionists may have considered the CPUSA to be a band of indigenous American radicals, but the Soviets had a different view of the matter. And the fact that the top Party leaders were willing to risk such intimate cooperation with Soviet intelligence despite what exposure could have done to their movement speaks volumes about their priorities.

While the opening of the Russian archives and the release of the Venona documents have ended—or should have ended—a number of disputes, they have exacerbated others. Not surprisingly, the underlying reason is political. While acknowledging the widespread cooperation of the CPUSA with Soviet intelligence, Ellen Schrecker, Maurice Isserman, Scott Lucas, and others have accused Haynes and myself of "triumphalism," pointing to the use of our data and arguments by conservatives such as George Will as justifications for American anti-Communism and for taking delight in the Cold War victory of the United States. We plead guilty, although why anyone, even an historian, would lament the collapse of the Soviet empire, the discrediting of a totalitarian ideology, or the self-immolation of Communism is a puzzle to me.

Surely, the revisionist historians, of all people, should not be complaining about allowing one's political perspective to help focus one's scholarship. Ellen Schrecker declared in *Many Are the Crimes* her sympathy for and agreement with much of the political agenda of her subjects. A number of revisionists have been quite vocal in asserting that it was and is an American tragedy that the Communist movement was defeated, claiming that during the 1930s it embodied much of what was decent and honorable in American life. Schrecker blamed anti-Communism for a litany of crimes, ranging from retarding the development of the civil rights movement to crippling American higher education.[8]

What united many traditionalists was the conviction that whatever its virtues—its opposition to racism, support for unionism, and periodic hostility to fascism—the CPUSA's professed commitment to democracy was a sham, belied by support for one of the bloodiest dictators in history. And they found it odd that some of the same historians who trumpeted the Communists' support for victims of fascism and repression around the world and in America had little to say about the millions of victims of Communism—including Communists. Arguably, Stalin killed nearly as many Communists as Hitler. And, Joseph Stalin repressed more American Communists than J. Edgar Hoover, HUAC, and Pat McCarran put together. More than a thousand American Finns died in the Gulag, as did assorted other émigrés. Writing the entry on Finnish-American Communists in *The Encyclopedia of the American Left*, Mike Karni couldn't be troubled to mention what happened to these people and revisionists free with the word "fascism" to characterize the United States have demonstrated no interest in their fate. We demonstrated in *The Soviet World of American Communism* that some of those victims were assisted to their fates by denunciations from fellow American Communists.[9] When Ellen Schrecker asserted that opposition to Communism during the Cold War "tapped into something dark and nasty in the human soul," she slandered the noble cause of anti-Communism and ignored the cultural, religious and ethnic links that ensured that the millions of victims of Communism are and were not just a remote issue for many Americans since so many—Poles, Jews, Ukrainians, Letts, Lithuanians, and others—lost relatives to Stalin. As Aileen Kraditor has documented, it was the CPUSA itself that insisted in its propaganda and internal Party training and education that the USSR was a model of democracy, so when it called for democracy and insisted that America was not one, most Americans could be pardoned for believing it was either lying or dangerous, whatever its rank and file members believed.[10]

I am confident that continuing different political and ideological perspectives will ensure that revisionists and traditionalists continue to interpret the evidence emerging from Russian archives differently. I can admire and appreciate the diligent and comprehensive research of Bruce Craig into the life of Harry Dexter White, which demonstrated White's cooperation with Soviet intelligence services, while deploring his conclusion that White's was an honorable life well-lived.[11] What is more disturbing is another trend to refuse to confront evidence or to distort it in unprofessional ways. Haynes and I have discussed a number of examples in our book *In Denial* and I will not repeat them here, other than to note that it is one thing to make a mistake or err in an assertion and correct it when called and another to refuse to respond to criticism or refuse to provide documentary evidence for implausible or risible claims.[12]

Haynes and I have admitted to errors, including confusing someone code-named Louis with another figure code-named Louis-Morris Cohen. We thus incorrectly argued in *The Secret World of American Communism* that CPUSA was involved in atomic espionage through Cohen in the Second World War. But I would also point out that Leona Cohen—Morris's wife—was involved in atomic espionage during that period, serving as a courier for Ted Hall, that Morris was involved in atomic espionage after the war and that Venona material has implicated the CPUSA in atomic espionage. Some revisionists will neither admit mistakes nor provide evidence for their assertions. Paul Buhle has still refused to respond to our challenge made several years ago that he provide evidence for his assertion in *The Encyclopedia of the American Left* that American Communists were prominent among those who died fighting in Israel's war of independence or that illegal aid to Israel by radicals in the late 1940s dwarfed the clandestine support given to Soviet intelligence by American Communists. And Peter Carroll's only response to our demonstration that he had incorrectly credited the Abraham Lincoln Brigade veterans and the CPUSA leadership with defying Soviet policies was to call our work "pseudo-research" that only "appears to have the trappings of bona fide scholarship." Despite repeated requests, no one has yet been able to demonstrate that the U.S. government labeled veterans of the ALB "premature anti-fascists" but revisionists keep repeating the claim. No matter what our political views, averting our eyes from the evidence ensures only blindness.[13]

Notes

1. Maurice Isserman, "Three Generations: Historians View American Communism," *Labor History*, 26 (Fall 1985).
2. Ibid., 539-540.
3. Norman Markowitz, "The New Cold War Scholarship," *Political Affairs*, 62 (October 1983), 27-38; Gerald Horne, "Communists in Harlem during the Depression," *Political Affairs*, 63 (September/October 1984), 36-38.
4. Harvey Klehr and John Earl Haynes, *The American Communist Movement: Storming Heaven Itself* (New York: Twayne Publishers, 1992), 4.
5. James R. Barrett, *William Z. Foster and the Tragedy of American Radicalism* (Urbana: University of Illinois Press, 1998), 45.
6. Mark Solomon, *The Cry Was Unity: Communists and Afro-Americans, 1917–1936* (Jackson: University Press of Mississippi, 1998), preface; Harvey Klehr, John Earl Haynes and Kyril Anderson, *The Soviet World of American Communism* (New Haven, CT: Yale University Press, 1998), 39-40.
7. Steve Nelson, James R. Barrett, and Rob Ruck, *Steve Nelson: American Radical* (Pittsburgh: University of Pittsburgh Press, 1981), 284; Katherine Sibley, *Red Spies in America* (Lawrence: University of Kansas Press, 2004).
8. Ellen Schrecker, *Many Are The Crimes: McCarthyism in America* (Boston: Little, Brown, 1998).
9. Michael Kazin, "Finnish Americans," in Mari Jo Buhle, Paul Buhle, and Dan Georgakas, eds., *Encyclopedia of the American Left*, 2nd ed. (New York: Oxford University Press, 1998), 227; Klehr et al., *The Soviet World*, 218–227.
10. Schrecker, *Many Are The Crimes*, 46; Aileen Kraditor, *"Jimmy Higgins": The Mental World of the American Rank-and-File Communist, 1930–1958* (New York: Greenwood, 1988).
11. Bruce Craig, *Treasonable Doubt: the Harry Dexter White Case* (Lawrence: University of Kansas Press, 2004), 276.
12. John Earl Haynes and Harvey Klehr, *In Denial: Historians, Communism, and Espionage* (San Francisco, CA: Encounter Books, 2003).
13. Ibid., 112-113, 124-134; Peter Carroll, "The Myth of the Moscow Archives," *Science and Society*, 68 (Fall 2004), 338.

24

Reflections on Anti-Anticommunism

Since Whittaker Chambers was a pioneer in the exposure of the Soviet espionage underground in the United States, the following reflections on the implications of the recent revelations from the Russian archives and the release of the Venona decryptions should begin with a story about him. In *Witness,* Chambers discussed the controversy he evoked after Henry Luce appointed him editor of foreign news at *Time* magazine in 1944. His fiercely anticommunist slant on the news enraged *Time*'s European and Asian correspondents who signed a round-robin letter demanding his removal. To Chambers's enemies, this story was just another example of his inability to understand the tenets of journalism; as an ideological warrior he distorted and deformed news reports which did not fit his own ideological views.[1]

The Venona messages recently declassified by the National Security Agency, the Federal Bureau of Investigation and the Central Intelligence Agency shed fresh light on this issue. Two of the most hostile Time correspondents were John Scott and Richard Lauterbach. The latter, described by Sam Tanenhaus in his superb biography of Chambers as "the correspondent Chambers trusted least," had been reporting from Moscow. In December 1944, just as he was attempting to get Chambers fired, Lauterbach was being considered for recruitment by the KGB. One cable from Soviet agent Jack Soble noted that Lauterbach was a secret member of the Communist Party and, upon his return from Moscow, had passed along information complaining about *Time*'s anti-Sovietism; the cable recommended formally recruiting him as a KGB agent. Vladimir Pravdin, a Tass correspondent in Washington and New York and himself a KGB officer, began to study Lauterbach, assigned him a cover name and asked Moscow to check on his activities when he had been stationed in the Soviet Union. No reply was ever decrypted.[2]

John Scott, another of Chambers's enemies, had been an active KGB source under the cover name Ivanov when he worked in the OSS in 1942 and 1943.

Originally published in *Continuity*, Spring 2003, and reprinted with permission.

And for good measure Stephen Laird, who supervised *Time* correspondents, was yet another KGB agent, operating under the cover name Yun, who regularly turned over reports and background material sent to the magazine by its employees. When Laird left *Time* to go to work for RKO in Hollywood, his new KGB contact used the opportunity to plead with Moscow for an adjustment in his budget to buy a car, noting that without one "in a town like Los Angeles I should simply be walked off my feet."[3]

Beyond providing additional confirmation of Chambers's story, this little episode says a great deal about the war waged over communism in the United States in the 1940s and 1950s. One side included a number of people pretending to be noncommunists. Hiding behind the cloak of being progressives or liberals or just objective observers, they were in fact secret members of the Communist Party and sometimes agents of Soviet intelligence. Many of their liberal allies were often reluctant, unwilling, or unable to consider that possibility and preferred to regard truth-tellers like Chambers as liars, deceivers, and morally reprehensible.

The passage of time and the explosion in recent years of material from Russian and American archives that has confirmed the extent and significance of Soviet espionage in the United States and the duplicitous and pernicious activities of the American Communist Party has modified but not eliminated this tendency.

Consider for a moment the recent imbroglio over the special Academy Award given to Elia Kazan. Prominent Hollywood figures denounced him as an informer. There was a fierce media debate about whether he deserved this honor. Compare the treatment of this genuinely talented artist, who testified honestly about his past, to that of Walter Bernstein, once blacklisted, winner of a Writers Guild Award for Lifetime Achievement, and a filmwriter among whose widely praised screenplays is "The Front," a denunciation of those who, like Kazan, cooperated with the House Committee on Un-American Activities. Bernstein is mentioned in Venona as a source for Soviet intelligence. Yet, as far as I can tell, not one journalist has asked him to explain his past behavior. No Hollywood dignitary has demanded that he apologize. There have been no outraged editorials denouncing him for apparently cooperating with the KGB. Can one imagine a Hollywood movie today making Kazan a hero? We live, after all, in a cultural world where the left never sees the need to apologize.[4]

Let me digress briefly to tell how I got involved in this kind of research. By 1989 I was thoroughly sick of studying American communism. I had published five books on the topic and had engaged in a number of nasty academic arguments about my interpretation of American communism. It was negative, and many of my colleagues believed that the CPUSA had been a democratic, progressive organization committed to civil rights and labor organizing. They further believed it had been destroyed by the illegal and repressive activities of the FBI, and they mocked my argument that the CPUSA had been controlled from Moscow. My Cold War views were denounced in academic reviews as a throwback to old, discredited interpretations that had been superseded by younger scholars with more open minds, many of whom, not coincidently, were veterans of the New Left of the 1960s. In the academic world, at least, communists were being rehabilitated. Veteran party warhorses published sanitized autobiographies or were eulogized by admiring younger scholars. The revisionist school was in full flower.

But still, I had considerable intellectual capital invested in the topic, so I had begun working on a biography of David Karr, a fascinating man who had begun life as a young communist in Brooklyn and ended it as a mysterious capitalist entrepreneur in Paris. Since Karr had many Russian connections, I wrote to archives in Moscow and was assured that I could examine material they had on him. By the time I arrived in the summer of 1992, the failed coup against Mikhail Gorbachev had led to the dissolution of the Soviet Union and the outlawing of the Communist Party. When the archive that had promised me access to Karr material suddenly withdrew its offer, I was forced to spend all of my time at the archive that housed the records of the Communist International. John Haynes, my co-author, and I later learned that the files of the CPUSA were also controlled by this archive. After a wait of one year, while a new law was passed by the Duma that ended the CPUSA's legal right to control this material and the massive file was retrieved from a warehouse outside Moscow, Haynes and I became the first Americans to research it.

When I began to look at this material, I worried that my academic reputation was about to be destroyed. Would I find a memo from the Soviet Politburo ordering the CPUSA to stop requesting guidance and make its own decisions? Letters from New York refusing to accept Moscow gold? Would I have to confess that twenty years of work had been wrong? No, I would not. I discovered that the revisionists had been wrong—spectacularly wrong—about every aspect of the history of American communism. And my enthusiasm for studying American communism was reignited.

One reason some of the archivists in this former stronghold of the Soviet Communist Party were nice to me and cooperative was that they were under the mistaken impression that I must be an American communist since they could not imagine who else would be interested in this stuff. When I began going through the Comintern material—and I was the first Westerner to look at most of it—I was astounded to discover many documents labeled top secret. I marked them for copying without trying to translate them; there were so many files to examine and my time was limited. After three weeks, I left Moscow with a reel of microfilm, many of whose exposures would have gotten me locked up just a year before—documents that detailed the intimate ties between the CPUSA and Soviet intelligence. Returning home to Atlanta, I had the material translated and began to marvel at what I had scooped up. I was fortunate too in that the political scene in Moscow was still in flux and chaos. The Russians did not know exactly what was in their files. After *The Secret World* of *American Communism* was published in 1995, John Haynes was back at the archives and learned that the SVR, successor to the KGB, had been investigating how we had been allowed access to this material. Many of the documents in the book have since been "resecretized" and one can no longer get access to them in Moscow even though they have been published abroad.[5]

It was not only Russian archives that began to disgorge documents. Shortly after our book was published John and I received a call from Senator Daniel Moynihan, who was heading a commission to examine issues of government secrecy. He had read our book and wanted us to testify about the internal security issues that had done so much to create many of the government's regulations about classification. When we did, we pleaded for the further opening of American records about Soviet espionage to match what was then available in Russian archives, specifically citing Venona, traces of which we had discovered in the Russian archives. Senator Moynihan turned to John Deutch, a presidential appointee to the Commission (who had just recently been appointed head of the CIA) and asked him to look into declassifying Venona. Deutch made no promises, but did agree to consider the issue. What we did not know was that within the intelligence community a number of people were already pushing to release the Venona material, and late in the summer of 1995 the first batch was declassified. Since then Allen Weinstein and Alexander Vassiliev have gained access to KGB files, and Christopher Andrew has told us of the fascinating material from KGB files copied by Vasili Mitrokhin.[6]

What is quite remarkable about this material is that all of it is largely consistent. The Comintern files, the CPUSA files, the KGB files and the Venona decryptions fit together, reinforce each other and give us great confidence that each is accurate. And, this material confirms, in astounding detail, the stories of Soviet espionage told by Whittaker Chambers as well as by Elizabeth Bentley, who broke with Soviet intelligence in 1945 and told the FBI about several dozen government officials who had provided her with confidential government documents.

It has been a bad decade for those who have denied Soviet espionage, like *Nation* editor Victor Navasky. But they have been resilient. Here are some examples of how they have dealt with these unpleasant new facts.

One of the more interesting historical tidbits emerging from the archives involved Harry Bridges, the long-time president of the International Longshoremen's and Warehousemen's Union, headquartered in San Francisco. Bridges had been a very controversial figure. From 1938 to 1956 the U.S. government tried to deport the Australian-born Bridges, alleging that he was a communist. In four different federal hearings, Bridges denied under oath that he was a member of the CPUSA. In the files of the Comintern in Moscow, we found a list of CPUSA members elected to the Central Committee of the party in 1936; on that list is a Comrade Rossi, identified in an accompanying biography as the pseudonym of Harry Bridges. So, not only was Bridges a communist, he was a member of the Central Committee. He lied and committed perjury in immigration hearings in 1938 and 1941, deceived a majority of the U.S. Supreme Court in 1945 when it overturned his deportation in a 5-4 decision, committed perjury at his naturalization hearing in 1945, and lied again at his 1949 trial for perjury.[7]

And what has been the reaction to these revelations? In 1992, the University of Washington accepted money to establish the Harry Bridges Endowed Chair in Labor Studies. In 1999, the San Francisco supervisors renamed the plaza in front of the San Francisco Ferry Building in his honor. Early in 1999, the president of the ILWU gave the keynote speech to the Southwest Labor Studies Association, and to the whoops and shouted approval of his academic audience, denounced these new efforts to use materials from Russian archives since, he claimed they were probably all forgeries, and proclaimed that he didn't give a damn whether Bridges was a communist or not.

Harry Bridges is not the only perjurer honored by a chair at an American institution of higher education. Bard College in New York has established the Alger Hiss Chair of Social Studies which is currently occupied by a suitably appropriate figure, Joel Kovel. Kovel, who ran for senator of New York in 1998 on the Green Party ticket, is a practicing psychotherapist. In 1988, he orchestrated a conference on anti-communism at Harvard University that was dedicated to the proposition that anti-communism had deformed American political, cultural, and social life. The conferees, who included John Kenneth Galbraith, Angela Davis and Howard Fast, cheered the imminent collapse of American capitalism.

The demise of the Soviet Union and its East European empire within three years did not daunt Kovel, who promptly wrote a particularly illuminating book, *Red Hunting in the Promised Land,* a few years later. In a breathtaking synthesis of American history, Kovel traced the roots of American anticommunism to the first red scare-the encounter between Puritan and Indian, during which the reds were unjustly persecuted, setting the stage for the 1940s. True to his psychological training, Kovel offered an interpretation of Hubert Humphrey's liberal anti-communism as "a ritual of male bonding within which the signifier 'father' links Hubert Humphrey, Jr., Hubert Humphrey Sr., Lyndon Johnson and the whole ethos of America as a land where real men stand tall and stand together." For J. Edgar Hoover anti-communism "might be interchangeably a womb or anus in addition to having moral and racial implications."[8]

As new information about the crimes and criminals of the past has piled up, the response of much of the academic and journalistic left has been to evade or deny the truth. In this, they are akin to current day Holocaust deniers who distort evidence and ignore the plain facts of history in order to sustain their own bankrupt political ideals. Take the case of some American victims of the Gulag.

When Memorial, the organization dedicated to remembering the victims of Stalinism, uncovered a mass grave in Russia in the summer of 1997, few

Americans took notice. Located in a rural area near Sandermakh, in Russia's Karelian republic, the gravesite contains more than 9,000 bodies in some 300 separate burial pits. Individual lists identify more than 6,000 people by name, place and year of birth, occupation, and date of execution.[9]

The victims included a wide variety of targets of Stalin's terror: four Russian Orthodox archbishops, thirty Roman Catholic priests, three hundred Ukrainian intellectuals, twenty Tatar leaders, a group of Belarusian officials, as well as thousands of Russians from every walk of life. But also on the list are 119 Americans. To mention only a few: Eino Bjorn, a tractor driver born in Minnesota and shot on February 10,1938, at the age of twenty-six; Walter Maki, a thirty-one year-old carpenter, also a Minnesota native, shot on May 15, 1938; and Logan Siren, yet another Minnesotan, an electrician at a paper plant who was shot on February 11, 1938. Matvei Kartinen, a mechanic born in Ironwood, Michigan, Andrew Hannula, a truck driver born in the state of Washington, and Karl Huuke, an Ohio native and cabinet maker, were executed on December 28, 1937. Helen Hill, who had been born and raised in Minnesota, had arrived in Karelia in 1931 with her parents at the age of fourteen. She was working as a dispatcher at a lumber camp when she was arrested. On April 22, 1938 an NKVD executioner shot her.

The Memorial researchers concluded that in many cases the dead appeared to have been executed on site. The position of the skeletons and other remains suggested that the prisoners had been stripped to their underwear, lined up next to a trench with their hands and feet tied, and then shot one at a time in the back of the head with a pistol.

Between 4,000 and 7,000 American and Canadian Finns caught "Karelian Fever" and emigrated in the early 1930s, aided by the Karelian Technical Aid Bureau, headed first by Matti Tenhunen and then by Oscar Corgan, both Finnish-American communists. Most were committed communists, eager to help build socialism. Within a few years several hundred returned home, but as many as a thousand were arrested or executed, including Tenhunen and Corgan, whose remains were found at Sandermakh.

The American government was indifferent to their murder. So, too, was the Finnish-American community, deeply split between the majority "White" or "Church" Finns (reflecting the central role of Lutheran churches in their community life) and a sizable minority of "Red" Finns who were aligned with the Communist Party. The former were ashamed of their radical brethren, hostile to their politics, and did not concern themselves with their fate.

For their part, the Red Finns remaining in the United States were also silent. When Lawrence Hokkanen returned to Michigan, after seeing dozens of his friends disappear, his own mother and sister refused to believe him. At a welcome home party, a representative of the CPUSA gave a speech asserting that "no innocent people had been arrested" in the Soviet Union. Lawrence later wrote that between the pressure of the party and his family "I remained silent."[10]

Oscar Corgan's American-born daughter recalled years later that the survivors "placed our faith in the Communist parties of the US and Canada to which our parents had devoted the best years of their lives. When the purges began and our parents began disappearing, we were sure those Communist parties would interfere and stand up for their comrades."[11]

It was a false hope. Earl Browder, head of the CPUSA in the 1930s, had personally known both Matti Tenhunen and Oscar Corgan. When they disappeared, however, he made no inquiry about their fate, despite exchanging letters and cables on a weekly basis and visiting Moscow annually to consult communist leaders regarding his party's activities.[12]

Not even Khrushchev's denunciation of Stalin's crimes in 1956 could bring the CPUSA to own up to its role in hiding the murder of hundreds of its former members. Ironically, the leader of the CPUSA from 1959 until shortly before his death in October 2000, Gus Hall, was himself a Finnish-American, born Arvo Holberg in Iron, Minnesota, in 1910. Considering the small size of the Finnish immigrant community, it is likely that he knew many of the families who emigrated to Karelia and whose bodies lie in the pits of Sandermakh.

Aside from a few articles in journals devoted to Finnish ethnic matters, the fate of the Finnish-American emigrants to Karelia has been ignored by most American historians and journalists. Somewhere among the 9,000 bodies buried near Sandermakh in far off Karelia are those of Helen Hill and other young Americans, murdered by the society which they tried to adopt, abandoned by the political movement from which they came, and ignored by the nation that gave them birth. Can you imagine the reaction if a mass grave was discovered in Germany from the Nazi era and the remains of several hundred Americans were uncovered? There would be stories on television, in mass circulation magazines, and in newspapers demanding congressional investigations and efforts to find out who was responsible—and demands that the murderers be brought to justice, if only before the bar of history.

Yet, American historians have ignored this issue. Take the widely praised reference work, *Encyclopedia of the American Left,* published by Oxford University Press, one of the more prestigious academic presses in this country. Hailed by historians as a monumental achievement, it has now gone to a second edition, almost a thousand pages long. Its entry on Finnish-American communists mentions the emigration of Finns to Karelia but says not one word about their fate.[13]

The same encyclopedia, by the way, has an entry on the Hiss case written by William Reuben, former correspondent for the *National Guardian,* who has since 1950 maintained that the Rosenbergs were framed and that no atomic espionage at all took place. Reuben, writing in 1998, deals with the Venona decryptions and new material from Russian archives by never mentioning them. In another essay on "Secret Work," Paul Buhle, one of the editors, sagely explained that "as of the late 1990s, documents examined in the Soviet Union or reprinted for scholars offered little that was new in regard to illegal or secret work by Soviet sympathizers."[14]

Ignoring the hundreds of Americans who died in the Gulag, the left also has not had much to say about the hundreds of Americans who spied for the Soviet Union and were never punished. The NSA had determined that the Venona decryptions would never be used in court, so the only spies they uncovered who could be prosecuted were those against whom independent evidence could be developed. And even some of these, like Judy Coplon, escaped conviction because of legal technicalities. Ted Hall, surely one of the most damaging atomic spies, a man who provided more information to the Soviets than Julius Rosenberg, got off free. Although most of the Venona spies have long since died, a handful remain alive–Donald Wheeler, Harry Magdoff, Judy Coplon. With the exception of Hall, none has been pursued by the press or subject to public denunciation. In the *Nation* magazine, Victor Navasky has pleaded with them to offer an alternative narrative of what they did to counter the lies being peddled by John Haynes, Alan Weinstein, Herb Romerstein, and myself, but silence has followed Navasky's plea.[15]

Ellen Schrecker's recent book, *Many Are the Crimes: McCarthyism in America*, complains that during World War II, the FBI and military intelligence "operated on the common assumption that, despite the wartime patriotism of the Communist party, its members remained a potential threat." She neglects to mention that Venona demonstrates that assumption was correct. Virtually every one of the 125-odd spies identified by American intelligence from the decryptions was a member of the American Communist Party. But it is Schrecker's apologia for espionage that is most interesting. After casting doubt on how extensive the Soviet espionage revealed in Venona was, after suggesting that Elizabeth Bentley remains an unreliable witness, after asserting that the jury is still out on Alger Hiss and, after hinting that none of the identifications in Venona is entirely reliable, she asks, "Were these activities so awful?" and pleads for a more "nuanced" view of espionage. After all, the spies mostly turned over innocuous material. Someone like Judy Coplon was just embarrassing the FBI, not damaging American security. By and large, no actual harm was done to American interests. "And many of the alleged Soviet agents did not consider their activities spying," she writes, but thought they were leaking material. And they did it for "political, not pecuniary, reasons" and "it is important to realize that as communists these people did not subscribe to traditional forms of patriotism; they were internationalists whose political allegiances transcended national boundaries." (Which, by the way, sounds like a very good reason to try to find communists working in the federal government and fire them). And, the U.S. and the USSR were allies when all of this happened, so why did people get so upset?[16]

In short, after years of denying that any espionage took place, the new argument is that it happened, and so what. It shouldn't be a crime, it was motivated by idealism, and nobody got hurt. What's the big deal? Wasn't it silly of Americans to get so exercised about some communists helping the Soviet Union? While this nonsense may at first make one yearn for those who used to claim that all those accused of espionage were innocent, it is, I think, actually grounds for optimism.

To recount these lies, evasions, and morally obtuse views is to see that they are the desperate flailings of a doomed viewpoint. The truth about communism and Soviet espionage in America is penetrating the mass media and opinion leaders and even intellectuals and academics. There are still holdouts, of course, but they are increasingly shrill and increasingly silly and fewer and fewer people take them seriously. Perhaps that explains why Hollywood is one of the last bastions. Just as the Holocaust deniers are today treated with contempt and scorn for their vile efforts to rewrite history, so too will the Schreckers, Buhles, and Navaskys be relegated to that bin where crackpots and fools ply their trade.

Notes

1. Whittaker Chambers, *Witness* (New York: Random House, 1952), 496-504; Sam Tanenhaus, *Whittaker Chambers: A Biography* (New York: Random House, 1997), 177-93.
2. Tanenhaus, *Chambers,* 182; Venona 1754 KGB New York to Moscow, 14 December 1944; 20 KGB New York to Moscow, 4 January 1945.
3. Venona 1681 KGB New York to Moscow, 13 October 1943; 207 Moscow to New York, 8 March 1945; 483-484 KGB San Francisco to Moscow, 13 September 1945.
4. In his autobiography, published before the Venona material about him was released, Bernstein tells several stories to suggest that he may have been approached by Soviet intelligence. He never confronts the story, head-on, however. Nor am I aware that any reporter has asked him about Venona. Walter Bernstein, *Inside Out: A Memoir of the Blacklist* (New York: Alfred A. Knopf, 1996), 124,228.
5. Harvey Klehr, John Haynes and Fridrikh Firsov, *The Secret World of American Communism* (New Haven, CT: Yale University Press, 1995).
6. Allen Weinstein and Alexander Vassiliev, *The Haunted Wood* (New York: Random House, 1999); Christopher Andrew and Vasili Mitrokhin, *The Sword and the Shield: The Mitrokhin Archive and the Secret History of the KGB* (New York: Basic Books, 1999).
7. The documents about Bridges are discussed in Harvey Klehr and John Haynes, "The Comintern's Open Secrets," *American Spectator* (December 1992), 34-43.
8. Joel Kovel, *Red Hunting in the Promised Land: Anticommunism and the Making of America* (New York: Basic Books, 1994), 156, 101.
9. I am indebted to Carl Ross, who provided a translation of an article that appeared in *Helsingin Sanomat,* July 17, 1997 and obtained a copy of the list of names. See also Peter Day, "Stalin's American Victims," *Weekly Standard* (January 4-11, 1979), 23-26.
10. Lawrence Hokkanen and Sylvia Hokkanen, *Karelia: A Finnish-American Couple in Stalin's Russia, 1934-1941* (St. Cloud, MN: North Star Press, 1991), 1, 125.
11. Mayme Sevander, *Red Exodus. Finnish-American Emigration to Russia* (Duluth: Oscat, 1993), 48.

12. See Harvey Klehr, John Haynes, and Kyrill Anderson, *The Soviet World of American Communism* (New Haven, CT: Yale University Press, 1998), 227-43.
13. Michael Karni, "Finnish Americans," in Mari Jo Buhle, Paul Buhle and Dan Georgakas, *Encyclopedia of the American Left* (New York: Oxford University Press, 1998), 226-27.
14. William Reuben, "Hiss Case," in ibid., 315-18; Paul Buhle, "Secret Work," in ibid., 735-737.
15. Victor Navasky, "Dialectical McCarthyism(s)," *Nation* (July 20, 1998), 28-31. Wheeler died in December 2002.
16. Ellen Schrecker, *Many are the Crimes: McCarthyism in America* (Boston: Little, Brown and Co., 1998),160-200.

Part 4

Espionage/Scholarship on
Venona Documents

25

The Strange Case of Roosevelt's "Secret Agent"

Josephine Truslow Adams, an obscure woman bearing a distinguished name, appeared before an executive session of the United States Senate Internal Security Committee on 16 January 1957. One month later an excerpt from her testimony was published in which she explained that she had served as a liaison between Franklin Roosevelt and Communist Party leader Earl Browder during World War II, meeting the president personally nearly forty times at both Hyde Park and the White House. Aside from communicating Browder's views on a variety of issues, Adams also brought Roosevelt documents received from the Chinese Communists, requests for favors (on such personal matters as the pending deportation of Mrs. Browder), and useful political gossip. According to her testimony, Miss Adams established so solid a relationship with Roosevelt that he jokingly called her "Dr. Johnson," after the famous conversationalist.[1]

Her story had the imprimatur of the only one of the principals still alive. Robert Morris, the Senate Committee's counsel, announced that while Earl Browder did not want to testify, he had confirmed her account. Right-wing anti-New Dealers have used the tale over the years to insinuate that Roosevelt harbored either sympathy for or naiveté towards Communists. Even such sympathetic historians as Joseph Lash have admitted that Adams had used the First Lady as a "mailman" for letters between Earl Browder and the president, and discreetly made no mention of her charges before the Senate Committee.[2]

There was something odd, however, about the whole episode. When stories of her activities briefly surfaced in 1953, Adams denied acting as a liaison and noted that she had only been at the White House once in 1939 as part of a group presenting a petition. Even more surprisingly, little was heard of her after the 1957 revelations were made public. David McKay Publishers advertised her book, *I Was Roosevelt's Secret Emissary,* for the Fall 1957 list, but never

Originally published in *Encounter*, December 1982.

brought it out. From Josephine Truslow Adams herself there was no further word or news. She vanished.

The Josephine Adams story is both a personal tragedy and an instructive lesson. It demonstrates very little about Franklin Roosevelt, but more about Earl Browder and the Communist Party, and a great deal about the ethics, judgment, and intensity of at least one Congressional subcommittee. For Josephine Truslow Adams was a political fraud, and a mentally-ill woman of long standing. While her ties to the Roosevelts were very tenuous and Earl Browder was deceived by her, the Senate Internal Security Subcommittee knew the extent of her delusions when it released her testimony smearing Franklin Roosevelt.

Born in Brooklyn in 1897, Josephine Adams graduated from Pratt Institute and began a career as an artist and teacher. From 1934 to 1941 she taught art at Swarthmore College. During this period she first got involved with Communist Party causes, attracted by the Party's support of loyalist Spain. By the late 1930s and early 1940s she was a staple on Party front organisations. She briefly became a *cause célèbre* in 1941. Early in the year she testified before the House Judiciary Committee in opposition to a bill legalising wire tapping in felony cases, claiming that because of her civil liberties work, her telephone had been tapped. Two weeks after her appearance Swarthmore notified her that she would not be re-hired the following year. Adams charged that she was "a hot potato" because of her political activities but also blamed her troubles on a faculty cabal of "Union Now" supporters, and hostility from the president of the College whose supposed anti-Semitic policies she had denounced. A brief flurry of protests by her friends and political supporters could not save her job.[3]

While her name was "in the news" Adams first met Eleanor Roosevelt. Esther Lape (a friend of the First Lady) had hired Adams to paint a picture which she gave to Mrs. Roosevelt. That in turn had led to occasional correspondence between Adams and Mrs. Roosevelt. When the latter visited Swarthmore in April 1941 they met. After this encounter, Adams sent her another painting and was soon bombarding Mrs Roosevelt with innumerable long letters.[4]

It was her ties, however tenuous, to Mrs. Roosevelt that brought Josephine Adams into the confidence of Earl Browder. From the day Browder entered the Atlanta Penitentiary in 1941 to begin serving a four-year sentence for passport fraud, the Communist Party had been demanding his release with greater frenzy. There were claims that his offence had been a mere technicality, the sentence unduly harsh. After Pearl Harbor, pleas on his behalf emphasised how his freedom would serve "national unity." Adams had been involved with several organizations defending the civil liberties of Communists; she quickly became a mainstay of the "Citizens' Committee to Free Earl Browder."

Although Adams later claimed that her first extended conversation with President Roosevelt took place at Hyde Park in August 1941 where she discussed the need to free Browder, there is no record that she was ever there or ever had an individual appointment at the White House. Just before Pearl Harbor she did write a letter to Eleanor Roosevelt asking that Browder be freed; she got a brief, noncommittal response. More than four months later, in April 1942, Adams addressed another plea to Mrs. Roosevelt, including a number of documents produced by the "National Free Browder Congress." She also mentioned that Elizabeth Gurley Flynn had asked her to raise the Browder issue and suggested that Mrs. Roosevelt agree to meet Flynn to discuss it. Mrs. Roosevelt promptly responded that she did not feel she should ask her husband about Browder. Moreover, since Flynn was a Communist "she would carry no weight" in Browder's behalf and it was useless to meet her. Adams wrote back, defending Flynn and suggesting that a non-Communist spokesman for Browder be allowed to meet her, but adding, "This is the last time I shall speak of it to you." Mrs. Roosevelt did not answer the letter.[5] The president finally gave the Party leader a pardon in May. Adams first met Browder on 4 July at a Party gala, convinced him that she had been instrumental in negotiating his release, and soon became a frequent family visitor. His confidence in her White House links was buttressed by a complicated affair that Adams soon orchestrated.

When Westbrook Pegler, a conservative anti-Roosevelt columnist, published a letter from an unnamed tank worker at the Baldwin Locomotive Works near Philadelphia claiming that production slow-downs were the result of union malfeasance and feather-bedding, Adams wrote to Eleanor Roosevelt on 4 December alleging that Pegler had obtained his information from "out-and-out Nazis" and suggesting an investigation was in order. The president himself spoke to J. Edgar Hoover about the affair and an FBI probe was soon under way. The Communist press also joined the hunt, identifying Pegler's source as one Andrew Hercha, a riveter at Baldwin who had quit immediately after Pegler's column had appeared. The leads Josephine Adams had provided were not productive and, after a cursory investigation, Hoover wrote to Mrs. Roosevelt on 5 January that no credible evidence tied Hercha to the Nazis. Mrs. Roosevelt sent a copy of this letter to Adams, presumably as a courtesy, since it was Adams who had first brought the case to her attention.[6]

Josephine Adams quickly used this ammunition to inflate her relationship with the White House. An FBI informant present at a party she attended on 9 January heard her boast of talking to "Eleanor" about the Hercha case. Adams quoted the First Lady as accusing Hoover of covering up for the fascists, claimed that the president had called him "Fascist" and "Himmler-like" and showed fellow-guests the letter from Hoover to Mrs. Roosevelt to demonstrate how intimate her relationship to the Administration was. The nervous FBI director ordered a more thorough investigation of Hercha which did turn up vague hints that he might have had Nazi sympathies—among other things Hercha had visited Germany several times as a seaman between 1934 and 1936.

In later years Josephine Adams insisted that the president had put Hoover on the carpet for botching the investigation, and had encouraged her to conduct an independent study. According to Adams, she met Mrs. Roosevelt twice to pass along her collected material. No evidence exists to support these claims; indeed it strains credulity that a president burdened by a world war could possibly care about Andrew Hercha, nor was there a scintilla of evidence that he had done anything illegal.

Adams did undertake her own investigation, and twice offered to supply the results to Mrs. Roosevelt. The beleaguered Eleanor refused. Finally on 23 February her secretary wrote a pleading letter to Hoover asking him to explain how he arrived at his conclusions about Hercha, "so she can explain to Miss Adams and convince her? . . ." Even before Hoover had a chance to reply, the indomitable Josephine had mailed more accounts of her interviews and conclusions about Hercha. The FBI pointed out the discrepancy between what Adams said she had been told and what the same sources had told FBI agents. Hoover also informed Mrs. Roosevelt that three people at Baldwin interviewed by Adams reported that she had claimed to be representing the Roosevelts. Mrs. Roosevelt was outraged; she quickly fired off a letter to Adams castigating her for such presumption. Adams denied the charge, falsely claimed to have been secretive about her ties to Mrs. Roosevelt, blamed everything on FBI persecution, and wept, "Your letter was such a shock that it has made me physically ill." Kindly Eleanor promptly wrote back, "Of course I believe you."[7]

Convinced by the Hoover letter of her bona fides, Earl Browder quickly decided to take advantage of this conduit to the White House and Adams's letters to Mrs. Roosevelt soon began to be filled with Browder's views, accounts of some of his activities, and interesting and occasionally spicy political gossip. During the 1944 campaign, Adams sent along information that Carl Byoir, a public-relations man once accused of being a Nazi propagandist, was advising the Dewey campaign. Another letter relayed information from Browder that Governor Dewey, busy criticizing Communist support for the president, had made deals to obtain Party support in his earlier campaigns for district attorney and governor in New York.

Mrs. Roosevelt soon recognized what was being offered and sent many of Adams's letters to the president. In January 1944, she forwarded one with a notation that "I know nothing about her reliability." One month later Eleanor wrote Adams a brief response to another letter, noting: "I gave it to the President." On 13 July she informed Adams, "I think you should know that your letters go directly to the President. What then happens I do not know." Such assurances convinced Browder that he had a pipeline to the White House. Adams went even further, however, and led him to believe she was visiting FDR at the White House. Browder talked to her regularly, providing information and advice that he thought the president should have. Adams would reappear with Roosevelt's supposed answers, comments, and requests. Years later, Earl Browder still could not believe that Adams had the political sophistication to "have held up her end" by inventing FDR's responses.[8]

In fact, she had. White House records do not reflect any visits by her from 1943 to 1945. In one letter to Mrs Roosevelt, Adams mentioned the FBI's interest in learning if she visited the White House. She had told one agent who asked that she did so "every Thursday," but "he did not take it as a joke at first." The only indication that the president even read any of her letters was his handwritten note on one, dealing with a political crisis in Bolivia, that "this should be taken up with State Dep't." Moreover, despite all her letter writing, Adams was hardly a household word in the White House. Early in October 1944, she sent the president a letter cautioning against "answering red-baiting with red-baiting" and signed J. Truslow Adams. An aide prepared a standard thank you note and, with the president's signature, it was sent off to its presumed author—the famous historian James Truslow Adams. Josephine received the letter at her own address, and wrote to Mrs. Roosevelt that she had burned it so no harm was done. Ironically, this letter was the only one which Josephine Adams ever received from Franklin Roosevelt—and he didn't even write it to her. Nor did she burn it—it was in her scrapbook which she showed to an FBI agent in 1951.[9]

Adams' elaborate deception was not the only sign of her emotional instability. Her letters to Mrs. Roosevelt were disordered and rambling. Handwritten, they meandered across pages and pages, often continuing up the margins as she ran out of space, and becoming less and less legible. Often two different kinds of paper were used. In between the nuggets of information supplied by Browder were pages and pages of dross.

None of this, of course, is *prima facie* evidence of mental imbalance but Adams's obsession with conspiracies was, to say the least, suggestive. She had charged that her telephone was tapped in 1940. During the Hercha case she had hinted that the FBI was interfering with her mail. Just before that she had complained to Mrs. Roosevelt that her home had been robbed because of her political activities. Several letters in 1944 were filled with warnings about a Catholic-Trotskyite-Social Democratic-Nazi alliance in Latin America designed to thwart the Soviet-American coalition. One came complete with a hand-drawn chart showing A. A. Berle of the State Department directing an anti-Roosevelt pro-Nazi cabal with strings of influence running through the "Trotskyite" *Reader's Digest,* Max Eastman, James Carey of the CIO, Bishop Fulton Sheen, a "Dubious Lady," and the Catholic Church to an anti-Popular Front coalition of fascists.[10]

Franklin Roosevelt died in the spring of 1945; a few months later Earl Browder was abruptly removed as leader of the American Communist Party following the publication of an article by the French Communist Jacques Duclos criticizing his "revisionism." Over the next several years, Adams developed a closer relationship with the FBI, volunteering her services as an occasional informant in 1950 and unsuccessfully offering to be a liaison between Browder and the Bureau. One year later she permitted an agent to photograph her scrapbook. He examined the perfunctory letters from Mrs. Roosevelt and the one communication from FDR. "No indication is shown in these documents," he reported, "that Adams acted as a liaison between Earl Browder and President Roosevelt under the name of Mr. Johnson or any other name as claimed by her previously." While Adams continued occasionally to provide the FBI with information, J. Edgar Hoover concluded in March 1954 that her lack of forthrightness, her unreliability, and her "exaggerated statements concerning her relationship with the Roosevelts" disqualified Adams from being considered a confidential source.[11]

One FBI report from the early 1940s had described Adams as "in an emotional and intellectual state of unbalance." The agent who interviewed her in 1950 was struck by her manner. "She is extremely nervous as is particularly evident in her continuous, unceasing conversation." By 1956 her obsessions had become overwhelming. Interviewed by an agent at the New York Infirmary early in September, Adams insisted she was merely painting a mural and residing at the hospital until it was finished. In her next breath, however, she complained of being given unauthorized psychiatric treatment and of a doctors' plot to commit her to a mental institution. She also was convinced that in August she had been subjected to a lobotomy by means of an "ice-pick treatment" which left no scars. Her knowledge of all this came from nurses' "voices" which she could hear from long distances away. In the space of a few days, Adams called the FBI's New York office twice to give reports on her condition; agents there logically concluded that she was suffering from mental illness.

It was in this state of mind that Josephine Adams told Robert Morris of the Senate Committee on 28 December that "communist doctors" had been busy giving her shock treatments and performing lobotomies in an effort to convince her she was mentally ill. Inexplicably, they were also injecting her with truth serum. Her only protection, she told Morris, was to put her full story on the record. In spite of all her delusions and the patently ludicrous story she had told, Adams was allowed to leave the Infirmary and testify in executive session in January before a subcommittee of the United States Senate. Only a portion of her testimony was ever released, perhaps because, as one FBI agent who examined the complete account noted, much of it was "rambling and unorganized" and counsel "had difficulty at times in eliciting responsive and precise answers." Even the published portion is hardly a model of clarity; what remained unpublished can only be guessed from Adams's mental state. After finishing with the subcommittee Adams returned to the infirmary.

Following her testimony, she signed a book contract, with Isaac Don Levine, a veteran anti-Communist journalist, as her ghost writer. By March 1957, however, Levine began to complain about her tardiness in producing the documentary evidence she claimed to have about her ties to the president. When it finally arrived, Levine became very suspicious.[12]

There were more than a score of letters from FDR to Adams, sprinkled with the same irreverence and flightiness as Adams's own correspondence. Of the twenty-one dates on which FDR supposedly wrote from Washington, he was not there on ten. Some of Adams's letters to the president were so prescient about future events that it was hard to avoid the conclusion that they had been written after the fact. One had the salutation "Dear Little White Father."

All of them were forgeries. Levine found a handwritten note by Adams (dated 28 March 1945) with reminders to write letters on various topics. Indeed, Adams admitted the fraud. In a 1958 letter to Levine pleading for the return of her genuine correspondence with Mrs Roosevelt, she plaintively asked whether "the *good* letters [were] in the package you left at Bella's or were they with the publisher?"

I Was Roosevelt's Secret Emissary was quietly dropped from McKay's list. Adams's sister returned the publisher's advance, and her brief moment in the limelight ended.[13]

Her exposure as a forger did not bring Josephine Adams back to reality. She merely transferred her paranoid delusions to a new set of villains—Mrs. Roosevelt and Esther Lape who had conspired to "put me under neuro-therapy and other things at night." Adams communicated with J. Edgar Hoover in May 1958 to complain in a rambling and incoherent letter that Mrs. Roosevelt and her sister were seeking to have her committed and that the latter had instigated the lobotomy. She pleaded with the director for help: "I would feel indeed lost if I could not count on you to defend my right to be heard no matter how barmy."

Josephine Adams was soon thereafter committed to the Norristown Sanitarium in Pennsylvania. She died there more than a decade later. Were it not for her ties, however tenuous, with the Roosevelts and Earl Browder, her tragic, troubled life would not merit such prolonged voyeurism. Because she made herself an historical figure with her charges, however, her obsessions become a matter of public interest and concern.

The most shocking aspect of this whole affair was the willingness of the Senate Internal Security Subcommittee to sponsor the public airing of a story it must have at least suspected was flawed. Not only did it conceal knowledge of her psychiatric problems, it released an edited version of her testimony which minimised its disorganisation. The FBI informed Robert Morris that Adams's version of the Hercha story was inaccurate, yet that apparently did not stay the Committee's confidence in her version of other events. The most charitable interpretation of its behavior is that it was so ready to believe the worst about Franklin Roosevelt that it suspended disbelief. More plausibly, it was prepared to use whatever was at hand, no matter how tainted, to suggest that the late president had secretly dealt with domestic Communists.[14]

Josephine Adams certainly did not have the influence she claimed on the Roosevelts. The information from Browder that she transmitted to Roosevelt was mostly innocuous. Browder certainly proffered suggestions about political strategy and foreign policies, but there is no evidence that they were heeded.

Moreover, by 1943 neither the president nor his wife had any illusions about American Communists. Mrs. Roosevelt's letters to Adams made it quite clear that she did not trust them and that the president would not credit them. Of less historical note, but more intriguing, is the influence Josephine Adams had on Earl Browder and, hence, on the Communist Party. Convinced that he and the president were exchanging views, did Browder make decisions based on the word of a mentally deranged woman? How could such a sophisticated man fail to see what an FBI agent quickly discerned in the early 1940s?

Years later, Browder could recall only one significant act directly attributable to Adams's supposed conversations with FDR. In 1943, she reported the president's eagerness to minimize independent third parties in the coming election. The Minnesota Democratic and Farmer-Labor parties had been discussing merger for some time. Browder told Adams to assure the president that if the Democrats would cooperate there would be no problem. He then urged Communists and their sympathisers in the Farmer-Labor Party not to be obstructionists, and the unification sailed through early in 1944. Quite likely, it would eventually have come anyway, but Josephine Truslow Adams perhaps deserves some credit for helping to create the Democratic Farmer-Labor Party by deceiving Earl Browder.[15]

Her indirect influence may have been far more substantial. Browder later insisted that, knowing Roosevelt's views so intimately, he was able to formulate his own policies with more confidence. His decision to dissolve the Communist Party in 1944 and replace it with a political association designed to function within the two-party system may well have been influenced by his belief that the president approved of the action and that Communists would be tolerated in the Democratic Party. Because he did not hide his supposed connections with FDR, Browder also guaranteed that the Russians would hear of them. Did this non-existent relationship worry them enough to lead to Browder's political elimination? Neither assertion can be confirmed, but both are plausible.

Why was Josephine Adams able to hoodwink Earl Browder? There was a surface plausibility to her story, supported by bits and pieces of documentation. Some of the very character traits that can be adduced as evidence of Adams's imbalance were not outside the range of acceptable Communist behavior. This is not to imply that Communists are mentally ill, but only to suggest that any small, millennial, extremist organisation attracts discontented people, some of whom have serious psychological debilities. The atmosphere of secrecy, intrigue, and danger appeals to some people. Paranoia can be regarded as a rational response to political persecution, and conspiracy theories accepted as a matter of course.

Communists in particular were liable to see conspiracies everywhere. Since they were sure of the inevitable march of history, Communists came to believe that obstacles to their plans were the result of sinister cabals by their numerous enemies. Even very disparate enemies could be lumped together "objectively." Despite their differences, for example, socialists and fascists were charged with cooperating in the early 1930s, and during the Moscow Purge Trials the Soviets blamed their ills on a conspiracy of "Bukharinites, Trotskyites, Social Democrats, wreckers, and Nazis," all united to destroy the great October Revolution.

Is it any wonder that Josephine Adams's fantasies did not seem beyond the pale? Possessed of a certain glibness and an active imagination, she played Earl Browder for a fool. The Senate Internal Security Subcommittee could have done more to discredit American Communism by exposing her than by trying to use her to smear President Roosevelt.

Notes

1. *Scope of Soviet Activity in the United States,* Park 54, US Senate Judiciary Committee (85th Congress, 1st Session, 1957), pp. 3,590-3,600. While the complete transcript of Adams' testimony has never been released, her full story of the dealings with both Roosevelt and Browder was told by ex-Communists Frank Meyer and John Lautner to the Senate Internal Security Subcommittee. A taped interview Adams made with Earl Browder and Theodore Draper on 21 April 1956, hitherto unavailable, covered her story in detail. It is now in the Draper Papers at Emory University. I also obtained the FBI file on Adams, 10022337. Unless otherwise indicated, all quotations are taken from this voluminous file.
2. Joseph Lash, *Eleanor and Franklin* (1981), pp. 202-204.
3. *New York Times,* 23 May 1941, p. 24; *Philadelphia Inquirer,* 11 February, 24 May 1941; *Philadelphia Record,* 24 May 1941. Although Josephine claimed to be a member of *the* Adams family, she was not.
4. Esther Lape Interview with Theodore Draper (13 February 1957, in Draper Papers).
5. Adams interview with Draper, *Scope of Soviet Activity,* p. 3591, Adams to ER, 1 December 1941; ER to Adams, 8 December 1941; Adams to ER, 15 April 1942; ER to Adams, 27 April 1942; Adams to ER, 2 May 1942; Adams to ER, December 1942 (in Eleanor Roosevelt Papers, Hyde Park).
6. In addition to Adams's FBI file, those of Andrew Hercha, 100-168918, and Robert Heineman, 62-36434, contain information on the case. In Mrs Roosevelt's papers there is a typed note on the top of Hoover's 5 January letter indicating that a copy was sent to Adams on 8 January.
7. JTA to ER, March 1943; ER to JTA, 18 March 1943 (in the Eleanor Roosevelt Papers).
8. JTA to ER, January 1944; ER to JTA, 12 February 1944; ER to JTA, 13 July 1944; Adams and Browder Interview with Draper, Browder Interview with Draper, 13 March 1957 (in Draper Papers).
9. JTA to ER, 4 July 1944; JTA to ER, 29 November 1944, ER to JTA, 13 January 1945 (in ER Papers). President's Office File 5621. Mrs Roosevelt chided General Watson that "everyone knows James Truslow Adams, the historian, would not write the President—and certainly not as she does."
10. JTA to ER, 11 February 1944 (in ER Papers).
11. Adams attempted to interest the Truman White House in her stories, but with little success. She also wrote one letter urging Browder's deportation. JTA to Mr Ross, 9

November 1945, JTA to Mr Hassett, 29 December 1945, JTA to President Truman, 24 September 1945 (in Truman Library).

12. Levine to Bella Dodd, 21 March 1957, Levine to JTA, 6 June 1957, Levine to Dodd, 12 June 1957 (in Isaac Don Levine Papers). Mr. and Mrs. Levine kindly allowed me to examine their entire file on Josephine Adams and answered extensive questions during an interview on 9 July 1979.

13. All of the forgeries are in the Levine papers. The information about the dates comes from a letter from Herman Kahn of the FDR Library to Grace Tully, 8 August 1957 (in Levine's Papers). Bella Dodd, an ex-Communist, was Mrs. Adams's lawyer. Mrs. William Troy, Interview with Klehr, 18 January 1978.

14. Robert Morris is usually spoken of in very engaging terms even by people on the opposite side of the political fence. Phillip Jaffe, for instance, wrote that he was "honest and reliable even with those whose politics he abhorred" (The *Rise and Fall of American Communism*, p. 164). Mr Morris did not respond to my request for help and information.

15. Earl Browder, Interview with Draper, 13 March 1957; Adams and Browder, Interview with Draper. In all the JTA-ER correspondence there is only one reference to the Minnesota situation—a letter from JTA to ER, January 1944 (in the ER Papers). It was to this letter that Mrs Roosevelt attached a memo to FDR saying she knew nothing of Adams's reliability.

26

Spy Stories

with John Earl Haynes and Ronald Radosh

Does anyone doubt, decades after the fact, that Senator Joseph McCarthy was a bully and a political opportunist? Why, then, did the *New York Times* take the unusual step of running a lead editorial on October 23 on "Revisionist McCarthyism," a historical issue fifty years old? Perhaps the editorial writers felt the need to comment on Ethan Bronner's October 18 lead article in the paper's Week in Review section, "Witching Hour: Rethinking McCarthyism, if Not McCarthy," which discussed our work on the McCarthy era and American communism. The editorial complained that "a number of American scholars"—the editorial mentioned no names—"[a]rmed with audacity and new archival information...would like to rewrite the historical verdict on Senator McCarthy and McCarthyism." The editorial conceded that there was more significant Communist infiltration of the U.S. government than McCarthy's critics have acknowledged but still implied that efforts to document the story are somehow illegitimate.

The *Times* editorial goes on to suggest that much of the recently published National Security Agency Venona intercepts and other new evidence of Soviet espionage is "opaque and ambiguous," even, perhaps, partly made up by Soviet field agents anxious to impress gullible superiors in Moscow. None of this evidence, the *Times* editors imply, should be allowed to stand in the way of the consensus that it was McCarthyism—much more so than any Soviet espionage or Communist infiltration of government—that "was a lethal threat to American democracy."

If Americans are ever going to understand their history, it is essential that McCarthyism and anti-communism be disentangled. We have no idea which

Originally published in the *New Republic* November 16, 1998 and reprinted with permission.

"scholars" the *Times* had in mind. For our part, we, along with historians such as Allen Weinstein and Richard Gid Powers, have always argued for just such a distinction. We have insisted that McCarthy was a demagogue whose reckless, irresponsible charges slandered innocent people.

In *The Secret World of American Communism*, two of us stated that "[i]n McCarthy's hands, anticommunism was a partisan weapon used to implicate the New Deal, liberals, and the Democratic Party in treason. Using evidence that was exaggerated, distorted, and in some cases utterly false, [McCarthy] accused hundreds of individuals of Communist activity, recklessly mixing the innocent with the assuredly guilty when it served his political purposes." And, in *The Amerasia Spy Case*, two of us made the point that "precisely because Senator McCarthy was reckless and made false charges, actual Communists who engaged in and contemplated espionage sought to claim the status of victims."

It is not so much that McCarthy exaggerated the threat of domestic communism as that he did not know what he was talking about. The people he accused of abetting the "conspiracy so immense"—for example, Dean Acheson and George C. Marshall—were not only major architects of the response to postwar Soviet expansionism but were themselves clear opponents of communism. McCarthy was simply incapable of identifying real Communists and spies, and he elided the differences among spies, Communists, fellow travelers, and liberals.

Let us be clear. There is simply no evidence in the Comintern or Communist Party of the United States (CPUSA) archives in Moscow, or in the recently released decoded KGB cables, that supports the general charge by Joe McCarthy that the Roosevelt and Truman administrations were part of, or assisted, a Communist conspiracy. Nor is there evidence for his accusations against Marshall, Acheson, and Truman. Nor is there any evidence supporting McCarthy's charge that the old China hand Owen Lattimore was "the top [Soviet] espionage agent in the United States," much less Alger Hiss's "boss." Nor did McCarthy's allegations that China hand John Service was a spy prove to be accurate. Lattimore was a pro-Soviet fellow traveler who defended the Soviet purge trials, and Service foolishly got mixed up in an abortive espionage scheme—but neither were Communists or Soviet spies.

We'd venture two explanations for the editorial's false statement that scholars "would like to rewrite the historical verdict on Senator McCarthy." The simplest and most judicious is that the editors may not have read the new books, ours included. The editorial argues that the deciphered Venona KGB codes are perhaps "embellished" or perhaps not even "accurate at all." Were Soviet intelligence agents making up all of their reports? The KGB and GRU had elaborate procedures for recruiting agents and running them. Sources were frequently shifted from one control officer to another. Moscow headquarters sent requests for specific information that sources were expected to provide, and Moscow required that sources provide copies of documents or reports they wrote themselves: KGB officers could not get by with reporting only information delivered verbally. KGB officers were encouraged to complain to Moscow about deficiencies in their colleagues' activities or tradecraft. Lying about sources could not long go undetected or unpunished. Certainly there are ambiguities in the status of such persons as I. F. Stone and J. Robert Oppenheimer, for example. [In our newest book, Spies: The Rise and Fall of the KGB in America, Haynes and I demonstrate that Stone was, in fact, an agent of the KGB and that Oppenheimer was not] But, for the overwhelming majority of the Soviet spies identified in the cables, the evidence is unambiguous.

The second possibility is that the *New York Times* does not want to disentangle McCarthyism from anticommunism. To say that there was a significant issue of Soviet espionage in post-World War II America is not to vindicate McCarthy. Most Americans who spied for the Soviet Union, we now know, were members of the CPUSA. The organization even had an underground apparatus that co-operated closely with both the KGB and GRU checking out prospective spies, providing safe houses, recruiting couriers, and supplying false passports. The head of this apparatus, Rudy Baker, met regularly with Earl Browder, the general secretary of the CPUSA. This did not mean that every American Communist was a Soviet agent. But the CPUSA was not just another American political party, operating according to the regularly established legal rules of political organizations. Its Soviet ties defined its very raison d'être, and those ties made it, as Sidney Hook argued at the time, in part a conspiracy and not a body of independent-minded heretics. Somehow, in the last several decades, a myth has grown that has erased the anti-Communist liberalism of that era from history. The myth's devotees insist that anyone who linked American Communists to Soviet espionage was a McCarthyite and that those accused of Soviet espionage were innocent victims of McCarthyite persecution. There were innocent victims of McCarthyism, but one bizarre feature of the myths that have developed is that persons who betrayed the United States and assisted Stalin's Soviet Union through espionage are portrayed as heroic victims.

Moreover, it is quite clear from new evidence that a number of guilty people escaped any punishment whatsoever—Ted Hall, a major atom bomb spy, is perhaps the most visible example. American intelligence unearthed information that more than 350 Americans had covert relationships with Soviet intelligence agencies in the 1940s. Only about half were ever identified, and no more than a dozen were ever successfully prosecuted. Soviet spies had infiltrated every significant agency of the U.S. government, ranging from the State and Treasury Departments to the Manhattan Project. High-ranking officials, including Harry Dexter White, assistant secretary of the Treasury; Laurence Duggan, chief of the State Department's division of American republics; and Lauchlin Currie, an administrative aide and State Department liaison to presidents Roosevelt and Truman, gave secrets to Soviet agents. White even met with a Soviet agent while at the San Francisco conference establishing the United Nations, revealing to him the American negotiating position on a number of issues.

It has been nearly fifty years since McCarthy burst on the scene with his inaccurate list of Communists in the State Department. The combination of newly opened Soviet archives, newly opened FBI records, and newly released deciphered KGB messages allows us to reconstruct with far greater precision what actually happened: There were hundreds of Communist spies in the United States, and we now know who many of them were. What remains a mystery is why the *New York Times* would try to label the effort to tell an accurate, documented story of American communism and Soviet espionage an effort to rehabilitate Joe McCarthy.

27

Reflections on Espionage

In 1995 the United States National Security Agency (NSA), the Central Intelligence Agency (CIA), and the Federal Bureau of Investigation (FBI) made public the story of a forty-year American intelligence operation code-named Venona. Shortly after the Nazi-Soviet Pact in 1939, American military intelligence had ordered companies that were sending and receiving coded cables overseas, such as Western Union, to turn over copies to the U.S. government. Hundreds of thousands of cables were sent or received by Soviet government bodies. Beginning in 1943, spurred by rumors and concerns that Stalin might conclude a separate peace with Hitler, the U.S. Army's cryptographic section began work trying to read these Russian cables. It had very limited success until 1946, by which time the Cold War was already underway. Some twenty-nine hundred cables dealing with Russian intelligence activities from 1942 to 1946 eventually were decrypted successfully in whole or in part as a result of Soviet technical errors in constructing and using "one-time pads" that American codebreakers were able to exploit. These cables implicated more than three hundred Americans as having been involved with Soviet intelligence services during World War II, a time when the United States and the USSR were allies.[1]

The Venona documents have sparked a renewed interest in issues of espionage, although in truth there has hardly been a time in the past fifty years that espionage has not generated public fascination, not only in the United States but also in Great Britain. One of the remarkable aspects of the response to Venona has been the effort by a number of people to defend Westerners who spied for the Soviet Union. The moral status of spies and spying has been debated for a long time. In the twentieth century, the advent of Communism and the willingness of so many citizens of democratic countries to spy on its behalf against their own nations gave this debate added urgency. That so many writers and intellectuals continue to see justifications for espionage against their

Originally published in *Social Philosophy and Policy*, Winter 2004 and reprinted with permission.

own countries after the collapse of Communism warrants a new look at the connections between morality and espionage, connections that are illuminated by a more precise and nuanced view of the moral status of the spy. Justifying espionage directed against democracies is not easy, and the recent attempts to do so have not been successful.

Espionage is almost as ubiquitous a historical phenomenon as it is a reviled profession. Intelligence gathering and the use of spies have a long pedigree. The history of intelligence organizations has been traced back to the societies of ancient Egypt, Babylonia, Assyria, Persia, and the Hittite Empire.[2] In Homer's *Odyssey*, Odysseus disguises himself to infiltrate Troy. The ancient Greeks wrote at length about the variety of spies, distinguishing among fake deserters, merchants, neutrals, and those recruited from within an enemy's population.[3] English journalist Phillip Knightley has called spying the world's second oldest profession.[4]

While recognizing its necessity, commentators have also accepted its moral ambiguity. Spying requires deception and secrecy. Those who engage in it must violate a variety of laws and moral principles. A historian of ancient Greek espionage notes that spies who betray their fellow citizens "have always been perceived in the Western tradition as corrupt and corrupting."[5] But even those who spy for a democratic society must walk a fine moral line. Paul Seabury notes that in a democratic society practitioners of spying need to be "able to maintain their integrity while being liars and obfuscators."[6] An international law text written during the American Civil War quotes a commentator who noted:

> Spies are generally condemned to capital punishment, and not unjustly; since we have scarcely any other means of guarding against the mischief they may do us. For this reason, a man of honor, who would not expose himself to the by the hand of a common executioner, ever declines serving as a spy. He considers it beneath him, as seldom can be done without some kind of treachery.[7]

Democratic societies have always been troubled by the use of spies. It is not simply that democracies rely on public discussion and abhor secrecy. They also struggle with the moral compromises that are required by their own spying and the reprehensible characters of many spies. Popular modern spy novelist, John Le Carré, has one of his most memorable characters, Alex Leamas, angrily explain, "What do you think spies are; priests, saints and martyrs? They're a squalid procession of vain fools, traitors too; yes; pansies, sadists and drunkards, people who play cowboys and Indians to brighten their rotten lives."[8] And yet, democracies also admire the self-sacrifice that they imagine motivates some spies. The first popular spy novel written by an American, based on American history, and set in the American countryside was James Fenimore Cooper's *The Spy*. It is an account of Harvey Birch, a member of General Washington's espionage corps who pretends to be a British agent and, pledged to secrecy, nobly suffers the "ostracism and hatred" of his neighbors to his dying day.[9]

The Morality of Espionage

For almost as long as there have been spies there has been debate about the morality of espionage. In the Hebrew Bible the first mention of spies suggests how dangerous a false charge of espionage can be. It comes when Joseph's brothers arrive in Egypt to buy grain. Joseph, as governor, meets them, learns who they are, and, remembering their ill treatment of him, charges them with espionage: "You are spies, you have come to see the weakness of the land."[10] Despite their repeated, frantic denials, Joseph demands that they prove their bona fides by leaving one brother hostage, returning to Canaan, and bringing their youngest surviving brother, Benjamin, back to Egypt. Joseph repeatedly tests his brothers, plants false evidence against them, and deceives them as to his motives before revealing his true identity. Significantly, the first accusation of espionage in the Bible is a false charge, made for ulterior purposes. Just as significantly, its targets are themselves not blameless but harbor a guilty secret, making them vulnerable to manipulation.

The first account of actual espionage in the Bible is likewise revealing. It is a botched operation. God tells Moses to "send men to spy out the land of Canaan." He suggests that one prominent figure from each of the twelve tribes be selected; Moses tasks them to "see what the land is, and whether the people who dwell in it are strong or weak, whether they are few or many, and whether the land that they dwell in is good or bad, and whether the cities that they dwell in are camps or strongholds, and whether the land is rich or poor, and whether there is wood in it or not. Be of good courage, and bring some of the fruit of the land."[11]

It takes this band of spies forty days to complete their mission. Upon their return they meet with Moses and Aaron and the entire Israelite population to report that the land of Canaan flows with milk and honey, but "the people who dwell in the land are strong, and the cities are fortified and very large." Despite the pleas of two of the spies that the Israelites forge ahead and conquer the land, the other ten insist that the task is hopeless, inciting the population to agitate for a return to Egypt. This first espionage mission ends in ignominious failure for the society. Commentators have argued that it was doomed from the start. Although God had already promised the land to the Israelites, their lack of faith in His word had led them to demand a group of spies to reconnoiter the territory. (In Deuteronomy 1:22, Moses reminds the Israelites that "all of you came near me and said, 'Let us send men before us, that they may explore the land for us, and bring us word again of the way by which we must go up and the cities into which we shall come.'" Angered, God told them through Moses to send out the spies "they pleased," but determined to punish the Jews.) After the debacle of their public report, God announces that the Israelites will be required to wander in the desert for forty years, one for each of the days "that you spied out the land." He further denies entry into the Promised Land to everyone over the age of twenty, with the exception of the two spies who had argued for the invasion, Caleb and Joshua, the latter of whom would actually lead that invasion years later.[12]

One intelligence analyst notes that this operation was doomed from the start. Those selected as spies were public figures; their names are provided in the Bible. Each one had significant political and military responsibilities that affected his evaluation of the information that he was gathering. The collected intelligence was openly discussed at a public meeting. Although no details are given of how they gathered their information, there is no indication that the spies spoke to anyone or did anything more than observe the inhabitants and their cities. All in all, the Israelites mounted an intelligence operation that lacked professionalism and violated a number of essential precautions. Having launched a risky venture, they paid a heavy price for its failure.[13]

Later espionage operations described in the Old Testament are far more successful. Moses sends out spies who wind up capturing Jazer.[14] More significantly, Joshua, a veteran of the earlier failure, recruits two anonymous spies, ordering them: "Go, observe the land and Jericho."[15] Arriving in Jericho, these unnamed men befriend a harlot named Rahab who is willing to hide them when the authorities learn of their presence and try to arrest them. In return for her help and insight into the public mood, they agree to spare her and her family during the coming battle. When they return, the spies report directly and confidentially to Joshua and note to him that even though Jericho is well fortified, its inhabitants fear the Israelites because of their previous military successes and the evidence of God's miracles. Joshua then promptly launches his successful attack on the city.

Other biblical stories describe spy operations ordered by David and Absalom.[16] In none of these stories does spying upon one's enemy incur any moral taint. There is, however, a clear contrast between the ingredients of a successful and an unsuccessful espionage mission. Joshua's anonymous spies never receive any credit for their actions. Their primary source is not some notable or upstanding citizen but a prostitute who, in return for her assistance in betraying her countrymen, is promised and receives protection. There is no suggestion that the spies somehow acted ignobly by concluding a deal with someone of ill repute. Unlike Moses' spies, who slipped in and out of enemy territory without being discovered, Joshua's operatives had to flee for their lives but still succeeded. As in another verse from the Hebrew Bible that explicitly mentions espionage, the spy is someone acting on behalf of his own people: in Judges, the tribe of Dan sends "five able men" to spy on a land that they intend to conquer.[17]

There is one notable exception to this positive portrayal of spies. Although she is not called a spy, Delilah, the Philistine woman who betrays Samson, acts much like one. Approached by Philistine leaders who ask her to "see wherein his great strength lies, and by what means we may overpower him," Delilah deceives her lover in return for money. Her first three efforts to learn his secrets fail, but she finally succeeds in wresting from him the secret of his strength, cuts his hair, and delivers him to the Philistines.[18]

The New Testament offers a more negative view of spies and espionage. In contrast to the Old Testament, where most espionage is carried out by Israelites responding to God's command to conquer the Promised Land, in the New Testament spies betray Jesus Christ.[19] In the one case, the Israelites are the beneficiaries of espionage; in the other Jesus is the victim. In the Gospel of Luke, for example, the scribes and high priests, anxious to discredit Jesus and to trick him into violating the law, "watched him, and sent spies, who pretended to be sincere, that they might take hold of what he said, so as to deliver him up to the authority and jurisdiction of the governor." These spies ask Jesus if they should give tribute to Caesar, to which he cannily and notably replies, "Render to Caesar the things that are Caesar's, and to God the things that are God's."[20] Likewise offering a negative view of spies, in his Letter to the Galatians Paul warns against "false brethren secretly brought in, who slipped in to spy out our freedom which we have in Christ Jesus, that they might bring us into bondage."[21] The spy here is someone pretending to be loyal or a friend but actually serving the interests of the enemy. He is the agent provocateur, encouraging actions designed to discredit the cause that he ostensibly supports.

The archetype of the betrayer, the man who pretends to be a loyalist but who is secretly working for the opposition, is, of course, Judas. One of Christ's disciples, he is willing to betray his teacher and master for money. Bought by the high priests for thirty pieces of silver, he identifies Jesus to the soldiers by kissing him on the cheek. His reward proves empty, and he hangs himself. Judas gave his name to all the spies who sell out their friends and compatriots. Unlike Joshua and his spies, he is not a patriot sent behind enemy lines but a disciple betraying his own people.

Historically, the spy who betrays his friends, his country, or his people has been a mercenary. Delilah, Judas, and Benedict Arnold all were bought with cash payments. No doubt the moral revulsion evoked by spies is linked to the motives for pecuniary gain that has driven so many of them. Montesquieu expresses the sentiment in *The Spirit of the Laws* (1748) when he notes that "the trade of a spy might perhaps be tolerable were it practiced by honest men; but the necessary infamy of the person is sufficient to make us judge of the infamy of the thing."[22]

While some have been repulsed by the sordid motives that drive many spies, others have worried about the impact of spying on the moral health of the regime that employs them. Immanuel Kant warns that even in wartime, a state is "permitted to use any means of defense except those that would make its subjects unfit to be citizens." The first restraint he deduces from this rule is that "means of defense that are not permitted include using its own subjects as spies; using them or even foreigners, as assassins or poisoners...or using them merely to spread false reports-in a word, using such underhanded means as would destroy the trust required to establish a lasting peace in the future."[23] Kant seems to leave open the possibility of employing foreigners as spies, provided they neither lie nor cheat nor kill, although exactly how useful they would be if they were required to be honest about what they were up to is an open question. Spying for Kant is a dishonorable profession that taints those who acquiesce in its use. A life of deception taints not only the one doing the deceiving, but also those who connive in it.

Such high-minded idealism has always had to confront the realities of the world of nation-states. Justifications for spying have ranged from its usefulness to rulers to its acceptance in international law. Thomas Hobbes argues that it is "necessary to the defense of the city, first, that there be some who may, as near as may be, search into and discover the counsels and motions of all those who may prejudice it." For Hobbes this means that rulers require spies: "[T]hey who bear rule, can no more know what is necessary to be commanded for the defense of their subjects without spies, than those spiders" who learn by the movement of their webs' threads when danger threatens.[24]

Similarly, Machiavelli would not have felt that there was any moral dilemma in using spies. Although he never explicitly discusses espionage, Machiavelli not only accepts but also praises a ruler who uses whatever means are necessary to learn about the intentions and capabilities of his enemies, both foreign and domestic. (He does warn that conspiracies rarely succeed because they will usually be betrayed by some disgruntled conspirator.) He warns the leader and would-be leader not to assume that Christian virtues can result in a successful and well-ordered state. It is necessary, he asserts, to understand that "he who abandons what is done for what ought to be done, will rather learn to bring about his own ruin than his preservation. A man who wishes to make a profession of goodness in everything must necessarily come to grief among so many who are not good. Therefore it is necessary for a prince, who wishes to maintain himself, to learn how not to be good."[25] If the prince himself must be able to lie and deceive, to present himself as what he is not, how can such stratagems be avoided by those citizens or employees who serve his purposes?

Machiavelli makes explicit throughout his writings that deceit, subterfuge, covert operations, and even political assassination are part of the arsenal that a ruler may have to employ. A successful ruler must "know well how to use both the beast and the man." To understand how to act as a beast, "he must imitate the fox and the lion, for the lion cannot protect himself from traps, and the fox cannot defend himself from wolves. One must therefore be a fox to recognize traps, and a lion to frighten wolves."[26]

One animal Machiavelli never mentions, however, is the mole, that creature of the underground that does its best work in the dark. It is no accident, as Marxists are wont to say, that Karl Marx was inordinately fond of the mole and that he himself was known as "the Old Mole." Marx compared the struggles of the working class to the burrowing of the mole, laboring out of sight in capitalist society until the moment when revolution erupts. The Old Mole's doctrines provided a heady rationale for hundreds of the twentieth century's most successful moles, who were able to burrow into positions of authority in capitalist societies and work to undermine them.[27]

Espionage per se is not illegal in international law. In the seventeenth century, Hugo Grotius noted the paradox that it is perfectly legal for a state to dispatch or employ spies but also perfectly legal for the target state to punish spies if it catches them: "[T]he law of nations unquestionably permits the sending out of spies...yet if they are caught they are commonly treated with great cruelty.... If there are men who refuse to employ the aid of spies, when it is offered them, their refusal must be attributed to loftiness of mind and confidence in their own revealed resources, not to any idea of what is lawful or unlawful."[28] Virtually every country engages in espionage and understands that others do as well. It may well be illegal in every country (or at least in those with minimal standards of individual rights) to intercept private communications, but every country in the world encrypts and encodes its diplomatic and sensitive communications, recognizing that others will attempt to break into them, without protesting that some kind of violation of international law is occurring.

Although the United States has employed spies from the Revolutionary War onward, there has always been a strain in American life that has regarded spying with distaste. Part of the reason, no doubt, has been the belief that a healthy and vibrant democracy need have no fear of any enemy and has nothing to hide from one. In a similar vein, Pericles boasted that open, democratic Athens did not have to rely on subterfuge:

> It was "an open city and do[es] not, by periodically expelling foreigners, keep them from seeing and learning things, lest some enemy benefit from what is open to his view. We trust less to our equipment and guile than to our personal courage in action."[29]

Another factor has been the belief that espionage is a dishonorable activity that runs counter to democratic values. Because it requires secrecy, it cannot be subject to the same demand for transparency that is usually made regarding political issues. It is difficult for representative bodies to exercise control and oversight. The methods and techniques of espionage often raise disturbing questions of propriety and legality. The individuals attracted to it or indoctrinated in its culture are often perceived as dangerous to democratic values. Consequently, many Americans have regarded espionage, particularly in peacetime, as a blight on our moral standards. Shortly after he was appointed secretary of state in 1929 Henry Stimson received a series of decrypted diplomatic telegrams from the American Black Chamber, the office run by

Herbert Yardley that had been successfully breaking foreign codes since 1919. Stimson "regarded it as a low, snooping activity, a sneaking, spying, keyhole-peering kind of dirty business, a violation of the principle of mutual trust upon which he conducted both his personal affairs and his foreign policy." As he later noted, "Gentlemen do not read each others' mail." His opposition led to the dissolution of the American Black Chamber.[30] Similarly, in October 1945 President Harry Truman disbanded the Office of Strategic Services (OSS), which had been created during World War II to serve as a national intelligence agency, amid fears that it could become an "American Gestapo." Concern with "dirty tricks" perpetrated by American security agencies prompted Congress to restrict what American spies could do following the Church Committee hearings in 1975 and in the 1990s led to rules that forbade the CIA from recruiting human rights violators as sources.

This distaste for the secret world of espionage, however, has generally given way, particularly in the twentieth century, to realistic concerns about national security. As secretary of war in the 1940s Stimson overcame his scruples to allow extensive spying. The CIA was created in 1947 and the following year received authorization to conduct covert operations. Following the terrorist attack on America on September 11, 2001, earlier restrictions on CIA recruitment of unsavory characters were lifted. Even when elected officials have tried to limit or restrict the activities of intelligence agencies, few Americans have gainsaid the need for this country to spy on enemies, adversaries, potential enemies, and, even perhaps, friends. Employing spies is regarded as part of the necessary business of governing. But if the need for the government to spy is widely recognized, Americans remain ambivalent about the people so employed and what they should be allowed to do. It is one thing to seek to ascertain the capabilities of a potential enemy, another to try to recruit a foreign politician to act in a certain way, and still another to bribe or coerce or threaten someone to obtain information.[31]

Varieties of Spies

In discussions about morality and espionage it is useful to recall that there are different types of spies. A country may employ its own nationals or citizens to obtain information about another country, or it may seek to use citizens of that other country to obtain information. Both types of recruits may be engaging in espionage and be labeled as spies, but their activities, behavior, and characters elicit very different evaluations.

Citizens of a country who spy for it are patriots. We may not approve of the country that they serve. We may deplore the tactics that they use or the methods that they employ to gather their information, but their actions are not much different than those of soldiers engaged in a particularly difficult or dangerous mission. Unlike soldiers they do not wear uniforms, and this difference may subject them to punishments from which soldiers are exempt under international law. Like Joshua, these spies are willing to go behind enemy lines to ferret out information that the enemy wishes to conceal.

There are actually two types of patriotic spies and international law treats them rather differently. Every modern intelligence agency employs the first type: officers or employees who recruit, supervise, and give orders to agents who obtain secrets. These officers are almost always citizens of the government that employs them and are loyal to its principles. Many of these men and women serve in diplomatic positions, often as minor functionaries or bureaucrats in an embassy or consulate, while their major task is to obtain secret information about the country to which they are posted. They have diplomatic immunity from arrest and punishment by their host government. In the modern world every state understands that such "spies" are a normal part of a country's diplomatic mission. If caught in the act of obtaining information from a source, they will be declared persona non grata and expelled. Such activities, however, are part and parcel of the normal relationship among nation-states. Even spies are protected by diplomatic immunity provided that they have the correct credentials. Under international law, even if some of the American diplomatic personnel who were held hostage by Iran in the late 1970s were CIA officers, the Iranians were obligated not to arrest and punish them.

The second type of patriotic spy is a citizen of one country who lives under cover in another country to spy on it; these spies are at greater hazard and in a more morally ambiguous position than the first type. While spies with diplomatic immunity are perceived to be serving the interests of their government, merely disguising their espionage work, the undercover spy, or agent in place, pretends to be a normal inhabitant of the country that he is seeking to undermine. He must disguise not only his job but also his loyalties. Many of the fictional and true-life heroes of popular espionage lore fall into this category. Since international law provides that a spy captured behind enemy lines is subject to the death penalty, such espionage carried on in wartime requires considerable bravery and a willingness to take enormous risks. No American spy better symbolized this than Nathan Hale, hung by the British in 1776, a statue of whom adorns the CIA'S Langley, Virginia, headquarters. Whether or not he ever uttered the famous phrase that is attributed to him, regretting he had but one life to give to his country, Hale's willingness to spy even though it was considered a dishonorable task for a gentleman and a graduate of Yale College, reflected a recognition that loyalty to one's country sometimes requires personal sacrifices.[32] James Fenimore Cooper's fictional spy, Harvey Birch, likewise linked valor and personal sacrifice as essential elements in the success of the Revolutionary War and the creation of a nation.

Americans have admired and honored spies who are willing to risk their lives to provide vital information about America's enemies. Nor are Americans alone. Every country has its mythic heroes who disguise their identities to blend in with the enemy and ferret out his secrets. Even when these spies have been adversaries, Americans have had a grudging admiration for their exploits. No nation used more "illegals" than the Soviet Union. Living under false identities in America, England, occupied France during World War II, and other nations throughout the world, such agents did not enjoy diplomatic immunity. "Illegals," however, shared with KGB and GRU officers assigned to embassy positions an allegiance to the Soviet Union.[33]

Not all "illegals" were Soviet citizens. A number of dedicated Communists had enlisted in the intelligence service of the Communist International, or Comintern, in the 1920s and shifted over to Soviet intelligence work late in the decade or in the 1930s. Regarding themselves as soldiers in an international army, such people were among the most effective and romanticized KGB and GRU officers. Multilingual, at home in working-class bars and corporate boardrooms, cultured and dedicated, many of them lived lives that were stranger than fiction. Their actions, activities, and fates mirror the moral ambiguities and horrors of the twentieth century.

Theodore Mally, a one-time seminarian studying for the priesthood in Hungary, was drafted into the army of the Austro-Hungarian Empire and taken prisoner in World War I. The Bolsheviks converted him to Communism in a prisoner-of-war camp. Assigned to the Cheka, the USSR's first internal security agency, he grew disillusioned with the internal repression that accompanied the collectivization drives of the 1920s, and secured a transfer to foreign intelligence. His longest assignment was to Great Britain; in 1935 he became the illegal resident for the KGB in London, where he oversaw the early espionage work of the "Cambridge spies," Kim Philby, Donald Maclean, Anthony Blunt, and Guy Burgess. In 1937, at the height of Stalin's purge of the Soviet intelligence services, Mally was recalled to Moscow. Responding to a friend who pleaded with him not to go back to certain death, he noted that "he could be killed abroad as well as in Moscow" and that "it would be better for him to meet his fate in the cellars of the Lubyanka." He was shot in 1938. Today his portrait hangs in a "History Room" honoring heroes of the Soviet intelligence service at the headquarters of the Russian intelligence service (SVR).[34]

Léopold Trepper, a Polish Jew, immigrated in the 1920s to Palestine, where he joined the Communist Party. Sent to France to work among Jewish immigrants, he later moved to Moscow for training in Comintern schools. Disillusioned by the purges of the 1930s that swallowed up hundreds of his old friends, he joined Soviet intelligence to better fight Nazism. As head of the "Red Orchestra," a huge Communist spy network, he operated under cover as a raincoat manufacturer in Paris and Brussels until he was arrested by the Gestapo. Trepper built a continent-wide circle of agents, used innocent people as fronts for his activities, betrayed a number of his agents in order to save others, pretended to cooperate with the Germans while feeding them false information, and managed to escape and remain in hiding until World War II ended. Upon returning to the Soviet Union in 1945 he was jailed as a traitor, rehabilitated after nine years, and reunited with his family. They returned to Poland, where he assumed a position within the decimated Jewish community. Appalled by the upsurge of anti-Semitism in 1967, he launched a campaign to be allowed to immigrate to Israel. For years the Communist authorities harassed him before finally allowing him to leave Poland in 1973.[35]

The Soviets used illegals like Mally and Trepper because they had the sophistication and skills to blend in with their surroundings. They, in turn, served the Soviet Union because they were convinced that its triumph would advance the cause of humanity. In the service of that cause they willingly risked their lives and sought to subvert and weaken enemies of the Soviet Union. While their unhappy fates were partially linked to suspicions that as foreigners and, in Trepper's case, as a Jew, they were inherently suspicious, under Stalin even native-born intelligence officers were frequent victims of waves of purges that swept through the intelligence agencies. Part of the admiration for their exploits, no doubt, is connected to the punishment to which they were subjected by the regime that they had so loyally served.

The Soviets used "illegals" as spies in the United States because they knew that American counterintelligence agencies carefully watched and monitored the activities of Soviet diplomatic personnel in order to detect their involvement with espionage. Although the KGB station chief in the United States during much of World War II, Vasili Zubilin, nominally a second secretary in the Soviet consulate in New York, was able to evade surveillance at times and meet with agents, it was a time-consuming process and not always successful. For example, one FBI bug planted in the home of an American Communist official in California in 1944 overheard Zubilin offering money in return for the use of a group of sources.[36]

The illegals, however, were unknown to the FBI. At the same time that Zubilin was being followed, Ishak Akmerhov was living under an assumed name in Baltimore, Maryland, posing as a fur merchant. Akmerhov was a Tatar and a veteran KGB officer who had served illegally in the United States in the 1930s and returned illegally in the early 1940s. He supervised a number of spies who were able to meet with him and turn over material that they had filched from the government offices in which they worked. Akmerhov sent fifty-nine rolls of microfilm to Moscow in 1942, 211 in 1943, 600 in 1944, and 1,896 in 1945.[37] He returned to Moscow in 1946, received a decoration, and continued to work for the KGB until his retirement. Not until after he left the United States did American counterintelligence learn about his activities.

Soviet citizens arrested in the United States for spying might not enjoy diplomatic immunity, but their status was different from American spies. In 1957, for example, the FBI arrested a man known as Rudolph Abel. His real name was William Fischer. Born in Great Britain to a Russian émigré family that returned to Soviet Russia when he was a young boy, Abel was later recruited into the KGB. In 1948 he entered the United States on a false passport, and then lived quietly in New York, posing as an artist, while running several agents, including Ted Hall and Morris and Lona Cohen (discussed below).

Abel, who had left his wife and children in the Soviet Union, was arrested in 1957 after his assistant, a Soviet illegal with a severe drinking problem, turned himself in to U.S. authorities. At the subsequent trial, Abel's defense lawyer attempted to discredit this man, Reino Hayhanen, by noting that "he entered the United States on false papers...he has lived here every day only by lying about his true identity, about his background, about every facet of his everyday life...he was trained abroad in what his 'cover' should be here, meaning that he was trained in the art of deception. He was trained to lie. In short, assuming that what the government says is true, this man is literally a professional liar."[38] The jury found the argument unpersuasive because it described Abel as much as Hayhanen. Every illegal has to be a professional liar. After serving several years in prison, Fischer was exchanged for Francis Gary Powers, pilot of the U-2 spy plane that had been shot down over the Soviet Union in 1960. Abel earned the grudging admiration of his American captors for his professionalism, dedication, and discipline.

If the first category of spies consists of those who serve their country or adopted nation, the second is comprised of those who betray it. Beginning with Benedict Arnold, Americans have been harshly unforgiving of those citizens who have provided enemies with America's secrets or turned on their own country to serve another. Even when a spy's employer has been a country with which America is friendly, both the public and the government have reacted with fury. When Jonathan Pollard was arrested in 1985 for spying for Israel, an ally of the United States, the Justice Department sought and received one of the harshest punishments ever for peacetime espionage, despite Pollard's claim that he never intended to harm the United States.[39]

The citizen who spies for another country violates one of the most basic clauses of the democratic social contract; by his actions he threatens the ties that bind a country of individuals together. Having freely consented to become a citizen or choosing to remain one despite the option of leaving, an American is regarded as a traitor (in fact if not in law) if he or she places loyalty to another country above loyalty to America. The sense of betrayal is relevant in a way that it is not if the spy is a resident alien or other kind of noncitizen. (Only in recent years has the issue of dual citizenship and dual loyalty become a complicating factor.) While a noncitizen resident in America is expected to obey American laws, only a citizen owes loyalty to the nation.

The disdain in which such spies are held is linked to the motives that most have for spying. Like Judas or Benedict Arnold, most are not very admirable people. In recent years, virtually every American citizen charged with and convicted of espionage has spied for base motives. Aldrich Ames, a CIA officer arrested in 1994 for spying for the Soviet Union and providing information to the KGB that led to the deaths of at least ten Soviets who were cooperating with American intelligence, was greedy. He sold to the Soviets, in return for direct payments of $2 million to support a lavish life style, the names of more than two dozen "human assets," as well as information compromising CIA officers and covert operations.[40] John Walker, Jr., who had recruited his own son, brother, and best friend to spy for the Soviet Union, likewise had no ideological ax to grind. Arrested in 1985, this retired Navy man and a one-time member of the Ku Klux Klan had supplied the Soviets with highly classified communications and encryption information over a seventeen-year span, simply for money.[41] Robert Hanssen, an FBI counterintelligence agent who received a life sentence in May 2002 for spying for the Soviet Union and then Russia, from 1985 until his arrest in February 2001, appears to have been motivated by a desire to demonstrate that he could outsmart people whom he regarded as his intellectual inferiors.[42]

It is usually human weaknesses that lead people to turn on their own countries, even when those countries have despicable regimes. For example, Reino Hayhanen, Rudolph Abel's assistant who betrayed him, was no devotee of democracy. Hayhanen had just been recalled to Moscow because his drinking was interfering with his work. He turned himself in to the American embassy in Paris rather than face demotion and punishment in Moscow. By all accounts, he was far less impressive a human being than Abel, even though the latter faithfully served an unpalatable regime.

The three hundred or so Americans exposed by the Venona decryptions were not, with possibly an exception or two, spies for such base reasons as ego, money, or avoiding disgrace. Not all of the people revealed in the decryptions, in fact, were conventional spies, stealing secrets and turning them over to another government. Some were talent spotters, identifying potential recruits for Soviet intelligence; others were couriers, ferrying information from a spy to a KGB officer; others operated safe houses where KGB officers could meet their sources; and still others performed various kinds of support work that enabled the spy rings to flourish. Many of these people incurred expenses and were reimbursed. A few were supported full-time to enable them to work exclusively for Soviet intelligence. During this period only a tiny handful of Soviet spies, however, were bought and paid for. KGB records shown to an American historian identify one particularly remarkable mercenary spy, Congressman Samuel Dickstein, a New York Democrat, whose chief claim to fame is that he introduced the resolution that created in 1938 the first Special Committee on Un-American Activities, known as the Dies Committee. Code-named Crook, demonstrating that the KGB had a sense of humor, Dickstein hoped to use the Committee to develop information on Nazi activities in America that he could then turn over to the Soviets for money. History sometimes takes ironic turns, but few more devilish than this. The KGB aided and abetted the creation of what would become the symbol of anticommunism in America: the House Committee on Un-American Activities. Eventually concluding that Dickstein's information was not worth what they were paying him, the KGB dropped him from its roster, and he moved from the House of Representatives to a New York judgeship.[43]

Justifying Espionage

Most of the Americans who spied for the Soviet Union in the 1930s and 1940s did not do so for money. A few received bonuses or expenses but virtually all of them spied because of ideological enthusiasm. They were Communists or Communist sympathizers, committed to the Soviet Union. In the Venona decryptions, the KGB's code name for American Communists was "Fellow Countrymen." And for many spies, the Soviet Union was, if not their native land, a second homeland, more deserving of loyalty than the land of their citizenship.

Three examples are representative of these ideological spies. Nathan Gregory Silvermaster, a government economist and leader of a productive spy ring that included Harry Dexter White, an assistant secretary of the U.S. Treasury, first volunteered his services to Soviet intelligence after the Nazi attack on the USSR. Upon being awarded a medal for his work, Silvermaster told his Soviet controller, Ishak Akmerhov, that "his work for us is the one good thing he has done in his life."[44] Philip Jaffe was a wealthy, pro-Communist, greeting-card manufacturer, editor of a left-wing magazine (*Amerasia*), and an aspiring Soviet spy. In 1945, an FBI wiretap overheard Jaffe explain that a real radical had to be prepared to defend the Soviet Union at all times: "I would say that the first test of a real radical is, do you trust the Soviet Union through thick and thin, regardless of what anybody says? It's the workers' government, the one shining star in the whole damned world and you got to defend that with your last drop of blood."[45] In late 1948 or early 1949, Julius Rosenberg told his brother-in-law David Greenglass, whom he had recruited for atomic espionage when the latter served at Los Alamos during World War II, that "we've got to be like soldiers. It doesn't matter if Stalin is sending his troops to be killed. What difference does it make as long as the victory is ours?"[46]

This vicarious identification with the Soviet Union had several sources. Many of the spies or their parents had been born in Russia. A visceral Russian loyalty animated them. Many were Jews who believed that the Soviet Union had abolished the anti-Semitism that had driven their families to America. Most were convinced that the USSR was building a shining new egalitarian society that would usher in the kingdom of heaven on earth. Others saw Stalin as the great bulwark against fascism and were filled with admiration for the heroism and sacrifice of the Russian people in standing up to Hitler.

Harry Gold was not a Communist, but scarred by exposure to American anti-Semitism and convinced that the USSR was embarked on a noble economic experiment, he agreed to provide industrial secrets to the KGB and then to work as a courier for Los Alamos physicist Klaus Fuchs and Army sergeant David Greenglass. Morris Cohen was a New York high school football star who attended Mississippi A&M College. He joined the Communist Party of the United States (CPUSA) in 1935, and two years later he enlisted in the International Brigades to fight the Franco forces in Spain. Wounded in battle, he volunteered for special assignments and soon entered a select Soviet school in Barcelona to train intelligence operatives. "[T]he Soviet comrades," he later told an interviewer, "suggested that fighting against fascism could be advanced by going into [their] Service.... So I said to the comrades: 'Yes.'"[47]

Cohen did not reveal his espionage activities to his wife, fellow-Communist Lona Petka, until after they were married. She was initially horrified and accused him of treason, but Morris explained to her that "if I betrayed America for money, or if I had betrayed the party or my convictions, that would have been a different thing since I would have betrayed the ideas which made up my credo."[48] Lona was persuaded and herself became a courier for a Soviet spy ring that smuggled atomic secrets out of Los Alamos. The Cohens quietly dropped out of sight and left the United States as members of Julius Rosenberg's spy ring were being arrested in 1950. They themselves were arrested in 1961 in Great Britain, where they had been posing as rare-book dealers, using the identities of a deceased couple, Peter and Helen Kroger, while working for Soviet intelligence. In 1967, they were exchanged for a British academic falsely accused of espionage by the Soviets. This is the only known case of the USSR repatriating spies who were not Soviet citizens, although they both later received Soviet citizenship and died in Russia.

One of the Cohens' espionage contacts while they were in the United States was Theodore Hall, who offered yet another high-minded motive for committing espionage. One of the major surprises of the Venona documents was the revelation that Hall, a young, Harvard-educated physicist, had been an important Soviet spy at Los Alamos during the development of the atomic bomb. Hall had graduated from Harvard College in 1944 when he was only eighteen years old. He was immediately recruited by the Manhattan Project and dispatched to New Mexico, where he did work on the physics of implosion. Returning home on leave in October, he told his college roommate, Saville Sax, like Hall a fervent young Communist, the nature of his work. They agreed that the Soviet Union should be informed. Sax meandered around New York looking for a KGB officer and was eventually led to Sergey Kurnakov, a Russian journalist who worked for Soviet intelligence. Kurnakov met with Hall and found him to be "politically developed," but asked nonetheless why he was willing to turn over American secrets. Hall responded, according to Kurnakov's report to Moscow, that "there is no country except for the Soviet Union which could be entrusted with such a terrible thing." He worried that after the war the United States might blackmail the Soviet Union if the U.S. had a monopoly on atomic weapons.[49]

When his espionage activities were disclosed in 1995, Hall was living in retirement in Great Britain. Although the FBI had investigated and questioned Hall in the 1940s and 1950s, it had never been able to gather enough evidence to indict or to try him. As a matter of policy the government had determined never to use in court any Venona material. So, even though the government knew he had been an important Soviet atomic spy, it would not indict him unless it could develop other admissible evidence that demonstrated his guilt. No American scientist turned over more significant information about the atomic bomb than Hall. (Klaus Fuchs, who was convicted of atomic espionage by the British in 1950, was not an American, but a German-born British physicist who had worked and spied at Los Alamos. Robert Oppenheimer, director of Los Alamos during the war, has been accused of being a Soviet source. His relationship with Soviet intelligence is still not entirely clear, although recent evidence suggests that he did cooperate with the KGB. If true, this would demote Hall to the second most important American atomic spy.)[50]

After release of the Venona material exposing him, Hall was unapologetic about his actions. He explained that "during 1944 I was worried about the dangers of an American monopoly of nuclear weapons if there should be a postwar depression" because it might encourage a fascist America to launch a nuclear war. While admitting that he had been mistaken about "the nature of the Soviet state," he still believed that he had contributed to world peace by ensuring a nuclear balance of terror: "I still think that brash youth had the right end of the stick. I am no longer that person; but I am by no means ashamed of him."[51] After his death in 1999 Hall's wife, Joan, was more vehement, defending his "humanitarian act." His daughter praised his espionage and called for a new generation of scientists "who dare to come forward as he did."[52]

There is a clear difference between explaining the motives that led people to betray their country and justifying that betrayal. That Ted Hall believed the United States would become a fascist country after World War II and that the Soviet Union needed to be able to protect itself may explain why he gave the KGB vital defense information. It hardly justifies his act, as the Hall family seems to believe. In any case, the justifications for their actions offered by the spies themselves must be taken with a large dose of skepticism. By his own admission Ted Hall, who was in the army at Los Alamos, violated his oath of allegiance, to say nothing of the fact that he lied to and deceived his coworkers, security officials, FBI interrogators, and numerous other people about his actions over the years. Documentary evidence also demonstrates that Hall's belated justification for his treachery, that he wanted to contribute to a nuclear balance of terror, is an ex post facto rationalization. His explanation to Kurnakov in 1944 suggests that he was providing atomic information to the Soviet Union because he had more faith in Stalin's Russia than he did in the United States. It was, he thought, the only country that could be trusted with such information. In addition, Hall did more than give the KGB data while the war was raging. He remained in touch with Soviet intelligence after he left Los Alamos in 1946 and helped it recruit at least two other atomic scientists over the next few years.

Despite his daughter's portrait of Hall as a courageous dissenter, he did not "come forward" to protest American policies that he opposed or thought dangerous. He never "took credit" for what he had done; he only admitted his espionage after he was publicly exposed by Venona material released fifty years after his actions. Hall, in fact, had an opportunity to come forward and to take credit for enabling the USSR to construct an atomic bomb. Shortly before the Rosenbergs' execution, Hall, consumed by guilt, suggested to his KGB controller that he should go to the authorities. Since in sentencing them to death, the judge had blamed the Rosenbergs for giving the Russians "the secret of the atomic bomb," Hall thought that confessing his own, far more important role in atomic espionage might save them from their fate. The Russian disagreed. So did his wife to whom he had confessed his espionage activities before they were married. Faced with this moral dilemma, Ted Hall did nothing. On the day of the Rosenbergs' execution, the Halls drove past Sing Sing prison on their way to a dinner party. They were distressed.[53]

The emotional loyalty of children to their parents should also not blind us to the costs that spies impose on their families. Since 1975, the Rosenberg children have attempted to rehabilitate their parents' reputations, charging in books, articles, interviews, and documentaries that they had been framed and persecuted by a corrupt and vengeful government.[54] Even the Venona decryptions and the revelations of the Rosenbergs' onetime KGB controller, Alexander Feklisov, in his autobiography and in film interviews, about Julius's key role in espionage, have elicited only their grudging admission that Julius might have been a low-level spy.[55] What these now-adult offspring have been unable to confront is that their parents, who could have saved their lives by confessing to espionage, chose to become martyrs and consciously made their children orphans rather than admit what they had done.

In the wake of the Venona revelations other commentators have adduced a variety of additional justifications for the espionage committed by American citizens during this era. For decades, defenders of spies such as Alger Hiss, Harry Dexter White, or the Rosenbergs based their arguments on the innocence of their subjects. They were not spies but had been framed. Cold War tensions, a repressive and corrupt FBI, and a coterie of liars and perjurers had resulted in a series of miscarriages of justice. Patriotic Americans, guilty of nothing more than progressive sympathies, had been tarred and, in the case of the Rosenbergs, murdered after falsely being accused of espionage. There was, in other words, no need to justify espionage because none had taken place. But, it turns out that documentary evidence from multiple sources demonstrates that Hiss, the Rosenbergs, and White, among many others, did cooperate with Soviet intelligence. This evidence has led to a number of efforts to minimize, rationalize, or justify espionage.

The most famous rationale used to justify espionage comes from a remark by British novelist and essayist E. M. Forster. Anthony Blunt, eminent art historian and pillar of the British art world, when he was publicly exposed as a Soviet spy in 1979, quoted Forster's remark of 1939: "[I]f I had to choose between betraying my country and betraying my friend, I hope I should have the guts to betray my country."[56] Blunt was being rather unfair to Forster. Taken in context, Forster's remark was a condemnation of not only patriotism, but Communism as well. Immediately before making his choice between friend and country, Forster noted: "[P]ersonal relations are despised today. They are regarded as bourgeois luxuries, as products of a time of fair weather which is now past, and we are urged to get rid of them, and to dedicate ourselves to some movement or cause instead. I hate the idea of causes." And just after defending personal relationships—that bourgeois affectation—Forster defended democracy as "less hateful than other contemporary forms of government" because of its assumption that the individual is the basic unit of society.[57]

Blunt's rationale is, in any case, not very persuasive. Far more than Great Britain, which was a real country inhabited by real people with real institutions, communism was an ideal vision. A spy like Blunt did more than betray an abstraction like the state. For a cause, he also betrayed family and friends and coworkers, who believed him to be what he was not—a loyal citizen and an honest man. The number of relatives and friends he betrayed dwarfed the handful of fellow spies and Communists whom he protected in the name of loyalty.

Several historians have recently suggested that those Communists who spied out of idealism were premature citizens of a global world. Notions of patriotism that stress loyalty to a single nation are, they believe, either outmoded or inappropriate to understanding ideological espionage. Ellen Schrecker, author of several books on McCarthyism, and former editor of *Academe*, the journal of the American Association of University Professors, has conceded that American Communists spied for the Soviet Union, but asks "were these activities so awful?" She notes that "it is important to realize that as Communists these people did not subscribe to traditional forms of patriotism; they were internationalists whose political allegiances transcended national boundaries. They thought they were 'building…a better world for the masses,' not betraying their country."[58]

Likewise, Bruce Craig, director of the National Coordinating Committee for the Promotion of History, attempting to justify Harry White's espionage, has linked it to Franklin Roosevelt's policy of friendship with the Soviet Union: "In his [White's] mind he could justify transmitting oral information to the NKVD… and, based on the assumption the information he was providing did not harm American interests, he was willing to give his handlers his personal opinions and observations on the future course of American politics." Peering retroactively into White's mind, Craig judges that "he probably believed that by answering questions posed by representatives of the Soviet underground he would be able to provide America's present and future friend with an insider's view of the American bureaucracy and thereby advance the goal of Soviet/American partnership." For Craig, "in the final analysis White's loyalties transcended any that he might have felt for his ancestral homeland of mother Russia or for the country of his birth."[59]

Craig ignores inconvenient facts. White did more than provide answers to innocuous questions about the bureaucracy or his personal views: one Venona cable shows White providing a KGB agent with the details of America's negotiating position at the first United Nations conference in San Francisco. He also had worked for Soviet intelligence since 1936, well before there was any "partnership" with the USSR. And while "his ancestral homeland" of Russia knew about his loyalty, or lack thereof, the United States, his country of birth, did not know about his loyalty to Communist Russia. Like Schrecker's transcendence, Craig's is asymmetrical.

The Soviet Union's American spies did not provide information to some mythical transcendent authority or some nonexistent world government but to the intelligence services of a foreign country. It is true that the United States and the Soviet Union were allies when much—but not all—of the espionage revealed by Venona took place. The USSR had suffered greatly resisting Nazism. Ted Hall argued that it therefore deserved to receive any information that would be of use to it. Robert Meeropol, son of the Rosenbergs, thinks that atomic scientists like Fuchs and Hall were simply "sharing information with their Soviet counterparts." While some people regard such activities as spying, others, like Meeropol, think of them simply as acts of "international cooperation."[60] Likewise, Victor Navasky, former editor of the *Nation*, has contended, "There were a lot of exchanges of information among people of good will, many of whom were Marxists, some of whom were Communists, some of whom were critical of US governmental policy and most of whom were patriots."[61]

Such arguments substitute the individual judgment of a single citizen for the legal authority of a democratic government. If Franklin Roosevelt had decided to share atomic information with Joseph Stalin, then it might have been a wise or a stupid policy decision, but Roosevelt was legally authorized to do so. He was answerable to the people of the United States. If Ted Hall had moral qualms about building an atomic bomb, then he was free to leave Los Alamos; at least one prominent scientist, Joseph Rothblatt, did. If Hall believed that classified scientific information should have been shared with Russian scientists, then he might have argued for such a policy. However, neither the law nor his fellow citizens authorized Hall to give sensitive information to anybody he chose, much less an intelligence officer of another country. And Hall did not ask anyone's permission. He did not choose to renounce his American citizenship after the war ended and move to the USSR to help it build an atomic bomb. Most tellingly, the information about the atomic bomb had nothing to do with helping the Soviet Union fight Germany, nor did all of the details about American diplomatic and military matters that these spies gave to the KGB. Most of the information was useful in helping undermine American interests or advance Soviet interests in the postwar world. Even if the spies believed that they were advancing the cause of Communism in the United States, their chosen means provided a direct benefit only to the Soviet Union. In fact, their spying required them to avoid participation in above-ground Communist activities for fear that FBI agents monitoring the Communist Party might stumble over espionage activities.

Another justification offered by apologists or the spies themselves for having committed espionage is that the spies actually assisted the United States. Hall hinted at this in his belated admission, maintaining that the information enabled the Soviet Union to resist American hegemony and thus benefited the cause of world peace and, ultimately, America. Historian Athan Theoharis has similarly argued, "American spies may have aimed to further Soviet interests and betray their own nation, but the effect of their actions compromised neither long-term nor immediate U.S. security interests." In fact, argues Theoharis, the theft of American secrets was actually in America's interests: "[T]he information about U.S. industrial productivity and military strength provided by the Silvermaster group—the numbers being overwhelming—might have deterred Soviet officials from pursuing an aggressive negotiating strategy."[62]

Like several other attempts to excuse espionage, this one fails to meet minimal tests of accuracy about the facts. A great deal of the information that was passed on to the USSR in the 1940s remains unknown because the Venona decryptions largely deal with tradecraft and not the actual espionage "take" that was shipped to Moscow in diplomatic pouches. Much of the data that was sent to the USSR by American spies enabled it to develop nuclear bombs, radar, jet engines, proximity fuses, and other high-tech weapons. Science and technology espionage saved the USSR billions of rubles over the years and enabled it to maintain military parity with the West.[63] Other information enabled the Soviet Union to know in advance American negotiating tactics at such sensitive meetings as Yalta and the United Nations conference in San Francisco. The claim that such espionage prevented World War III is far less credible than the assertion that by strengthening the Soviet Union it prolonged and worsened the Cold War.

Conclusion

All countries spy. Since the United States has engaged in espionage, how can its government or citizens become indignant or mount a moral high horse about Soviet espionage? Theoharis writes,

> Nor was it particularly unusual that Soviet agents operating in the United States during World War II recruited ideologically driven sources. Both U.S. and Soviet intelligence operatives paid the sources they recruited, and both also looked for recruits who for ideological reasons were willing to betray their country's secrets-whether they were committed American Communists and Communist sympathizers (for the Soviets) or disaffected Soviet Communists (for the United States).[64]

There are numerous flaws in this comparison, beginning with the inconvenient fact that neither the United States nor Britain aggressively spied on their Soviet ally during World War II. Trying to read Soviet coded cables was a passive kind of spying far less intrusive than the use of hundreds of active American agents recruited by Soviet intelligence. In fact, when key Soviet agents Kim Philby, Guy Burgess, and Donald Maclean reported to the KGB that Great Britain had suspended efforts to spy on the USSR during World War II, Stalin concluded that they must be lying and were most likely double agents. He could not believe that any capitalist government would forgo the opportunity to spy on the Soviet Union; after all, his regime had mounted an extraordinarily large espionage assault on the United States and Britain precisely when they were allies. As a result of Stalin's incredulity, for several years the KGB seriously believed that its most well-placed British spies were feeding it disinformation.[65]

Theoharis also implies that the nature of the regime for which one works is irrelevant. Is a disaffected Soviet citizen who spies for America because he believes in democracy the moral equivalent of a disaffected American citizen who spies for Russia because he thinks that America is a bourgeois dictatorship and Stalin's USSR a real democracy? Both may "legally" be put to death by the regimes that they betray, but the regimes themselves are not morally equivalent. In any kind of moral calculus, the regime that a spy serves is relevant. Spying for an ally, like the Soviet Union during World War II, is morally and legally different from spying for an enemy such as Nazi Germany. But there is also a moral difference between spying for a democracy and spying for a totalitarian regime.

Just as the regime that one serves must be taken into account in any moral calculus, so must the regime one betrays. Many of the spies exposed by Venona had taken explicit oaths of allegiance to the United States, either when they became naturalized citizens, or when they joined the armed forces or entered government service. They had agreed to security restrictions. They lived in a democratic country with laws that prohibited them from transmitting secret or sensitive information to any unauthorized person. Lauchlin Currie, a Harvard-trained economist, was a Canadian who became a naturalized American citizen in 1934, the same year that he went to work for the U.S. Treasury Department. In 1939 Whittaker Chambers, a one-time Soviet spy who exposed Alger Hiss, told a State Department official that Currie had assisted a Soviet espionage ring. Currie is identified in Venona as being an important Soviet source while serving as a presidential assistant and administrator of the Foreign Economic Administration. Currie chose to become an American citizen and chose to work for the American government. He did not turn over confidential information to other American allies but only to the Soviet Union. When he appeared before the House Committee on Un-American Activities after being named as a spy by Chambers and by Elizabeth Bentley (another defector from Soviet intelligence), Currie lied under oath. He then moved to Colombia and eventually became a citizen of that country. His allegiance to the United States may have been fleeting, but it was in force when he turned over confidential information to the KGB.[66]

All of these spies betrayed their country, but virtually none renounced his American citizenship or the privileges it provided. (Currie is one of the few exceptions.) When a number of these spies were subpoenaed before congressional committees, they exercised their rights under the Fifth Amendment to refuse to answer and were not punished. Most of the American citizens identified in the Venona decryptions were never prosecuted because the government could not develop additional corroborating evidence and did not want to publicly divulge the Venona project. Despite unequivocal evidence of their guilt contained in Venona decryptions, the American legal system protected them from summary arrest and conviction. Some lost government jobs or suffered public humiliation or scorn, but otherwise they escaped the legal consequences of their actions. The American legal system and its constitutional protections that they worked so zealously to subvert spared them.

To be a spy is to engage in deception and lying. Even if spying does not directly involve betrayal, it requires encouraging others to betray their country. It may lead to preying on human weakness and greed. Yet, the gentlemanly view that spying is always dishonorable is both naive and dangerous. Whether deception and betrayal are justified cannot be determined in the abstract. Some regimes are so odious that remaining loyal to them taints an individual. Some enemies are so dangerous that their defeat transcends other reservations. Some motives that lead to betrayal are base and dishonorable, but others may be admirable. Good regimes and good motives may not, of course, always coincide. That many Americans who spied for the Soviets were idealists does not compensate for their betrayal of American secrets. German Communists who spied for the Soviet Union during World War II were in a very different situation. By the same token, Soviet citizens who betrayed their country because they believed in democracy surely merit a different evaluation than Americans who chose to spy on behalf of the Soviet Union. Perhaps E. M. Forster got it wrong when he denigrated the value of causes and insisted on remaining loyal to his friend. There are countries whose values are worth defending, even if that defense sometimes requires betraying one's friend or other unpalatable deeds. Some causes are not worth betraying either friend or country: Communism was one of these causes.

Notes

1. For a complete description, see John Haynes and Harvey Klehr, *Venona: Decoding Soviet Espionage in America* (New Haven, CT: Yale University Press, 1999).
2. Francis Dvornik, *Origins of Intelligence Services: The Ancient Near East, Persia, Greece, Rome, Byzantium, the Arab Muslim Empires, the Mongol Empire, China, Muscovy* (New Brunswick, NJ: Rutgers University Press, 1974).
3. Frank Russell, *information Gathering in Classical Greece* (Ann Arbor: University of Michigan Press, 1999), 105.
4. Phillip Knightley, *The Second Oldest Profession: Spies and Spying in the Twentieth Century* (London: A. Deutsch, 1986).

5. Russell, *Information Gathering in Classical Greece,* 106.
6. Paul Seabury in *Covert Action,* no. *4* of *Intelligence Requirements for the 1980s,* ed. Roy Godson (Washington, DC: National Strategy Information Center, 1981), 107.
7. Henry Halleck, *International Law* (San Francisco: H. H. Bancroft & Co., 1861), 406.
8. John Le Carre, *The Spy Who Came in From the Cold* (New York: Bantam Books, 1963), 210-11.
9. James Fenimore Cooper, *The Spy: A Tale of the Neutral Ground* (New York: Hafner Pub. Co., 1960). The quotation is from the introduction by Warren S. Walker, 6.
10. Gen. 42:6-17. The Oxford Annotated Bible, Revised Standard Version (New York: Oxford University Press, 1962).
11. Num. 13: 1-20.
12. Num. 13:21-31; and Deut. 1:22-38. Nehama Leibowitz, *Studies in Bamidbar (Numbers),* trans. Aryeh Newman (Jerusalem: World Zionist Organization, 1980), 135-41.
13. John M. Cardwell, "A Bible Lesson on Spying," *Studies in Intelligence* (Winter 1978), available on-line at http://www.parascope.com/ds/articles/ciaBibleStudyDoc.html [accessed in January 2003].
14. Num. 21:32.
15. Josh. 2.
16. 1 Sam 26:4, and 2 Sam 15:10.
17. Judg. 18:2.
18. Judg. 16.
19. One significant exception to this negative portrayal is Rahab, the woman who had aided Joshua's spies. In Heb. 11:31 she is praised "By faith Rahab the harlot did not perish with those who were disobedient, because she had given friendly welcome to the spies."
20. Luke 20:20. In Matt. 22:15 it is the Pharisees who send not spies, but some of their own disciples.
21. Gal. 2:4.
22. Charles de Secondat, baron de Montesquieu, *The Spirit of the Laws* (1748; reprint, trans. Thomas Nugent, New York: Hafner Press, 1949), 202.
23. Immanuel Kant, *The Metaphysics of Morals,* trans. Mary Gregor (Cambridge: Cambridge University Press, 1991), 154.
24. Thomas Hobbes, *De Cive* (Garden City, NJ: Anchor Books, 1972), 13:7.
25. Niccolo Machiavelli, *The Prince and the Discourses* (New York: Random House, 1950), 56.
26. Ibid., 64. In *Discourses,* bk. 3, chap. 6, Machiavelli treats at length of conspiracies and conspirators but these are not, strictly speaking, spies.
27. Marx compared the communist revolution to a mole, paraphrasing Shakespeare's *Hamlet,* 1.5.162: "Well said, old mole!" Marx added:
    But the revolution is thoroughgoing. It is still traveling through purgatory. It does its work methodically. By December 2, 1851, it had completed half of its preparatory work; it is now completing the other half. First it perfected the parliamentary power in order to be able to overthrow it. Now that it has attained this, it perfects the executive power, reduces it to its purest expression, isolates it, sets it up against itself as the sole target, in order to concentrate all its forces of destruction against it. And when it has done this second half of its preliminary work, Europe will leap from its seat and exultantly exclaim: Well-grubbed old mole! Karl Marx, *The Eighteenth Brumaire of Louis Bonaparte* (1851-1852; reprint, Moscow: Foreign Language Publishing House, 1983), 121.

28. Hugo Grotius, *The Law of War and Peace* (1670), trans. Louise R. Loomis (New York: Walter J. Black, 1949), bk. 111, chap. 4, p. 302.
29. Thucydides, *The Peloponnesian War,* Walter Blanco and Jennifer T. Roberts, eds. (New York: Norton, 1998), *73*.
30. David Kahn, *The Codebreakers: The Story of Secret Writing* (New York: Charles Scribner's Sons, 1996), 360.
31. See, for example, David L. Perry, " 'Repugnant Philosophy': Ethics, Espionage, and Covert Action," *Journal of Conflict Studies* 15, no. 1 (1995): 92-115, for an effort to determine the moral limitations on espionage.
32. See, for example, William Ordway Partridge, *Nathan Hale, the Ideal Patriot: A Study of Character* (New York: Funk & Wagnalls Co., 1902).
33. A word on nomenclature. The USSR's main foreign intelligence organization, commonly known in the West as the KGB, used a variety of names from its origins as the Cheka shortly after the Russian Revolution. For simplicity, I have used KGB throughout this essay to refer to its various incarnations. The GRU, or military intelligence, is a separate organization that often had a fierce bureaucratic rivalry with the KGB.
34. William Duff, A *Time For Spies: Theodore Stephanovich Mally and the Era of the Great Illegals* (Nashville, TN: Vanderbilt University Press, 1999), 156.
35. See Leopold Trepper, *The Great Game: Memoirs of the Spy Hitler Couldn't Silence* (New York: McGraw-Hill, 1977); and Gilles Perrault, *The Red Orchestra,* trans. Peter Wiles (New York: Simon & Schuster, 1969).
36. See Haynes and Klehr, *Venona,* 230-31.
37. Christopher Andrew and Vasili Mitrokhin, *The Sword and the Shield: The Mitrokhin Archive and the Secret History of the KGB* (New York: Basic Books, 1999), 111, 118, and 129.
38. Louise Bernikow, *Abel* (New York: Trident Press, 1970), 155.
39. Wolf Blitzer, *Territory of Lies: The Exclusive Story of Jonathan Jay Pollard, the American Who Spied on His Country for Israel and How He Was Betrayed* (New York: Harper & Row, 1989).
40. David Wise, *Nightmover: How Aldrlch Ames Sold the CIA to the KGB for $4.6 Million* (New York: HarperColllns, 1995).
41. Pete Earley, *Family of Spies: Inside the John Walker Spy Ring* (New York: Bantam Books, 1988).
42. Elaine Shannon and Ann Blackman, *The Spy Next Door: The Extraordinary Secret Life of Robert Philip Hanssen, the Most Damaging FBI Agent In U.S. History* (Boston: Little, Brown, & Co., 2002).
43. Allan Weinstein and Alexander Vasiliev, *The Haunted Wood* (New York: Random House, 1999), 140-50.
44. Venona 1635 KGB New York to Moscow. November 21, 1944.
45. To the Director from SAC Guy Hottel; June 14, 1945; FBI File 100-267360-531, Box 120, Folder 6, Philip Jaffe Papers, Emory University.
46. Ronald Radosh and Joyce Milton, *The Rosenberg File: A Search for the Truth* (New York: Holt, Rinehart & Winston, 1983), 73.
47. Joseph Albright and Marcia Kunstel, *Bombshell: The Secret Story of America's Unknown Atomic Spy Conspiracy* (New York: Times Books, 1997), 32.
48. Ibid., 48.
49. Weinstein and Vasiliev, *The Haunted Wood,* 196.
50. On Oppenheimer see Jerrold and Leona Schecter, *Sacred Secrets: How Soviet Intelligence Operations Changed American History* (Washington, DC: Brassey's, 2002), 50.

51. Albright and Kunstel, *Bombshell,* 288-89.

52. Joan and Ruth Hall, interviewed in "Family of Spies," *Secrets, Lies, and Atomic Spies,* a NOVA television production (Boston, MA: WGBH Educational Foundation, 2002). Transcript available on-line at http://www.pbs.org/wgbh/nova/venona/fami_joanhall.html.

53. Albright and Kunstel, *Bombshell, 240.*

54. See, most notably, Robert and Michael Meeropol, *We Are Your Sons: The Legacy of Ethel and Julius Rosenberg* (Boston: Houghton Mifflin, 1975). The Rosenberg children were adopted and their last names were changed.

55. Alexander Feklisov and Sergei Kostin, *The Man Behind the Rosenbergs,* trans. Catherine Dop (New York: Enigma Books, *2001);* and Robert and Michael Meeropol, interviewed in "Family of Spies," *Secrets, Lies, and Atomic Spies;* transcript available on-line at http://www.pbs.org/wgbh/nova/venona/fami_meeropol.html.

56. Miranda Carter, *Anthony Blunt: His Lives* (New York: Farrar, Straus, & Giroux, 2001), 178.

57. E. M. Forster, *Two Cheers for Democracy* (New York: Harcourt, Brace & Co., 1951), 68-69.

58. Ellen Schrecker, *Many Are the Crimes: McCarthyism in America* (Boston: Little, Brown & Co., 1998), 178-79, 188.

59. Bruce Craig, " 'Treasonable Doubt': The Harry Dexter White Case" (Ph.D. diss., American University, 1999), 581, 585-86, and 588.

60. Robert and Michael Meeropol, "Family of Spies," *Secrets, Lies, and Atomic Spies.*

61. Victor Navasky, "Cold War Ghosts," *Nation,* July 16, 2001. As cited on-line at http://www.thenation.com/doc.mhtm1?i=20010716&s=navasky.

62. Athan Theoharis, *Chasing Spies: How the FBI Failed in Counterintelligence but Promoted the Politics of McCarthyism in the Cold War Years* (Chicago, IL: Ivan R. Dee, 2002), 16-17.

63. Andrew and Mitrokhin, *The Sword and the Shield,* 216-20.

64. Theoharis, *Chasing Spies,* 237-38.

65. Nigel West and Oleg Tsarev, *The Crown Jewels: The British Secrets at the Heart of the KGB Archives* (London: HarperCollins, 1998), 159-68.

66. On Currie, see Haynes and Klehr, *Venona,* 145-50. Roger Sandilands, a protégé of Currie and a British academic, has denied that Currie was a spy. See Roger Sandilands, "Guilt by Association? Lauchlin Currie's Alleged Involvement with Washington Economists in Soviet Espionage," *History of Political* Economy 32, no. 3 (2000): 473-515.

Index